Contents

PETER COLEMAN

Christian Attitudes to Homosexuality

LONDON
SPCK

First published 1980
SPCK
Holy Trinity Church
Marylebone Road
London NW1 4DU

ACKNOWLEDGEMENTS

Thanks are due to the following for extracts from:

Jerusalem Bible published and © 1966, 1967 and 1968 by Darton, Longman & Todd Ltd. and Doubleday & Co. Inc. and are used by the permission of the publishers.

Revised Standard Version of the Bible, copyrighted 1946, 1952, © 1971, 1973 by the Division of Christian Education of the National Council of the Churches of Christ in the USA, and are used by permission.

Authorized Version of the Bible, which is Crown Copyright, are used with permission of Eyre & Spottiswoode (Publishers) Ltd.

New English Bible, Second Edition © 1970, by permission of Oxford and Cambridge University Presses.

The Symposium by Plato, translated by Walter Hamilton, are used by permission of Penguin Books Ltd.

Printed in Great Britain by Spottiswoode Ballantyne Ltd.
Colchester and London

ISBN 0 281 03756 6

PART D
Old Morality or New

PART E
Conclusions

Preface

From the time of St Paul until the middle of the present century, the Christian attitude to homosexual behaviour remained unchanged and seldom questioned. It was an unnatural offence, not to be named among Christians. Ever since the Wolfenden Committee report of 1957 recommended a change in the law concerning homosexual behaviour among adult men, the traditional view that such behaviour was sinful has been re-appraised. It has been argued that modern understandings of human sexuality provide compelling reasons for revising the old view.

The distinction now commonly made between the homosexual orientation as such, and physical activity that may or may not result from that orientation, has led many Christians to regard the biblical prohibitions, on which the traditional view is based, as properly applying only to acts of genital intimacy between homosexuals and not as a general judgement on the many millions of men and women in the world who find themselves incapable of feeling either romantic or erotic attraction to their opposite sex. Some Christians have gone further, and responding to the arguments for what has now come to be called Gay Liberation, judge that it may be unfairly discriminatory to prohibit homosexual behaviour among Christians, provided that the relationship between the partners contains a quality of love and stability sufficient to make it in some sense, albeit limited by the lack of procreative potential, the nearest equivalent to heterosexual marriage available for homosexuals.

While the understanding of homosexuality as a permanent state is by now probably widespread, official church teaching on this subject since 1957 tends to reiterate the conviction that abstinence from physical expression is the proper response a Christian should make to the discovery that he or she is in fact of a settled homosexual orientation. But the case for toleration is continually pressed, and receives some reinforcement from the evident fact that sexual activity is now regarded more positively than in the past.

The Christian teaching about heterosexual love has itself been subject to much modification in recent years, its relational significance now being accorded greater prominence as the problem of population growth becomes more pressing. Has the moment now come when Christian teaching should be modified to allow homosexual people to express love for each other in ways that simulate heterosexual intercourse?

There has been a steady flow of reports by working parties of varying expertise and authority, and a great number of individual studies published reflecting on this question, and the debate is at the time of writing in no sense resolved, except for those who find no sufficient cause to question the traditional teaching. The debate has become world-wide, involving all the major denominational Churches and the trans-denominational loyalties reflected in the various theologies of post-reformation Christianity. Since it has also been a matter of public concern, Christian and secular views have been exchanged through the mass media of communication.

Despite this great stir of interest, the issue may seem insignificant by comparison with the major tasks that face the contemporary Church in mission, pastoral care and social responsibility, but it is clear that for many people the dilemma the Churches face concerning homosexual behaviour cannot be resolved without considering fundamental questions about the meaning and abiding value of the relevant scriptural texts, the teaching authority of the Church throughout the ages, and the significance Christians should allow to modern understandings of human sexuality. The morality or otherwise of homosexual behaviour has therefore become something of a test case among Christians, challenging long held certainties and probing for the future what the consequences might be in other aspects of Christian thought if a change were to be made.

This book is described as a survey of Christian attitudes, and is not intended to be polemical on behalf of any of the views expressed within it. Most space is given to the biblical texts and the historical record. The particular position of the Church of England in relation to the State seems to justify some detailing of its participation in the Parliamentary process of changing the law in 1967. Quotations are taken from many sources, and inevitably the selection is arbitrary and often too brief to do justice to their authors' arguments. Keeping to a reasonable length, while attempting to provide a comprehensive view of the past and present Christian attitudes has required omitting many sources which, valuable in themselves, contain information already provided elsewhere.

I conclude this preface with a personal note.

In preparing this book I have sometimes been asked what kind of readership I have in mind, and my answer has been the general reader and those who would count themselves theologically literate, but not the specialist theologian, who will readily detect that an amateur has been browsing in his field, whether that be Church History, Biblical Studies or Moral Philosophy. In the notes I have tried to list books that are generally available, as well as those only likely to be found in comprehensive libraries. The short bibliography is limited to standard books recently published.

Perhaps I may end this preface with a word of appreciation to a number of people who have helped me at various stages in its evolution. First to students of King's College, London, who many years ago bore with my tentative first lectures on Christian Ethics and asked good questions. Secondly to Professor Kenneth Grayston, head of the Theology Department and Mr Peter Powesland of the Psychology Department of the University of Bristol who supervised a modest research project on the subject. Also to Dr Sherwin Bailey who, as a Canon at Wells, showed me great kindness and shared many documents with me as I began to trace his pioneering and learned studies. To my secretary, Miss Betty Millard, who conquered my awful script and made it fit for the publishers. To the Staff of SPCK for risking another publication on an already well covered theme.

Finally, to my wife and four children who have endured without complaint my pre-occupation with research and a book, though they could never quite decide why I was interested in this particular topic. To that question I offer two answers. The first comes from a comment by Bishop Ian Ramsey at the seminar on Natural Law he was conducting with a group of us in Church House, Westminster, in 1964. He said, 'The Church has always been opposed to homosexuality—I don't know why'. The question seemed worth pursuing. Once started on it I have often recalled a dialogue between Hamlet and Polonius concerning the accommodation to be provided for the players. 'I will use them according to their desert', says Polonius. 'God's Bodkin, man, much better!' replies Hamlet, 'Use every-man after his desert and who shall 'scape whipping' (*Hamlet* II 2.531).

PART A
Understanding Homosexuality

1 Understanding Homosexuality

A Introduction

Some recognition of homosexual behaviour is to be found in most forms of human society, ancient and modern. This is as true of China and Greece in the past as it is of Europe and America today. The written records of all cultures provide this evidence and it is not necessary to follow the anthropologists to the Pacific Islands to demonstrate its universality. Since most human beings are heterosexual, it is not surprising that the minority who are attracted to their own sex have been usually regarded as in some sense deviant and therefore ostracized or mocked. The modern name for this disapproval is 'homophobia', and like other forms of discrimination, it can be expressed in a wide range of attitudes, from tolerance and pity through scorn and rejection, to legal prohibition and mob violence. 'Queer bashing' as it is called, has led to murder in England in this decade, even though since the Sexual Offences Act of 1967 homosexual behaviour in private is no longer punished by the law.

When the Government appointed the Wolfenden Committee in 1955, it was perhaps hoped that public opinion had reached a sufficient understanding of the complex facts of human sexuality to make it no longer acceptable for the old law against homosexual behaviour to be used to prosecute otherwise respectable citizens who expressed their sexual preference in this way. The trial of Lord Montagu of Beaulieu evoked a quite different reaction in the Press from that of Oscar Wilde some sixty-five years before. But it took ten years for Parliament to come to a decision that the Wolfenden Committee's recommendation could be implemented by Statute, and it would be hazardous to recommend even now that a man or woman would incur no risk to their career or public acceptance by 'coming out', that is declaring openly that their sexual orientation is of a homosexual kind. Homophobia remains a deep-set attitude in present society, as it appears always to have been, and the enormously increased amount of information about homosexuality from the mass media, plays, films, television, newspapers, as well as a great number of books on the subject, and a generally increased reference to it in professional textbooks has not, as yet, set at rest the anxieties which heterosexual people have when confronted with this difference.

In this chapter an attempt is made to set out what may be claimed as generally accepted facts about homosexuality as they have emerged in a century of medical and psychological study. In one sense, such an attempt is doomed to failure, for it is very clear that as research proceeds, no easy solution to the question of aetiology has been found, nor is there any longer much confidence in the probability of treatment and cure. Indeed, medical opinion seems to have moved on to the view that the homosexual condition as such is not pathological, and therefore, as such, calls for no interference by doctors. That which is not an illness calls for no treatment. It remains true, of course, that some people who are homosexual do need treatment, and their sexual anxiety may be part of a more complex problem which does call for help, though that can equally be said of heterosexual people.

The tempo of research into all aspects of human sexuality has increased enormously in recent years, and to some extent public interest has been served by a spate of publications on the medical and psychological investigations which have now become readily available in paperback editions. It remains true, however, that a great deal of what is now known is published only in the technical journals of the specialisms involved, and it is an impossible task to report this information adequately in précis.

In the Sections that follow there is first offered an indication of many of the words frequently used. This is followed by a brief account of physical and genetic factors relevant to human sexuality. The work of psychologists and psychiatrists is obviously of equal importance to that of the geneticists and started earlier in respect of homosexuality, but these sciences now have many branches. Among the pioneers Freud is justly famous and is considered in some detail; for subsequent work notes and bibliography are provided for the more specialist reader to pursue. Brief mention is made of some anthropological studies and of Kinsey's work, and some approaches to the question of treatment are described. Among church people, the particular methods of Dr Frank Lake are well known, so an example of clinical theology is also included. Nothing is said in this section of the views expressed about themselves by homosexual people. Extensive and important though that material is, it seems best to consider it later as part of the assessment of the present position in Part D. The movement for Gay Liberation is best dealt with then.

It remains true that human sexuality is a subject of deep and abiding interest to everyone, whatever their age or sexual orientation. The inadequacy of what follows in terms of personal feeling and even more in terms of affection and love will be readily apparent. But equally, reticence and embarrassment have long been powerful influences in the Christian tradition concerning homosexuality, and if that tradition is now confronted with an excess of explicitness and pornographic polemic, then the commonplace facts are worth setting down briefly, even if they can do little more than challenge some misunderstandings.

B Words and Meanings

In modern English, medical terminology usually makes use of Latin and Greek words, and the related sciences psychology and psychiatry thus refer to reasoning about 'the soul' and its treatment. Some confusion may be caused when roots of both the ancient languages are combined, and this is the case with *'homo-sexuality'* which seems to have been first coined by the Swiss Doctor K. M. Benkert in 1869, and introduced into England by Havelock Ellis at the turn of the century. Only since the Wolfenden Committee reported in 1957 has it been in general use. The Greek prefix *homo* has been added to the Latin *sex* to indicate an attraction or sexual preference for the same sex, in distinction from the more usual 'hetero-sexual' attraction, where the prefix means 'other' or 'different'. The confusion occurs where *homo* is mistakenly taken to represent the Latin word for 'man', thereby apparently implying that the homosexual choice is concerned with males, whereas in fact, it was also applicable to females. Female homosexuality is also described as *'Lesbianism'*, taking its name from the Island of Lesbos, where the Greek poet Sappho once lived in a female community and wrote erotic poetry which is often, though need not be, interpreted as predominantly homosexual in tone. The term *'homophobia'* has recently emerged to describe the reaction of fear and dislike which the heterosexual majority tend to express to homosexual culture and people.

The terms 'homosexual' and 'heterosexual' can be used in a range of meanings. Narrowly, they indicate the direction of the sexual drive, that is, the sexual gender to which a person will be attracted in terms of eroticism or sexual behaviour. Whether or not any action ensues depends, of course, on circumstances and intentions, and therefore to designate a person as being homosexual need not imply actual sexual activity with the same sex any more than it does with heterosexual people. But in popular and more pejorative use identifying a person as having a homosexual character is often taken to mean that he or she is sexually active as one. One way of distinguishing the direction of sexual drive from the implication of sexual behaviour is to describe the first as the condition of homosexuality, but this is in some ways unsatisfactory, for it seems to indicate a clearer separation between disposition and action than the nature of human sexuality warrants. A person's awareness of another's sexuality does not operate in such distinct categories, and the components of interest, attraction, friendship, love and physical expression present in relationships, are influenced by moral and practical considerations as they develop or diminish rather than by simple switching from 'condition' to 'behaviour'. That said, it is useful to be able to indicate when actual physical 'love-making' is being referred to, and in this book, *'homosexual behaviour'* is used to describe this.

Such terms as 'sexual behaviour' and 'love-making' are, of course ambiguous and are not necessarily limited to descriptions of vaginal or anal intercourse among heterosexual and homosexual couples respectively. Although *anal intercourse*, also known as sodomy or buggery, is still technically illegal, even within marriage, it occurs between heterosexual couples as a means of contraception or as a variant form of sexual pleasure. Some male homosexuals, but probably a minority, prefer it, but the majority of them seem to find mutual masturbation and other forms of erotic contact more satisfactory. Aesthetic and hygienic considerations also may be relevant. Among Lesbians similar behaviour is found. The terms *'fellatio'* and *'cunnilingus'* refer to oral stimulation of male or female genitalia, both being practices referred to in ancient and medieval times between hetero- and homosexual couples. In recent times, the original Latin terms, used chiefly in ascetic theology, have been replaced by the expression *'oral sex'* and quite widely recommended in some magazines and manuals concerned with sexual techniques. Research in America has suggested that oral masturbation by such methods may be as popular among homosexual couples as manual masturbation.[1]

An important aspect of the changing conventions about sexual morality at the present time is the open recognition of wide-spread extra-marital sexual behaviour. It remains to be seen how far contemporary Christian commendations of chastity and modesty can be persuasively argued as good in themselves at a time when the prudential considerations which once buttressed them have collapsed with the arrival of widely available contraceptive methods for the unmarried. This point must be examined later in Part D, but is introduced now as a corrective to any impression that sexual behaviour and love-making among homosexual people can be discussed apart from the contemporary sexual *mores* of society generally.

Before the present day terminology emerged, other expressions to describe homosexuality were used, mostly implying explicit physical contact. Among such expressions were *'pederasty'*, *'unnatural vice'*, *'sodomy'* (from the biblical tradition) and *'buggery'*, which is now an archaic legalism, but originated as a term of abuse for a group of Christian heretics in Bulgaria, who were supposed to match their false beliefs with perverted sexuality. Among slang terms, *'gay'* has become a popular description among homosexual people themselves, etymologically based on the legend of Ganymede, and *'fairy'*, *'pansy'* and *'queer'* are slang homophobic expressions. Of more importance are the terms *'inversion'* and *'perversion'*, used by the early psychologists and Freud to distinguish between those whose condition was exclusively homosexual and those whose sexual drive could be directed either way. The expressions *'bi-sexual'*, *'ambi-sexual'* or *'inter-sexual'* mean, according to context, either those whose physical structure is hermaphrodite, or those whose sexual orientation is neither exclusively hetero- or homo-sexual.

Paedophilia is the modern term for all kinds of sexual relationships between adults and young children of the same or opposite sex. *Pederasty* is sometimes still used for this, but originally among the Greeks referred only to homosexual relationships between adult males and post-pubertal male youths. *Paedophilia* describes both heterosexual and homosexual relationships, where an ante-pubertal child is involved. By the Sexual Offences Act of 1967, adults over twenty-one may consent to homosexual behaviour in private, but the general law concerning heterosexual intercourse places the age of consent at sixteen years. Current medical opinion suggests that *paedophilia* is best regarded as a sexual abnormality and, like *voyeurism* and *fetichism*, may require treatment or restraint where others are at risk or affronted. Since such problems occur for heterosexual people as well as homosexuals, they are not further considered in this book.

C Physical and Genetic Factors

Human sexuality can be described in a number of ways. The most obvious is physical appearance. At birth, the baby is designated male or female from observation of its external genitalia, though it is now possible to discover the gender of a foetus by examination of the amniotic fluid that surrounds it in the womb. Body shape, appearance, voice and styles of dress usually conform to the genetic distinction in broad terms, though the wide range of human physical types, as well as changes in fashion, can deceive a casual observer.

The physical distinction between male and female results genetically from the chromosomal pattern established at conception. Human cells normally contain 23 pairs of chromosomes, of which one pair, usually called XX or XY, determines the sex of the person, as female or male respectively. Women produce in the ovary eggs having X chromosomes, and male spermatozoa develop in the testes having either an X or a Y chromosome. At the moment of conception the fusion of the male X with the female X establishes a female, while that of a male Y with a female X establishes a male. Since a man produces equal numbers of X and Y spermatozoa, the sex of the child is random and should be statistically approximately equal. In fact, some 6 per cent more boys are conceived, especially among younger parents, but men are slightly less robust so that by the age of thirty-three the numbers of men and women living have evened out.

Chromosomal abnormalities occur in a small number of conceptions where an extra or missing chromosome leads to untypical development. Thus an additional chromosome on the twenty-first pair leads to Down's syndrome or mongolism, present in perhaps one in seven hundred viable babies, and rarer additions to other pairs of chromosomes are known. Such variation has also been found in the sex chromosomes, notably XO and XXX in females, and XXY and XYY in males. XO females, suffering from Turner's syndrome, may not develop properly at puberty, and similar effects may be found where the XXX pattern is present. Among males, the XXY pattern (Klinefelter's syndrome) may result in reduced sexual drive and poor genital development, while the XYY pattern produces men who can be unusually tall, but not thereby exceptionally masculine. In fact, there is some evidence that this category includes a higher than expected proportion of men who suffer from psychiatric conditions and perhaps criminal tendencies.

Research into these chromosomal variations is relatively recent. The sex determination factor itself was not firmly demonstrated until 1959 although the chromosomal differences between males and females were observed earlier in this century. While progress has been rapid, greatly assisted by new microscopic techniques in conjunction with cell staining, no clear evidence has yet been found of a chromosomic origin for homosexuality in any direct sense.[2]

After conception, the basic physical pattern of the developing foetus is female, but from the seventh week onwards the sex glands or gonads follow the already established genetic 'instructions' and begin to secrete hormones, androgens for males, and oestrogens for females. Both hormones are, in fact, produced in every foetus, oestrogens being a development from androgens and the balance of each is important. Provided this is normal, male or female internal and external genital organs develop in the familiar anatomical pattern, while certain brain cells act as receptors for these hormones and build up patterns which eventually form the basis for male and female characteristics.

After birth, but probably within the first five years of life, the child learns its gender type and behaves accordingly. This process, sometimes called 'imprinting' is complex, partly a response to external influences—learning to correspond with being a boy or a girl as society and the family demonstrate the two roles, and partly an expression of all that has been 'laid down' by genetic distinction and hormonal influence. When the hormonal chemistry is not balanced in the normal way, variations in development of the internal and external sex organs takes place, and this leads to various kinds of inter-sexual characteristics. A person may grow up with apparently male or female external genitalia, but in fact have the opposite chromosomal pattern. If detected early in childhood, injection of the correct hormone may assist the formation of the correct physical organs, genetically speaking, and in later life, so-called 'sex-change' operations can sometimes remedy the chemical mistake by anatomical adjustments. These inter-sexual problems are rare and do not, in themselves, explain homosexuality, though they may cause some people uncertainty about their sexual role and homosexual behaviour may result.

It remains to note the more familiar fact that the normal process of sexual development is completed at puberty, when the pituitary gland stimulates the sexual glands to produce more of the appropriate hormones, the secondary sexual characteristics develop and the various components of the reproductive systems become fertile. It is often through the process of medical investigation of infertility or incapacity for satisfactory intercourse, that the underlying genetic and hormonal imbalance comes to light and steps can be taken to alleviate its consequences.

Reports of research in progress on rats and other small mammals suggest that artificially introduced alterations in the hormonal balance at early stages of development can lead to homosexual characteristics being demonstrated later. Workers in this field suggest that the neurophysiology of humans is much more complex, and probably includes other as yet unidentified transmitters as well as the sex hormones, so it would be precipitate to claim at this stage that the causes of homosexuality are hormonal, or could be corrected at the foetal stage by appropriate injections.[3]

Hormonal injections have been found to affect the intensity of the sexual drive in humans, but the effect is to strengthen or diminish the drive in the already established direction, not to alter its direction. Since the technology required to measure the minute quantities of the hormonal fluids in the body has only recently been developed, it is probable that further experiment will help our understanding of the importance or otherwise of this body chemistry as a physical factor in the aetiology of the homosexual condition. There is some evidence to suggest that such a genetic factor may dispose towards certain personality traits which, in turn, increase the likelihood of homosexuality emerging. Whereas at one stage, environment was considered highly influential, hormones are now recognized as being perhaps of equal significance.[4]

D Social and Cultural Factors

These are not now thought to be as significant for adult homosexuality as once supposed, except in so far as special situations can cause a temporary change in the direction of the sex drive.

Anthropological studies by B. Malinowski, Margaret Mead and others of the sexual mores in primitive societies, made in the late nineteen-twenties, suggested that homosexual practices among the South Sea Islanders were mostly confined to adolescents. Similar findings for New Guinea and other South West Pacific Islands were reported in 1965 and recent studies by Ford and Beach[5] have shown a general occurrence of some homosexual behaviour among animals, and in a wide range of human cultures. On the basis of these findings, Dr Wainwright Churchill has argued that it is mistaken to describe the sex-drive as 'instinctual'. He prefers to limit the naturalness of the drive to consist only in the desire to relieve tension, and thinks that the choice of like or unlike partners is entirely culturally conditioned.[6]

The recognition that the drive of human sexuality is not consistently and exclusively directed towards the same or opposite sex, but is better represented as in varying degrees flexible in aim, was demonstrated in a convincing way by Kinsey and has been confirmed by subsequent research. He suggested a seven point scale, reflecting his findings that the majority of the men and women interviewed could recall some interest in sexual activity other than that which now predominated. His statistics showed that among a large and carefully checked group of white Americans, 37 per cent of the males had at least some overt homosexual experience between adolescence and old age, and that 8 per cent of the males were exclusively homosexual for a period of three years between the ages of 16 and 55. The study of women, published five years later and based on a smaller sample, showed that 13 per cent of women had overt homosexual experience by the age of 45 years. These findings do not, of course, permit of a precise deduction of how many men and women in present day society are predominantly homosexual, but there seem good grounds for concluding that the oft-quoted figure of 5 per cent is a reliable minimum estimate. The data collected by Kinsey's interviewers of the range of experiences between exclusive heterosexual and exclusive homosexual behaviour, recalled by their respondents, has made a most significant contribution to present understandings of human sexuality. Subsequent research by the Institute that bears his name has confirmed and elaborated the appropriateness of the flexible scale model.[7]

The consequences of recognizing this flexibility involve several adjustments to traditional thinking. First, it provides a ready explanation for the transient emergence of homosexual interests among those who have previously been predominantly heterosexual but find themselves confined to one-sex institutions such as prisons or the Armed Forces. On release, the heterosexual orientation revives. Secondly, bisexuality can be understood as arising from the lack of a marked exclusive disposition either way, and it may well be that the proportion of human beings who occupy the middle ground of the scale, and are therefore capable under the appropriate stimulus to relate temporarily or for a long period, to either their own or the opposite sex in behavioural terms, may prove to be higher than those classified as exclusively homosexual. The strength of their sexual drive may, of course, not be so strong as those at the ends of the scale, and a distinction needs to be made between capacity for sexual arousal by a member of the same sex in some circumstances, and a real sexual preference.[8]

E Psychological Investigation

(a) THE PIONEERS

During the nineteenth century, psychiatry emerges as a distinct form of medical science, concerned with diseases of the mind. The first systematic lectures on the subject in Britain were given by Sir Andrew Morrison of Edinburgh in 1823.[9] Similarly at this time psychology, which in a loose sense had been part of the study of philosophy from the time of Aristotle onwards, begins to be recognized as a separate science, encouraged by the earlier reflections of Kant and Leibnitz and the English empiricists, Locke and Hume.[10] Hume had suggested that 'reason is and ought only to be the slave of the passions, and can never pretend to any other office than to serve and obey them'. He does, of course, qualify this statement by explaining that passion surrenders to reason when we realize that the objective of our passion is not, in fact, in our own self-interest.[11]

The work of the Utilitarian philosophers is also important, and in particular the argument central to John Stuart Mill's essay 'On Liberty', published in 1859. Mill writes:

> The object of this Essay is to assert one very simple principle, as entitled to govern absolutely the dealings of society with the individual in the way of compulsion and control, whether the means used be physical force in the form of legal penalties, or the moral coercion of public opinion. That principle is, that the sole end for which mankind are warranted, individually or collectively, in interfering with the liberty of action of any of their number, is self-protection. That the only purpose for which power can be rightfully exercised over any member of a civilised community, against his will, is to prevent harm to others. His own good, either physical or moral, is not a sufficient warrant.[12]

Although Bentham and Mill were primarily concerned to commend Utilitarianism as a basis for social and legal reform, the essay on liberty reflects in part the more personal struggle that Mill endured through his love for Harriet Taylor, and his inability to marry her until her husband died. The argument that protection of others was the only ground for interfering with personal liberty was not welcome in England at this time. The Oxford Movement was tightening up the Church to conform to a corporate discipline, the social reforms going through Parliament stressed the importance of the group rather than the individual, and so the effect of Mill's plea was only slowly felt; it was of crucial importance for the Wolfenden Committee a hundred years later.

Meanwhile, this philosophical background, stressing empiricism and liberty, was helpful as the early psychiatrists and psychologists began to explore the wide range of human consciousness which was seen to include not only those ideas that were clearly present to the mind at any given moment, but also those barely perceived, and beyond them an unconscious area that was exerting a powerful but previously undetected influence on human choices and activities. As patients described their sexual fears, difficulties, and exploits, the clinicians began to see that a whole new approach to human sexuality was needed, particularly for those involved in the many varieties of deviant behaviour.

One of the first articles on homosexuality to appear in a professional journal in England was that in the *Medical Times and Gazette* for 1867, recording the tendencies of some men to feminine occupations and women to masculine occupations. In October 1884, Sir G. Savage described a case of sexual perversion in the *Journal of Medical Science*. The editor of this Journal was Dr D. H. Tuke, a noted London physician and alienist, who was a friend of the Symonds family.[13] Tuke's son, Jack, was a painter who lived in Falmouth, and J. A. Symonds wrote to him in praise of his paintings of adolescent bathers. Havelock Ellis was also a friend of Jack Tuke, and through these and other mutual friends, Symonds and Ellis came to know each other and collaborate on the preparation of the famous study 'Sexual Inversion'. This was first published in German translation as *'Das Konträre Geschlechtsgefühl'* in 1896 and a year later in an English edition which was quickly suppressed.

The book subsequently became one of the four volumes of Ellis' study in the *Psychology of Sex* which went through a number of editions until 1936. In the original, a good deal of the material was supplied by Symonds, including case histories and large parts of his essays. In later editions Ellis reduced the part supplied by Symonds progressively, and tried to suggest that Symonds' contribution was slight and unwelcome. The evidence of the letters exchanged between them in 1892 and 1893 shows, however, a much greater eagerness for collaboration; Symonds was an eager propagandist against the Labouchère amendment, and after his death, and the hostile public opinion created by the Wilde trial, Ellis' preference for a cooler detached approach is understandable.

Although Ellis' *Psychology of Sex* in its successive editions has been one of the most widely read of such books available in English, his contribution to the study of homosexuality was paralleled by a number of similar continental studies. Among them, Westphal, Professor of

Psychiatry in Berlin, published some case studies on inversion in his *'Archiv für Psychiatrie'* of 1870 (he called it *Konträre Sexualempfindung*—literally 'contrary sexual feeling'). Krafft-Ebing, Professor of Psychiatry in Vienna at the same time, recorded over two hundred cases of sexual inversion in his *Psychopathia Sexualis*, and Dr Magnus Hirschfeld, also of Berlin, considered the whole question from a medical legal viewpoint in his long and detailed study *Die Homosexualitat des Mannes and des Weibes* of 1914.

The bearing of all this accumulated new knowledge on the moral attitudes was carefully considered by Westermarck, a Finnish anthropologist who became Professor of Sociology at London University in 1907, having published *The Origin and Development of the Moral Ideas* the previous year. Dr Sherwin Bailey has drawn attention to a number of inaccuracies in the writings of both Ellis and Westermarck, who, he suggests, were inclined by anti-ecclesiastical and anti-christian prejudice to 'attribute to the Church every idea or development of which they disapproved'.[14] While it is true that these and indeed contemporary secular writers have a tendency to blame the Christian tradition, rather than the whole society of which it was a part, for the harsh attitude taken to homosexual behaviour, the accumulated clinical experience of these writers served to reveal not only how many people had some homosexual experience, but also how great was the misery they endured in a society which neither accepted them nor held out any great hope of cure.

It is often suggested that Kinsey's much later finding that about 5 per cent of adults were homosexually orientated was both novel and exaggerated, but in fact Ellis made the same estimate fifty years before. The risk of blackmail was serious, and Hirschfeld noted in 1913 that in Germany, where the law was similar to that in England, 'among 10,000 homosexual persons, hardly one falls victim to the law, but over 3,000 are victimized by blackmailers'. The case histories seldom refer to blackmail, though the fear of it sometimes drives patients to seek advice, but they give frequent evidence of jobs being lost and attempted suicide. The effect of publishing these histories was, of course, to create temporary scandal, but it eventually led to increased pressure that the laws of other European countries be brought into line with the humane provisions of the Code Napoléon. There was little that the doctors could do beyond assuring their patients that their condition was congenital rather than blameworthy, and encourage them to confine their sexual relationships to consenting partners on as permanent a basis as possible. Various theories emerged as to the causes of the homosexual condition. Hereditary predisposition, biological factors, experiences in early life, glands, and theories based on the assumed bisexuality of human nature were all put forward, but no consensus was reached at this period.

(b) THE NEW APPROACH OF S. FREUD

As a pioneer in the study of human sexuality, Sigmund Freud's work can rightly be regarded as a new departure even though he accepted some of the premises and findings of his predecessors. His general theory was concerned with the development of the sexual drive or libido towards the opposite sex, and he suggested that homosexuality could best be described as the retention or reversion of this drive to the same sex. The key to understanding homosexuality is to be found, therefore, in the circumstances which prevent some men and women from achieving the ability to choose their opposites as sexual partners. He makes an important distinction between inverts and perverts; inverts are limited in choice to their own sex with whom they seek to share sexual expression of a usual kind as far as anatomy permits; perverts have a more inhibited libido which seeks expression in diverted and abnormal ways through fetichism, voyeurism and similar 'horrors' as he calls them in his introductory lectures.

But he reassures his audience that indignation and disgust at unusual forms of sexual satisfaction are not enough. They represent a field of phenomena widely distributed. 'If we do not understand these morbid forms of sexuality, and cannot relate them to what is normal in sexual life, then neither can we understand normal sexuality.'[15]

In Freud's view, therefore, inversion and perversion are best regarded as fixations on sexual objects short of that normally achieved in adult life. The object of the libido remains where it was in childhood or adolescence, attached to objectives not fully differentiated from the individual concerned. Through analysis, it may be possible to retrace the forgotten experience which, retained within the unconscious part of the mind, continues to inhibit further development. Freud suggests that the inhibition is characteristically an irrational fear that heterosexual intercourse threatens castration or violent penetration. This is, of course, unrealized, and indeed may be symbolic—it is not the actual fear of sexual mutilation which matters so much, as the relational demands these fears signify which are, in reality, creating the anxiety and inhibition.

Freud's earliest substantial account of his understanding of homosexuality was set out in the first of his *Three Essays on Sexuality* published in 1905, and he amplified this by extensive footnotes in later editions up to 1920. In addition to the references in the *Introductory Lectures* of 1919, he considered further case histories in *Jealousy, Paranoia and Homosexuality* published in 1922 and in later contributions to Journals.

The first of the essays on sexuality deals with 'sexual aberrations'. Freud notes at once that he has drawn information for this essay from Krafft-Ebing, Havelock Ellis, Hirschfeld, and others, but he quickly imposes his own pattern of thought, distinguishing the sex object from the sex aim, the object being the person 'from whom sexual attraction proceeds', and the aim being 'towards which the instinct tends'. Numerous deviations occur in respect of both object and aim. Freud suggests:

The popular view of the sexual instinct is beautifully reflected in the poetic fable which tells how the original human beings were cut up into two halves—man and woman—and how these are always striving to unite again in love. It comes as a great surprise therefore to learn that there are men whose sexual object is a man and not a woman, and women whose sexual object is a woman and not a man. People of this kind are described as having 'contrary sexual feelings', or better, as being 'inverts' and the fact is described as 'inversion'. The number of such people is very considerable, though there are difficulties in describing it very precisely.[16]

There seems no reason to doubt that Freud is here referring to the androgynous myth set out by Aristophanes in Plato's *Symposium*[17] and he then distinguishes three types of inverts:

Absolute —exclusively drawn to their own sex
Amphigenic—equally drawn to both sexes
Contingent —drawn to their own sex when the other is inaccessible or imitated.

He then notes that inverts vary in attitude as to the peculiarity of their instinct, some accepting it as the natural course of things, while others rebel against what they feel as a pathological compulsion. Time is also relevant, for some inverts remember nothing else, some notice it after puberty, some regard it as a temporary episode in normal development, for some it develops late in life after a long period of normal sexual activity. Sometimes the libido changes over to an inverted sexual object after a distressing experience with a normal one.

The next section of the essay concerns deviations in sexual aim and is characterized by the same blend of calm observation of variant sexual behaviour and refusal to accept previous theories which do not explain adequately the range of actual human sexual activity. Instead of tracing this aspect of Freud's thought further in the first essay or his brief references to homosexuality, as he calls it later, it seems that a more balanced picture of his views can be gained by comparing a very different kind of writing from the essays or lectures. This is to be found in a biographical sketch of Leonardo da Vinci which Freud wrote and several times revised during the same period as the essays were composed.

In *Leonardo*, Freud offers an explanation of the painter's reputed homosexuality in terms of the significance of the emotional experiences of his early years as these could be understood by the psycho-analytic method. In this fascinating study, Freud fastens on the fact that Leonardo was an illegitimate child, brought up in his early years by his natural mother, and then, aged five, taken into his father's household when his wife proved childless. Noting also Leonardo's slow rate of work in certain assignments, he suggests an inhibition and finds evidence of this in the famous pictures, the 'Mona Lisa', and the 'Madonna and Child with St Anne'. The secret smile in the former represents that of his mother, the curious composition in the latter—two heads from a single body as it has been described—represents the two women he had to relate to in childhood. Further, Leonardo's drawing of 'human coition' in which Freud sees repugnance on the man's face and anatomical inaccuracy of a kind quite untypical of the artist, confirms the diagnosis.

The study has been criticized as fanciful, and dependent upon inaccurate evidence about Leonardo's life, and for the 'coition' sketch it has been established that the features Freud found significant were put in by his colleague Wehrt, who had made the copy Freud used, and are not in the original. Despite these criticisms, the *Leonardo* is an important document for its demonstration of Freud's method, and it has been used since by many imitators who have lacked his case experience and clinical intuition. The pattern was thus set for the commonplace assumption that the causes of homosexuality can be readily identified where there is evidence of disturbed relationships in infancy, and this doctrine has become entrenched in popular folklore on the subject in this century as had the notion of disease previously. Freud himself makes his own more cautious claim in a footnote to the sketch added in 1919:

> Psycho-analytic research has contributed two facts that are beyond question to the understanding of homosexuality, without at the same time supposing that it has exhausted the causes of this sexual aberration. The first is the fixation of the erotic needs on the mother . . .; the other is contained in the statement that everyone even the most normal person, is capable of making a homosexual object-choice and has done so at some time in his life, and either still adheres to it in his unconscious, or else protects himself against it by vigorous counter-attitudes. These two discoveries put an end both to the claims of homosexuals to be regarded as a 'third sex' and to what has been believed to be the important distinction between innate and acquired homosexuality.[18]

(c) POST-FREUDIAN PSYCHOLOGY AND PSYCHIATRY

A very brief review must suffice. Both Jung and Adler produced explanations of homosexuality in terms of their own positions, and Fenichel particularly expanded and emphasized Freud's suggestion that fear of female genitalia was a major factor in the origins of male homosexuality.[19] In the psychiatric field, I. Bieber and his associates used psycho-therapy with 106 male hospital patients and concluded from their findings that childhood conflict in the nuclear family, the presence of 'detached-hostile fathers' and/or 'close-binding-intimate' mothers were factors occurring more frequently in the histories of these patients than in a matched group of heterosexual patients. In their view the sins of the parents were visited on their children, or as they expressed it, 'The homosexual son emerged as the interactional focal point on whom the most profound parental psychopathology was concentrated.'[20]

Further studies by E. Bene, F. E. Kenyon, J. Hopkins and others[21] have aimed to provide more objective information about factors that might predispose towards homosexuality in early experience and about personal characteristics of adult male and female homosexuals. While these studies have produced significant results among the groups tested, their value as a general guide is not apparently fully accepted, partly because those available for the survey have usually been highly selected from hospitals or drawn from organizations concerned with advancing education about homosexuality, including the Albany Trust, and partly because some of the findings seem contradictory. It seems true at the moment that expert opinion is agreed on the relevance of infant and childhood experience, but that adult homosexuality includes a wide range of conditions for which the attempt to identify a single over-riding cause has proved simplistic.

The weight of research evidence on psychological factors substantiates the view that parental abnormalities are frequently found in case histories of adult homosexuals, but allowance must be made for the influence of the pioneer analysts in suggesting that this was the case. It is not certain that weak fathers or possessive mothers always predispose towards homosexual children; many homosexual adults have normal parents, many inadequate parents have heterosexual children.

A balanced and useful scheme for indicating how a range of psychological factors can be considered for relevance to homosexual imprinting has been suggested by Bancroft.[22] He distinguishes between *Push* factors which have a negative effect on the development of heterosexual behaviour and *Pull* factors which have a positive effect towards homosexuality.

Included in the *Push* factors are:

(1) *Anxiety and fear.* Typical fears are of venereal disease, pregnancy, injury by female sex organs, ridicule of one's sexual inadequacy.
(2) *Hostility and resentment.* Hostility and rivalry towards the other sex is commonly expressed by established homosexuals, though it is not clear if this attitude precedes or follows the original development of the orientation.

(3) *Disgust.* Disgust of female sex organs may turn some men away from women and in the predisposed make homosexuality more likely.
(4) *Inhibition.* Parents can create inhibitory attitudes in their children, either to sexual activity as such—by calling it sinful or dirty for example, or by inculcating disparaging notions and discouraging appropriate role play.

Included in the *Pull* factors are:

(1) *The strength of the sexual drive.* The desire for sexual contact with another person is basic for most humans, and a homosexual object choice is one alternative for meeting the desire.
(2) *Need for warmth.* If the father–child relationship has been unsatisfactory, and heterosexual relationships are unfulfilling, there may be a need for an emotionally and physically warm relationship with an older male.
(3) *Fulfilment of basic human needs.* Where strong feelings of heterosexual inadequacy are present, an alternative relationship of possessing and being possessed and sharing a common life and domestic arrangements with a homosexual partner will seem fulfilling and reinforce initial sexual object choices.

F Possibilities of Treatment

Possible methods of treating homosexuals have obviously been related to the various supposed causes. One of the attractions of the theory that it was an inherited or inherent trait was that this implied less moral blameworthiness and little expectation of cure. As the psychological studies were advanced, hopes were raised that once the inhibitory incidents were recalled through analysis, re-orientation of the sexual drive would follow, but Freud himself did not think this likely. He thought rather that the original bi-sexuality could be restored to a sufficient degree for the patient to be free to choose heterosexual activity, even if homosexual objects were still preferred.[23]

In a subsequent comment on the prospects for treatment, Freud wrote to an American woman who had asked for advice about her homosexual son, that he could not promise in a general way to abolish homosexuality and make normal heterosexuality takes its place:

> In a certain number of cases we succeed in developing the blighted germs of heterosexual tendency which are present in every homosexual, but in the majority of cases it is no more possible. It is a question of the quality and the age of the individual. The results of treatment cannot be predicted. What analysis can do for your son runs in a different line. If he is unhappy, neurotic, torn by conflicts, inhibited in his social life, analysis may bring him

harmony, peace of mind, full efficiency, whether he remains a homosexual or gets changed.[24]

The Wolfenden Committee considered what kind of help homosexuals should be offered and listed three objectives: a change in the direction of sexual preference, a better adaptation to life in general, and greater continence and self-control. They noted that none of their medical witnesses were able to provide any reference in medical literature to a complete change in orientation, and they concluded that it was unlikely that more than a shift on the Kinsey scale could be achieved. They therefore suggested that:

A homosexual, like any other person who suffers from maladjustment to society, may be regarded as successfully treated if he is brought to a more nearly complete adjustment with the society in which he lives .... It is perhaps worth adding that there may be good grounds, from a medical point of view, for not attempting any fundamental re-orientation of the sexual propensity of a homosexual who is already well adjusted and is a useful member of society.[25]

This commonsense view about the objectives of treatment was possibly influenced by the evidence already available to the Committee in 1957 that the prospects for change in orientation by any of the means then available were not very encouraging. The Committee had been told that of the 1065 men in prison for homosexual offences at that time, only some 60 were undergoing treatment in the prison psychiatric units. Some others, who might have been suitable, did not wish to be treated, and there was always some risk that prisoners would feign re-orientation to expedite their release.

In subsequent paragraphs of the Report, the Committee noted the obstacles to success in psychotherapeutic treatment for prisoners, including the low intelligence of the patient, and his lack of co-operation in a form of treatment which he feared might take away the only form of sexual satisfaction he knew without any certainty of providing an alternative. They recognized that some prisoners might be best kept in prison to protect society, but recommended extended use of probation.

Peter Wildeblood and others have derided the value of the measure of psychiatric help available to those in prison and, no doubt, the expense and availability of trained therapists affected the real position.[26] How much was achieved in private practice is unknown, for confidentiality and anonymity would have been carefully preserved until the passing of the 1967 Act. Many of the patients treated in hospital were there for mental conditions not necessarily associated with their homosexual orientation, but it has been among them, as volunteers, that most treatment seems to have been attempted.

Counselling services for homosexuals have proliferated in the past decade, but these are mostly concerned to give support rather than recommend change or treatment.

In 1967, MacCulloch and Feldman published results of treating 43 homosexuals with Aversion Therapy.[27] The method was not new, involving the administration of unpleasant but not unbearable electric shocks to patients when they responded to pictures of a homosexually erotic character with erections, but had been previously thought ineffective. Using the method involves assumptions about learning theory, and it is still uncertain whether or not more than short term—less than twelve months—changes in orientation can be achieved. Bancroft in a similar trial in 1969, achieved long term success with one out of ten of his patients, but notes that aversion is a technique that should be used in conjunction with drug and counselling therapy and, because it is inherently unpleasant, needs further controlled testing before its use can be justified regularly.[28]

Since the outlook for treatment of the homosexual condition in the present state of knowledge is confined to these rather uncertain procedures, and it is anyway clear that a large number of homosexual people, and probably the majority, do not seek treatment or wish for change, it is worth asking the question, What justification for treatment is there? Bancroft and others active in this field speak of more patients seeking their help than they can cope with, but given the possibility that 5 per cent of the adult population is homosexual, it seems that most of them consider themselves already within the Wolfenden definition of being sufficiently well-adjusted to their society as they are.

G Clinical Theology

Dr Frank Lake, the Christian missionary doctor who in the past 25 years has pioneered the Clinical Theology movement for pastoral training and care, particularly among clergy, from his centre in Nottingham, has made considerable use of neo-Freudian understandings. In his work with homosexual patients, mostly clergy, Dr Lake has used the drug LSD to assist in the recall of the earliest experiences of infancy, and he has focused attention on the particular experiences of birth itself. The struggle out of the womb, with its threat of asphyxia, the pains of withdrawal of life-sustaining attention by the mother in the first months of life, and similar traumas, can lead, he suggests, to the kind of distrust of women and mothers which predisposes towards adult homosexuality, and, indeed, to most kinds of neurotic illness.

All the fifty male homosexual patients to whom Lake and his colleagues administered LSD within the years 1955–66, relived, he reports, a traumatic incident or painful period of babyhood in which life in the woman's care had been horrific. He cites Otto Rank and Melanie Klein as original proponents of the theory that birth experiences were crucial, confirmed by the evidence of those who, in using LSD for psychotherapy, found that memories of these earliest moments could be recalled. Lake writes:

> The two forms of sexuality which impel men and women to love and to be drawn physically to members of their own and the opposite sex cannot be equated simply as genetic or constitutional variants. If a man's deep and natural love for a woman is analysed down to its depths, the roots will be found to reach down, not into pain, but into the exquisite bliss of union between the mother and the baby. To analyse, to the same depth, the homosexual element in a man's love, is to find invariably that this represents the hectic attempt to salvage something human and loving from the holocaust of dread in which all previous trust of the mother perished. Homosexual love in men for men, exactly like the hysterical woman's love of men, is impelled by dread. But the remedy for dread is not genital intimacy but spiritual intimacy.[29]

Lake also disagrees with the Wolfenden Committee conclusion that the homosexual propensity is no less controllable than the hetero-sexual one. He writes:

> To control that which is the free outgoing of a soul at peace with itself is entirely a different matter than the control of a need-love which is driven by the fierce panic of the most terrible deprivation known to the mind of man, that of a mother's love withdrawn from a baby.[30]

Lake claims several thousand clergy as being connected with his movement. This is not surprising, especially as it is fundamental to his method to work with Christian theological positions throughout. Writing from his pastoral viewpoint, Lake suggests that the Church has a therapy for homosexual men, who as clergy, while carrying it as a burden themselves, in another sense ceased to do so because they had surmounted it in their life in Christ. Further, the Church is said to provide the only fellowship for many lonely men and women, and therefore no one in training for the ministry can overlook his responsibility to understand and treat homosexuality.[31]

Perhaps the most obvious difficulties presented by Lake's findings are the comparatively unexplored technique of using LSD, and the possibility that the only certain deduction that can be made from his treatment of homosexual clergy with it, is that they suffered birth trauma *and* are homosexual, not that the first *caused* the second.

The question of religious conversion as a means of helping neurotic patients is too large for proper consideration here, though it may be noted that the B.M.A. Report to the Wolfenden Committee contained an appendix prepared by the Secretary, Dr E. E. Claxton, in which he provided ten case histories of homosexual people whom he considered had been helped in this way. Ever since William James published *The Varieties of Religious Experience*, the Gifford Lectures for 1901, it has been recognized that certain experiences permit both a religious and psychological explanation, and it is not surprising that the effects of LSD should equally be explainable in the same ways.[32]

H Some Tentative Conclusions

If the incidence of homosexuality among adult men and women is conservatively estimated at 5 per cent, it follows, for example, that more than a million such people live in England at the present time. Of these, only a few will seek for any kind of treatment leading to a change in the direction of their sexual drive, and even for them no great confidence of successful change can be offered.

The situation among bisexual people, possibly a far greater number, is less certain. Since the causes of homosexuality remain obscure, and the factors so far identified serve as little more than indicators of the complex processes by which human sexual drives are established or changed, there are no substantial grounds for supposing that the size of this substantial minority will be reduced in the near future. It could also be hazarded, at least in the opinion of the author, that a minority of similar proportions has usually existed in previous ages and societies. The homosexual condition is not one that waxes and wanes with the state of permissiveness in sexual behaviour of any given period.

What is known about the aetiology of sexual preference, heterosexual or homosexual, indicates that it is non-voluntary in terms of individual choice. The life style chosen by each person is, of course, a different matter, and unless a strict determinist view is taken of human nature, some measure of decision-making and moral responsibility remains. The traditional Christian teaching has been that homosexual people must remain physically inactive, or celibate, on the ground that the only form of legitimate sexual behaviour is between heterosexual couples married to each other.

The basis of this teaching is to be found in the interpretation given to certain biblical texts and the undeviating tradition of the Christian Church until modern times. This basis must now be examined in detail.

PART B
The Biblical Texts

2 Preliminary Questions

A Introduction

References to homosexuality in the Bible are infrequent and not easy to identify. Indeed, although the word has been in general use since the publication of the Wolfenden Report in 1957, it occurs only once in the New English Bible of 1970, and not at all in the Jerusalem Bible of 1966, nor in the Common Bible, an ecumenical edition of the Revised Standard Version, published in 1973. There are, however, several biblical texts widely regarded as being concerned with homosexual behaviour. In the Old Testament, a clear condemnation of male homosexual behaviour is found twice in the Holiness Code of Leviticus. Other Old Testament passages which very probably include reference to homosexual behaviour are the story of the destruction of Sodom in the book of Genesis and a somewhat similar event at Gibeah described in the Book of Judges. The denunciation of Temple prostitution in Deuteronomy and in the Books of the Kings may be relevant.

Within the New Testament, the Gospels do not mention homosexuality, but male and female homosexual behaviour are condemned in St Paul's Epistles to Corinthians, Romans, and Timothy.

In the inter-testamentary period, the Apocryphal writings and Rabbinic literature provide useful additional information. Some texts in the Apocrypha maintain the condemnation found in Leviticus, but also associate it strongly with the story of Sodom's destruction, and traces of this emphasis are also found in the New Testament Epistles of Peter and Jude. Through this association, unknown in the Old Testament proper, Sodom has lent its name in subsequent history to the practice of anal intercourse, but it should be noted that in the Gospels, the wickedness of Sodom is regarded as idolatry, inhospitality, and general sinfulness, rather than homosexuality, in this respect continuing the Old Testament tradition. Rabbinic literature follows Leviticus in condemning homosexual behaviour, and takes much the same generalized attitude to the sin of Sodom as found in the Old Testament.

B Problems of Translation

The biblical texts examined in detail later in this section are quoted from the New English Bible of 1970. Where significant alternative translations of the passages are to be found in other widely used English versions of the Bible, these are noted. Where the precise meaning of Hebrew or Greek words is important, transliteration is used, and attention is drawn to words in the older English versions which have a different contemporary meaning. An obvious example of the need for precision occurs with the Hebrew word *'yadha'* rendered as 'to know' in the Authorized Version, and variously in the newer translations. Its Hebrew meaning is important for a proper understanding of the Sodom story. An example of different contemporary meaning is 'sodomy', used of various kinds of sexual vice in the Authorized version, including temple prostitution and not confined to homosexual behaviour as we might perhaps assume. Care about translation is obviously necessary for a correct understanding of the original text, and while it is true that recently discovered biblical manuscripts pre-dating those used by earlier translators have led to some minor corrections and clarification among possible variant readings, notably with the help of the Qumran documents for the Old Testament, it does not appear at the time of writing that any of the passages considered here are affected.

C The inclusion of non-canonical sources

The version of the Old Testament usually available to the first Christians was the Greek translation called the Septuagint, and quotations from the Old Testament found in the New Testament come from it. The Septuagint included the Apocryphal writings, as did the Latin Vulgate, so familiarity with these writings continued in the Western Church until the Reformation, and in the Catholic Church since then. The Reformers, however, used the Hebrew Bible without the Apocrypha for their translations of the Old Testament, and only with the latest versions have the Apocryphal books reappeared bound into the popular editions, interspersed in the traditional way as in the Jerusalem Bible, or collected between the Canonical Testaments as in the New English Bible.

The long standing debate about the status of the Apocryphal books between the Catholic and Protestant churches cannot be pursued here,[1] but their significance in the developing Christian attitude to homosexuality justifies reference to them in this section.

Rabbinic literature originating in the inter-testamental period is proving to be an important source for extending our understanding of the background to Christ's work and teaching, and comparative study is fast developing now that the traditional antipathy between Judaism and Christianity is waning. Such comparison raises, of course, problems about the measure of continuity to be expected between the old teaching and the new, but at least it can be said that Jesus and Paul were familiar with the views of the Rabbis of their time. Converts from Judaism in the Palestinian Church would have been in the same position, and probably suspicious of the Apocryphal writings, unlike their kinsmen of the Greek-speaking diaspora around the Mediterranean who were accustomed to the Septuagint.

D The authority and interpretation of the Biblical Texts

The Bible is regarded by Christians as their primary source of guidance in questions of faith and morality. The precise way in which this guidance is thought to be found has varied in Christian history, reflecting not only the traditions of the Churches and the importance given to sacred Scripture in their teaching, but also the changing presuppositions which Christians have brought to the study of the texts. It is not always realized that methods of interpretation of Scripture have varied from the earliest times to the present, as much, for example, between Jerome and Augustine, Eusebius and Bede, Luther and Calvin, as between the better known biblical commentators of the nineteenth and twentieth centuries. Augustine's suggestion in *De Doctrina Christiana*, *c.* 400 CE that he who would read the Bible correctly must be skilled in Greek and Hebrew and ought to be well grounded in history, local customs, and institutions, has a modern ring.[2]

Those Christians who seek detailed ethical guidance direct from the text of the Bible will find no difficulty in confirming that the traditional attitude of hostility to homosexual behaviour is derived from Scripture. The references in Leviticus and Paul's Epistles are unambiguous even to readers who would hesitate to adopt an unqualified literalism. Other Christians find this direct approach unsatisfactory in a number of ways. The new understandings of human sexuality provided by the medical and behavioural sciences, reviewed in the preceding section, seem for them to raise questions about how far it is still legitimate to read off such directions from biblical texts which originated, it is assumed, at a time of comparative ignorance about the nature of the homosexual condition. Without abandoning the concept of the authority of the Bible, it can be argued that since homosexual behaviour was clearly a minor matter for the biblical writers compared with their overriding responsibility to record God's saving work in history, we should take serious note of any relevant texts but feel free to interpret them afresh in the light of current knowledge.

New understandings of human sexuality have been matched with new approaches to biblical scholarship. As Augustine suggested, but probably in a far more thorough-going way than he would have envisaged, archaeological discoveries in the Middle Eastern lands of the Fertile Crescent have in this century greatly increased our knowledge of the cultural, religious, ethical, legal, and social aspects of the life of Israel and its surrounding nations. However, early confidence as to how much information for interpreting the Bible could be obtained from these discoveries has been modified recently, for it now seems there are limits to the value of other documentary sources and the Bible has to be interpreted, to a large extent, *sui generis*.

While taking careful note of archaeological evidence, biblical scholars are now more inclined to regard archaeology as a related but distinct field of study from their own, and they have paid increasing attention to the literary structure of the biblical writings, hoping to discern the oral and written traditions from which the final canonical texts of the Bible as we know it have been formed. An obvious and well-known example for the Old Testament is the recognition that the Pentateuch has a complicated literary history in which at least four original sources can be distinguished with some certainty, and in the same way St Paul's two Epistles to the Corinthians are thought to have been compiled from an original correspondence, not all of which is now available. Both these examples will prove relevant to the texts about homosexuality.

Another concern of contemporary biblical scholarship which affects the interpretation of particular texts is the conceptual framework within which the original writings were framed. The controversies which have arisen over the findings of Galileo, Darwin, Freud, and in our own day, the dymythologizing school in theology, are familiar examples of the continuing need to assess the relationships between the concepts of different ages.

Ways of describing truth, accepted without question in one age, can seem apparently incompatible with those of another. The unique status of the Bible in Christian thought implies that we cannot treat its conceptual frameworks as lightly as we are now accustomed to do with, say, scientific models of thought, enunciated with the expectation that they will be shortly modified or superseded. The Christian mind has to wrestle with the dilemma arising from the recognition of a certain givenness in the scriptural revelation, from which the Holy Spirit draws forth illumination for every generation, set against the obvious fact that the biblical writers were men of their own time, earthed in actual situations amongst which they hoped to discern the will of God and obey it. The dilemma has been well expressed in Leonard Hodgson's famous question and answer:

> What must the truth have been if it appeared like this to men who thought and spoke like that? . . .
> We must be content to see what we can from the standpoint of our own circumstances. Our task is to expound the revelation as we see it to our contemporaries, leaving it to future generations to discount whatever in our vision and exposition has been of only passing worth.[3]

Whatever view is taken with regard to the authority and interpretation of the Bible (and it may be noted in parenthesis that some antagonism between evangelical and Gay Liberation groups seems to be related more to the question of biblical authority than to texts about homosexuality), most Christian writers in the past twenty years concerned with the problem of homosexuality have felt it necessary to scrutinize the biblical texts. These writings are reviewed in Part D, and it will be seen that they are greatly indebted to the pioneer and comprehensive research of Dr Sherwin Bailey, whose careful and wide-ranging work originally appeared in a paper prepared for the Church of England Moral Welfare Council and submitted to the Wolfenden Committee. An expanded version was subsequently published as *Homosexuality and the Western Christian Tradition*, in which the first third of the book is devoted to an examination of the biblical evidence.[4]

Most commentators on the biblical texts since Bailey have accepted his distinction between the definite references to homosexual behaviour, namely Leviticus and St Paul's Epistle, and the possible references in Deuteronomy and the Apocrypha, but his arguments for excluding the Sodom story have proved more controversial. Although the distinction between definite and possible references makes for clarity in examining the texts, it does of course involve prior decisions about their interpretation, and implicitly imposes an external pattern on the way we approach the texts. In view of recent developments in biblical scholarship, that distinction is not followed here. Instead, the texts are taken in chronological order of composition. This historical order has the advantage that it makes easier any comparison with other writings or evidence of a similar period, though it must be admitted that assigning dates to biblical texts is a complex task and precision is not always possible. Nevertheless, to anticipate a conclusion from the examination of the texts that follow, it will be argued that this historical method shows how antagonism to homosexual behaviour was expressed intermittently in the early traditions of Israel, and among its surrounding nations. By the fifth century before the Christian era, this antagonism had become established as a firm prohibition in Old Testament law and St Paul reiterates it, seeing homosexual behaviour as a feature of the pagan lifestyle to be avoided by Christians.

3 Old Testament Texts

A The Destruction of Sodom and Gomorrah Genesis 19

(a) THE NARRATIVE

The catastrophe that overtook these two cities of the plain at the base of the Dead Sea is described in Genesis 18.16—19.29, and the sequence of events set out there has been traditionally interpreted by Jewish, Islamic, and Christian commentators as a clear demonstration of God's wrath at those who attempted homosexual intercourse. But the destruction of Sodom is part of a much longer narrative, the story of Abraham, which continues from chapter 12—24 of Genesis, and a consideration of the whole story helps towards the interpretation of the events at Sodom. The lives of the patriarchs in these chapters have been called sagas, by which is meant not merely records in a factual sense, but the expression in literary form of how people 'think of their history'. These patriarchal traditions, therefore, though they contain history, are for belief, not just for information about the origins of the Israelites.[1]

Abraham is the first Old Testament 'personality', the pioneer of Israel's faith, and the saga records the development of his special relationship with God. Lot, Abraham's nephew, appears in the saga as a relatively less satisfactory character. Originally a settler in Sodom, preferring the comforts of urban life to the spartan style of Abraham, Lot is captured in a tribal raid but he is rescued by his uncle and returns home. Abraham is visited by the Lord and two companions and is promised an heir. Then the Lord says he must visit Sodom and Gomorrah to see for himself whether or not the outcry against them justifies their destruction.

Abraham intercedes for Sodom, and the Lord agrees that he will not destroy it if ten good men are found there. The Lord then departs and his two companions, now identified as angels, once the presence of the Lord is removed, travel at great speed to Sodom and meet Lot at the gates of the city. Lot appears to recognize the true identity of his visitors, and after the appropriate courtesies of eastern culture for offering hospitality to distinguished guests have been exchanged, they agree to come home with him. After supper the townspeople surround the house and it is made clear that the whole male population is involved.

They called to Lot and asked him where the men were who had entered his house that night. 'Bring them out' they shouted, 'so that we can have intercourse with them.' Lot went out into the doorway to them, closed the door behind him and said, 'No, my friends, do not be so wicked. Look I have two daughters, both virgins; let me bring them out to you, and you can do what you like with them, but do not touch these men, because they have come under the shelter of my roof.' (New English Bible, Genesis 19.5–8)

Lot's offer of his daughters is rejected and he is threatened as an alien in the city with worse than they have in mind for his visitors.

Once the immediate danger from the mob is averted by striking them blind, the total destruction of Sodom is deferred long enough for Lot and his family to escape. They leave reluctantly. Lot's wife is turned into a pillar of salt for looking back, and Lot eventually settles in the isolated region of Zoar. No husbands are available for his daughters and so he begets children from them himself, and these are said to be the original ancestors of the Moabites and Ammonites, Israel's traditional enemies. On this apparently sarcastic note, the story of Sodom and Lot ends, and the contrast is thus firmly drawn between the long-term consequences of Abraham's free response in faith and Lot's grudging obedience.

(b) COMMENT

The investigation of the oral and written sources of the books of the Pentateuch has been a major task of Old Testament scholars for some two centuries, and only a brief outline of some generally accepted conclusions can be given here, but they will prove a sufficient basis for the contention that the Sodom narrative can be regarded as the earliest indication of hostility to homosexual behaviour in the Old Testament.

The supposition that Moses was the author of the whole Pentateuch, the Law of the Hebrew Bible, appeared in the second century before the Christian era, despite the difficulty that his own death is described within it, but this is seldom accepted today.[2] Instead, the basic formation of the text as we now know it seems to have resulted from a process of collection, reflection, and editing over a period of some five centuries. The process began early after the setting up of the monarchy around 1000 years BCE, and ended with the re-establishment of Israel after the exile in the sixth century BCE, though it has to be recognized that the existing Hebrew texts come from copies made after the time of Christ.

The original oral traditions of Israel now found in the Pentateuch, and once supposedly memorized and recited at the worship centres of early tribal settlements were collected by two authors, the Yahwist (J) from the Southern Kingdom, and the Elohist (E) in the north. To these were added the Deuteronomist (D) in the middle of the period, and the final assimilation and editing was made by a Priestly group (P) at the end of the exile, *c.* 538 BCE. It must be regarded as not yet settled how far the material used by these four sources was extant at the beginning of the monarchy (in which case there was a kind of common pool of tradition from which the authors chose that which suited their theological perspective), and how far each author took from that which was current at his own time.[3]

In either case the Yahwistic material has been long regarded by some scholars as containing at least two early but distinct blocks of traditional material, and among those who take this view, the story of Sodom's destruction is assigned to the earliest block, and this included Genesis chapter 13, as well as chapters 18 and 19. This assignment implies that the successive editors of the Pentateuch, as far as we can tell, have regarded the Sodom narrative as an ancient one, worth preserving intact and unaltered, though it has been suggested that the stories of Abraham and Lot were originally separate and woven together by the Yahwist or just before his time.[4]

The precise sites of the five cities of the plain, including Sodom and Gomorrah, have proved difficult to identify, though they are usually placed at the southern end of the Dead Sea, and possibly are now submerged. The region has been subject to earthquake and subsidence, and is, of course, within the northern part of the great Rift Valley running down from Syria to the African Lakes. The presence of sulphurous springs, oil, and bitumen at the east bank of the sea have led some commentators to suggest a natural explanation for the destruction of the cities, especially when this geological information is associated with archaeological evidence of the abandonment of a possible site around 2400 BCE.[5]

To the questions how, when and why was Sodom destroyed, there can bc few confident answers apart from those suggested in the narrative itself, and those who press beyond the Yahwist's explanation of divine intervention suggest that the actual natural disaster was still remembered at the time of Abraham, and a theological or aetiological explanation was attached to the memory as the tale was told. Alternatively, later than Abraham, but before the conquest of Canaan, observation of the destroyed sites during the patriarchal period and the migration northwards was used as a didactic opportunity. In either case, the description of Sodom as a place of wickedness worthy of divine indignation and judgement became entrenched in the saga of Abraham.[6]

As the Yahwist presents the story of Sodom, however, the chief focus of interest lies not in the wickedness of the city itself, but in the development of the relationship between God and Abraham, so that Abraham becomes, *inter alia*, convinced of God's justice. Sodom is, from the beginning, a city destined for destruction and this is made plain in chapter 13, verses 11 and 13: 'The men of Sodom were wicked, great sinners against the Lord'. But before God acts, he decides to take Abraham into his confidence and explain the action he feels bound to take. The ensuing discussion (chapter 18.17–38) develops several major themes. Among them is the universality of the just judgement of God, who hears and responds to the cry of the oppressed from the cities of the plain, in no sense places belonging to Israel. Then there is the theme of communal responsibility, and its contrast, drawn out by Abraham's plea, of communal merit, for it is not suggested that the ten righteous, if such be found, should save only themselves. There is further, in the whole narrative, an underlying motif of great significance later in the Bible, that the just shall live by faith. Abraham does, profoundly, and Lot attempts to, but the inadequacy of his commitment is shown by the difficulty the angels have in persuading him to leave the city in time. With all these themes introduced into the discussion that precedes the events that precipitate the city's destruction, it is clear that the wickedness of the men of Sodom is generalized and established in advance. What happens when the angelic visitors accept Lot's hospitality is an illustration of that wickedness, further evidence of an abominable state of affairs which requires God's justice to be expressed in punishment, and not in itself the cause of that judgement.[7]

That the wickedness of Sodom was understood in broad terms within the Israelite tradition can be demonstrated from the other references to Sodom in the Old Testament. In the later writings, various sins are suggested within the general conviction that Sodom represents in an archetypal way the alienation from Yahweh that provokes his destructive wrath. Thus in Isaiah chapter 1 insincere sacrifice, injustice, and oppression are considered the major sins of Sodom: in Ezekiel chapter 16 they are pride and neglect of the poor, and in Jeremiah chapter 23, adultery and hypocrisy are mentioned.[8] It seems then that both in the introduction to the events at Sodom and in subsequent reference to it in the Old Testament, no special emphasis in placed on homosexual sin, but it is nevertheless clear that the narrative itself suggests an attempt at homosexual assault which Lot attempts to defeat by appealing to the code of hospitality and the offer of an heterosexual alternative.

The theme of hospitality has been introduced into the narrative at the beginning of chapter 18 when Abraham entertains the three visitors and in a similar way Lot insists on receiving the angelic visitors to Sodom, who were prepared at first to spend the night in the streets. The townspeople invade their privacy, and the communal responsibility for this offence is stressed. What they demand, according to the New English Bible translation, is intercourse with the visitors, and this makes explicit that sodomy was intended, conforming to the traditional interpretation of the text, of which the older translation, from the Authorized version onwards was 'that we might know them'.[9]

The Hebrew word here translated as intercourse is *'yadha'*, which is very commonly used in the Old Testament and usually means 'to know' in the ordinary sense of 'being acquainted with'. Apart from this usual meaning, *yadha* is also occasionally used to imply sexual intercourse or coital knowledge, and this special use is familiar from the King James and subsequent English Bibles, and in the legal term 'carnal knowledge', now somewhat archaic. *Yadha* occurs ten times in the Old Testament with this meaning of sexual intercourse, and in each case apart from the Sodom narrative (and Judges chapter 19 infra) heterosexual intercourse is clearly intended and a child results. Thus in Genesis chapter 4, where the conception of Cain (v. 1), Enoch (v. 17) and Seth (v. 25) are described by *yadha*, the older translations use 'knew' and the New English Bible uses 'lay with'.

The possibility of ambiguity in the use of *yadha* in the Sodom story and thence of the exclusion of any reference to homosexual assault has attracted a good deal of attention among commentators in this century who are not primarily Old Testament scholars. The ambiguity was, in fact, recognized by Calvin in his commentary on this verse in Genesis, where he suggests that the townspeople deliberately used this word to conceal their real intentions towards Lot's guests, as they had, until then, prevented him from discovering this to be one of their vices. But Calvin has no doubt that this attempted atrocity was the final proof that God's judgement on them could no longer be deferred.[10]

More serious doubt was expressed early in this century by G. A. Barton who suggested that there was no actual necessity to give *yadha* the sexual meaning found in Genesis chapter 4.1 and that the townspeople may have only intended to give the visitors a beating. He further noticed that in the Bishops' Bible and King James' Bible, sodomy was a term used of sexual vice including bestiality, fornication, and cult prostitution, as in Deuteronomy and Kings,[11] where it refers to temple prostitutes.

This view was thoroughly examined by Bailey,[12] who argued that the assumption that *yadha* has the untypical sexual connotation in the Sodom narrative is mistaken. In his view the story makes better sense if the ordinary meaning of *yadha* is understood, for then the townspeople of Sodom simply exercise their civic right to enquire who the strangers are. They wish to establish for themselves the harmlessness of the foreigners, for after all, Lot himself is an alien, the times are dangerous, and the visitors may be spies. It is a sensible precaution to check the credentials of strangers within the walls. If this view is accepted, the wickedness of the townspeople can be said to be adequately shown by their refusal to allow Lot to exercise hospitality and their attempt to break into his house.

Although Bailey's argument has found a ready acceptance among some subsequent writers on the biblical attitude to homosexuality, and does, if it stands, cast serious doubts on the traditional interpretation,[13] there are probably stronger arguments for continuing to hold that the Yahwist intended to preserve the tradition that the men of Sodom were so wicked that they did not even hesitate to attempt buggery with strangers. The practice of inflicting this indecency on defeated enemies in the Middle Eastern countries in ancient times has been clearly established, and homosexual assault on the young and on other vulnerable people was forbidden in the laws of other nations in the Fertile Crescent during the period of the Patriarchs.[14] It is not, therefore, intrinsically unlikely that the Israelite tradition would contain such a derogatory tale. We have already seen that the detail of the story is not of much importance to the Yahwist, but that he seems to have accepted the narrative as a whole.

Further, there seems to be a macabre symmetry about the tale as it is traditionally interpreted. Modern readers, no doubt, find the offer of the daughters as a substitute distasteful, but it has to be remembered that the place of women was inferior and it would have been regarded as moral for Lot to preserve his angelic visitors and protect the honour of the Lord whom they represented by making such an offer. Presumably the townspeople were not aware of the status of the visitors, and Lot's offer of his daughters would seem something of an over-reaction if all that was being asked was a check on the *bona fides* of the visitors. No doubt women were expendable at this time in a way abhorrent to twentieth-century minds, but the Yahwist uses the word *yadha* again in verse 7, the daughters 'have not yet known a man' ('both virgins' in the New English Bible translation), so a rather extraordinary subtlety is inferred in the narrative if the word changes its meaning from 'acquaintance' to 'intercourse' as the dialogue proceeds.

The story of Sodom's destruction may be held therefore to be one of Israel's ancient traditions, taken into the Pentateuch unchanged, woven into the saga of Abraham and Lot, and establishing primarily the universal justice of God. Whether the tradition stems from a memory of the natural disaster that overwhelmed the cities of the plain at or soon before the time of Abraham, or is an aetiological myth about ruins that had never been known to have been inhabited, the story as we have it is a rich source of theological truth concerning Abraham's spiritual odyssey. It has to be said, too, that among the various wickednesses attributed to this foreign city inhospitality and homosexual assault are included. While there seem to be insufficient grounds for asserting that the Sodom narrative is the definitive text in the Bible for condemning homosexual practice, it remains the case that the Pentateuchal editors from first to last evidently thought such condemnation appropriate.

B The Rape of the Levite's concubine at Gibeah Judges 19

(a) INTRODUCTORY NOTE

Although this narrative is found in the Hebrew Old Testament after the Pentateuch, in the group of books known as the former Prophets, and may have reached its final form as late as the fifth century BCE, it refers to the period of the Israelite settlement in Canaan, and has some obvious similarities to the Sodom story. It is therefore convenient to consider it now, before the references to temple prostitution in Deuteronomy, and the prohibitions of the Holiness Code in Leviticus.

(b) THE NARRATIVE

The story begins with a Levite from the hill country of Ephraim taking as wife a concubine from Bethlehem. In a fit of anger she returns to her father's home, but the Levite follows her, and after a family reconciliation, he sets out with her and a servant to return north to Ephraim.[15] They pass by Jerusalem, not at this time occupied by the tribes of Israel, and arrive at Gibeah in Benjamite territory. They are offered hospitality for the night by an old man who lives in the town but who is himself a stranger (*ger*) to the townspeople, and also an Ephraimite. As they settle down to supper, they are interrupted:

> While they were enjoying themselves, some of the worst scoundrels in the town surrounded the house, hurling themselves against the door and shouting to the old man who owned the house, 'Bring out the man who has gone into your house, for us to have intercourse with him'. The owner of the house went to them and said 'No, my friends, do nothing so wicked. This man is my guest; do not commit this outrage. Here is my daughter, a virgin; let me bring her out to you. Rape her and do to her what you please; but you shall not commit such an outrage against this man.' But the men refused to listen to him, so the Levite took hold of his concubine and thrust her outside for them. They assaulted her and abused her all night till the morning, and when dawn broke, they let her go. (*New English Bible*, Judges 19.22–25)

The concubine dies as a result of this outrage, and the Levite dissects her body and sends a portion of it to each of the other eleven tribes, blaming the Benjamites for their refusal to deal with the offenders themselves. The consequence is a punitive 'Holy War' between the eleven tribes and the Benjamites, which ends, after a good deal of killing, with a reconciliation.

(c) COMMENT

The Book of the Judges covers the early period of the Israelites' settlement in Canaan in the thirteenth and twelfth centuries BCE, and points towards the need for the establishment of the monarchy—when everyone did that which was right in his own eyes, there was no King in Israel (21.25). The original compilation of these traditional stories about local heroes and rulers during the settlement period may have been made by a pre-deuteronomic editor, and his work is thought to have been several times revised, so that the version we now have is probably post-exilic. The twelve tribes are described as settling into their allotted areas, knowing themselves bound together in principle by their committal to or covenant with Yahweh, and in practice struggling to form an institutional relationship with each other, while at the same time maintaining an uneasy peace both with the previous inhabitants of their territories, and with powerful surrounding nations. The relationship between the tribes has been described by Alt as an 'amphictyony', a term adopted from the supposedly similar arrangement existing among the Greek city states, but this may be misleading in that it suggests a closer and more legally structured federation than the tribal league had developed at this time.[16]

The final five chapters of Judges are additions to the main part of the book, and chiefly describe the tribe of Dan's migration north, and then the war between Benjamin and the remaining tribes, for which the cause, or as some scholars suggest, the pretext, is the rape of the Levite's concubine. Gibeah was a town just east of the main road north from Jerusalem, and is now called Tel-el-Ful. Recent excavations there indicate that a violent destruction of the site took place in the twelfth century BCE.[17]

Although no reference to Sodom is made in the Judges story, the apparent similarities between the townspeople's assault at Sodom and the scoundrels' rape at Gibeah are marked, and it has often been suggested that the Judges version is the old tale reworked for a new didactic purpose. In both stories there is a serious breach of hospitality, the Levite is entitled to respect as the angels were, and the demand to bring out the man (men) that we may have intercourse with them is identical, though only a few men are involved at Gibeah, and the corporate responsibility theme is applied to the Benjamites as a tribe not to the actual attackers. The Hebrew word *yadha* is used for the demand, and in reference to the virgin daughter who has not 'known' men. Like Lot, the old man offers his daughter as a substitute, but at this point the stories diverge. Instead of the intervention of the angels, the Levite surrenders his concubine, and the assault follows, the Hebrew words making clear its brutality. The theme of providing descendants, illustrated after Sodom by Lot's incest with his daughters, reappears in the sequel to the Gibeah incident. After the war, the continuity of the tribe is provided by the capture of young women who are taken to Shiloh and there forcibly married to the remaining Benjamite men.

The main didactic purpose of the Gibeah narrative seems to be to draw out from the memory of the feuds among the tribes a warning that the lack of a central ruler was a serious disadvantage for the emerging notionally united tribal league. It is doubted how far there was, in fact, at this time a sufficiently united structure among the tribes, around a sanctuary or in terms of political organization, for a relatively unimportant man like the Levite to summon the tribes to corporate action against the Benjamites. It is unlikely also that there existed among the tribes in the twelfth century BCE any common codified system of criminal law, but there may well have been some consensus that breach of hospitality to the Levite and sexual violence to his woman were serious crimes. Such precepts would not have been unique to Israel in the twelfth century BCE.[18] A post-exilic editor, adding these chapters as an appendix might, however, be glad to imply ancient witness to such structure and law.

The narrative itself poses intriguing textual problems. In some verses there is an economy of style reminiscent of the Yahwist. The return of the woman to the threshold, arms stretched out, dead but not so described, is poignant. But there is also a good deal of repetition and untidiness in the text, notably about the status of the woman, whether she was angry, or unfaithful as the Hebrew text has it, how long they stayed with the father-in-law, whether the old man at Gibeah offered his daughter and the concubine, or simply stated she was a virgin. (See footnote to Revised Standard Version, etc.) In his account of what happened, in chapter 20 verse 5, the Levite says the attack was intended to kill him and rape his concubine.

It seems likely, therefore, that a conflation of two stories has taken place here, and it is fairly simple to disentangle them. From J the men of the city surround the house, demanding that the man be brought out that they may know him. The host offers two women instead, denouncing their wickedness. From another source comes a story of attempted murder on the Levite by scoundrels who beat on the door and accept instead the opportunity to rape his wife. Conflating the two stories, and achieving a measure of verbal harmonization with the Genesis account, would not have been a difficult task for an editor who may also have been aware of the Holiness Code, and a Levite himself.[19]

The ambiguity about the meaning to be given to *yadha* by translators of the Gibeah narrative reflects the same hesitancy as that noted for the Sodom narrative. The Septuagint, both in the version of Grabe and later of Swete, has 'given recognition or permission' (*sungeneumetha*) for Sodom, and 'acquaint ourselves with' (*gnomen*) for Gibeah. Calvin noticed this Septuagint difference, used 'know' (*cognoscemus*) for his Latin version, but with the meaning noted above. The Vulgate has 'know' (*cognoscemus*) and the Douai English translation of 1609 renders the Vulgate Latin as 'know'. Similarly, Luther preserves the ambiguity in his Bible, using 'know' (*erkennen*) in Genesis and Judges, but the Zuricher Bibel published in 1931 to mark the four-hundredth centenary of Zwingli twice uses 'cohabit' (*beiwohnen*), clearly sexual in the context. The English Bibles from the Authorized Version to the Common Bible have the ambiguous 'know' except the New English Bible, as quoted above, and the Good News Bible, which describes the men of Gibeah as sexual perverts who want to have sex with the Levite. The French Jerusalem translation has 'know' (*connaissons*) in Judges whereas 'abuse' was used in Genesis, but this rather surprising variant is removed in the English version of Jerusalem which has 'abuse' in both narratives, though a footnote to the Judges text stresses the offence against hospitality only.[20]

It would seem from this review of the major European translations that the ancient and reformation Bibles were uniform in preserving the ambiguity, and although the opportunity to choose either a sexual or acquaintance alternative seems to have been open to them from the Septuagint text and the Hebrew if they had them, this was not taken. The most likely explanation for this is that they would have been aware of the traditional interpretation and saw no reason to doubt it. By the end of the nineteenth century, the sexologists[21] had noted the doubts expressed by Christian and Jewish scholars, a view elaborated by Barton and later Bailey, and the reaction of the subsequent biblical translators has been either (a) to retain the ambiguity in the translations which stem from the Revised Version and which are characteristically careful about literalism where possible or (b) to make the homosexual behaviour explicit, where the sense of the original dominates, as in Zurich and New English Bible, and in the Good News paraphrase. Given the Vulgate, it is improbable that the modern Jersalem versions intend a serious exclusion of homosexual reference from the Judges story.

Not surprisingly, Bailey has argued that *yadha* has the same 'examine their credentials' meaning in Judges as in Genesis, and also draws attention to the corruption of the Judges text, holding, therefore, that the Gibeah outrage has no importance for establishing the biblical attitude to homosexual behaviour.[22] This view, once widely followed, is now treated with more caution.[23] While respecting the care which Bailey has taken in examining the texts, it seems preferable to be rather more thorough-going in disentangling the two sources (at least) which lie behind the Gibeah narrative as we now have it. If it is the case, as modern commentators accept, that the J source contains the reference to homosexual behaviour, and it is the Yahwist who uses *yadha* with the literally ambiguous meaning, but makes clear what is implied by the context and restrained style, then it is proper to ask what is the significance of the conflation accepted or devised by the final post-exilic editor of Judges. Presumably out of respect for the tradition as he found it, or to harmonize this narrative with the Sodom and Leviticus texts, he provides this reiteration, stressing thereby a hostile attitude to homosexual behaviour of which he approved, or which he felt obliged to record. In other words, when the opportunity to reaffirm this hostility appeared, it was accepted, and for this reason the Judges narrative stands as distinct additional evidence of the attitude of the Old Testament writers, notwithstanding the J source from which it comes.

This conclusion, clear as it is, must not, however, obscure the fact that, like the Sodom narrative, the attribution of homosexual behaviour to the scoundrels of Gibeah is not the chief emphasis. As with the story of Lot in Genesis, which acts as a counterpoint to the obedience of Abraham, so in this appendix to Judges, the insignificant and inferior tribe of Benjamin is denigrated in comparison with the high calling of the whole tribal league. Sodom had been an alien place, inhabited by foreigners, and long known in ruins. The quarrels between the tribes were much more recent history, and the Gibeathites a disgrace to the family who were punished and reformed. The tale may have been sharpened in the telling, but then King Saul's birthplace had been Gibeah, as a later Jewish reader might have recalled with a wry smile.

C The Eradication of Temple Prostitution

(a) INTRODUCTION

The second section of the Hebrew Bible, known as the former Prophets, comprises the Books of Joshua, Judges, 1 and 2 Samuel and 1 and 2 Kings, which together record the history of Israel from the settlement in Canaan to the exile in Babylon. Recent scholarship, following a suggestion of Martin Noth, is inclined to regard these six books as a collection of historical records and legal codes woven into a composite work, for which the Book of Deuteronomy served as an introduction. This composition was completed during or soon after the exile, and is known as the Deuteronomistic History, but its unity was subsequently broken when the final form of the Pentateuch emerged, and the historical books were divided, somewhat arbitrarily to fit into convenient scroll lengths.

The 'history' is characterized by a theological premise that the decline and fall of the two kingdoms of Israel and Judah have to be explained, not by the weakness of the people before their invaders, but as a demonstration of the power and judgement of God on their disobedience. This premise is in a sense nothing other than the message of the major prophets, particularly Amos, but it is expressed in the Deuteronomistic corpus both in terms of the laws that should have been obeyed and in comment on the kings who are assessed in terms of their righteousness before God, rather than from the political or economic success of their reigns. One test of their orthodoxy is the degree of resistance they offer to the ever-present threat of syncretism with the religious practices of the Canaanites of which temple prostitution is regarded as an outrageous example.

There are, of course, a number of qualifications that have to be made to this theory of the Deuteronomistic history, outlined above in a simplified form, and the identification of this theological overview does not preclude the recognition of many sources, some of them ancient, within the corpus as it finally developed. It is the basic framework, and occasional comments in the text which indicate the Deuteronomist's work, and which justify considering together certain similar texts from Deuteronomy and 1 and 2 Kings which refer to temple prostitution. It will be argued that they have only marginal significance for our study of biblical attitudes to homosexuality.[24]

(b) THE TEXTS

There are five references to temple prostitution in Deuteronomy and the Books of the Kings.

The first reference, in terms of a direct prohibition, is in Deuteronomy 23.17

> No Israelite woman shall become a Temple Prostitute and no Israelite man shall prostitute himself in this way. (New English Bible)

The references in Kings are related to particular situations during the troubled years of the divided kingdom. In Solomon's declining years, the superficial unity of David's monarchy begins to collapse, and Jeroboam leads the Northern tribes into revolt while Rehoboam, who rules Judah in the south, is pre-occupied with the threat of invasion from Egypt. To discourage worship at the central sanctuary in Jerusalem, Jeroboam establishes hill shrines in the north, his own non-levitical priesthood and two sanctuaries at Bethel and Dan, complete with Golden Calves. The Deuteronomist comments that he thus 'brought guilt upon his own house and doomed it to utter destruction'.[25]

In Judah, Rehoboam follows the same policy:

> They erected hill shrines, sacred pillars and sacred poles, on every high hill and under every spreading tree. Worse still, all over the country there were male prostitutes attached to the shrines, and the people adopted all the abominable practices of the nations whom the Lord had dispossessed in favour of Israel. (1 Kings 14.23–24)

The subsequent record of Rehoboam is limited to the perhaps gleeful comment, from the editor's viewpoint, that Shishak's invasion was successful and Jerusalem was captured. These events took place about 920 BCE, and Hosea later comments on the calf-gods of Jeroboam disparagingly (Hosea 8.5–6), but it may be fair to say that Jeroboam thought he was re-establishing the religion of Moses, at the risk of syncretism, rather than embracing Canaanite ritual. Rehoboam took the further step of encouraging it.[26]

The narrative continues with a brief reference to Abijah as the next king of Judah, allowed to rule in Jerusalem out of respect for David, according to the record. He followed Rehoboam's syncretism, but the policy changes with the next king, Asa, who

> expelled from the land the male prostitutes attached to the shrines, and did away with all the idols which his predecessors had made. (1 Kings 15.12)

The history of 1 Kings continues with the growing strength of the Northern Kingdom under Omri and his son Ahab recorded disapprovingly, while chief attention is paid to the prophets Micaiah and Elijah, and the cautious re-alliance of the kingdoms under Ahab and Jehoshaphat. This latter king of Judah wins some credit, for though he allowed the hill shrines to remain and sacrifices there to continue,

> he did away with such of the male prostitutes attached to the shrines as were still left over from the days of Asa his father. (1 Kings 22.46)

The remaining reference to temple prostitution in Kings occurs much later, during the reign of Josiah from 619 BCE onwards. Josiah is the ideal ruler from the Deuteronomist's viewpoint, a religious reformer and a nationalist concerned to unite the kingdoms, making a fresh start after the heroism of Hezekiah and the recidivist villainies of Manasseh. In obedience to the Book of the Covenant, he cleans up Jerusalem and its surroundings of all traces of the Baal worship, and suppresses the heathen priesthood of the hill shrines:

> He also pulled down the houses of the male prostitutes attached to the house of the Lord, where the women wove vestments in honour of Asherah. (2 Kings 23.7)

(c) COMMENT

The text from Deuteronomy refers to both men and women Israelites—they are not to become temple prostitutes, but the references in Kings are to male prostitutes[27] said to be attached to the hill shrines in the first three instances, but to the Temple of the Lord at Jerusalem in the time of Josiah. Clearly, the problem was seen as a recurrent one, for what Rehoboam allowed Asa only partly suppressed: Jehoshophat made a further attempt, but Josiah faced the problem afresh, and dealt with it perhaps more ruthlessly. The broad question of how far the Israelites came to terms with the existing cultus of Canaan has no simple agreed answer. What these texts make clear is that the Deuteronomistic overview employs the test of attitude to the hill shrines as of crucial importance, and takes the presence of male prostitutes at them as a further intolerable factor.

The disapproval of the hill shrines in these texts reflects the primacy placed at later times on the importance of the central sanctuary at Jerusalem, a feature of Josiah's policy easier to maintain in principle than in practice, together with a dislike of the nature religion of the Canaanites in the eyes of those schooled in the astringent and exclusive traditions of the Yahwist and Elohist. Looking back, the Deuteronomist regards them as threats to orthodoxy, places where the Israelite settlers were all too ready to accept an uncontroversial syncretism.

From the evidence available since 1929 in the Ras Shamra tablets and the deciphered Ugaritic script, we now know that the Canaanite religion was a developed one, and that this culture had close affinities with that of the Israelites in some respects. Under the High God 'El', the storm God Baal, with his consort Astarte, as she is called in the Old Testament, controlled the climate and therefore the fertility of the land, a matter of crucial importance to the agricultural society of Palestine in its somewhat precarious environment. It was believed that this pair of gods could be encouraged to provide the right conditions by ritual acts of sexual intercourse by men and women at their shrines. The temple prostitutes performed this ritual of imitative magic among themselves at the appropriate seasons, and they could also be hired for an initial act of intercourse with ordinary citizens about to be married. This custom of sacred intercourse was widely accepted in the countries of the Fertile Crescent as a means of ensuring the marriage would be fruitful and is mentioned by Herodotus as practised by the Persians.

In contrast, the Hebrew concept of Yahweh required him to have no consort, and his character of creative generosity called forth a human response of thanksgiving and obedience. The imitative magic of Canaan, whereby Baal was obliged to act, was abhorrent to the biblical writers on theological grounds and the associated practice of child sacrifice[28] was an abomination. There are numerous references in the prophetic writings to hill shrines and the institution of temple prostitution, and it is clear throughout that the reason for their condemnation is this theological one, and not a disapproval of commercial prostitution as such, as a contemporary Christian might suppose. Von Rad writes of the prohibition:

> This verse has to do with a religious phenomenon alien to Western man, but all the more dangerous to early Israel, namely sacral prostitution, which was firmly embedded in the fertility cult (Ishtar-Astarte) of the whole ancient East

from Cyprus to Babylon. Deuteronomy is particularly harsh in attacking these Canaanite cultic practices, which had penetrated into Israel as well during the period of the monarchy.[29]

Tracing the attempts to eradicate temple prostitution described in the Deuteronomistic history, and the reasons for this policy, leaves open the question what relevance all this has to homosexuality. It would seem that if the purpose of the cult was to encourage fertility, the barrenness of homosexual behaviour would be inappropriate, except perhaps in the secondary sense that the orgiastic atmosphere of sexual licence, which appears to have pervaded the shrines, would not have actually discouraged it. No specific mention of homosexual behaviour is made in Deuteronomy or Kings, but of course, the Deuteronomist may have considered the stories of Sodom and Gibeah, if these traditions were available to him. Whether or not they were can only be conjecture, for the D material in the Pentateuch, apart from Deuteronomy itself, may have been added later, and the appendices to Judges are also post-deuteronomic. What is otherwise known about the Canaanites does not suggest that homosexual behaviour was exceptionally prevalent in their communities, but it may have been common knowledge among the Israelites that this was a feature of life at the shrines. There is no conclusive evidence either way.

The problems of translation and of changed meaning of words need brief mention. The Hebrew *kadesh* used in these texts is translated as 'prostitute' in the Septuagint and as 'Sodomite' in the English Authorized and Revised Versions, though the latter adds a footnote: 'Hebrew Kadesh'. The Revised Standard Version makes the change to 'cult-prostitute', the New English Bible has 'temple prostitute' and the Jerusalem Bible has 'sacred prostitute', though the English Vulgate used 'fornicator' for Deuteronomy and 'effeminate' in the verses from Kings.

In view of the universal translation of *kadesh* in modern Bibles to indicate temple prostitution, it only needs to be said that readers of the Authorized or Revised version, or of concordances based on these Bibles, may be misled in assuming that all these texts refer exclusively to homosexual behaviour. The modern translations may be too definite in referring always to male prostitutes, not only because the Hebrew masculine plural form can include the female, but also because the introductory reference in Deuteronomy itself mentions both, and other evidence about the cultus indicates that male prostitutes and hierodules were present. The word 'sodomy' was used in Cranmer's time to mean sexual vice generally, and served as a suitable rendering of *kadesh*, but is now confined in English use to the more precise 'anal intercourse' especially in legal terminology, or as a general term of abuse, not necessary homophobic.[30]

Although the fundamental opposition to the shrines and their employees in these texts springs from a zeal for a kind of worship appropriate to God as Israel understands him, the denigration of sexual licence is a predictable reaction from the Israelite tradition, especially since great emphasis is placed on family life. Repudiation of the fertility cult lies deep in the religious consciousness of Israel, and homosexual behaviour is clearly associated with it in the Holiness Code of Leviticus, as it also seems to be in the letter of St Paul to the Corinthians, one of the few Hellenistic cities where the cult survived into New Testament times.

D The Friendship between David and Jonathan 1 and 2 Samuel

The establishment of the monarchy under Saul and its development by David described in the Books of Samuel precede, of course, the controversy over the hill shrines after the kingdom was divided. The tales of intrigue and heroism during which the succession passes to David need no elaboration here, and the whole work seems to have a unity in composition which the Deuteronomist left undisturbed.[31] The devious King Saul was unable to prevent the developing friendship between his son Jonathan and David, but he did persuade David to marry his daughter Michal, who is said to have loved him. They became separated and David was involved with a number of other women, although wishing eventually to have her back.

The strong terms in which David describes his affection for Jonathan when he learns of his death with his father in battle, have sometimes been interpreted as implying a homosexual relationship. Thus:

> I grieve for you, Jonathan, my brother; dear and delightful you were to me; your love for me was wonderful, surpassing the love of women. (2 Samuel 1.26)

The evidence given of David's marriage to Michal, and then to Abigail, and the incident with Bathsheba, suggest he had an active heterosexual life, but the friendship with Jonathan is also described in terms which go beyond political association. It may be that Jonathan was attracted to the warrior in an intense and personal way, though it seems clear that he was himself a mature man, and there is no hint of pederasty or erotic behaviour. The two men bind themselves in what the New English Bible translates as a solemn compact (1 Samuel 18.3) and in Hebrew custom this would be a formal bond of friendship and loyalty for which there is no obvious modern equivalent. The bond is further stressed in chapter 20, verse 14, where Jonathan says to David, 'I know that you will show me faithful friendship, as the Lord requires: and if I should die, you will continue loyal to my family for ever'. Jonathan is then said to have 'pledged himself afresh to David because of his love for him, for he loved him as himself'. A similar phrase occurs in the earlier passage (18.2) where Saul 'saw that Jonathan had given his heart to David and had grown to love him as himself'.

David's attitude to Jonathan is not recorded, except in the Lament, which may not be his own composition, so it appears that there is inadequate evidence to deduce that David was bisexual. Equally, the co-operation between David and Jonathan against Saul seems to be recorded with approval, and therefore the stress put on Jonathan's love and loyalty may serve another purpose. A hint of what this might be could be found in the fact that in both Hebrew and Greek the same word is used for this relationship as for that between Yahweh and Israel. What is said of Yahweh's love in Deuteronomy, and in the neighbourly love commandments in Leviticus 19, is expressed by the same Hebrew word, for the Hebrew language has no distinct words for the three aspects of love familiar to Christians from the Greek. Thus in the Lament itself, the same word appears, and the Septuagint translates all by the single word *agapan*. It follows then that any homosexual or erotic significance discerned in the story of David and Jonathan depends upon our modern perception. No clear indication of it is given (or probably could be) in the biblical text as written.[32] In fact, as will be seen in chapter 10, some very recent writers have used the David and Jonathan story as a commendable biblical model of a non-genital male friendship which homosexuals could be encouraged to copy.

E The Holiness Code Leviticus 18 and 20

(a) INTRODUCTION

While many of the exiles from Jerusalem sat down and wept by the waters of Babylon, some of them were busy writing. They had brought with them the priestly traditions of the Temple, now in ruins, and also the great epic story of Israel, already composed from the original works of the Yahwist, Elohist and Deuteronomist. Into this story they inserted the Jerusalem tradition, at appropriate points, to complete the Pentateuch. The major new block of material, concerned with cultic and ritual matters, was called Leviticus in the Septuagint version.

Within Leviticus, chapters 17—26 are usually identified as a separate section, first distinguished by Klostermann in 1877, and named 'The Holiness Code'. Its main concern is purity of worship, for both the priests and lay Israelites, and many of its injunctions end with the phrase 'I am the Lord'. Although chapter 19 of Leviticus contains the 'love your neighbour' commandment, once called the Heart of Torah and highlighted by Jesus, the general subject matter has been of slight interest within the Christian tradition, but in chapter

18 and again in chapter 20 there are direct prohibitions of male homosexual behaviour.

(b) THE TEXTS

Both references to homosexual behaviour occur in lists of regulations concerning family life.

> You shall not lie with a man as with a woman: that is an abomination. You shall not have sexual intercourse with any beast to make yourself unclean with it, nor shall a woman submit herself to intercourse with a beast; that is a violation of nature. (Leviticus 18.22–23)

> If a man has intercourse with a man as with a woman, they both commit an abomination. They shall both be put to death; their blood shall be on their own heads. (Leviticus 20.13)

(c) COMMENT

Although the narrative setting of the Holiness Code indicates that it consists of speeches made by Moses to the Israelites gathered at Sinai, a study of its precepts suggests an association with Jeremiah and Ezekiel at the end of the sixth century BCE. But it may be of later composition in its present form, and Martin Noth suggests that the Code passed through several stages of editing, and contains both substance and phrasing very much older. It is probable that both chapter 18 and chapter 20 once existed separately as legal codes, dealing generally with the same sexual offences, but with marked differences in style and order. During, or soon after the exile, they were combined and eventually used in services at the second Temple, set out in a liturgical style, somewhat akin to the recital of the Decalogue in Cranmer's prayer book, the phrase 'I am the Lord' being the congregational responses. This would have been soon after 400 BCE.[33]

The second chapter of the Code, Leviticus 18 in the modern numbering, begins with a brief narrative section. The Israelites, waiting at Sinai, are not to follow the institutions of the Egyptians 'where you once dwelt' nor those of the land of Canaan 'to which I am bringing you'. They must keep God's ways and institutions—He is the Lord. There follows in verses 6–18 a list of prohibitions of sexual intercourse by a man with his female blood relations. Its scope is wider than a list of prohibited degrees for marriage, extending probably to all those living in the camp or group of tents. The New English Bible rendering 'intercourse' is more satisfactory than 'uncover the nakedness' of the Jerusalem translation, which is also retained by the Common Bible and its antecedents. Although this is an alternative meaning in the Hebrew it is euphemistic and perhaps misleading in the context here.

The following verses (19–23) contain a miscellaneous list of sexual malpractices, not necessarily concerned with family life, and may have been a separate code originally. Intercourse during menstruation, or with a neighbour's wife, offering children for temple prostitution, male homosexual behaviour, and bestiality are forbidden. The chapter concludes with an explanation that the land of Canaan became unclean because the inhabitants behaved like this, and God has driven them out in punishment. If the Israelites do the same things they will be cut off from worship—our word would be excommunicated—but they will not be sent into exile.

The next section of the Holiness Code (chapter 19) is more general and marked by a strong humane sense of care for the under-privileged and aliens, and chapter 20.1–9 reverts to the issue of child prostitution and child sacrifice. This horrible practice, repudiated in Genesis and by Jeremiah and Ezekiel, took place at a shrine in the valley of Ben-hinnom near Jerusalem until suppressed by Josiah.[34]

The second list of sexual offences, in chapter 20.10–21 covers most of the same matters as chapter 18, but set out in a different order, with some new clauses and, significantly, adding a range of appropriate punishments to each prohibition. Whereas the wording in the first list is cast in the apodeictic style, that is direct command, the second list of offences is expressed conditionally—*if* men behave homosexually together, they commit an abomination and shall be put to death, a sentence that the community would have to implement.

Anthony Phillips has noticed a basic distinction between pre-exilic and post-exilic Israelite criminal codes in that, after the exile, and the replacement of the Old Covenant by the New, the death penalty is no longer required. There was an interim stage when the Israelites were under Persian control and could not carry out execution themselves, and offenders had to be left to divine retribution, but once the Temple was restored, the sanctions for maintaining cultic purity became temporary suspension or permanent exclusion (cutting off) from the worshipping life of Israel. Since the list of punishments allotted in chapter 20 include execution, this appears to be the earlier list, and therefore the crimes said to merit capital punishment, such as adultery, incest, bestiality and homosexual behaviour were treated thus in pre-exilic times. Eichrodt has suggested that they may have been transposed from the Book of the Covenant, after Exodus 22.17, and Phillips thinks that the list of miscellaneous offences attached to chapter 18 as verses 19–23 are, in fact, a summary of the code in chapter 20 transferred to chapter 18 to make that list complete.[35]

In simplified form, the development can be set out in chronological order:

LIST A was Leviticus 20.10–21 and is pre-exilic

LIST B was Leviticus 18.6–18 dealing with blood relations only and post-exilic, at least in its apodeictic form

LIST C was a summary of those offences in List A not found in List B, and therefore inserted into Leviticus 18 as vv. 19–23 to make List B complete for liturgical use in the apodeictic form.

The neatness of this suggested development does not correspond precisely with the arrangement of verses printed in the Bible. The reference to child prostitution (surrendering them to Moloch) occurs in the earlier part of chapter 20, and the prohibition of adultery with a neighbour's wife in List A is extended in List C to the wife of a fellow countryman, but this is consistent with the teaching in chapter 19. The prohibition of male homosexual behaviour re-occurs unchanged, and the section on bestiality is expressed more briefly. These differences can be readily explained by editorial licence, and the implication is that an ancient law of Israel, making male homosexual behaviour a capital offence, has been retained in the Priestly tradition after the exile, but the death penalty for it has been dropped.

Martin Noth views the development of these codes somewhat differently. He suggests there is a link idea between the miscellaneous provisions of List C, namely the misuse of semen (seed) and this includes the consequence of intercourse, children, and hence the reference to child sacrifice. List C would therefore be a separate list, not a summary of List A. He further thinks that List A is later, designed to be used in worship, the conditional style and reference to the death penalty being used didactically as an illustration from the Old Law that holiness is always taken very seriously in Israel. He concludes that there is no necessary literary link between the codes, nor an original common nucleus, each having had its own *sitz im leben*.[36]

It would seem that whichever view is preferred as to the formation of these two codes, the old tradition was that homosexual offences were a capital crime, or so at least the Priestly editors suggest. There is no indication of such punishment being carried out in the Old Testament records, except in a diffuse way in the Sodom and Gibeah narratives.

There are no serious difficulties in translation of these texts. The New English Bible expression, 'lie with a woman as with a man' (chapter 18), seems less specific than 'intercourse with a man as with a woman' (chapter 20), but the Hebrew phrase is identical. It does not mean 'lie down' in a sense of getting off one's feet, but 'adopting the position for intercourse' or most literally, 'crouching in a coital position'. The Common Bible and its antecedents, and the Jerusalem, preserve the expression 'lie with' for both verses and use the same for the preceding verses prohibiting intercourse with blood relations.[37] It is not clear if seminal emission was required for the commission of these offences, or whether a wider range of sexual contact or juxtaposition, including some degree of nakedness, would have been sufficient as the euphemistic language suggests. Legal precision concerning actions of such a private and personal kind is notoriously difficult to achieve. A comparison may be made with the ambiguity of the English expression 'to sleep with someone'.

The word 'abomination' (Hebrew—*to'ebah*) needs some explanation. In English the word expresses disgust or disapproval, but in the Bible its predominant meaning is concerned with religious truth rather than morality or aesthetics. Among the range of meanings in the Old Testament it is used, for example, in the closing chapters of Genesis to describe the Egyptians' dislike of foreigners and their eating habits, and in Exodus chapter 8 to draw a distinction between the respect of the Egyptians for animals and the Hebrew's sacrifice of them. These are probably J sources. The Prophets see the worship of idols and the cult of Canaan as abominable to the Lord and deceit in business is an abomination—false scales—in Proverbs 11.1. In Deuteronomy and Kings, 'abomination' is used as in Jeremiah and Ezekiel, to describe the Canaanite idolatry, focused on the hill shrines, their ritual and their prostitutes, permitted, as we have seen, by Rehoboam, Ahaz and Manasseh, and banned by Josiah, only to return later (Jeremiah 7.31).[38]

In the Holiness Code *to'ebah* is used only in regard to homosexual behaviour (18.22 and 20.13), and in the summary (18.26–30). In the 'cleanness regulations' referring to animals in Leviticus chapter 11, most English translations use 'abomination' for those thought unclean, but the New English Bible draws out the difference in the Hebrew text by using 'vermin'. The distinction between clean and unclean animals in the Jewish tradition may have begun by the recognition that the so-called unclean animals were used in alien religious rites, so the attribution may have deeper significance than mere dietary or health considerations. It seems, however, in the Holiness Code that the association of homosexual intercourse with the Canaanites' temple prostitution and child sacrifice is firm.

It may not, however, be a full explanation of the reason for prohibiting homosexual behaviour that it is a Canaanite practice based on a wrong theology of creation. Nor has the suggestion that it is a waste of seed much cogency, even if this is the linking theme of List C, the miscellaneous provisions of chapter 18.19–23.[39]

Thus far, in the consideration of the Holiness Code, it has been established that by 400 BCE the Jewish people were being warned in their Torah that male homosexual behaviour was an abomination to the Lord. It had once been a capital crime, but now it was regarded as making them unclean and therefore must imply excommunication from the worship and also from the fellowship of Israel. The concluding verses of Leviticus 18 make this clear. Declaring such behaviour abominable placed it in a well-recognized category of sin, somewhat equivalent perhaps to mortal sin in traditional Catholic spiritual discipline.

There is one further example of uncleanness in the list C which is not only called abominable, but a violation of nature. That is bestiality, and the word 'violation' can also be translated as perversion, or more literally as confusion. The confusion caused by sexual actvity with an animal is the breaking down of the natural division of species from the creation, described in the Priestly narrative that opens the book of Genesis. Perhaps Noth is right to see this as one form of misuse of semen, but it also has reference to the supposed cultic ritual of intercourse between humans and sacred animals, another form of imitative magic at the Canaanite shrines offensive to the Israelites.[40]

In condemning bestiality as a violation of nature, the concept of what is abominable to God takes on a further meaning, in which it has some embryonic sense of natural law. This sense is entirely personalized in the will of God, not part of the framework of the universe, as it is later understood in Greek and scholastic Christian thought. For the Hebrew mind, natural aversion and the sense of the good are not separate categories from the will of God, and their theocratic and theonomic perceptions make no distinction between sound religion and good morals. Nevertheless, confusion in sexual behaviour disturbs the extensive but close-knit family structure which the Holiness Code is commending and therefore this added explanation for condemning bestiality in List C could be seen to add a further reason for condemning homosexual behaviour and adultery. It is taken seriously by St Paul in the Epistle to the Romans.[41]

F Summary of the Old Testament evidence

This extensive review of the texts in the Old Testament that have some reference to homosexual behaviour has included what some readers may find a surprisingly detailed study of the literary sources of the passages in which these references appear. The justification for this, as suggested in the introduction to this section, is to make possible an evaluation of texts in terms of a continuing tradition, rather than in isolation, or by the frequently used method of distinguishing one text from another by the measure of its directness in referring to homosexual behaviour. What seems to emerge from this study is the existence of derogatory tales about Israel's enemies and wicked colleagues, as represented in the early traditions of Sodom and Gibeah, followed by a fierce confrontation with all that was involved in the temple rituals of the Canaanite religion.

The ancient precepts of the criminal law are reshaped to commend ritual cleanness in the Holiness Code, and here is found express condemnation of male homosexual behaviour. But it needs to be said that these progressive steps in the formation of the tradition of hostility to homosexual behaviour are the product of the saga of the Jewish people, who guarded and modified their beliefs and practices in the light of their experience of God's election and promise, providence and judgement. The composition of the Deuteronomistic history and of the final Priestly canon of the Torah was not the work of scissor-and-paste sub-editors, but of religious men pondering the paradox of their faith and their failure. Clearly, homosexual behaviour was never an important issue, but equally they never struck it out of the tradition where it appeared in material they were revising. Nor, until the Holiness Code, is any attempt made to show why such behaviour was thought wicked, but this tantalizing question must now be considered.

It is possible that there is no actual reason, in terms of religious morality, for the hostility to homosexual behaviour in the Old Testament. In modern terms, it can be explained by the ordinary homophobic reaction of heterosexual people in every age to this perplexing difference. The absence of any specific consideration of the question may lend weight to this view. Secondly, there may be combined with this ordinary homophobic reaction, an assimilation into the laws of Israel of the attitude to homosexual behaviour taken by other cultures and legal systems of the Fertile Crescent.

Undoubtedly the customs and laws of Israel were in some respects similar to those of surrounding nations, but similarity does not necessarily imply copying. This explanation requires a review of the evidence which is given in the following chapter. Thirdly, there is the possibility that it is an indirect result of the confrontation with the Canaanite cultus, and although there is insufficient evidence to assert with confidence that homosexual practices at the shrines were a particular emphasis, it could have been so. However, the basic objection to this view stands, that the chief purpose of this ritual was to encourage fertility, for which heterosexual patterns seem likely to predominate. That leads to the fourth and perhaps most cogent explanation, though again it may not be an exclusive one, but rather the leading motive in a complex attitude in which the consensus of the Semitic peoples against homosexual behaviour coalesced with ordinary homophobia and was then strengthened and perhaps transmuted by a doctrine of creation and sexuality that came to understand human sexual nature as intended to find its physical expression only within certain recognized limits.

Men were to have intercourse with women, not with each other or with beasts; slaves and foreigners were not to be raped without responsibility for the future; divorced wives were to be compensated; family and kinship were to be respected; there were bars to incest and to marriage outside acceptable groups; and so the whole family law was built up, piece by piece, as in any other race, culture, or civilization. That it was the will of Yahweh to follow these rules was the particular insight of Judaism, and the precepts of the Torah were for obedience, not question. This is, perhaps, a somewhat disappointing conclusion to the search for reasons for the Old Testament attitude, but, in fact, puzzlement about the reasons can be shown in the writings of later Judaism and, of course, in the Christian tradition as well.

G Attitudes to Homosexual Behaviour in Cultures surrounding Israel

Christian thought has always taken serious note of Greek and Roman civilizations as the dominant cultures in European history to which its 'Good News' was addressed. For the major churches of the West, the older cultures of the Near East were of little interest and, indeed, little understood until the growth of historical studies in the nineteenth century and easier travel facilities spurred the archaeologists to search the Fertile Crescent, as it was called, for evidence of the ancient civilizations of Egypt and Babylon.

The importance of archaeological discoveries for biblical scholarship was immediately apparent, not only for comparison with biblical history, but also in providing a far better understanding of its language, as the inscriptions and manuscripts of the Semitic peoples were deciphered. From the mass of new material, amongst many subjects of interest, studies of cult prostitution and sodomy began to be published, of which the articles by Professor G. A. Barton on 'Hierodouloi' and 'Sodomy' in Hastings' *Encyclopaedia of Religion and Ethics* are significant examples widely quoted. With regard to the Old Testament text, useful collections have been made since by Driver and Miles, Pritchard and Beyerlin.[42]

Comparison of the laws and customs relating to sexual matters in these ancient documents with those found in the Old Testament, indicates many similarities concerning the status of women, respect for marriage, virginity, and legitimacy and in some respects early Israelite laws appear harsher, for example, than those of Babylon. There are also marked distinctions, not least in the intolerance of Israel towards prostitution, cultic or secular, from the time of Amos onwards, and also in the diminution of class difference. Scholars disagree on whether the development seen in the Old Testament is a process of decline and restoration, in which the distinctiveness of Israel's morality was blurred during the settlement in Canaan, and revived with the

Deuteronomist or whether, in fact, it was a more or less straightforward process from common Semitic customary law to the sharply distinct characteristic shown in the final edition of the Pentateuch.

Probably, as Soggin suggests, some process of synthesis has taken place, but we have in the Old Testament the distinctive religious ethic of Israel together with everyday law from its neighbours.[43]

The co-existence in the Old Testament of the distinctively religious ethic of Israel and commonplace regulations, customs, and attitudes to everyday life not dissimilar to those of the other Semitic nations makes it virtually impossible to identify what is distinctive, and what is common for such an infrequently mentioned subject as homosexual behaviour.

If the early date of the Sodom and Gibeah tradition is accepted, recorded by the Yahwist but from an oral tradition which may go back at least to the period of Abraham, we may ask if there is any other contemporary evidence for similar prohibition or derogation. Such evidence is sometimes thought to be present in the Epic of Gilgamesh. This is the legend of the King of Uruk, south of Babylon, and describes his search for immortality. Although he is of semi-divine origin, this bliss finally eludes him, but the story centres on his great friendship with Enkidu, created by the gods as his companion. Ishtar, the mother goddess of love, unsuccessfully woos Gilgamesh, and the love of the two warriors for each other, their wrestling and embracing, and Gilgamesh's desolation when Enkidu dies may suggest a homosexual theme, even though both men are sexually active with women. But the epic is chiefly concerned with the religious quest, and the friendship aspect is an early example of the recurrent tale of physical and emotional attraction between male heroes, found in literature of all ages, notably among the Greeks, but also in the Bible story of David and Jonathan.

Abraham may be dated around the eighteenth century BCE, and texts of the Gilgamesh epic are known of around 2000 BCE, though the story itself may be much older. If a subsidiary theme of the epic is the jealously of Ishtar at the homosexual friendship and not merely the thwarting of her own attraction, something of an insult by Gilgamesh, then there might be seen here an implied criticism of homosexual behaviour, but this is unlikely, as clearly the story regards Gilgamesh as the hero, and it is a misunderstanding of its purpose to make too much of the details. Barton suggests that Enkidu enjoyed bestiality before being enticed by a harlot and finally becoming committed to Gilgamesh.[44]

The most important Law code of patriarchal times is that of Hammurabi, King of Babylon in the nineteenth century BCE of which the best known and nearly complete text was found on a stone shaft or stele at Susa, now in the Louvre. Havelock Ellis, Kinsey, and others have suggested that the code contains references to homosexuality, but Bailey noted that this is not expressly mentioned.[45] The suggestion is also made by Barton[46] referring to section 187 of the code. The context of this section is a series of regulations concerned to protect the priestesses of the temple and others who worked there. Paragraph 187 deals with adoption, laying down the right of adoptive parents to resist the attempts of Chamberlains and others to reclaim their children:

The adopted son of a Chamberlain or the adopted son of an epicene shall not be reclaimed. (Laws of Hammurabi 187, trans. Driver (1955), p. 75)

Barton argues that the word translated as 'Chamberlain' by Driver is either *Nersega* or *Girsega* (Driver transliterates it thus) and may be an euphemism for male temple prostitute. Driver finds no necessary reason for the Chamberlain or temple guard to be involved in the sexual rituals, and makes the, perhaps tongue in cheek, remark that for an Egyptian father to offer his daughter to the temple was the equivalent, in the Christian era, of sending her to a nunnery.

The epicene (*salzikrum*)—literally woman-man—is possibly, Driver suggests, a man or woman whose function was ritual transvestism. It appears that in this part of Hammurabi's code there is evidence of cult-prostitution in some respects similar to that of Canaan, with the same question unresolved concerning the presence of homosexual practices. Whereas Israel condemned the cult, this Babylonian law gives the temple employees some measure of protection, and it may be suggested, encourages the adoption of any offspring, instead of their sacrifice.

From Egypt, there is the legendary reference to sodomy in the tale of the rivalry between the gods Horus and Seth, perhaps best regarded as an early indication of the view that this was an appropriate indignity to inflict on the vanquished, but there is a clear disapproval of pederasty in the Confession Section of the Book of the Dead, an old tradition of which the extant texts are probably from the fifteenth century BCE. The penitent makes his confession before the gods, expressed in negative form, and the list gives a wide indication of Egyptian religious morality of the period, not dissimilar in many respects from Old Testament teaching. In the Beyerlin translation verse 16 reads:

I have not had sexual relations with a boy and I have not satisfied myself. (Quoted from Beyerlin, *Texts*, op. cit., pp. 65–6)

Beyerlin notes that the exact meaning is obscure, but that homosexuality was strictly taboo. Since the contacts between the

Egyptians and Israelites may well have been strong at this period[47] the possibility of a common tradition cannot be excluded, though this need not imply unreflective assimilation.

Apart from Egypt in the south west, and Babylon in the south east, the three other strong Empires that impinged on the territory of the Israelites were the Assyrians, the Hittites, and the Persians. A simplified chronology indicates that in the Middle Bronze Age, 2000–1500 BCE, the Egyptian strength was matched by that of Babylon under Hammurabi, and towards the end of this period, the Hittites, *c.* 1600–1200 BCE, destroyed Babylon and remained powerful until checked by the Egyptians at the battle of Kadesh *c.* 1275 and by the Assyrians soon after. The Hebrew Exodus from Egypt took place about 1250 BCE and the full conquest of Canaan about a century later. From the beginning of the Iron Age, 1200 BCE, Egypt declined, and Assyria dominated from then until 612 BCE when the Babylonian empire revived briefly, until 539 BCE. The Persians then ruled until their defeat by the Greeks under Alexander from 334 BCE onwards. The exile from Palestine took place under the Babylonians, but Cyrus the Persian allowed their return in 538 BCE.

There is little evidence from Hittite and Middle Assyrian Laws of prohibition of homosexual behaviour, and it was regarded as a capital offence in the Zoroastrian religion of the Persians.

Apart from the brief references to the Hittites in Genesis, where Abraham and Esau have contact with them, the chief interest for Old Testament scholars has been in the Hittite treaties with their vassal states, which seem to have influenced the notion of covenant in the Old Testament.[48] Among the incomplete codes of the Hittite Laws found so far, and dating perhaps in the fifteenth century BCE, there is a regulation concerning 'violation' by a man on his mother, daughter, or son, and step-mother if the father is still alive. Such a prohibition of incentuous sexual assault is hardly surprising, though the inclusion of the son has been noted by some commentators. There is insufficient knowledge of Hittite Laws to judge if homosexual behaviour outside the family was permitted.[49]

Among the Assyrian Law Codes discovered at Ashur from 1903 onwards, ascribed to Tiglath-Pileser in the twelfth century BCE, but probably some three centuries older in origin, Tablets 19 and 20 refer to homosexual behaviour, the first in connection with defamation, and the second direct.

The two readily available translations of Tablet 19 by Pritchard and Driver respectively differ in wording, and are too long for full quotation here. There is no significant difference in meaning and the text of the prohibition can be summarized thus:

> If a man accuses his neighbour by rumour or in quarrel that he practices sodomy frequently and fails to prove the charge, his punishment shall be a

beating, forced labour, castration and a fine. (Pritchard, op. cit., p. 181, and Driver, op. cit., p. 391)

Tablet 20 reads:

If a man has defiled his neighbour and charge and proof have been brought against him, he shall be defiled and made a eunuch. (Driver, op. cit., p. 391)

Pritchard's version is substantially the same, and Driver notes that the defilement is clearly that of homosexual behaviour, while Pritchard uses the familiar phrase 'lay with'. The word 'neighbour' is used to translate *tappau* by Driver,[50] while Pritchard has 'seignior' for 'man'. *Tappau* has a range of meanings in these laws, from business associate to anyone living nearby or in a dependent relationship to the offender. Seignior is used to represent a man of free standing, that is, neither a nobleman nor a slave. The severity of the punishments, including forced sodomy and castration, may be noted, though punishment is usually harsh and often capital in these laws relating to sexual offences. Thus, rape of a married woman was a capital offence, and so was adultery for both partners if the woman consented and was known to be married. Unmarried women were much less well protected. It is not possible, therefore, to argue from this evidence that homosexual behaviour was regarded with exceptional severity, but equally clearly it was not condoned among free consenting men, and a defamatory allegation of it was fiercely punished.

The presence of such severe laws for sexual offences might be taken to imply a policy of reaction against an excess of such activity, and a contrast can be drawn with the mildness and tolerance of the Babylonians, Assyria's neighbours some three hundred years earlier, as already noted in Hammurabi's code. Driver has suggested that between the compilation of the Babylonian and Middle Assyrian codes, the attitudes of the Eastern Semites towards unnatural offences underwent a change, and that this development was parallelled among the Western Semites about the time of the exile, and is reflected in the Holiness Code. Phillips agrees that this is possible.[51]

The gap in time between the Middle Assyrian Laws and the post-exilic version of the Holiness Code may well be seven hundred years, and therefore copying seems to be unlikely. A reasonable speculation might be that the common law of the Semitic people contained prohibitions of homosexual behaviour, at least among those in certain close or well-defined relationships, and that these prohibitions were sharpened or ignored at various times according to circumstances. Such variation can be seen in Greek and Roman history, and indeed in modern times, of which the trials of Oscar Wilde, German generals in the Hitler era, and Lord Montagu are well-known examples.

Zarathustra, the Persian prophet who may have lived as late as the sixth century BCE, is remembered for the ethical monotheism of his teaching, and his movement, short lived in Persia itself with support from Darius but abandoned by Artaxerxes II by 404 BCE, lived on in Zoroastrianism, and still does among the Parsees in India. Among the sacred books of this religion is the Vendidad, a book of ritual legislation somewhat similar to Leviticus,[52] and this contains fierce denunciation of homosexual behaviour, the unnatural vice which incurs capital punishment on earth and torment in the other world. However, only the Gathas are now regarded as containing the teaching of Zarathustra himself, and the Vendidad is to be dated several centuries later, a code of the Zoroastrian priests. There is a very remote possibility that the specific prohibition of homosexual behaviour found in the Holiness Code could have been influenced by the teaching of Zarathustra while the Israelite priests were in exile in Babylon, or that this teaching from the older criminal codes was highlighted after the exile to conform to the Persian view, as an expression of respect to Cyrus. But it is not thought that Zarathrustra was an innovator so much as a collector of the best moral notions of his time, and so it may be best to regard the Vendidad prohibitions as late and irrelevant to the Holiness Code, but perhaps reflected in the inter-testamental period writings of Judaism.

This survey of attitudes to homosexual behaviour in cultures surrounding Israel during the period from the Patriarchs to the completion of the Pentateuch suffers from the obvious limitation that the evidence is very slight and fragmentary. If further information becomes available from inscriptions and papyri, the picture will become more complete, and only tentative conclusions can be offered at the present time. In brief, hostility to homosexual behaviour can be found in the religion of Egypt and in the Hittite and Assyrian cultures for close relatives and neighbours. The existence of male temple prostitutes in Babylon, as in Canaan, does not prove homosexual behaviour to be an important feature of the cult. Abhorrence of it in the tradition of Israel arises perhaps chiefly because such men were dedicated to the service of a false god, though it may be that the Old Testament attitude in this respect is, in fact, a synthesis between this uniquely Israelite perception among the Semitic people and their common legal tradition of prohibiting homosexual behaviour in some circumstances. The precepts of the Holiness Code may demonstrate this synthesis clearly.

4 The Inter-Testamental Period

A Introduction

There was an interval of some three hundred years between the completion of the Old Testament Books eventually included in the Hebrew Canon and the composition of the major writings of the New Testament. This interval was of great significance in Palestine, both in terms of political changes and religious developments, and of crucial importance to an understanding of Christianity. Within this inter-testamental period, as it is called, Judaism was forced to take the decisive step of becoming a religion based on a book rather than a building, for the Temple was desecrated and later destroyed. Within this period Jesus of Nazareth was born, and by its end, the essential characteristics of Christian doctrine and ethics were being settled.

By this time, the Jewish people had long ceased to be a close-knit group in central Palestine. Some stayed behind in Babylon after the exile, and a prosperous Jewish community developed there. It was later to be an influential centre for Rabbinic learning. Both commerce and captivity had taken Jews to the west, notably to Alexandria. Jerusalem itself was becoming internationalized through trade as well as occupation forces, Greek, Egyptian, Syrian, and Roman, and added to these was a steadily increasing flow of pilgrims to the Holy City.[1]

B The Threat from Hellenism

From the seventh century onwards, Palestine had known Greek trading and increasing seaborne contact, and this increased after the exile. Following the destruction of the Persian Empire by Alexander the Great and his early death in 323 BCE, the Egyptian Ptolemies ruled in Palestine and southern Syria for a hundred years until the Syrian Antiochus III wrested Palestine from them. Like the Persians, these Egyptian rulers of the Hellenistic empire allowed religious affairs in Jerusalem to remain under Jewish authority represented by the new office of High Priest, and the council of influential families called the Sanhedrin. In terms of culture, commerce, and intellectual pursuits, the urban Jews were much impressed by Greek thought, and became accustomed to Greek settlers and the renaming of their towns in the Greek language.

As they lost their knowledge of Hebrew, Palestinian Jews became bilingual, learning their Scriptures in Aramaic translations (Targums), and using Greek a good deal in everyday life. While they came to terms with the Greek immigrants in their homeland, many other Jews left Palestine as captives or traders to settle in the cities and ports of the extensive Greek empire around the Eastern Mediterranean, and this movement was called the exile (*golah* in Hebrew) or the more familiar scattering (*diaspora* in Greek). The different nuance of meaning between these words indicates the conscious nationalism of the Jews which has been, of course, of marked significance in their subsequent history. Reacting to Syrian aggression this nationalism found a vigorous expression in the Maccabean revolt from 166 BCE onwards, but after an uneasy truce, Jewish orthodoxy had to contend with the unsatisfactory rule of the Hasmoneans, combining religious and secular authority until the Roman Pompey made Judea a province of that empire from 63 BCE onwards. The Temple was finally destroyed by Titus in 70 CE.[2]

Although it seems to be true that the Jews of Palestine found the invasion of the Hellenistic culture in some respects less objectionable than that of earlier assailants, and the Diaspora Jews had no choice but to conform to the local alien rule, the Jewish self-consciousness in religious and moral terms led them inevitably to resist some aspects of Hellenism. This resistance was inevitable in so far as the challenge was presented, not in the cool detached terms of classical Greece, but in the mystery religions, ludicrous to the Jewish mind, and in the sensual crudities bequeathed by Alexander's soldiers and practised in the Mediterranean ports. Zoroastrian dualistic influences were strong and the cult of Astarte was widespread and, of course, both Syrian and Egyptian forms of Hellenism were syncretistic, not sudden transformations obliterating the old cultures.

In Jerusalem itself, the establishment of the Gymnasium and the participation in the public games of Jewish youths, naked in the Greek fashion and sometimes undergoing an operation to conceal their circumcision, was a great affront to orthodox Jews. An account of this is given in 1 Maccabees 1.11–15, and it is not difficult to understand the offence of such developments to the Jews who saw in them, not merely the disregard of their traditional reticence with the body, but the abandonment of the sign of the Covenant and the religious and moral corruption of their young people by foreign soldiers, traders, and brothel keepers.[3]

C Inter-Testamental Jewish writings

The Jewish religious writings of the inter-testamental period can be conveniently treated in three somewhat loosely classified groups: apocryphal, pseudepigraphical, and rabbinic. The apocryphal writings were known and used by the Christian Church in its early period, being part of the Septuagint and familiar to the Diaspora. The attractiveness of these works to the Christians may have been at least in part their emphasis on a future hope, now seen to be fulfilled in Christ. Written in Greek, and having assimilated Greek ideas, their language and conceptual framework were perhaps easier for non-Palestinian Christians than orthodox Rabbinic writings, and they formed a useful bridge for evangelism among the liberal Jews.

The Pseudepigraphical books have been traditionally disregarded in the Christian tradition, not only as non-canonical, but also because until recently they were often known only in Ethiopic or Slavonic translations. The discovery of the Dead Sea Scrolls and the Qumran Library in 1947 has made available fragments of these works which must be dated not later than 68 CE, and it has been increasingly recognized in the past twenty years that the pseudepigrapha were widely read and influential in the inter-testamental period. The programme of translation and publication of these books is by no means completed, but as they become available, they provide much new evidence of the life and thought of the time.

The Rabbinic writings are, in principle, the investigation and exegesis of the Torah, protecting it by interpretation, as the development of the literature has been described. It takes two forms. The first 'Midrash', meaning deduction, originated with the appointment of a group of authorized leaders after the time of Ezra, continued in the practice at synagogue of reading a section of the Pentateuch and adding narration and explanation, and developed finally into written commentaries on the Pentateuch, compiled at the Rabbinic academies or by later respected teachers. The second form, 'Mishnah', is a codification of the teaching of the Rabbis on the Torah, but arranged by subject matter in a series of tractates, the biblical texts themselves being omitted. Further codification of Mishnah and other teachings led to the Talmuds, dating from the fifth century CE, and produced in authoritative versions in Palestine and Babylon. To represent this tradition adequately, texts from the Mishnah and Midrash on Genesis are followed by consideration of the much later commentary by Rashi, and finally, for comparison, reference is made to the writings of Philo and Josephus.

The reaction of orthodox Judaism to the Hellenization of Palestine was to resist syncretism, to see the new situation as a renewal of the old battle with the Canaanites over idolatry and the behaviour which sprang from it, and to abide by the old tradition to which the ancient scrolls bore witness. The Jews of the Diaspora, however, regarded the new apocryphal writings as part of the Wisdom literature of their religion, a supplement to the Torah and the Prophets.[4] The latest works in the Apocrypha may well have been written just before or during the life of Jesus, and both the writers of the New Testament and the early Church fathers were familiar with these books and quoted from them. Although the early Church accepted them as part of Scripture, they were distinguished from the Hebrew Canon, at least in principle if not so clearly in practice, and eventually in the fourth century CE, St Jerome named them *libri ecclesiastici* not *libri canonici.*[5]

It would be misleading to suggest, however, that the canon of the Hebrew Old Testament was settled before the Apocryphal books were written. Indeed, only at the Council of Jamnia, around 90 CE, were Ecclesiastes and the Song of Songs accepted, and discussion continued for two further centuries among the Rabbis. Regular use in the synagogues was probably an important factor in final acceptance, as the Jewish religion became more centred on 'The Book' after the destruction of the second Temple. Judaism shares with Christianity the characteristics of development, so that whatever official status is bestowed on a particular religious text, its existence always tells something of the views of the time.[6] In this chapter, therefore, references to homosexuality are considered from the three sources—the official Apocrypha, the contemporaneous Jewish writings known as the Pseudepigrapha, and the commentaries of the Rabbis.

D References to Homosexual Behaviour in the Apocrypha

It has already become clear from study of the Hebrew Bible, that references to homosexual behaviour are often elusive, but can be detected with some certainty in association with four other offences which the Israelite tradition condemns. These offences are: the sin of Sodom: temple prostitution: sexual activity between different species: and unnatural intercourse. It is also clear that in the tradition these topics are often associated and overlap, so that it is not easy to disentangle what exactly was in the mind of a writer when he lists them in a general way as if they were already familiar to his readers. The references to these offences in the Apocrypha are of this general kind, and can best be understood as denunciation of the alien culture in familiar and oft repeated terms, by a nation in crisis, committed to the belief that only by obedience to the Law will they escape the Lord's judgement and survive under his protection.

Within the apocryphal books of Ecclesiasticus and the Wisdom of Solomon, Sodom is referred to four times, and homosexual behaviour appears to be included in one reference to foreign idolatrous cults.

(a) ECCLESIASTICUS

This book was written in Hebrew about 190 BCE and accepted into the Septuagint by the Christian Church with its title in Greek, the Wisdom of Ben Sirach.[7] Chapter 39.12–35 contains one of the doctrinal hymns characteristic of this work, and reference is made to God's watch over creation and his judgement:

His blessing is like a river in flood which inundates the parched ground. But the doom he assigns the heathen is his wrath, as when he turned a watered plain into a salt desert. (Verses 22–23 New English Bible)

This passage is similar to Psalm 107.34, 'He turns fruitful land into salt waste because the men who dwell there are so wicked.' These quotations simply maintain the original J view that the cataclysm at the base of the Dead Sea was an expression of God's judgement.

The other reference to Sodom in Ecclesiasticus occurs in an earlier section of the book illustrating the same theme. God's anger against sinners:

There was no pardon for the Giants of old, who revolted in all their strength, there was no relief for Lot's adopted home, abhorrent in its arrogance. (Ecclesiasticus 16.7–8 New English Bible)

The latter verse shows once again the standard use of Sodom as the synonym of resistance to God and his response, but verse 7 refers to the Giants who were said to have resulted from the intercourse between the sons of God and human women in Genesis chapter 6, a precipitating cause of the Flood. Detailed consideration of the legendary stories developed around this incident is left for consideration later, as its sources are the lost Book of the Giants, and the pseudepigraphical work 1 Enoch, but it can be noted here that the legend marks an attempt in the inter-testamental period to deal with the problems of evil by the interpolation of intermediaries between God and human beings. Two groups of angels are postulated, Michael, Gabriel, and others who remain with God and act for him on earth, and a second group who were disobedient, confused their species with humans, and though judged, liberated evil spirits on earth to assault and to deceive mankind.[8]

(b) THE BOOK OF WISDOM

This has been dated between 100 BCE and 40 CE and is a composite work from Jewish sources in Alexandria, written in Greek.[9] The early parts deal with righteousness and wisdom, but from chapter 10 onwards begins a history of Israel from Adam to the Exodus. Within this history is inserted an interpolation about idolatry comprising chapters 13—15. In chapter 10, surveying the survival of Noah and Lot as attributable to the saving power of Wisdom, the destruction of Sodom is described:

She saved a good man from the destruction of the godless, and he escaped the fire that came down on the five cities, cities whose wickedness is still attested by a smoking waste. . . . Wisdom they ignored, losing the power to recognize what is good and leaving by their lives a monument of folly, such that their enormities can never be forgotten. (Wisdom of Solomon 10.6–8, New English Bible)

The activity of God is here expressed in terms of the divine Wisdom, and suggests that the author has been influenced by Platonism.

The second reference is similar, but concentrates on the hatred of strangers and foreigners, presumably with reference to the Egyptian treatment of the Israelites after Joseph, and then in parenthesis includes the men of Sodom among those who, with the Egyptians, were struck blind:

They were struck with blindness also, like the men at the door of the one good man, when yawning darkness fell upon them, and each went groping for his own doorway. (Wisdom of Solomon 19.17, New English Bible)

The context of this verse is a contrast between the 'others' who had refused to welcome strangers, and the Egyptians who had made slaves of guests and benefactors. The Revised Version and Jerusalem Versions by italicization or footnote make clear the reference to Sodom, though the New English Bible and the Common Bible leave the literal translation 'others' unexplained, presumably because the reference to Sodom is clear enough already.

There is, however, one reference to sexual perversion in Wisdom. This occurs in the interpolation on idolatry, chapters 13—15, a beautifully written and sharply derisive description of its origins and futile consequences. With fierce irony, the writer sets out how bereavement or political obsequiousness leads to the setting up of images and their subsequent deification. Once this fundamental error is made, then every kind of moral evil flows from it. The passage is typical of the period, and since it has some similarity to that in the Epistle to the Romans, chapter 1, it is quoted at length:

Then, not content with gross error in their knowledge of God, men live in the constant warfare of ignorance and call this monstrous evil, peace. They perform ritual murders of children and secret ceremonies and the frenzied orgies of unnatural cults; the purity of life and marriage is abandoned; and a man treacherously murders his neighbour or corrupts his wife and breaks his heart. All is chaos—bloody murder, theft and fraud, corruption, treachery, riot, perjury, honest men driven to distraction; ingratitude, moral corruption, sexual perversion, breakdown of marriage, adultery, debauchery. For the worship of idols, whose names it is wrong even to mention, is the beginning, cause and end of every evil. (Wisdom 14.22–27, New English Bible)

How far, in fact, child sacrifice was still practised in the mystery cults of the Near East at this time is uncertain, and the whole tone of the denunciation is polemical, perhaps to the point of exaggeration. In every age, some observers see decadence all around, but allowing for that, the list of offences mentioned is reminiscent of those found in the final form of the Holiness Code, and four kinds of sexual sin are enumerated in verse 26. The first one presents difficulty in translation, for although the New English Bible has 'sexual perversion', which probably means homosexual behaviour, the best literal meaning seems to be 'changing of kind', though the Greek expression (*geneseos enallage*) is unusual.

The Jersalem Bible has 'sins against nature' which has a consistent homosexual meaning in that translation. The older translations indicate the difficulty with alternatives: Changing of kind, or sex; Confusion of kind or sex; and the Common Bible has sex perversion. There is here another example of a change of language between the older and newer translations to make the homosexual meaning clearer. Certainly changing of sex would be quite misleading to a modern reader. Since 'kind' meaning 'species' (Hebrew: *mishpachah*) is rendered in the Septuagint as *genesis* and hence reflects the creation of the different species and perhaps of male and female nature, the notion of confusion, contrary to God's order, may be present here and the modern translations are correct. It was noted earlier, in connection with the prohibition of bestiality in the Holiness Code, that confusion of the natural order was the basis of that offence, and child sacrifice and homosexual behaviour were prohibited in the same section. There is no mention of bestiality in this passage in Wisdom, but the whole tenor of it suggests a reiteration of the traditional code and its precepts. It is, perhaps, unlikely that the reference to homosexual behaviour would be dropped, since this was a notorious feature of Hellenism.[10]

To sum up, in the apocryphal books of Ecclesiasticus and Wisdom the traditional attitude to Sodom as the synonym of general wickedness, folly, and inhospitality, is thrice repeated, and in the Wisdom interpolation about idolatry, the prohibition of homosexual behaviour seems probably to be reiterated.

E References to Homosexual Behaviour in the Jewish Pseudepigrapha

The tracts for the times by Jewish thinkers known as the Old Testament Pseudepigrapha have historical value though their ascriptions to wellknown Old Testament characters are usually fictitious. For the most part composed in Hebrew or Aramaic by Palestinian authors, the Pseudepigrapha circulated widely among the dispersed Jews in Greek translations and were as well known as the Apocrypha to the early Christian apologists and New Testament writers who refer to them.[11]

The discoveries at Qumran have shown that the community there valued these writings as Scripture and fragments of them found in the caves help to authenticate some of the texts. More needs to be done in this respect to increase the credibility and usefulness of the Pseudepigrapha for inter-testamental study, since the major texts now available are often much later translations of translations, with interpolations by Christian writers. The largest collection of Pseudepigrapha translated in English at present remains that by R. H. Charles of 1913, apart from extracts in Qumran documents.[12]

The Pseudepigraphical literature is, of course, voluminous even in English translation, and there is more to come. It is questionable how far it is useful at this point to provide direct quotations from it concerning homosexual behaviour and the meanings given to the sin of Sodom. Since these writings have always been excluded from the Canon and only serve as a guide to religious thought of the time, reflecting both the perceptions and prejudices of their many authors, often now unidentifiable, it would be perhaps adequate to give only a summary for the general reader at this point. However, it is the case in modern times that some of these writings, chiefly the Books of Enoch, Jubilees and the Testaments of the Twelve Patriarchs, are cited to substantiate the argument that the origins of the Christian attitude of hostility to homosexual behaviour are to be found here.

This argument tends to be pressed by those who place more emphasis on the late identification of the sin of Sodom with homosexual behaviour than on the tradition derived from the Holiness Code. While it is clearly true that such identification can be found in some of these writings, the general pattern they present is more complex, reflecting the actual situation at the time. It has to be recognized also that, as in the canonical books, homosexual behaviour is only mentioned in passing, as a feature of sexual licence in paganism or as a temptation to Jews forbidden by the long established Law and, for some authors, part of the sinfulness for which Sodom was destroyed. Only extensive quotation can actually demonstrate the complexity and inconsistency of the references, but such detail may prove wearisome to the general reader. It seems best, therefore, to set out at this point a summary of the evidence from the pseudepigraphical books, and to provide a detailed examination of the relevant passages as an excursus for whose who wish to pursue the matter further, but would have difficulty in reading the sources for themselves.

Several pseudepigraphical books provide abbreviated histories of Israel, notably 1 Enoch, Jubilees, the Genesis Apocryphon and the Testaments of the Twelve Patriarchs. In these, as in Ecclesiasticus already noted, the legend of the Fallen Giants who conceived children with human women, is linked with the destruction of Sodom. The breach of the natural order, or the confusion of species here identified, is held to apply to the attempted homosexual rape on the angels at Sodom. This 'confusion' argument stems presumably from exegesis of the Holiness Code.

The use of Sodom as a prototype of general wickedness in terms of arrogance and idolatry is widespread in the Pseudepigrapha, not only in the histories of the origins of Israel already cited, but also in 3 Maccabees which contains a similar history but mentions only the boldness of the Giants and the arrogance of the Sodomites. It needs to be stressed for those more familiar with the Christian tradition, that the habitual explanation of the causes of evil in the world and frustration of the hopes of Israel was centred at this time on the events which preceded the flood and not so commonly in the Fall in the Garden of Eden. The dispensation to Noah and his descendants bound all men, as the Law given to Moses bound the Jews, and the Noachic commandments as they were called are the standard by which God will judge pagans. These are of great importance in interpreting St Paul's references to pagan vices as we shall see later. Criticism of male homosexual behaviour and of pederasty as pagan customs contrary to natural law appears in the Letter of Aristeas, and in some of the earlier sections of the collection of Jewish and Christian Pseudepigrapha known as the Sibylline Oracles. Here, and in the Psalms of Solomon, references to unnatural intercourse among the daughters of Israel may include not only the usual list of confusions and prohibited sexual activities with males, such as incest, fornication, adultery, and intercourse *per anum*, but also bestiality and lesbianism.

EXCURSUS ON PSEUDEPIGRAPHICAL REFERENCES

Among the many pseudepigraphical writings, nine of those available in English contain references to the Watchers, the Destruction of Sodom and its sins, and sexual offences which demonstrate attitudes to homosexual behaviour. These writings are considered in chronological order as far as reasonably accurate dating permits. Interpolation of Christian glosses or amendments to sources of Jewish origin has very probably taken place, but these cannot be readily detected. The works referred to are:

1 Enoch
The Second Book of Enoch
The Book of Jubilees
The Psalms of Solomon
The Genesis Apocryphon
The Testaments of the Twelve Patriarchs
The Letter of Aristeas
The Sibylline Oracles
3 Maccabees

Except where stated, quotations come from Charles, *Pseudepigrapha*, op. cit.

(a) 1 ENOCH

This is also called Ethiopic Enoch because the first full text known in modern times was in that language, and dates from 164 BCE. Portions of it have been found at Qumran. It is a composite work in five parts of which the first, after an introduction, quotes from an earlier work, the Book of Noah. The quotations are woven into an account of the origin of evil, which is attributed to the action of the sons of God (Genesis 6.3), who descend to earth from their proper realm and mate with human women. The early J account of this leads on to the story of the flood and the preservation of Noah, but 1 Enoch chapters 6—16 elaborates the story of the Sons of God in some detail. They are destined for destruction, but Enoch pleads for them unsuccessfully to the Lord of Heaven. The Sons of God are also described as fallen angels or the Watchers, and the offspring are the Giants.

In 1 Enoch 10.9 the unfallen angel Gabriel is told by the Lord to 'proceed against the bastards' and destroy the children of the Watchers, 'Children of fornication', by sending them to destroy each other in battle. In verse 11, Gabriel's colleague, Michael, is instructed to bind fast the Watchers themselves until they are destroyed in the day of judgement. The Watchers are said to 'have united themselves with women so as to have defiled themselves with them in all their uncleanness'.[13]

The sins of the Watchers are fornication (chapter 10.9), and also intercourse with women during their menstrual period—'in their uncleanness' in v. 11 may be equivalent to defiling themselves with the blood of women. A wider definition of their sin occurs in chapter 106.14,17, a detached fragment also from the Book of Noah, where the Watchers are said to have transgressed the law in uniting themselves with women, marrying them and having children with them, and producing giants, not according to the spirit, but according to the flesh. It is not marriage and children that are objected to, but the breach in the natural order and confusion of the distinction between angelic and human beings. Hence, in the legend, the monstrous offspring result. It may be recalled that the visitors to Sodom were angels, and in the Babylonian Jewish Midrash, Gabriel and Michael are named as the two angels who visited Sodom. There is, therefore, a possible new link here, or at least one not noticed before except in Ecclesiasticus, in that by the second century BCE, the offence of the Watchers is paralleled by the offence of the men of Sodom although in reverse. The Watchers confused the created order by intercourse with women, while the men of Sodom attempted the same confusion in their assault on Gabriel and Michael.[14]

(b) THE SECOND BOOK OF ENOCH also known as the Slavonic Enoch or the Secrets of Enoch, contains what appears to be a clear denunciation of pederasty:

> Those who dishonour God, who on earth practice sin against nature, which is child-corruption after the sodomitic fashion. (2 Enoch 10.4, Charles' translation, op. cit., p. 435)

2 Enoch has some affinity in content to 1 Enoch, and if it dates from approximately the same period, would provide in this verse a clear identification of the sin of Sodom as pederasty, but this theory seems untenable. Charles regarded 2 Enoch as authentic work of the inter-testamentary period, but this has been doubted by Rowley and subsequent commentators such as Vaillant who suggested it was a third century counter to 1 Enoch by a Christian author. The whole problem of dating and composition has been thoroughly examined by Milik who concludes that its original author was a Christian monk of the ninth–tenth century writing in Greek, whose text still existed in the thirteenth century, but now remains only in Serbian and Russian translation. This being so, the identification of the sin of Sodom with homosexual behaviour shown in the verse quoted, reflects the long established tradition of the Christian era.[15]

(c) THE BOOK OF JUBILEES was written in Hebrew about 150 BCE or soon after. The earliest full text is in Ethiopic translation, but since the discovery of a large number of fragments at Qumran, Jubilees has been regarded as evidently a popular book of the inter-testamental period. It is closely associated with the community at Qumran and some scholars suggest it was written there.[16]

Jubilees has been called the little Genesis because it is a re-writing of that Book and the first twelve chapters of Exodus in forty-nine periods of forty-nine years—a Jubilee of Jubilees. Within this calendar framework it concentrates on the Law as delivered by the Lord to Moses on Mount Sinai, and it is Midrashic in style, adding interpolations from later traditions. It has a good deal to say about sexual sin, and the author knows the Book of Noah and 1 Enoch, or at least the Legend of the Watchers and Giants they record. He elaborates Genesis 6.1–4 as Enoch does, quoting him at the end of chapter 7. Earlier in this chapter, Noah is said to enjoin upon his sons the commands 'and all the judgements he knew'. These are, 'to bless their creator, honour father and mother, love their neighbours and guard their souls from fornication, uncleanness and all iniquity.' The passage continues:

For owing to these three things came the flood upon the earth, namely, owing to the fornication wherein the Watchers against the Law of their ordinances went a-whoring after the daughters of men, and took themselves wives of all which they chose: and they made the beginning of uncleanness. (Jubilees 7.21, Charles, *Pseudepigrapha*, p. 24)

References to Sodom in the Book of Jubilees show how the name is being used in this period as both the universal symbol of disobedience associated with idolatry to God, and also the catchphrase for sexual depravity. Thus in the first sense:

The men of Sodom were sinners exceedingly. (Chapter 13.17)
As the children of Sodom were taken away from the earth so will all those who worship idols be taken away. (Chapter 22.22)
But on the day of turbulence and execration . . . with flaming devouring fire as he burnt Sodom, so likewise will he burn his land and his city. (Chapter 36.10)

The contexts of these three quotations are, respectively: the first part of the story of Lot, Abraham's final blessing of Jacob, and Isaac's final command to Jacob about, *inter alia*, brotherly love between him and Esau.

In the sense of sexual depravity, Sodom is also referred to three times as follows:

They defile themselves and commit fornication in the flesh, and work uncleanness on the earth. (Chapter 16.5)
And he told them of the judgement of the Giants and the judgement of the sodomites, how they had been judged on account of their wickedness, and had died on account of their fornication and uncleanness, and mutual corruption through fornication. (Chapter 20.5)

In the following verses (6–10) there is a general plea in poetic form that Abraham's sons should love the God of heaven and keep all his commandments, avoiding fornication and uncleanness to escape the curse of Sodom, keeping away from idols and the uncleanness and vanity they represent.

The contexts of these three quotations are: the second part of the story of Sodom where God executes his judgement (chapter 16); and Abraham's summons to Ishmael and Isaac and their sons, where he gives them commandments similar to those of Noah, but with dire threats against fornication and uncleanness, particularly for the women, who are to be burnt. Nor are the sons to marry Canaanites.

These three references to Sodom in terms of sexual depravity are similar to those already noticed in Ecclesiasticus, 1 Enoch chapter 10, and the earlier reference to the Watchers in chapter 7 of Jubilees, with whom the 'uncleanness' began.

In one sense it is no surprise that the men of Sodom are accused of fornication, a common enough sin, and Jeremiah has previously described them as adulterous. But the fornication of the Watchers was of a special kind, and so there is further emphasis here on the confusion noted in Enoch's account. There is also, of course, a different meaning to fornication which may be included here since the poem refers to Canaan and idolatry. That is the sense in which the prophets Hosea and Jeremiah describe the unfaithfulness of Israel as fornication, or in other words, apostasy.[17] It may be necessary at this point to allow the possibility that 'fornication' in the use of the inter-testamental writers is a broad one, representing a fundamental view that religious apostasy usually also implies sexual licence and every other kind of sin.[18]

(d) THE PSALMS OF SOLOMON

Since the Pseudepigrapha are likely to be unfamiliar to modern Christians and the texts from Qumran are not yet widely circulated, it seems useful at this stage to add in parentheses two further references to sexual offences in connection with apostasy and the Watchers to illustrate how common such references appear to have been at this period. In the Psalms of Solomon, dated between 80 and 40 BCE, the second Psalm concerns the violation of the Temple, presumably by Antiochus. 'Because the sons of Jerusalem had defiled the holy things of the Lord, God had allowed this to happen'; and, 'The daughters of Jerusalem were defiled in accordance with thy judgement because they had defiled themselves with unnatural intercourse.' (Psalms of Solomon 2.3,13,15, Charles' translation.)

In a similar passage in Psalm 8, adultery, incest and intercourse during the menstrual period are mentioned, and the Greek text for Solomon's Psalm 2.15 suggests confusion and inappropriate mingling, as does Solomon's Psalm 8.10, where the confusion of incest is followed by uncleanness at worship. Incest seems the most likely translation though lesbianism or intercourse *per anum* could be possible alternative meanings. In Judaism of this period there were strict rules about when intercourse might take place and since this caused ritual impurity, cleansing was necessary before prayer. In the same vein, pilgrims to the Temple had to be abstinent within the precincts.

(e) THE GENESIS APOCRYPHON

Among the documents discovered at Qumran are fragments of Bible commentary, one of which is called the Genesis Apocryphon. The fragment refers to the birth of Noah, which his father Lamech suspects was due to the Watchers or the Giants. His wife Bathenosh assures him rather wrathfully that 'The seed is yours and the conception is from you. This fruit was planted by you, and by no stranger or watcher or Son of Heaven.' Lamech asks his father Methuselah to consult Enoch who would know the truth, but unfortunately the fragment does not contain any answer Enoch offered.[19]

(f) THE TESTAMENTS OF THE TWELVE PATRIARCHS

These examples set the scene for another set of pseudepigraphical books, known as the Testaments of the Twelve Patriarchs. These books purport to be the final death-bed instructions of the twelve sons of Jacob to their descendants, predicting their subsequent history. Charles dated the Testaments in the second century BCE with Christian interpolations while de Jong thought they were clearly books of the Christian period, around 200 CE; they also contain Zoroastrian dualism and notions of resurrection. However, the testament of Levi has been found at Qumran in Aramaic and that of Naphtali also, but in Hebrew.[20]

It may be best to assume, as Milik does, that the earliest present full texts of the Testaments we have in Greek are the work of a Christian author who makes use of earlier Hebrew writings as found at Qumran and very possibly others, and admit that it is impossible to know how far this Greek text corresponds with the Hebrew original.

There are five references to Sodom, from the Testaments of Asher, Benjamin, Levi, and Naphtali respectively, but these may include later Christian interpretation of its sin. They are, in fact, quite similar to other such references in the Pseudepigrapha and can be summarized briefly:

(1) *The Testament of Asher*
'Sodom sinned against the angels of the Lord.' (Chapter 7.1)

(2) *The Testament of Benjamin*
'They commit the fornication of Sodom and renew wanton acts with women.' (Chapter 9.1)
This could be generalized, or reflect the non-J source of the heterosexual rape at Gibeah by the Benjamites, as Josephus does.

(3) *The Testament of Levi*
'Adultery, prostitution and marriage to gentile women is unlawful, like the union of Sodom.' (Chapter 14.6–7)

(4) *The Testament of Naphtali*
A passage which contrasts in dualistic fashion the will and order of God with that of the chief evil spirit Beliar. (Chapter 3.3–5)
As the sun and stars do not change their order, so the tribe of Naphtali are to obey God rather than the disorderliness of idolatry.
Recognizing in all created things the Lord who made them, they are not to become as Sodom which changed the order of nature, or the Watchers who changed the order of their nature, hence the flood.

Then in the next section, chapter 4, Naphtali predicts (from the writing of Enoch) that they will depart from the Lord, following the lawlessness of the Gentiles and the wickedness of Sodom. Of these references, only the first one from Naphtali is untypical, developing the connection between the natural law of creation and the moral law, though the conjunction of the Watchers and Sodom reiterates the familiar theme of confusing the species.

(g) THE LETTER OF ARISTEAS

This letter, of uncertain date after 200 BCE, written in Greek is chiefly of interest for its account of the origin of the Septuagint. Although probably not accurate history, it shows what may have been thought by the Jews of Alexandria at this time about the Septuagint, and the merits of the Jewish Law. It contains a section on sexual offences, suggesting that unlike the rest of mankind, Jews avoid sexual promiscuity and homosexual behaviour.

> We have been distinctly separated from the rest of mankind. For most other men defile themselves with promiscuous intercourse, thereby working great iniquity, and whole countries and cities pride themselves upon such vices. For they not only have intercourse with men, but they defile their own mothers and even their own daughters. But we have been kept separate from such sins. (The Letter of Aristeas, 151–3, Charles' translation)

(h) THE SIBYLLINE ORACLES

These are a collection of sayings by Jewish and Christian authors dating through the whole inter-testamental period and probably later. They are in the manner of a pagan original and were thought by Clement of Alexandria to provide useful external arguments for Christianity. Book Three of the Oracles was probably written *c.* 140 BCE, and Books Four and Five after the destruction of Jerusalem in 70 CE.

In Book Three, amid prophecy of doom, there are two predictions concerning homosexual behaviour:

> A stress of ungodliness shall fall on them, and male shall draw near to male, and they shall set their children in ill-famed houses. (Book 3, line 185, Charles' translation)

In contrast, a new God-fearing people will emerge who:

> are mindful of the purity of marriage. Nor do they hold unholy intercourse with boys, as do the Phoenicians, Egyptians and Latins and spacious Hellas, and many nations of other men, Persians and Galatians and all Asia, transgressing the holy law of the immortal God which he ordained. (Book 3, lines 596–600, Charles' translation)

(i) 3 MACCABEES

The final pseudepigraphical book to be considered is 3 Maccabees. This is a tale in Greek of Ptolemy's persecution of the Jews at Alexandria. He tries to enter their Temple and force idolatry on them, but they are miraculously preserved. Its date is uncertain, from 100

BCE onwards, and the title is misleading, as the book has nothing to do with the situation in Palestine during the Maccabean revolt except in the sense that it reflects typical thinking of Judaism at this period. The early Church regarded this story with respect, but only the Syriac Church now regards it as canonical.

Chapter 2 of 3 Maccabees contains a high-priestly prayer for deliverance which reviews what would now be called major events in the salvation history of Judaism, and the reference to Sodom occurs between the story of creation and the deliverance from Egypt.

For thou who hast created all things, and governest the whole world, art a righteous ruler, and judgest those who do aught in violence and arrogance. Thou didst destroy those who in aforetime did iniquity, among whom were giants trusting in their strength and boldness, bringing upon them a boundless flood of water. Thou didst burn up with fire and brimstone the men of Sodom, workers of arrogance, who had become known of all for their crimes, and didst make them an example to those who should come after. (3 Maccabees 2.3–5)

This passage from 3 Maccabees shows the reference to Sodom as the symbol of universal disobedience, and in typical fashion associates this also with the giants and the flood. The pattern of these pseudepigraphical references therefore, is that they are standard quasi-credal statements in which the saving acts of the Lord are contrasted with judgement stories from the patriarchal period. These judgement stories usually include the Giants, Sodom, the Flood, the Red Sea. Here idolatry is the complaint, the same illustrations often serve, with sexual offences included.

F References to Homosexual Behaviour in the Rabbinic Writings

From the beginning of the Christian era, the Jews of Palestine struggled for survival against the Romans, losing the first war and the Temple in 70 CE, and the second war and the remaining vestiges of political independence in 135 CE. With Jerusalem no longer available, a temporary patriarchate and Sanhedrin were established at Yabneh (Jamnia), but after the Bar Kokhba revolt, many Jews fled to Babylon and only small scattered communities remained in Judea. A new patriarchate was set up at Usha in Galilee and the religious traditions were preserved and studied in the Academy there. These traditions were eventually codified for worldwide Jewry in the Palestinian and Babylonian Talmuds. Although Midrash had been the earliest form of biblical commentary from the time of Ezra onwards, the legal codification of the Mishnah was the dominant part of the Talmud. Further Midrashim were written subsequently on the Pentateuch.

The Christian community in Jerusalem left the city after the Roman wars, but the Christian mission to the Gentiles led by Paul had already moved the focus of attention towards Rome and the major cosmopolitan cities of the Empire. It was the Hellenized Dispersion rather than the Jews of Palestine who faced the strongest challenge from the Christians and there was little need for the Christian apologists to learn Hebrew or Aramaic. Palestinian Judaism and mainstream Christianity were therefore seldom in direct conflict after the death of Paul. However, the Jews and Christians shared the Old Testament and the influence of the Jewish tradition on Christian biblical scholars continued at least until the Reformation.

Both traditions treat the Sodom story similarly, and in the Mishnah homosexual behaviour is listed as one of the capital offences.

In the Midrash Rabbah on Genesis, dating from the sixth century, the homosexual connotation of the sin of Sodom is maintained. This is reiterated in the Commentary by Rashi, of the eleventh century, of importance not only because he was a notable interpreter in the literal style, but also because of his influence on the Christian commentator Nicholas of Lyra to whom Luther was in turn indebted. In Reformation Europe, the traditions converged to some extent. Of more obvious significance for the Christian tradition in its early stages are the commentaries of the Alexandrian Jew, Philo, on Genesis, and the account of Jewish history written by the Romanized Pharisee, Josephus, both from the first century of the Christian era.[21]

(a) THE MISHNAH

The Mishnah has been described as a deposit of four centuries of Jewish religious and cultural activity in Palestine, dating from early in the second century BCE onwards. It was compiled by the Rabbi Judah who lived from 135–220 CE and it ranks second only to the Hebrew Scriptures in authority. It marks for the Jews the transition from Old Testament to Judaism as the New Testament marks for the Christians the emergence of Christianity. The fourth division of the Mishnah deals with legal matters, and within it the fourth section, entitled Sanhedrin, describes the legal council's jurisdiction, including capital offences and punishments. This court is composed of twenty-three judges and may award four types of death penalty according to the descending gravity of the offence: burning, stoning, beheading, and strangling. Homosexual behaviour is to be punished by stoning:

> These are they that are to be stoned: he that has connection with his mother, his father's wife, his daughter-in-law, a male, or a beast, and the woman that suffers connection with a beast, and the blasphemer and the idolater and he that offers any of his seed to Moloch. . . . (Quoted from the Mishnah, Sanhedrin 7.4, trans. H. Danby (Oxford 1933), p. 391)

The fifth division of the Mishnah, dealing with ritual law, sets out the severity of punishment for a list of offences similar to that in the tractate quoted above, but with the inclusion of intercourse with a menstrous woman, and the punishment is modified where there are extenuating circumstances. All such punishments are called *kerithoth*—literally 'cutting off' or excommunication, but stoning is required only for those who commit the transgression knowingly, after warning by witnesses; if the offence was committed in error, the penalty is a sin offering; if guilt is uncertain, a suspensive guilt offering is required. Minors or those asleep are not considered culpable.[22]

The list of offences and punishments in the Mishnah here given shows obvious similarities with the Holiness Code and the death penalty and excommunication are conflated. Whether or not these capital penalties were exacted in fact seems doubtful, not only because the Sanhedrin was seldom, if ever, in a position of sufficiently independent authority, but also because the general disposition of the Rabbinic precepts is to provide a system of appeals and checks which, while respecting the rigour of the law, avoids capital punishment whenever possible. Maimonides observes in his commentary on the Sanhedrin rules:

> It is the duty of the Court to be deliberate in capital cases, to exercise caution and patience. Any Court that condemns to death one man in seven years is branded as destructive. Nevertheless, if it is necessary to execute culprits every day, the Court must do so. (A. M. Hershman, *The Code of Maimonides*, Book 14 (Yale University Press, 1949), pp. 40–1)

Maimonides wrote this commentary in the twelfth century CE, but like the Talmud and Mishnah, refers back to a probably idealized situation in the time of Moses, but in fact, nearest to realization in the inter-testamental period under the Hasmoneans. The decision of the Sanhedrin to deliver Jesus to Pilate for execution will be recalled.

The sin of Sodom is twice referred to in the Mishnah. First in Sanhedrin 10.3 there are lists of those who will not share in the world to come, and these include the generation of the Flood, the men of Sodom, spies and those of the dispersion and the wilderness. In Aboth 5.10 those who claim to respect their own and others' property rights, but lack the generosity of the saints are, it is suggested, like men of Sodom, presumably meaning little more than somewhat legalistic or tight-fisted. Since the prohibition of homosexual behaviour in the Mishnah is clearly based on the Holiness Code, and the references to Sodom are insignificant, either as part of one of the usual lists familiar from the Pseudepigrapha, or as vague general wickedness, it might be argued that the link between Sodom and homosexual behaviour is not maintained in Rabbinic writing, but this is not the case as references to the Midrash Rabbah on Genesis and Rashi show. Before coming to these commentaries on Genesis, however, another aspect of human sexuality noticed in the Mishnah deserves brief consideration.

There are numerous references in the Mishnah to a special category—those of doubtful or double sex. These terms seem to imply androgyny or hermaphroditism in modern medical terminology, and in the Mishnah are applied to both human beings and animals, predominantly of the male sex. Where this condition is found, it acts as a bar in terms of suitability for ritual offering, and also disqualifies men from some masculine rights as adults, assigning them a lower status equivalent to women, although preserving the basic human rights under the laws concerning, for example, property, inheritance, and protection of the person.

The final section of the tractate Bikkurim defines what is meant by 'those of double sex' as 'in some ways like both to men and women and in some things like neither to men nor to women'. The details that follow suggest a range of characteristics found in various forms of hermaphroditism including perhaps defective genitalia and disinclination to sexual activity, but the emphasis in this and other references in the Mishnah is not on anatomy or sexual performance but on the difficulty of assigning sexual identity, and therefore appropriate status and obligations under the law. The reference to the 'androgynos' which concludes Bikkurim seems, Danby suggests, to be a later addition to the original Mishnah, intended to explain the meaning of the term, though even here it is observed that 'the androgynos is a creature by itself, and the sages could not decide about it whether it was man or woman'.[23]

It seems from these references to the special 'double sex category' in the Mishnah that the Rabbis were well aware of hermaphroditism, and since the criteria they used included both anatomical appearance and sexual behaviour or the lack of it, it may not be too far-fetched to discern here some awareness of the homosexual condition, not differentiated from chromosomal abnormality as modern medical science makes possible. The condition was clearly found puzzling, inconsistent with the usual sharply distinct sexual male or female classification, which is made of considerable importance in the Rabbinic tradition, and it is interesting that the basic human rights are granted, although in religious terms such persons are considered unclean. Many Jews thought that Adam had been bi-sexual until divided, thus interpreting Genesis 1.27.

(b) MIDRASH RABBAH–GENESIS

This commentary dates in its present form from the sixth century CE, though its antecedents may be much older and have some links with the Tannaitic Commentaries on the other books of the Pentateuch compiled in the inter-testamental period. It comes from Palestine, not Babylon. The sinfulness of Sodom is described in general terms in a comment on Genesis 13.13, where Lot is separating from Abraham to live near the town.

> There was no city more wicked than Sodom; when a man was evil he was called a Sodomite ... the men of Sodom were WICKED to each other; SINNERS in adultery; AGAINST THE LORD in idolatry while EXCEEDINGLY refers to bloodshed. (Midrash Rabbah XLI.7)[24]

Ascribing adultery, idolatry, and bloodshed to the men of Sodom is, of course, normal practice as we have seen both in the writings of the biblical prophets and in the inter-testamental period generally. On Genesis 19.5 the commentary specifies homosexual behaviour as the assault intended on Lot's visitors, who are named as Gabriel, sent to overturn Sodom, and Raphael who is to rescue Lot.

> Lot prayed on their (the men of Sodom's) behalf the whole of that night, and they (the angels) would have heeded him; but immediately the Sodomites demanded BRING THEM OUT UNTO US, THAT WE MAY KNOW THEM—for sexual purposes. (Midrash Rabbah L.5)[25]

A footnote to this comment adds 'i.e. pederasty, "know" being understood as in Genesis 4.1.'

In a further comment on Genesis 19.9 it is observed that:

> The Sodomites made an agreement among themselves that whenever a stranger visited them, they should force him to sodomy and rob him of his money. (Midrash Rabbah LVII)[26]

In noting these Midrash references, it has to be remembered that the text is a compilation of comments by noted Rabbinic teachers of the past, and it is obvious here that the general wickedness of Sodom and the particular mention of sodomy are brought together as parts of the tradition, so that anyone reading the commentary as a whole would have no doubt of the authenticity of the general and specific grounds of the condemnation. The commentary also elaborates the intercessory role of Abraham and Lot's equally unsuccessful imitation of it. The observation about the pact of the men of Sodom to inflict this indignity on strangers recalls the ancient custom of the Semitic peoples to prisoners, and is perhaps a fresh way of demonstrating the theme of inhospitality. The naming of the angels has also become part of the tradition in the Midrash, as in the Book of Enoch, but not in the canonical Pentateuch.

Earlier in this Midrash, there is a comment on Genesis 2.16, the commandment of God to Adam to eat from any of the trees in the Garden except the Tree of Knowledge. This is the second creation narrative in Genesis, and usually regarded as the earlier one, from a J source. The commentary quotes R. Levi as saying that six commandments were given, and these are, in fact, the so-called Noachic precepts which the Rabbis held were obligatory on Gentiles. They include the prohibition of idolatry, blasphemy, injustice, murder, incest, and theft. The prohibition against incest is explained by reference to Genesis 2.24: Adam is united to his wife, 'which implies not to his neighbour's wife, nor to a male, nor to an animal' (Midrash Genesis Rabbah XVI.6). An editorial footnote to this comment adds that in Hebrew usage 'incest' includes adultery, pederasty, and bestiality.

(c) RASHI—COMMENTARY ON GENESIS

Rashi, so called from the initials of his name Rabbi Solomon ben Isaac, was a French Jewish Biblical scholar, a Rabbi of Troyes, living from 1040–1105 CE. He wrote commentaries on the Talmud and most of the Old Testament, and his commentary on the Pentateuch was eventually printed in many translations from the seventeenth century onwards. Since this commentary is in a very simple form, the Hebrew scriptural text interspersed with concise observations about meanings and Rabbinic interpretations, it has been adopted as a book of devotion, laid out so that the obligation to read a portion of the Torah in Hebrew and translation weekly can be observed using only one volume. Modern translations of Rashi, therefore, are similar in form to Bible reading notes in the Christian tradition.

Rashi's treatment of the Sodom narrative indicates some reserve about the Midrash interpretation of Lot's character. Thus in the comments on Genesis 13.10–13, Rashi suggests the text means that Lot chose the area of Sodom as more fertile, not because he wished to identify with the immorality of the inhabitants. This view, of course, is textually accurate, but he does then maintain the traditional interpretation of verse 13, the wickedness of the men of Sodom being set down as guilt in the abuse of their bodies, abuse of their money and in knowing God who was their master and deliberately sinning against him.[27]

In his comments on chapter 19 Rashi takes seriously the themes of hospitality, and of a delay in the execution of God's judgement while the angelic visitors, not named, discuss with Lot how far all the men of Sodom are implicated. Having concluded (verse 4) 'that there was not even one righteous man among them', Rashi makes the sexual meaning of verse 5 explicit:

> That we may have unnatural connection with them, as it is said 'who know not men carnally'.

The restraint shown by Rashi in these comments compared with the Mishnah, Midrash, and Pseudepigrapha marks his concern to concentrate on the original text, and therefore references to idolatry are excluded. As will be seen later, the suggestions that the men of Sodom ignore the natural law and abuse their bodies, is followed by Luther, in his Lectures on Romans, where it seems masturbation is taken as the primary offence.

(d) PHILO

Living between 20 BCE and 50 CE in Alexandria, a rival city to Rome, with a large Jewish population, Philo was probably the most influential Hellenistic Jew of his time. Besides his philosophical and historical works, he wrote extensive commentaries on the pentateuchal books of Genesis and Exodus and on the laws they contained. His biblical work is characterized by a very broad style of allegorical interpretation and great freedom in allusion to aspects of life in his own time, and he is much influenced by Greek ideas, such as the development of the soul towards perfection or destruction. An example of this allegorical method is provided by his treatment of nakedness in Genesis which is given both a literal and a figurative meaning, the latter having the real significance, for through experience the soul learns to protect its nakedness from evil.[28]

In his commentary on the Laws, Philo takes the decalogue commandments in sequence, using the Septuagint text, and expanding his material to include a great deal of Jewish law on each subject in a style and method similar to that of the Mishnah. Thus after a personal introduction sections of Book Three of the Laws are concerned with the sixth commandment, against adultery. Under this heading not only marital infidelity, but all the items in the Holiness Codes referring to sexual offences are included and explained, such as incest, pederasty, bestiality and the bar to intercourse during the menstrual period. Although there is little in Philo's treatment of the Jewish teaching which is not already familiar from other inter-testamental writings, the early Christian fathers such as Clement, Origen, and Ambrose used his ideas freely, and therefore his views are of importance for the subsequent Christian attitudes to some sexual questions.

The commentary follows the order of Leviticus chapter 18, and applies the prohibitions strictly. Intercourse with a woman during menstruation is said to be contrary to the law of nature, because generative seeds must not be wasted 'for the sake of a gross and untimely pleasure'.[29] In Section 33, Philo elaborates this rule in terms of the human biology of his times, assuming the monthly flow functions to cleanse the womb and prepare it for successful seed laying, as a farmer waits till the winter flood subsides before sowing his field. His view that intercourse is intended only for procreation is reinforced in the next section where he likens the attempt to marry a woman known to be barren as equivalent to ploughing hard and stony ground. But he is realistic enough to observe that the men who do this are motivated by the wish for intercourse without the risk of conception, and he regards such men as lecherous and incontinent past all cure. They are said to copulate like pigs or goats and are adversaries of God. He concludes:

> For while God in His love both for mankind and all that lives spares no care to effect the preservation and permanence of every race, those persons who make an art of quenching the life of the seed as it drops, stand confessed as the enemies of nature. (Philo, Loeb, vol. 7, p. 497)

Having delineated the purpose of sexual activity in such strictly procreational terms, it comes as no surprise that he deals harshly with pederasty in Sections 37–42. In his Greek text, Philo uses the word *paiderastein* and not the phrase in the Septuagint 'lie with a man as a woman', and it is clear from the fifty-three lines he takes to deal with this subject that he is describing the association of mature men with youthful lovers, an institution of Greek and Roman cultures familiar to him, rather than the cult prostitution that had once worried the Israelites. He does mention religious festivities and rites in honour of Demeter where 'these hybrids of man and woman' head the procession, strutting through the markets, but his chief concern is the exploitation of the young and their own willing participation in the role put upon them in which the male nature is transformed to the female. Their hair, their scent, their clothes, their cosmetics, all offend Philo and he holds that such effeminacy makes them permanently impotent. The text is too long for full quotation, but Philo's reflection on the older partner gives a good indication of his attitude:

> He pursues an unnatural pleasure and does his best to render cities desolate and uninhabited by destroying (or wasting) the means of procreation. (Philo, Loeb, vol. 7, p. 499)

Philo next deals with bestiality. He cites the Cretan myth by which Pasiphae, wife of King Minos, conceived with a bull and gave birth to the Minotaur, and then refers to the Jewish rules forbidding cross-breeding among animals, and concludes that men and women who offend in this way, together with the animal involved, must be put to death. His argument refers to the Mosaic tradition against confusing species among animals, but adds that further reasons for the prohibition were 'decency and conformity to nature'.

In these comments on sexual offences, based on the sixth commandment and Leviticus chapter 18, Philo clearly greatly elaborates by comparison with the restraint of the Palestinian Mishnah and Talmud, and this conforms to his awareness of the Hellenistic culture and philosophy, though he also visited Rome at the time of

Caligula. His stress on natural law and the procreative purpose of sex is notable.

Philo also deals at length with the story of Sodom. In the introductory volume to the Laws, in the first section about Abraham, he comments on the land of the Sodomites in vehement terms, and this passage is more commonly quoted by present-day writers than that on the sex laws referred to above.[30] The argument is basically the same, though he gives free rein to his imagination and describes life in Sodom in terms which go far beyond anything depicted in the Genesis narrative or other inter-testamental writings. Indeed, it reads more like a passage from Suetonius or the Satyricon. The men of Sodom are said to owe their gluttony and lewdness to their excessive wealth, and so, unable to bear such fullness, they throw off the law of nature and apply themselves to strong drink, dainty feeding, and forbidden forms of intercourse. Adultery is followed by homosexual behaviour and leads to sterility, the degeneration of their souls and the corruption of mankind.[31]

Much of the text of Genesis is scrutinized by Philo in his further commentary 'Questions and Answers on Genesis'. In several references to Sodom and the Sodomites, Philo develops his argument that Sodom is the symbol of the blindness of the souls of men destined for destruction. His comment on Genesis chapter 5 merits quotation; the text of Philo available here is an Aramaic one, and he takes the meaning of the Hebrew *yadha* in the literal 'to know' sense rather than the ambiguous Greek of the Septuagint:

> What is the meaning of the words, 'bring them out to us that we may know them'? The literal meaning indicates servile, lawless and unseemly pederasty. But, as for the deeper meaning, lascivious and unrestrainedly impure men, raising a mound of desires, threaten with death those who are self-controlled and desirous of continence. To these they say 'let them come forth from their own wills, and from their choice of a constant, seemly and noble way of life in order that we may know them.' For they will be persuaded to change their ways and gladly accept ours, learning in the act that souls are not naked and incorporal so as not to be in want, but have something in common with the body which lacks many necessities. They should not treat it badly or dismiss it, but tame it and domesticate it by offering it the materials that belong to it.[32]

In the next section, Philo considers the inner meaning of Lot's offer of his daughters as substitutes, and here argues that although the text shows the Sodomites were literally pederasts, the real point is that the progressive soul follows masculine thoughts of wisdom and virtue rather than feminine thoughts dominated by bodily needs and passions. So Lot apparently did right to be prepared to abandon feminine thoughts to save masculine ones, a somewhat bizarre conclusion to modern minds, as much of Philo's writing must seem.

The tendency to philosophical mysticism shown in this kind of speculation demonstrates how far Philo is from the thought-forms of Rabbinic Judaism,[33] and it is somewhat tantalizing to find that he so confidently identifies the literal sense of Sodom's sins with general wickedness and the Greek and Roman institutionalized pederasty, while using all this symbolically as the basis of his ascetic teaching. These quotations serve as an early demonstration of the excesses to which allegorical interpretation of Scripture can lead, by comparison with which, the rewriting of Jewish history by Josephus seems commendably restrained.[34]

(e) JOSEPHUS

Josephus was a Palestinian Jew, trained in the Law and as a Pharisee. He was born in 37 CE, took part in the war of 66 CE and was captured by Vespasian, who took him to Rome, and provided for him an income from captured property in Palestine. Regarded as a traitor by the Jews, Josephus wrote in 77 CE an historical account of the Jewish war, based largely on his own recollections, and in a style sympathetic to the Roman viewpoint. Some twenty years later he completed a twenty-volume history of the Jewish people from the Creation to the start of the war, entitled 'Jewish Antiquities'. This longer work is based on the Old Testament, of which he seems to have used a Hebrew or Aramaic version in preference to the Septuagint, at least for the Pentateuch and early historical books. The story is told in honour of the Jewish race and represents probably an attempt at reconciliation with his own people in his final years. He died *c.* 100 CE.[35]

In the *Jewish War*, chapter 16, Josephus described Vespasian's campaign at the point when he enters a deserted Jericho, the inhabitants having already fled west to the hills between the Jordan valley and Jerusalem. There follows a description of the terrain and its vegetation, and then of the Dead Sea which, apart from a slight exaggeration of distances, reads as a careful eye-witness account of an area which appears much the same to a modern observer.[36] Josephus notes that south of the lake lies the land of Sodom:

> Once so rich in crops and in the wealth of its cities, but now dust and ashes. They say that owing to the impiety of its inhabitants it was burnt up by lightning; indeed, there are still marks from the fire from heaven. . . . To this extent, the stories about the land of Sodom are confirmed by the evidence of our eyes. (Josephus, *The Jewish War* (Penguin edn), p. 262)

It is perhaps worth noting that to see the southern end of the Dead Sea, Josephus would presumably have followed the road on the western side, and thus passed Qumran and Masada. The distances are short, Masada being little more than fifty miles from Jerusalem by road, but there seems no reason to doubt that Josephus would have been familiar with these communities and their traditions, as he was with the rabbinic writings. Since he described the destruction of Masada in later pages, observing that 'God was indeed on the side of the Romans' (op. cit., p. 385), it is not surprising that he describes the destruction of Sodom in such a reserved way, as if surprised that the folk tale has left such geological evidence. It might be impolite to draw attention to sexual sin but Roman religion would not be offended at impiety as the suggested cause of the catastrophe.

In the *Antiquities*, Book 1, Josephus describes the story of Lot and Abraham in an urbane style, softening the Genesis narrative to suggest that the character of these patriarchs was wholly respectable. Thus Abraham visits Egypt, not only to escape famine, but to explore the possibilities of theological dialogue with the priests. The attempted seduction of Sarah on this occasion and later with the Philistinian Abimelech is explained away as misunderstandings between gentlemen who, of course, respect each other's wife. In the story of Sodom, Lot goes there because it is more prosperous: the city is said to flourish, with many young people. Josephus also seems to think that the Salt Lake only emerged after the city was destroyed by lightning and submerged.

The final stages of the destruction of the city are recorded as a sad story of progressive moral decay against which God reluctantly has to act in punishment, despite Abraham's grief and pleading. Thus:

> Now about this time the Sodomites, overwhelmingly proud of their numbers and the extent of their wealth, showed themselves insolent to men and impious to the Divinity, insomuch that they no more remembered the benefits they had received from Him, hated foreigners and declined all intercourse with others. Indignant at this conduct, God accordingly resolved to chastise them for their arrogance. . . .[37]

The word 'intercourse' (Greek: *homilias*) in Josephus' text, clearly means companionship or association, not sexual behaviour, but while it seems that Josephus is stressing the inhospitality theme at this point the sexual nature of the intended assault is hinted at as the commentary proceeds.[38] Josepus continues:

> The angels came to the city of the Sodomites and Lot invited them to be his guests, for he was very kind to strangers and had learned the lesson of Abraham's liberality. But the Sodomites, on seeing these men of remarkably fair appearance whom Lot had taken under his roof, were bent only on violence and outrage to their youthful beauty. . . . God, therefore, indignant at their atrocities, blinded the criminals so that they could not find the entrance to the house, and condemned the whole people of the Sodomites to destruction.[39]

Lot's alternative offer of his daughters is described as an attempt to restrain the passions of the Sodomites and protect the guests from dishonour if they were so licentious that they needed the girls to gratify their lusts, but Josephus concludes that even this would not content them. There can be little doubt that Josephus believed the men of Sodom to have intended homosexual rape on the angels, and perhaps the interest of these quotations lies chiefly in the restrained way he records the narrative, and in the underlying concept of God these comments indicate, closer to that in Greek rather than Hebrew theology.

The story of the rape of the Levite's concubine at Gibeah from Judges 19, seems to have been ignored in the inter-testamental writings so far considered, and a single reason for this may be the distinction made at this time between the Law and the historical books. Since Josephus is providing a complete history in the *Antiquities*, the settlement of the tribe in Canaan is of obvious importance. Josephus does, therefore, deal with this story, though he transposes it from the appendix to an earlier part of Judges, after chapter 2, perhaps to allow time for the tribe of Benjamin to recover its strength before the emergence of Saul. He elaborates the biblical narrative making clear that the wife, as he describes her, does not at first reciprocate the affection of her husband, but makes amends in the final tragic moments and dies knowing her shame will make him inconsolable. The men of Gibeah are depicted harshly, for they have noticed the girl's beauty when she entered their town, and after argument with the old man who appeals to the laws of hospitality and protection for his kinsman, they seize the girl and carry her away. The old man's suggestion that if they must appease their lust they should use his own daughter rather than break the law of hospitality, is brushed aside. As Josephus tells the tale, there is no hint whatever of interest by the townspeople in the Levite, nor of homosexual intentions towards him. It may be that this omission is deliberate, for the tale is disgraceful to the tribe of Benjamin, and nothing good will come of repeating the homosexual assault sub-theme in first-century Rome. But it is, of course, possible that Josephus himself detected the unsatisfactory state of the text and removed the J interpolation, as suggested in the previous chapter. A further speculation might be that Josephus had a different Hebrew or Aramaic text to work from, since lost, in which this amendment and perhaps others, including the transposition of the appendix, had already been made. There are a number of places in the *Antiquities* where Josephus adds detail or varies it from what is now known of the Septuagint or Hebrew Bibles, and so the different text theory has some merit. Alternatively, he may have had a Midrash on the Pentateuch to hand, dating from the post-exilic period from which he derived interpolations of this kind.[40] In any case, while we have argued that the Gibeah narrative has to be taken seriously in the Canon of the Old Testament, the exclusion of homosexual elements from it by Josephus is an early indication of its subsequent eclipse in the Christian tradition.

G Summary of the Inter-Testamental Period

The evidence of the Apocryphal and Pseudepigraphical writings of the inter-testamental period show the emergence of a clearer denunciation of homosexual behaviour than is found in the canonical Old Testament, apart from the Holiness Code. This seems to have arisen in connection with the development of the legends of the Watchers and the Giants, and the association of them with the story of Noah, the Flood, and the destruction of Sodom as destruction sagas from the past which helped to explain the judgement of God the Jewish people felt on themselves in their own day. Sodom stands not only for general wickedness, arrogance, idolatry, and every kind of sexual sin in the past, as Hellenistic culture and Roman occupation do now, but homosexual behaviour and particularly pederasty were a great affront from these cultures, which it seemed to Jewish readers of Genesis at this time, God had once abhorred and judged.

Orthodox Palestinian Judaism, as it is represented in the Mishnah and Talmud, was more restrained, taking the precepts of the Holiness Code with full seriousness as part of the Law, to which obedience was the only hope of salvation from present miseries, but the Rabbis looked for reasons to alleviate the severity of its punishments. Later Jewish commentators on Genesis, the Midrash Rabbah and Rashi, have no doubt that among the sins of Sodom were inhospitality, arrogance, and male homosexual behaviour. Nor did Philo and Josephus query the tradition, though their interpretations were in quite different styles. All this evidence is somewhat untidy, but to anyone studying the Jewish teaching in Jerusalem or the Diaspora, both the Torah and the story of Sodom would have been cited to establish the abhorrence to homosexual behaviour generally adopted by the Jews. Jesus and Paul would have encountered this teaching, which brings us to the New Testament.

5 The New Testament

A Introduction

The canonical Books of the New Testament were formed into an authentic collection accepted by the Church over a period of some three centuries. The first Christians did not depend on sacred writings as their source of authority in faith and morals, but on the preaching and teaching of the Apostles. While those who had been 'eye-witnesses' of the Resurrection of Christ remained alive, their understanding of that event and of the Passion that preceded it formed the basis of the new faith. The new converts were taught the 'tradition' of the teaching of Jesus, and as time passed, selections of those teachings coalesced into carefully remembered and treasured groups of sayings. From these, eventually, the four evangelists constructed their written Gospels, adding sufficient narrative detail of the life of Jesus to make a coherent framework.

Most of the surviving eleven Apostles seem to have become missionary preachers, and nothing certainly written by them is known to have survived, although their recollections are obviously a major source of the Gospels. The twelfth man, Paul of Tarsus, was, however, an assiduous correspondent, and although not all the epistles attributed to him in the New Testament are thought to have come straight from his dictation, his corpus of writings is a major source of information about the Christian faith and life in the first century. His missionary journeys and his close links with the major churches at Ephesus, Corinth, and Rome need no emphasis here.

Apart from the Gospels and the epistles of Paul, a great number of other Christian writings emerged in the first two centuries. Among these were apocryphal Gospels, claiming apostolic authorship, a number of epistles of varying orthodoxy, and as church organization developed, genuine pastoral letters and sets of instructions from bishops and others in authority. Some books from the latter two groups were finally accepted into the Canon. Precise agreement about dating and authorship of the New Testament books has not been achieved among scholars but it is clear that Paul's letters were written between 48 and 65 CE, the Gospels and Acts follow within the next thirty years, and the remaining books are variously placed within this period or soon after. It is probable that the whole New Testament is the work of not more than a dozen authors spanning a period of perhaps 100 years.[1]

Christianity shares with Judaism a common inheritance of ethical monotheism, and in practice that has meant that the Old Testament is Part One of the Bible. The New Testament authors used the

Septuagint and were familiar with the inter-testamental writings. Both to explain Jesus to the Jews, and to reassure them that the basic purpose of the Torah was fulfilled by him, not abrogated, constant reference is made to the old tradition in the new. The primary task of evangelism among the Gentiles inclined the Gospel writers to emphasize the conflict between Jesus and the Scribes and Pharisees. The ecclesiastical authorities in Jerusalem are made to bear the chief blame for his condemnation, but in controversy with them, it is their interpretation of the Law, not its precepts as such, which Jesus challenges. Similarly, St Paul sees the new revelation as fulfilling the old, and strives continually to win round his erstwhile colleagues. From the Rabbinic point of view, no doubt the Old Testament texts chosen for this purpose are somewhat arbitrary, and the interpretations placed on them by the Christians unorthodox, but still there was at first much more common ground between the Christians and Jews than between the Christians and the Greek and Roman cultures: only slowly could suitable links be forged with them.

Among the beliefs of the early Church was the expectation that Christ would shortly return and sum up human history in a final judgement. This expectation gave Christian moral teaching for its own communities a somewhat interim character. Collections of the sayings of Jesus, such as the Sermon on the Mount were circulated.[2] Instructions from the Apostles and other teachers were provided, and other internal regulations were worked out within the fellowship in response to the Holy Spirit's prompting, but a serious critique of the morality of pagan society was scarcely attempted. That was part of the 'world' which would shortly pass away. For the time being, the realities of political power and government were accepted as ordained by God, Caesar was to be given his due, law was to be obeyed, social institutions like marriage and the family were to be continued, and even slavery could be tolerated if administered humanely.

Since the kingdoms of this world were shortly to pass away, no thorough-going Christian ethic of a universalist kind was worked out in the first years of the life of the Church. No effort to match in Christian terms the all-embracing designs of Plato's *Republic* and *Laws* seemed appropriate, and with their apocalyptic expectations the Christians saw little point in a revived and reformed deuteronomism. For the immediate future, the first Christian teachers, being themselves Jews, tended to maintain their old moral codes, except where they realized these were incompatible with the teaching of Jesus. His own approach had seemed to them to be largely a process of selection and re-emphasis rather than radically new in this respect. It is not surprising, therefore, that the New Testament contains many lists of virtues and vices which are very similar in content to those in Jewish writings, and indeed, sometimes Greek equivalents, of the inter-testamental period.[3]

Homosexual behaviour is repudiated in lists of pagan vices in Paul's letters to Romans, 1 Corinthians and 1 Timothy. The Gospels do not mention the subject, but there are several references to Sodom. In the Catholic Epistles, 2 Peter and Jude, Sodom and the fallen angels legends reappear in the style of the Pseudepigrapha. The absence of any references to homosexuality in the Gospels is not surprising, as the four evangelists seem to confine their records of the teaching of Jesus on issues of sexual morality only to those that were controversial among the Jews of his time, such as divorce and adultery. What he did say about these issues, however, illustrates his general approach to moral questions and is briefly considered later in this chapter. Some contemporary Christians assign more importance to his approach than to the specific texts from the Epistles which they regard as little more than unreflective reiterations of the Jewish polemic. References to Sodom in the Gospels treat it as a symbol of wickedness and inhospitality, a warning to self-righteous Jews.

B The Pauline Texts

In his Epistle to the Romans, St Paul denounces homosexual behaviour among men and women as a feature of paganism, and in the First Epistle to the Corinthians, he warns Christians that such activity would prevent them entering the Kingdom of God. In the First Epistle to Timothy 'perversion' is said to flout the moral law and the teaching of the gospel, and this probably refers to homosexual behaviour. In the New Testament, Romans is usually printed before Corinthians, to mark its theological pre-eminence, though there seems little doubt that Corinthians was written earlier. Since they were composed within a short period of, perhaps, three years, and their arguments closely related, they are considered here in the familiar order. It is also convenient to set out the text of the references to homosexual behaviour from all three epistles together, and then examine each in its context: the three passages are as follows:

In consequence, I say, God has given them up to shameful passions. Their women have exchanged natural intercourse for unnatural, and their men in turn, giving up natural relations with women, burn with lust for one another; males behave indecently with males, and are paid in their own persons the fitting wage of such perversion. (Romans 1.26–7)

Surely you know that the unjust will never come into possession of the kingdom of God. Make no mistake: no fornicator or idolater, none who are guilty either of adultery or of homosexual perversion, no thieves or grabbers or drunkards or slanderers or swindlers, will possess the kingdom of God. (1 Corinthians 6.9–10)

We all know that the law is an excellent thing, provided we treat it as law, recognizing that it is not aimed at good citizens, but at the lawless and unruly, the impious and sinful, the irreligious and worldly; at parricides and matricides, murderers and fornicators, perverts, kidnappers, liars, perjurers—in fact all whose behaviour flouts the wholesome teaching which conforms with the gospel entrusted to me, the gospel which tells of the glory of God in His eternal felicity. (1 Timothy 1.8–11)

(a) EPISTLE TO THE ROMANS

St Paul's Epistle to the Romans is his major theological contribution to the New Testament. He wrote it from Corinth between 56 and 58 CE, towards the end of his final stay in that city, and with his plans already settled to visit Rome after he had been to Jerusalem. His obvious interest in the increasingly important church of the Empire's capital city is matched by his awareness that the Roman Christians may not take the authenticity of his apostleship for granted. The congregation in Rome was probably mostly non-Jewish, and so he writes courteously, perhaps to make a good impression on people he has not met and for a church he has not founded. He suggests that the purpose of his visit is to be refreshed by their fellowship before he travels to Spain. The difference in style is quite noticeable between this Epistle and the correspondence with the Corinthians. With the Corinthians he is personal and passionate; with the Romans polemic is reserved for the unbelievers.[4]

After an introduction, the greater part of Romans 1—11 is a vindication of Paul's own understanding of the gospel. He writes of God's response to the universal human predicament. For Jews and Gentiles alike, the acceptance by faith of Jesus as Lord is the way to reconciliation with God and to membership of his Kingdom. But for this reconciliation to be received, it is first necessary to understand that the advent of the gospel makes clear that all men, Jews and Gentiles alike, rightly stand under the judgement of God. Paul then begins to explain why this is so.

In chapter 1.18–32 he describes the predicament of the non-Jews who 'have made fools of themselves by exchanging the splendour of immortal God for an image shaped like mortal man'. As Manson puts it, 'the two counts in the indictment are idolatry and immorality, idolatry being the tap-root of evil'. Paul sees such idolatry as disastrous, for all men are subject to God's laws and the divine wrath falls inescapably on those who flout them. Once men's minds are darkened by idolatry, their wills are corrupted and their bodies degraded.

The line of reasoning used in these verses by Paul is, of course, similar to that in the Book of Wisdom, particularly chapter 14, and the pseudepigraphical books as noted in the previous chapter. In a vigorous phrase, Karl Barth has commented that the Gentiles are subject to God's wrath because their religion 'consists of one great confusion between the Creator and his creatures'.[5] But the confusion here is not that between species of creation; it is the fundamental mistake of idolatry to obscure the difference between the divine and human roles. For St Paul the consequence is seen to be that men imitate the beasts they worship. God abandons them, they lose their moral sense, degrade their bodies in sexual sin, and commit the usual long list of anti-social offences on each other, breaking all rules of conduct.

Barrett observes in his comment on verse 24 that 'the process by which idolatry becomes moral evil is neither automatic nor impersonal; God hands them over to sin'.[6]

His comment on verses 26 and 27 continues:

> No feature of pagan society filled the Jew with greater loathing than the toleration, or rather admiration, of homosexual practices. Paul is entirely one here with his compatriots; but his disgust is more than instinctive. In the obscene pleasures to which he refers is to be seen precisely that perversion of the created order which may be expected when men put the creation in place of the creator. That idolatry has such consequences is to Paul a plain mark of God's wrath. (Barrett, *Commentary*, op. cit., p. 39)

Although the examples of shameful passion given by St Paul in verses 26 and 27 are apparently almost universally regarded by modern commentators as referring to homosexual behaviour, first between women and then between men,[7] the obligation of the biblical translators to render the Greek text as precisely as they can has slightly obscured this meaning. For verse 26 the New English Bible has: 'The women have exchanged natural intercourse for unnatural.' The Authorized Version has: 'changed the natural use to that which is against nature', and the Revised Version has the same. The Revised Standard Version, the Common Bible and the New International Version alter this to: 'exchanged natural relations for unnatural' and the Jerusalem Bible renders the phrase: 'their women have turned from natural intercourse to unnatural practices.' The Good News Bible has 'The women pervert the natural use of their sex by unnatural acts', and the Living Bible paraphrases: 'the women turned against God's natural plan for them and indulged in sexual sin with each other.'

The Greek words *phusis* and *chresis* used by Paul mean 'nature' and 'use'. So clearly, the Authorized Version translation is precise and literal, but it does not indicate what practices 'against nature' might, in fact, be, and the later versions are hardly more definite, except by implication. As with the 2nd Psalm of Solomon, it is possible that the women are here being accused of abnormal forms of intercourse with men, such as *coitus interruptus*, *coitus per anum*, or as Bailey suggested[8] intercourse in which the man lies below the woman, supposedly lessening the chance of conception. All such behaviour was disapproved of in the Jewish tradition, but it seems more likely that lesbian practices are repudiated here. Although generally ignored in the Jewish writings, female homosexual behaviour was well recognized in the Hellenistic world, whether or not rightly attributed to Sappho and her companions on the island of Lesbos, a point sometimes disputed.

The description of male homosexual practices in verse 27 is quite direct and produces no difficulty in the various translations. Paul links the shameless or indecent acts among men with their lust for each other, but does not expressly mention sodomy or pederasty. Some doubts have been expressed about the introductory phrase 'giving up natural relations with women', for this could mean that Paul is only condemning those men who have been first heterosexual and then deliberately pervert themselves with homosexual practices. If that interpretation is correct, then only this kind of pervert, and possibly men of bisexual nature, are being reproved, but it is probably unrealistic to suppose that Paul himself could have thought in this way. If the argument is pressed, then it could be that we have an example in these verses from Romans of the Church's later interpretation being mistaken in including genuine homosexual men and women with Paul's condemnation, but this is really an attempt to read the old texts with modern presuppositions. It seems better to accept the view that Paul is adapting for his purpose a standard piece of Jewish propaganda, familiar to all his readers and unquestioned at the time. The *Satyricon* and other similar writings give lurid descriptions of the secular permissiveness of the times, and Paul's condemnation could be taken as a typical piece of preacher's polemic against the sins of the day. The readers may be expected to fill in the details for themselves.

Among the Christians in Rome, therefore, those converted from Judaism would find little new or strange in Paul's argument at this stage of the Epistle. Gentile converts would probably have heard such condemnation from Stoic sources, and perhaps be aware that Roman law officially disapproved of homosexual behaviour, irrespective of rumours about disgraceful goings-on in the dissolute imperial court. It might seem, therefore, that Paul is expressing here little more than the conventional moral disapproval of secular vice, just as in chapter 3 he will string together a series of quotations from the Psalms to bring the Jews under condemnation. It all goes to demonstrate a topsy-turvy world in which the good is unachievable by Jew or barbarian, and therefore a world ready to be justified by God's free grace alone if only it will abandon its pride in either works or law. Undoubtedly Paul is determined to remove every excuse so that he may clear the way for the gospel, but the question remains how far his denunciation of the Gentiles is a reiteration of his Rabbinic traditions, and how far he has subjected them to re-assessment in the light of his Christian experience. More particularly, does the condemnation of homosexual behaviour here reflect a continuation of the Jewish attitude which Paul, at this stage in his thought, has seen no need to revise after his conversion, or is it a freshly worked judgement, a Christian view, which happens to be the same as the Jewish one?

The answer to this question is, of course, of some importance for the Christian tradition. In general terms, Paul has repudiated the Torah as a means of salvation, and certainly in his letter to the Galatians, he stresses that the Christians are no longer bound by its precepts. But equally, he has no time for antinomianism: the loving liberty of the Christians will fulfil and exceed all that the law requires in terms of human care and responsibility. It is one of the paradoxes of the Christian ethic that law and love will point in the same direction in most aspects of practical living. Having posed the question, the only honest answer seems to be that it is not possible to be sure whether Paul makes this judgement afresh or continues the Rabbinic attitude. Since he expresses the same view, but in more explicit terms in the Epistle to the Corinthians, and that the order of composition appears to be Corinthians, Galatians, Romans, within a period of not more than three years, and further, that the Christian ethic is more directly set out in the two earlier writings, then it seems more consistent to regard the denunciation in Romans as a Christian judgement, identical as it happens with the Jewish tradition, but no mere unreflective repetition.

These two verses in Romans chapter 1 are often cited as the clearest possible demonstration that homosexual behaviour is forbidden in the New Testament. It has been argued so far that there is no real reason for doubting their meaning, and that although they are used as part of the criticism of the secular world, a consequence of idolatry, they also stand as part of the Christian ethical precepts for the Church and the world of the future.

It is perhaps worth recalling at this point the existence of what are called the Noachian commands of the Jewish tradition. The Rabbis had long debated what was necessary for Gentiles to be saved. Obviously, they could not be expected to obey all the precepts of the Jewish Law, but as descendants of Noah, so their reasoning ran, there were seven minimal requirements, six of which have already been noted in the previous chapter as recorded in the Midrash on Genesis 2.16. The seventh, not to cut flesh from a living animal, was added later, and some Rabbis added further precepts, one such list totalling more than thirty prohibitions. Now it is clear that this Noachian list forms the basis for many of the household codes found in the New Testament, and their precepts are included in the lists given by Paul here in Romans 1 and also in 1 Corinthians 6.

The so-called Apostolic Decree settled at the Council of Jerusalem in 49 CE (Acts 15.28–9) contains three of the Noachian precepts and some early texts add the 'Love your neighbour' commandment in negative form. This minimal law for Gentile Christians, as the Jerusalem Church saw it, refers primarily to food laws, but with the prohibition of fornication added became a set of moral precepts. Paul was at this Council.[9]

This evidence suggests the Noachian code is being used in the New Testament as the basis of a natural law, as it had already served in the past. The Rabbis had explained its binding force on unbelievers in terms of the covenant made between Noah and his three sons, from whom the whole human race descended before the Jews were given their special covenants from Abraham and Moses. Paul seems to use the argument of the covenant of Noah in Romans 1.18–21. All men know enough of God to honour him and give him thanks. Further, the Rabbinic understanding of the Noachian commandment against adultery excluded all other forms of irregular sexual activity outside marriage, so it may be concluded that among the reasons available to Paul when he selects homosexual behaviour as the particular example of degradation are not only common disapproval and the Jewish tradition, but the conviction that it was contrary to natural law. He may also have been aware of Plato's teaching to the same effect, a point to be examined later. A fair conclusion seems to be that Paul, if asked, could have provided a number of reasons for his condemnation of homosexual behaviour in this Epistle.[10]

(b) 1 CORINTHIANS

This Epistle is part of the correspondence Paul has with the Church at Corinth. He writes from Ephesus around 55 CE to a city and congregation he knows well from his previous eighteen months stay. They are close to his heart, he has written before, their reply is to hand, and he has heard other disquieting news.

Corinth had been an old Greek city, geographically well placed for trade at the crossing point between mainland Greece and the Peloponnese. Although an attempt had been made to construct a canal, this project had been abandoned, and trade flowed through the port East and West, North and South. A disastrous fire had destroyed most of the city in 146 BCE, but it had now been rebuilt under the patronage of Julius Caesar and was in many ways a typical Roman provincial capital, commercial centre, and holiday resort.

There was a Jewish synagogue and the usual range of temples for Greek and Latin deities, reflecting the Roman tolerance of syncretism. No doubt the docks had their measure of vice, but the old legend, recorded by the Greek geographer Strabo, of the Temple of Aphrodite and her thousand cult prostitutes, was an exaggeration, at least by the time Paul visited the city.[11]

After a warm greeting, Paul deals with various points from their letter, justifying his own previous instructions against their queries which he regards as partly reflecting a worldly attitude, and partly the antinomian error. Paul argues that they are to be separate from the world's standards in morality, but they cannot live totally apart from other men.

In chapter 5 he comes to the particular problem of the man living with his step-mother. Presumably this was, in fact, a marriage of a kind forbidden in both Jewish and Roman law, not incest or mere fornication. Paul regards the situation as scandalous and worries that the Corinthians do not. No details are provided, presumably because they are already well known by everyone concerned, but it is virtually impossible that a marriage to the actual mother of the man would have been tolerated. She is a second wife to the father, divorced or widowed presumably, and so the man's offence is contrary to the law. For that Paul insists he must be rooted out of the community.

Chapter 6 begins with a further problem about law. In this case it is a dispute among Christians which they take to the secular and pagan courts for settlement. This should be dealt with inside the Christian community, either among themselves or by choosing their own arbiter. This prefigures, of course, the ecclesiastical jurisdiction and canon law of later times, but it is also a continuation of the Jewish practice. Paul inserts the Christian ethic at this point—it would be better to suffer injury than allow yourselves to break the commandments against theft and then seek secular redress. To amplify this point, in verses 9 and 10 of chapter 6 he reminds them that the unjust will never come into possession of the Kingdom of God, and then provides a list of offences that would exclude them.

The concept of the Kingdom of God is treated by St Paul, as generally in the New Testament, in two senses. Sometimes it is regarded as the present reality, realized eschatology as Dodd has named it, and sometimes it refers to the future hope and consummation of God's will. Here the future sense is implied. The unjust will have no part in the coming Kingdom. Some of the Corinthians had been sinners in the ways listed—Paul may have had personal knowledge of the previous life of some of the converts—but now they have been through the purifying waters, dedicated to God, and justified. They are free, but not free to do anything, as the Corinthians seem to be implying. The Epistle continues with a number of cases where Paul sets out in a casuistic style the moral obligations of the Christian life. In striking a right balance between Christian freedom and licence, Paul finds himself waging war on two fronts at the same time. He has to correct those who think the truly spiritual man can ignore petty moral conventions, and yet he has to reassure his Gentile converts that the Council in Jerusalem makes him free to protect them from any attempts by the Judaizing party to make them subject to the precepts of the Mosaic Law.

The list of offences which includes homosexual perversion as sins excluding from the future Kingdom is cast in the form of a rhetorical question. The precepts are broadly similar to those in Romans, but more specific and more focused on individual acts of sin concerning sex and property. The style is of a household code, a domestic list of things a Christian does not do. Such lists abound in the New Testament and opinions differ among scholars as to their sources. Clearly the Noachian code can be detected as one, and given the Rabbinic inclusion of homosexual behaviour as one form of fornication in this tradition, Paul could simply be reiterating that. But such lists from Plato and from Stoic sources were widely circulated in the Hellenistic world, and in the Gospels and some Epistles there is another form which seems to depend more on the Decalogue with the addition of the love commandment.[12]

This question of sources of such codes cannot be further pursued here, and perhaps W. D. Davies gets near the truth with regard to Paul's use of them in Romans and Corinthians by describing them as an Hellenistic dress on a Rabbinic body.[13]

It is difficult to be certain how far Paul chooses the particular offences in this list on the basis of what he knows of the previous life of the Christians at Corinth. It is a personal letter, and he continues 'Such were some of you' (v. 11). Commentators usually stress the immorality of Corinth and assume that such offenders had been converted and brought into the Church, but it is also possible that the list is unstudied, a reflection of the offences from the Holiness Code: once he has begun on incest, the other prohibited sexual activities are added for good measure. In any case, it is quite clear that Paul warns the Corinthians against homosexual behaviour, and in much more specific terms than in the Epistle to the Romans. He writes specifically 'catamites' and 'sodomites'.[14]

The Greek words *malakoi* and *arsenokoitai* have precise meanings. The first is literally 'soft to the touch' and metaphorically, among the Greeks, meant males (not necessarily boys) who played the passive role in homosexual intercourse. The second means literally 'male in a bed' and the Greeks used this expression to describe the one who took the active role. Whereas in other biblical texts referring to homosexuality, the translators have wrestled to make precise sense of vague expressions, in this verse of 1 Corinthians, the older versions have euphemistically avoided conveying Paul's bluntness to their readers. The Authorized Version had 'effeminate, and abusers of themselves with mankind', which to modern English readers would probably convey 'rather feminine types who indulged in mutual masturbation'. The Revised Version is the same as the Authorized, but the Revised Standard Version uses 'homosexuals' to include both the Greek words with a footnote 'two Greek words are rendered by this expression'. The Common Bible changes this to 'sexual perverts'.[15]

The New English Bible compromises between explicitness and euphemism by referring to 'homosexual perversion' but the Jerusalem translators into English have 'catamites and sodomites', following Moffatt's accuracy of 1913, rather than their own French antecedent which reads: 'ni dépravés, ni gens de moeurs infâmes'. Etymologically, the word 'catamite' is a Latin form of the Greek 'Ganymede'. Ganymedes, the son of King Tros, and the most beautiful of all Greek youths, was appointed wine pourer of the gods, and cup-bearer to Zeus. The myth is said to have gained immense popularity in Greece and Rome because it afforded a dubious but welcome religious justification for a grown man's passionate love for a boy.[16]

The Good News Bible has 'homosexual perverts', the Living Bible has 'homosexuals' following the unamended Revised Standard Version, and the New International Version has 'homosexual offenders'.

The general trend of these newer translations is to leave no doubt that Paul means to condemn homosexual behaviour, the Common Bible altering the Revised Standard Version to meet the objection that the emphasis is placed on behaviour or perversion, and not on the homosexual condition as such. Whether or not Paul would have understood the modern distinction between the condition and behaviour is unascertainable, but his choice of words here strongly suggests that he is warning the Corinthians against the institution of homosexual behaviour between mature men and youths, so commonly recorded in the secular literature of the time, and forbidden, as we have seen, in some of the inter-testamental writings. The words 'sodomite' or 'paiderastia' might have been used instead of these secular Greek ones, but it is clear from the vocabulary of the Pauline corpus of letters that *paidion* is only used in a positive sense, to render the ideas of childlikeness or teachability as Christian virtues. He does refer to Sodom once, in Romans 9.29, as a reminder of the forbearance of God who has saved a remnant, and not judged all Israel like Sodom. He does not use the word *malakos* except in this verse of Corinthians, and it otherwise appears only twice in the New Testament: in the synoptic Gospels of Matthew (11.8) and Luke (7.25) where it means soft living in contrast to asceticism, but there is no obvious sexual implication.

The word *arsenokoitai* re-occurs in the similar context of 1 Timothy 1.10. Perhaps it seems a pedantic point to labour the 'homosexual behaviour' meaning of this verse in Corinthians, but the range of translations shown above, and the very limited use of the words in the New Testament has led some modern commentators to query their meaning. It does, however, seem clear that Paul intended to be specific and that his Corinthian readers would have no difficulty in understanding what he meant.[17]

So far we have established that Paul's condemnation of homosexual behaviour in the Corinthian Epistle appears in a list of offences against sexual morality and respect for property and the context is a dialogue between the Corinthians and himself on certain precepts of his original letter which they question. He has dealt with incest, separation, arbitration within the community, and in parenthesis reminded them of the pagan life-style they have abandoned since their conversion. It would be possible to argue at this point that no special Christian reasoning has been offered for the disapproval of homosexual behaviour, but merely the reiteration of a standard Rabbinic and Stoic tradition. However, the construction of this Epistle is less ordered than in Romans, and a fresh approach to questions of sexual morality appears in subsequent verses. These provide in effect a Christian theological basis for repudiating all forms of sexual behaviour except within monogamous marriage.

In the remaining verses of chapter 6, Paul comments on an argument from the Corinthians that 'they are free to do anything'. He agrees as far as food regulations are concerned, having in mind, no doubt, the Apostolic Decree, but he disagrees with regard to the use of the body. The body is for the Lord and the Lord for the body, therefore human lust is excluded, since God who raised Christ's body will also raise ours. He then takes the example of the prostitute to illustrate this.

Paul argues that human beings are a union of body and spirit, and that the whole personality is involved in sexual intercourse. It is not just an external act 'outside the body' as some Corinthians may have supposed. Therefore, in the act of fornication, a Christian might be said to be joining a part of Christ's body, that is himself, with a prostitute. It is a vigorous metaphor, and obviously must not be taken literally, but it goes far to explain why Paul finds sexual relationships outside marriage so abhorrent. This abhorrence would apply even more forcefully to homosexual unions.[18]

In verse 18, Paul describes fornication as a sin against one's own body. Adultery and sodomy are equally intimate physical acts. Fornication here presumably extends beyond intercourse between unmarried people. The use of the Greek word *soma* translated 'body' is a complicated one in the New Testament, and especially so in 1 Corinthians, but it will suffice to say that Paul is using it in these verses to include intimate personal relationship. The Christian, indwelt by the Spirit, has an intimate relationship with Christ, and he takes the view, against the gnostics, that human flesh and spirit are so interdependent that they must be regarded as, in effect, a unity.

The reference to 'the twain shall become one flesh', from Genesis 2.24, by Paul in verse 16 is interesting because it posits a kind of ontological reason for the practice of chastity and monogamous marriage. The 'one flesh' relationship can be understood as a sacramental union of which intercourse is the effective sign, and those Christians who argue for the indissolubility of marriage, understand this to be the case. In the Hebrew tradition, man is thought to have been created by God as originally the androgynous Adam, and Philo for example comments 'when the true companion Eve is created, love supervenes, and brings together and fits into one the divided halves as it were of one being'. The same myth is referred to by Plato in the *Symposium*. This exegesis of Genesis 2.24 placed the Rabbis in a difficult position, recognizing as they did both polygamy and divorce. They therefore adopted a different interpretation, seeing the commandment to become one flesh as a Noachian one addressed, not to the Jews, but to the Gentiles and requiring them not to practice incest, homosexuality, or bestiality, thus bringing the verse into conformity with the Leviticus chapter 18 injunction for the Jews.[19]

It is most likely that Paul would have been aware of the Rabbinic interpretation of Genesis 2.24, and also familiar with Jesus' own repudiation of that exegesis and it may well be that he accepts the androgynous myth as to the nature of human sexuality. With this background and his typical Jewish reaction to homosexual practices, there seems no doubt that even though this is another generalized polemic against the pagan way of life, Paul would be ready, if asked, to justify his condemnation of homosexual behaviour in 1 Corinthians 6 as properly based on his theology of marriage as a one-flesh union between men and women exclusively.

Paul very rarely refers directly to sayings of Jesus, but in chapter 7 when he moves on to the next query from the Corinthians, he distinguishes clearly between the dominical principle against divorce, and his own observations on related matters concerning marital problems. This section starts with a quotation from the Corinthians: 'It is good for a man to have nothing to do with woman'. He disagrees with this ascetic view on several grounds, of which the negative one against fornication is not the most important. As most commentators point out, Paul is not in principle against marriage: in this respect he follows the Rabbinic precept that it is a duty, perhaps lessened if the parousia is imminent, and he himself has a special vocation to celibacy for the sake of his missionary calling. Times of abstinence are recommended, but this was also a Rabbinic precept. Divorce is prohibited, and he is clearly aware of the teaching of Jesus which reversed the Rabbinic view that Genesis 2.24 applied only to sexual offences outside marriage among the Gentiles. Polygamy and divorce are now banned though Paul is realistic enough to recognize that some women, under Jewish law, and some men, under Roman law, may have already found themselves legally separated. If reconciliation is not possible, he advises against second marriages, and where one partner is not a Christian, he does not find that an obligatory ground for divorce.

Paul's firmness over these matters is, of course, a matter of thorough scrutiny in connection with the present dilemma about remarriage, a subject outside our scope. For our purpose it is sufficient to note that Paul reflects the reinterpretation of Genesis 2.24 positively to stress the permanence of the 'one-flesh relationship', and negatively to exclude all other forms of sexual behaviour. It seems fair to conclude that taking the course of the arguments put in 1 Corinthians chapters 5 to 7, Paul's thoughts about human sexuality are expressed in terms of 'within marriage only' and that this is a new approach, following the teaching of Jesus, and marking a Christian viewpoint distinct from either the Rabbinic or secular traditions of his time. Given that approach, he evidently holds, but does not think it necessary to elaborate, the view that homosexual behaviour is to be rejected among Christians.[20]

(c) 1 TIMOTHY

St Paul's First Letter to Timothy appears from its introduction to have been written from Macedonia, with the intention of setting out formally the instructions Paul has already given to Timothy as the temporary leader or personal representative of the Apostle for the Church at Ephesus. If this was indeed the situation, the three references to homosexual behaviour in the Pauline corpus are conveniently addressed to three of the most significant original Christian congregations, at Rome, at Corinth, and at Ephesus. A possible date would be around 55 CE, the letter being written some months after 1 Corinthians and preceding Galatians and Romans.

Although traditionally regarded as a genuine Pauline letter, many scholars have recently doubted his authorship, identifying four main difficulties. These concern the theological content, the vocabulary used, the type of church organization described, and the apparent incompatibility between the biographical details given in the Pastoral Epistles and what is otherwise known of the Apostle's movements. No attempt to resolve the question of authorship would be appropriate here, but it can be said that among the possibilities to be considered, apart from the straightforward one outlined above, are that Paul wrote the letter towards the end of his life during a period when he was based on Rome and travelled to Spain, that he dictated it to a secretary who was free to use his own words and expressions to some extent, or that it was composed much later, well into the second century CE, and contains carefully worked out but spurious detail to simulate apostolic authenticity, with a few direct quotations from St Paul himself.[21]

At first sight, the question of authorship seems unimportant, for the reference to 'perverts' is again condemnatory, occurring within a list of offenders whose behaviour is said to 'flout the wholesome teaching of the gospel'. It is not suggested that the Ephesian Christians are doing such things, but that they are troubled by inadequate teachers of the moral law (v. 7). These are probably Jewish teachers, expounding the precepts of the Torah as binding on the Christians, though not perhaps Judaizers in the sense of insisting on the ceremonial precepts; they are inadequate, Paul suggests, in not understanding the full implications of the gospel of love and faith. This kind of interpretation of these verses fits well an early date for the Epistle, reflecting the controversies of the times, but those commentators who accept a later date see a more bourgeois morality implied here, less dependent on the Torah than on second-century conventional Gentile attitudes, to which Christianity is said not to be in opposition. In either case, the list Paul gives is more markedly cast in the decalogue form than those in Romans and Corinthians, and rather fierce examples are chosen. Paul uses the word *arsenokoitais* as in Corinthians, and this has resulted again in a wide range of translations.

The Authorized Version has 'them that defile themselves with mankind'; the Revised Version has 'abusers of themselves with men'; the Revised Standard Version has 'sodomites' which suggests that its translators' reticence in 1 Corinthians was a matter of style rather than of distaste for the word. The New English Bible has 'perverts' which is consistent with their translation of Romans and Corinthians, provided it is remembered that they have homosexual perversion in mind in each case. The average reader, without a Greek text to compare, might, of course, assume that the dropping of 'homosexual' in this third reference means that Paul is here referring to other forms of perversion. The French Jerusalem has 'les gens de moeurs infâmes', and the English Jerusalem recasts the whole phrase 'those who are immoral with women or with boys or with men', which is not a literal translation, but does try to express in a modern idiom what Paul probably thought.

The Good News Bible has 'sexual perverts', the Living Bible 'homosexuals' and the New International version has 'perverts'. Since the other offences in this list tend to be gross examples of offences within the decalogue categories, such as matricide, kidnap, and perjury, it seems most likely that homosexual behaviour is again being vehemently condemned.

Those who regard 1 Timothy as a second-century work note that this emphasis on serious and unusual crimes is not typical of Paul and reflects a more general approach, indicating, as perhaps the whole Epistle does, that there is no particular Church or setting in mind. Similarities have been noted with the style of Philo's commentary on Genesis, and the polemical lists of sins in some of the inter-testamental writings, and equivalent Hellenistic lists.[22] Phrases such as 'the wholesome teaching which conforms with the gospel' seems redolent of a more settled pastoral situation than existed in the Church at Ephesus after Paul's stay there and its tense conclusion, but this does not, of course, necessarily argue that the unknown later author was unaware of Paul's attitude to homosexuality. Indeed, even if this Epistle is contemporaneous with the *Didache*, considered later, there is no innovation at this point.

(d) SUMMARY

Taken together, St Paul's writings repudiate homosexual behaviour as a vice of the Gentiles in Romans, as a bar to the Kingdom in Corinthians, and as an offence to be repudiated by the moral law in 1 Timothy. In taking this attitude he conforms to the precepts of the Rabbis, to popular secular moralism, and also, by implication, to the dominical precept limiting sexual activity to monogamous and permanent marriage. If he wrote the relevant section of 1 Timothy, it would be consistent with his thought to call such behaviour forbidden by the moral law though that is not a characteristic expression for him.

All these references, however, arise in parenthesis and he assumes that homosexual behaviour will have been abandoned on conversion if it had occurred before. Since he suggests the man 'married' to his stepmother at Corinth should be excluded from the congregation—a similar punishment to being cut off from the worshipping community required by the Holiness Code for the Jews—it seems unlikely that he would have taken a different view of a homosexual offender, if he had been required to adjudicate on such a problem. At this very early stage of the development of the Christian Church, forgiveness is largely focused on sins before conversion, and the discipline of those who offend after baptism is still to be worked out in detail.

C The Gospels

The four Gospels are usually thought to have been composed within a period of thirty-five years from 60 CE onwards.[23] Although probably later than Paul's Epistles, and separated from the events they describe by two generations, the work of the four Evangelists is still taken as the primary record against which all the other writings of the period, inside and outside the Canon, have to be tested. Yet the Gospels are a unique kind of literature. They are not *bioi*-lives of Jesus; they are not *praxeis*-deeds of Jesus: they are not even *apomnemoneumata*-memoirs of Jesus. As Evans has vividly expressed it, the literary character of the Gospels is so distinct that the librarian of the famous Library in Alexandria in the second century would have been puzzled to decide in which section he should catalogue them.[24]

The Gospel writers are not setting down mere biographies of Jesus. They show little interest in the human aspects of his personality: they neither describe how he looked nor set out any of the mundane characteristics which distinguish one man from another. Their 'portraits' are in a sense contrived, to fit in with certain theological and evangelistic presuppositions, and the sequence of events they describe is governed more by the logic of these presuppositions than it is by any precise concern for historical or biographical accuracy. They have selected their material from a large mass of oral tradition no longer available, and a large number of interesting sayings of Jesus may have been lost.[25] This means it is not strictly possible to say whether or not Jesus ever made any comment about homosexuality. If he did, the evangelists did not record it, and none of the references in the Pauline Epistles already examined appear to be based directly on an otherwise forgotten dominical saying.

This absence of any reference to homosexuality in the Gospels in contrast to Paul's Epistles may be easily explained. The recorded sayings of Jesus about sexual problems seem to concern matters which were in dispute among the Palestinian Jews of his day, notably the controversies about marriage, divorce, and the status of women.[26] The orthodox Jewish teaching about sodomy and pederasty was clear, and although the Fourth Gospel shows Jesus to have had some contact with Hellenized Jews or Greeks in Jerusalem (John 12.20ff), his mission was primarily to Israel, and he moved about chiefly within the Jewish provinces of Galilee, Samaria, and Judea.

(a) GOSPEL REFERENCES TO SODOM

Jesus refers to the story of Sodom's destruction as an example of God's judgement obviously familiar to his hearers. His comments are noted five times in the synoptic Gospels, of which three are in Matthew (10.15; 11.23; 11.24) and two in Luke (10.12; 17.29).[27] In each case the context is a discussion of what will happen to those who reject the message of the gospel, and Jesus asserts that in comparison, the fate of Sodom and Gomorrah would be more bearable than theirs on the day of judgement. Thus, as part of his instructions to the newly chosen Apostles before he sends them on their first (abortive) mission, Jesus says to them:

If anyone will not receive you or listen to what you say, then as you leave that house or that town, shake the dust of it off your feet. I tell you this: on the day of judgement it will be more bearable for the land of Sodom and Gomorrah than for that town. (Matthew 10.14–15)

Some early texts of Mark include the reference to Sodom, etc. in similar words, and they are included in the Authorized Version translation in describing the charge to the Apostles. The modern Greek text, however, places the sentence as a footnote[28] and the New English Bible omits it. Luke does not include the reference to Sodom in his account of the instructions to the twelve, but does later, in the charge to the seventy, an incident that is mentioned only in his Gospel. The wording in Luke 10.12 is the same as in Matthew 10.15 and presumably some of the early copyists decided that they should include it in Mark on the assumption that it had been accidentally omitted from the text before them.

In the following chapter, Matthew again refers to Sodom in a similar vein, but with the additional point that they would have repented if they had seen the miracles performed in the Jewish cities by Jesus:

Then he spoke of the towns in which most of his miracles had been performed, and denounced them for their impenitence. 'Alas for you, Chorazin!' he said, 'alas for you, Bethsaida! If the miracles that were performed in you had been performed in Tyre and Sidon, they would have repented long ago in sackcloth and ashes. But it will be more bearable, I tell you, for Tyre and Sidon on the day of judgement than for you. And as for you, Capernaum, will you be exalted to the skies? No, brought down to the depths! For if the miracles had been performed in Sodom which were performed in you, Sodom would be standing to this day. But it will be more bearable, I tell you, for the land of Sodom on the day of judgement than for you.' (Matthew 11.20–4)

The final reference, in Luke's Gospel, is more distinctly eschatological. Answering a question from the Pharisees about when the Kingdom of God will come, Jesus tells them that it is 'among them', and then he explains to the disciples that the end will come unexpectedly, as it did at the time of the Flood and for Sodom:

As things were in Noah's days, so will they be in the days of the Son of Man. They ate and drank and married, until the day that Noah went into the ark and the flood came and made an end of them all. As things were in Lot's days, also: they ate and drank; they bought and sold; they planted and built: but the day that Lot went out from Sodom, it rained fire and sulphur from heaven and made an end of them all—it will be like that on the day when the Son of Man is revealed. On that day the man who is on the roof and his belongings in the house must not come down to pick them up: he, too, who is in the fields must not go back. Remember Lot's wife. Whoever seeks to save his life will lose it; and whoever loses it will save it, and live. (Luke 17.26–33)

This is the only reference to Lot in the New Testament apart from that in 2 Peter chapter 2, to be considered in the next section. Luke makes no comment on the character of Lot, using him as an illustration of the general principle that those who seek to save their lives will lose them.

Taken together, the five references to Sodom in the Gospels appear to be used in line with the Old Testament tradition as a symbol of general unspecified wickedness and rejection of God's messengers: the similarity of the references suggests that they are based on a quite simple teaching point made by Jesus.[29] Apart from the reference in Luke 17, the men of Sodom are said by Jesus to be no worse than those who are now opposing his message, indeed he suggests that they might be better.

It is normal in the Gospels for the sharpest condemnation to be directed at Christ's Jewish opponents, and it has been suggested that this features so strongly in the written records because the Christians are more fiercely persecuted by the Jews than by the Romans and anyway they remember that the Jews originally condemned him. Even if the evangelists are inclined to strengthen the anti-Jewish emphasis of Christ's teaching, there seems no reason to doubt that they are quoting one of his own sayings here, and its effect must have been startling. To say that God's judgement on the Jews will be worse than his judgement on Sodom is to go beyond the old criticism of Isaiah on Jerusalem which is said to be as desolate as Sodom apart from a remnant left in the land (Isaiah 1.7–10). Paul, incidentally, quotes this to the Romans (9.29). On the face of it, Jesus mentions Sodom to his Jewish audience in a way that would seem deliberately insulting unless they perceived the serious purpose behind it. If this is the correct exegesis of these passages, they seem to have nothing to do with homosexuality.

Such a conclusion, however, is based on the assumption that Jesus and his hearers would not associate the destruction of Sodom with homosexual practices unless they were specially mentioned. This assumption is easily made by later readers of the Gospels who have little knowledge of the inter-testamental period or of its writings. But it could be argued that in first-century Palestine, most people would have been aware of the controversy between the orthodox Jews and the Hellenistic culture, and that some at least of Jesus' hearers would associate the name of Sodom with sexual irregularities. Perhaps Jesus himself expected that they would, and if he intended to sharpen his challenge to the Jews in this way, then it would be in keeping with his frequent teaching that he had come for the lost sheep, and to call sinners rather than the righteous. More probably, however, Jesus refers to Sodom with the conventional usage of the Old Testament in mind, as a familiar allusion to general wickedness and as a warning to the Jews of the fate of those who in the past had rejected the messengers of God.

(b) JESUS' ATTITUDE TO SEXUAL OFFENDERS

Jesus was unmarried, and despite giving offence to some critics by attending dinner parties, he was basically ascetic in life-style, sharing an itinerant ministry with his group of male disciples. It is generally accepted that it would have led to hopeless misunderstanding at the time for him to have included women in his close circle, but he appears to have been a welcome guest to Peter's family home in Capernaum and at Mary and Martha's house in Bethany. He was ready to ignore the conventions by speaking alone to women when the pastoral situation demanded it and to encourage a penitent prostitute towards a new life.

Both during the Sermon on the Mount, according to Matthew, and in the discussion on the renunciation of riches, Jesus quotes the commandment against adultery with approval.[30] Given the Rabbinic understanding that this precept extended to all forms of extra-marital sex, Jesus might be assumed to have declared himself against homosexual behaviour, but such an argument from silence is precarious.

There has been occasional speculation in recent years that Jesus himself was of a homosexual disposition, and that Paul's harsh attitude to homosexuals was a result of repression of his own sexuality. The fact that neither of them were married does not justify this inference, even at a time when it was regarded as a normal obligation to marry. Paul claimed his celibacy as a special vocation and no doubt the same could have been said of Jesus. In a recent notorious trial, a poem suggesting that Jesus was homosexual was held to be blasphemy, but the speculation was given a more cautious examination at the Conference of New Testament Scholars held in Oxford in 1967. In a paper by H. Montefiore it was suggested that Jesus' unmarried state, the gospel witness that he was friends with women but loved men, and that at a deeper level such a characteristic would be fully consonant with the doctrine that in the incarnation God identifies himself with the outsider, could point to Jesus being homosexual in nature.

These ideas were widely reported in the press, out of context, and caused a temporary furore. When his paper was published[31] Montefiore added a footnote of explanation. He pointed out that:

> The word 'homosexual' when applied to human nature, does not contain or imply any moral connotation whatever. It is simply descriptive of a certain type of personality. It in no way implies or attributes any kind of sinfulness to Jesus. As readers of this lecture will notice, I have been careful to stress (because I happen to believe) the human perfection of Jesus and his entire obedience to his Father's Will. (p. 109)

It is very difficult to transfer such speculation in our contemporary modes of thought back to the Palestine of Jesus. Although the liberty of Jesus gave offence and hints were made of his uncertain parentage, no surviving literature of the time suggests that this kind of thinking was applied to Jesus or any other religious leader who chose to surround himself with a group of male disciples. It is likely that if homosexual behaviour was known to have occurred in Jesus' group, the Rabbis would have been able to use it as an immediate cause for condemnation.

The ethical teaching of Jesus merits more attention than space here permits. Although he is never willing to disagree with the Torah, his own approach of agapaistic love so completely extends the neighbour commandment, that it amounts to a new teaching. He extends the scope of the law, and yet is free from it. His precept 'Be ye perfect' in Matthew becomes 'Be ye merciful' in Luke and this demonstrates the paradox.[32] Jesus tells the Pharisees that 'the tax gatherers and prostitutes are entering the Kingdom of God ahead of you' (Matthew 21.31) and describes the elder son's comment to his father on the prodigal as having 'run through your money with his women' (Luke 15.31). Such examples give no suggestion that Jesus is soft on sexual sin, and that he is firm about it is very clear from the Sermon on the Mount and particularly the hard saying about adultery in the heart. But the paradox is clear in such remarks and is shown also in the incident at the supper party when the prostitute anoints Jesus and washes his feet with her tears. Luke gives this story in full (7.30ff) while Mark and Matthew insert it more briefly in the Passion Narrative (Mark 14.3ff and Matthew 26.6). Jesus says that her sins are forgiven, her faith has saved her, and she may go in peace. Tradition has identified this woman with Mary of Magdala, but the narrative does not state this explicitly.

The best known example of Jesus' repudiating the sin but accepting the sinner is, of course, the woman taken in adultery noted in St John's Gospel. The story does not appear in the earliest manuscripts of St

John though it was accepted by Ambrose and Augustine and included in the Vulgate by St Jerome as John 7.53—8.11. It is printed at this place in the Authorized and Revised Versions, but as a footnote in the Revised Standard Version and as an appendix to the Gospel in the New English Bible. It is, however, restored to the text in the Common Bible, the Good News Bible, The Living Bible and the New International Version, with a note that it is not found in the earliest manuscripts of St John.[33]

Various attitudes are taken to this story. It has some similarity with that of the anointing, and would fit well into the synoptic Gospels as an illustration of the saying in the Sermon on the Mount about not judging (Matthew 7.1 or Luke 6.37 for example) or with the Fourth Gospel declaration 'I judge no one' (John 8.15) to which, in the later versions, it seems to have been inserted as an introduction. Perhaps the Synoptists preferred the other story and this leaves open the possibility that it was an unattached incident from the oral tradition which was included here by an editor to preserve the memory of an illuminating encounter for Christian reflection. It could otherwise have been a teaching illustration of the early Church that Jesus accepts adulterers as well as prostitutes into his Kingdom. He neither condemns nor condones.

In favour of regarding the story as genuine, it can be suggested that perhaps the underlying point is a typical one of the Gospels, a criticism of self-righteousness among the Jews. Jesus seems to be in danger of the familiar trap: if he pardons the woman he ignores the law; if he adjudicates in favour of it he casts himself in the role of judge, to which he is not entitled and which he has previously refused. By writing in the dust he follows the judicial custom of setting down his judgement before announcing it: when it is read, the accusers find it impossible to implement. Attractive as this interpretation is, in detail the story lacks precise awareness of Jewish law, for a betrothed woman committing fornication would be liable to stoning. An adulterous woman and the man would be strangled, according to the Mishnah, though, as we have seen earlier, such sentences could scarcely have been passed without proper trial or carried out in Jerusalem at this time of Roman occupation, except by mob violence. Perhaps the conclusion has to be that in its present form this story is not original but a real event may lie behind it. That said, it is consistent with the general teaching of Christ's forgiveness of sexual sin, clearly regarded with some nervousness in the early Church lest it lead to antinomian licentiousness.

The story as set out evokes sympathy for the woman, especially for the modern reader, accustomed to a much more tolerant attitude to adultery and fornication than was found in first-century Judaism. If the concluding remarks are rightly attributable to Jesus then he seems to be dissociating himself from the view that such sexual sin merits the capital punishment set down in the Holiness Code and the Mishnah. It is also possible to see here an example of his concern to improve the status of women. The criticism he makes of Jewish divorce law not only serves to strengthen the institution of marriage; by implication it gives better protection to the wife against dismissal when she ceases to please, and this is consonant with a feeling which he perhaps had that the woman was unjustly regarded by the accusers as bearing the chief blame. The man could just as well have been brought before him. Beyond this it is not possible to go in interpreting the story in permissive terms, for the need for repentance is stressed, as it is at the anointing.

It is perhaps worth recalling that when the debate about the so-called new morality was at its fiercest in the 1960s the non-judgemental attitude of Jesus to sexual offences was much stressed by some theologians. A notable example was given by H. A. Williams in an essay entitled 'Theology and Self-Awareness'.[34] He referred to the sexual inadequacy portrayed by the chief characters in two popular films of the time—'Never on Sunday' and 'The Mark'. In the first film, a young sailor doubts his capacity for sexual intercourse and in the second a man assaults small girls. Both characters are 'healed' by acts of fornication with experienced women, and Williams commented, 'Where there is healing, there is Christ, whatever the Church may say about fornication.' It may be questioned whether in reality impotence or pederasty could be cured in reality as simply as in these fables, but the more serious aspects of the situationist ethic merit proper discussion later. A few years after the publication of this essay, J. Marsh felt it appropriate to comment that perhaps the original story of the woman taken in adultery was suppressed because it could be taken to encourage a 'misunderstanding of this kind'.[35]

(c) SUMMARY OF EVIDENCE IN THE GOSPELS

The references to Sodom in the Gospels indicate that Jesus used it as a general synonym for wickedness, but with a didactic purpose of warning those who rejected the gospel and its messengers, that they were if anything more at risk of destruction than the men of Sodom had been. He seems to place the emphasis clearly on rejecting the message rather than on the offence of inhospitality. This would have sounded a particularly fierce denunciation to Jewish hearers, especially if they had been aware of Sodom's significance in the inter-testamental writings and its association there with homosexual behaviour. Although no specific reference is made to homosexual behaviour, Jesus would presumably have regarded it as one of the species of sexual sin for which forgiveness and repentance were more appropriate than punishment. Since he expressed God's truth in terms accessible to a man of his time, some questions which arise in new forms in the twentieth century inevitably have no direct answers to be read off from the Gospel records.

D The Catholic Epistles: Jude and 2 Peter

These two Epistles purport to be written by a brother of Jesus, and the senior Apostle, but this is often doubted. Jude was probably an otherwise unknown church leader writing for Christians of Gentile origin about the year 90 CE, and 2 Peter is usually regarded as a pseudonymous epistle of the second century of the Christian era, possibly as late as 140 CE and therefore the latest document in the New Testament Canon. 2 Peter seems to be heavily dependent on Jude, which it quotes and expands in some sections, and this is quite noticeable in the references to Sodom. The purpose of Jude's Epistle is to set forward a defence of the Christian faith in its by now more defined form against the erroneous teaching of the gnostics, and 2 Peter is written to resist antinomianism and to reaffirm the orthodox teaching of the imminent parousia against a growing conviction that the world will continue as it always has done.[36]

The status of these two Epistles varied in the early Church. Jude's claim to be a brother of James—that is, the leader of the Jerusalem Church—and hence by implication of Jesus also, seemed spurious, but his thought was popular and his work is included in the Muratorian Canon, *c.* 200 CE. Despite its ascription, 2 Peter is nowhere referred to until the third century CE. Eusebius reckoned Jude and James as spurious but read in churches: 2 Peter as uncanonical but highly esteemed. Luther and the Reformers were doubtful of the importance of either Epistle, judging their content lightweight in terms of the gospel. J. A. T. Robinson, however, has reconsidered their dating and finds them addressing a situation very similar to that of the Corinthians, and has therefore advanced the hypothesis that both Epistles were written by Jude around 61–62 CE to churches of chiefly Jewish origin in Asia Minor.[37] In case it seems tedious to have raised again contrasting views of dating and authorship, it may be said that the references to the sin of Sodom in these Epistles bear a close resemblance to those in some inter-testamental writings and appear to assume familiarity among recipients with 1 Enoch and the legend of the fallen angels. This might suggest an early origin, and a church composed largely of Diaspora Jews. Against this view is usually argued the use by Jude of a polished Greek style and vocabulary which, it is suggested, would be unlikely for a man who grew up in Nazareth.

In refuting various heresies, both Epistles refer to examples in Jewish history of God's judgement falling on unbelievers, including in the usual way the story of Sodom's destruction. Jude refers to fornication and unnatural lusts, while 2 Peter has a more diffuse description of general dissolution. The two passages are as follows:

You already know it all, but let me remind you how the Lord, having once delivered the people of Israel out of Egypt, next time destroyed those who were guilty of unbelief. Remember too the angels, how some of them were not content to keep the dominion given to them but abandoned their proper home; and God has reserved them for judgement on the great Day, bound beneath the darkness in everlasting chains. Remember Sodom and Gomorrah and the neighbouring towns; like the angels, they committed fornication and followed unnatural lusts; and they paid the penalty in eternal fire, an example for all to see. So too with these men today. Their dreams lead them to defile the body, to flout authority, and to insult celestial beings. (Jude 1.5–8 New English Bible)

But the judgement long decreed for them has not been idle; perdition waits for them with unsleeping eyes. God did not spare the angels who sinned, but consigned them to the dark pits of hell, where they are reserved for judgement. He did not spare the world of old (except for Noah, preacher of righteousness, whom he preserved with seven others), but brought the deluge upon that world of godless men. The cities of Sodom and Gomorrah God burned to ashes, and condemned them to total destruction, making them an object-lesson for godless men in future days. But he rescued Lot, who was a good man, shocked by the dissolute habits of the lawless society in which he lived; day after day every sight, every sound, of their evil courses tortured that good man's heart. Thus the Lord is well able to rescue the godly out of trials, and to reserve the wicked under punishment until the day of judgement. (2 Peter 2.3b–9)

The New English Bible translation of Jude 7 as 'unnatural lusts' reads as a clear reference to homosexual behaviour, though this is not the expression used in 1 Corinthians or 1 Timothy. In fact, the Greek is *hetera sarx* which can be rendered most literally as 'other flesh' or perhaps 'different flesh', which is a clear way of expressing the inappropriate mingling of angels and men sexually. Many readers of the Bible would find this incomprehensible, and there is something to be said for the archaic 'strange flesh' of the Authorized Version. Some new translations follow the New English Bible and others use 'perversion', misleading if that is also used for Paul's references. The Jerusalem Bible has 'unnatural' but adds a footnote reference to Genesis and 1 Enoch. The Living Bible has 'lust of men for other men' which misses the point completely.

Taken literally, therefore, Jude is using the legend of the fallen angels and the destruction of Sodom in the customary way as a warning of God's judgement and not specifying homosexual behaviour. But in verse 8 he continues about the dreams which defile the body and this can be interpreted as licentious dreams, or as the fantasies of the gnostics which lead to all three offences, fornication, lawlessness, and irreverence. In either case the condemnation comes close to that usually applied to pagans and it would be possible for readers to assume that all forms of sexual malpractice were being alluded to here.[38]

The author of 2 Peter omits any mention of the sexual aspect of the Sodom story, and provides instead a reference to Lot, contrasted approvingly with the Sodomites in terms which owe more to the Book of Wisdom than to Genesis. The two passages, therefore, make use of the Sodom story in ways which are different from the Gospels. Jude follows the pattern of 1 Enoch while 2 Peter reflects an Alexandrine tradition in praising Lot. The gnostics are being condemned, like the fallen angels and the men of Sodom, but there is no invitation to repentance. Whatever the date of their composition, their attitude is rather dour and they offer nothing new about sexual morality, merely the commonplace derogation of inter-testamental Judaism.

In conclusion to this whole section on biblical attitudes, it seems worthwhile to set out a few references to the subject in the New Testament Apocrypha. These writings are a distinct category of Christian documents from the early period, claiming apostolic authorship though excluded from the Canon. Other Christian writings of the period are considered in Part C. Since the Christians confronted the Hellenistic culture and to a lesser extent that of Rome, it seems also valuable to recall at this stage briefly what these cultures seemed to believe about homosexuality. These notes are set out in Excursuses I and II respectively.

EXCURSUS I

References to homosexual behaviour in the New Testament Apocrypha

By the end of the second Christian century, there were what Papias called 'a mass of writings' from which the members of the Church could study their faith. The four Gospels and most of Paul's Epistles were already recognized as the standard or canon and increasingly vested with a unique authority. Some other writings were approved, read at worship, or treasured by particular congregations, and among these the *Shepherd* of Hermas, *The Didache*, and letters of church leaders and their apologias, such as those from Clement, Justin, and the later Fathers carried their own authority. A further group, called the Apocrypha because they were to be hidden from general readership in the Church, in fact circulated widely and many of them claimed apostolic authorship. In some ways these apocryphal writings stand *vis-à-vis* the New Testament in a somewhat similar relationship to that of the Jewish inter-testamental writings with the Old Testament. In them can be found quotations from the Gospels and Pauline Epistles, and in fact from the Old Testament as well, which in an oblique way confirm the texts we know and also show their familiarity among the Christian congregations. There are also a few quotations from Jesus in these writings which seem consistent with the sayings in the Gospels and perhaps represent authentic teaching from the oral period which was not included by the evangelists.

There are several references to Sodom in the New Testament Apocrypha which show a continuation of the kinds of use already well established in the canonical books. The discovery and printing of the Apocrypha from the early Christian centuries continues, so it is only possible to quote from a few examples here.[39] No attempt is made to discuss date of composition or authorship of the books from which these quotations are taken, but it is assumed that they were probably written by the end of the third century CE. The works of the Fathers within this period are considered later as part of the section on the Christian tradition.

(a) THE PSEUDO-EPISTLE OF TITUS

This work is concerned to advocate complete chastity, and abstention from marriage and all sexual activity for male and female Christians. Copious references from the Old and New Testaments are used to substantiate this theme, and these include Ezekiel chapter 16 to illustrate that Jerusalem is worse than Sodom. The strictures of Paul on the man who married his mother-in-law are invoked next from 1 Corinthians chapter 5 and the general effect is to show that the sin of Sodom is understood as heterosexual fornication. The sequel to the rape at Gibeah is mentioned in a similar way. Although this pseudo-epistle can be fairly said to wallow in ascetic denunciation of everything but stubborn resistence to the demands of the flesh, homosexual behaviour as such does not seem to be mentioned.[40]

(b) ACTS OF ST PAUL

This is an enthralling biography of Paul, quoting extensively from Acts, the Gospels and his Epistles and notable, *inter alia*, for the positive role given to women, some of whom are described as fellow-sufferers in persecution and sharing in his ministry. At one point Paul is sent into the arena at Ephesus, but the lion who is meant to devour him turns out to have been baptized by Paul at an earlier meeting; they converse, a hailstorm intervenes, and Paul escapes and sails for Macedonia. No complete text of this book has yet been discovered, but one fragment records his visit to Sidon. His preaching is not well received, he is cast into prison, prepared for sacrifice but part of the building collapses and he escapes again. In his speech he apparently attempts to persuade the people against some intended action by referring to an unseemly practice—'Have you not heard of that which happened, which God brought upon Sodom and Gomorrah, because they robbed. . . .'[41] The fragment ends here, so it is not possible to say whether more than robbery was intended.

(c) THE ASCENSION OF ISAIAH

In the first half of this book the martyrdom of the prophet is described; he is sawn in two. The story is probably of early Jewish origin and may be referred to in Hebrews 11.37. In chapter 3 of the story the saying of Isaiah (1.10) is quoted. He has called Jerusalem Sodom and the princes of Judah and Jerusalem he has declared to be the people of Gomorrah. Since in the previous verse Isaiah had referred to the Remnant and this was also mentioned by Paul (Romans 9.29) it seems possible to identify here a quotation from the prophet that was being generally used by the Christians at this period, Sodom symbolizing judgement.[42]

(d) THE FIFTH BOOK OF EZRA

This contains a cursory reference to Sodom as a place 'whose land lies in clods of pitch and heaps of ashes; this will I do to those who have not listened to me, saith the Lord the Almighty'. Recalling the comment of Josephus, the appearance of this area obviously impressed first-century travellers in this region.[43]

(e) THE CHRISTIAN SIBYLLINES

Jewish parts of this collection have been referred to in the previous chapter Excursus on Pseudepigrapha. In Book 6 there is a Hymn to Christ which ends by identifying Jerusalem with Sodom:

It shall be, when earth shall rejoice in the hope of a son,
But for thee alone, land of Sodom, evil woe lies waiting;
For thou in thy folly didst not perceive thy God
When he came in the eyes of men. But from the thorn
Thou didst weave a crown, and bitter gall didst thou mingle for an insulting drink.[44]

(f) THE APOCALYPSE OF PAUL

This purports to be a vision Paul had of Paradise which he subsequently wrote down. It was discovered in a marble box buried in the foundation of the house in Tarsus. Augustine thought it a bogus concoction. In his visit to the heavenly places, Paul is allowed to visit hell where he finds various categories of people in torment, including bishops and other ministers who failed to exercise their ministry with diligence. Adulterers are suspended by their hair in a river of fire, and other men and women covered in dust were in a pit of tar and brimstone. It is explained that 'they are those who have committed the iniquity of Sodom and Gomorrah, men with men. Therefore they pay the penalty unceasingly.' As women were in the pit as well as men, it seems clear that homosexual behaviour among both sexes is being punished here, and this is the only reference to Sodom in the New Testament Apocrypha that specifies the offence. Later Paul visits Paradise and meets Lot 'who was found righteous in Sodom'. He tells the story of his attempt to protect the angels from violation by the offer of his daughters and the moral is drawn that God will repay many times over.

(g) SUMMARY

This review of the references to Sodom in the Apocryphal New Testament writings suggests that it was regarded in a way generally similar to that found in the canonical Scriptures. Thus Sodom is a symbol of judgement as in Isaiah, Ezekiel, and the synoptic Gospels. Only in the Apocalypse of Paul is the homosexual interpretation mentioned.

EXCURSUS II

Greek and Roman attitudes to Homosexuality

(a) INTRODUCTION

In popular present-day caricature the culture of Greece is sometimes represented as philosophy and pederasty among superb buildings; similarly that of Rome is depicted as military and engineering genius abroad, while the old city by the Tiber remained a centre of brutality and sexual licentiousness. Certainly neither the Jewish nor Christian writings we have examined so far give a favourable impression of the classical world, though Paul had respect for the Roman legal system, based no doubt on a more cosmopolitan experience than the single impression left on the Gospel writers by Pontius Pilate.

These caricatures no doubt reflect some truth, and to set down a full picture of sexual life and ethics among the generality of Greek and Roman peoples over a period in excess of a thousand years is clearly impossible in this brief note. It has to be asserted, however, that Plato's reports on the Dialogues of Socrates concerning love between males, and the records of the Caesars of imperial Rome have to be set against a normal pattern of life for most Greeks and Romans which prized family and domestic life, protected and encouraged by the law. In particular, there is no reason to doubt that the great majority of Greeks and Romans were heterosexual and settled into stable family units in a similar fashion to those of other major civilizations, including our own. That said, it is also true that the surviving literature contains a great deal of evidence that homosexual friendship and pederasty were tolerated, and indeed commended, by authors who can in no sense be dismissed as trivial or pornographic in intention, though that is perhaps more true of the Greeks than the Romans.[45]

(b) GREEK MYTHOLOGY

Primitive Greek religion looked to a mother goddess, but she was replaced by the Olympian pantheon presided over by Zeus not later than 1000 BCE, as Homer indicates. Fuller details and the origins of these gods is provided by Hesiod in the eighth-century poem *Theogony*, and the Olympians remained the officially recognized deities until the Christian era, although other cults and mystery religions emerged in this period, partly borrowed from Asiatic cultures. With Zeus on Olympus were his wife, Hera, and ten other major gods. Among their courtiers and servants were the Graces and Muses and Ganymede the cup-bearer.

According to Homer in the *Iliad*, Ganymede, the most beautiful youth in the world, because of his good looks was kidnapped by the gods to be cup-bearer to Zeus.[46] Later legend suggests he was carried to Olympus by an eagle and Graves suggests that the legend gained popularity in Greece and Rome as a religious justification for pederasty. It is certainly asserted in the *Iliad* that Zeus was heterosexually inclined, that he slept with Hera before marriage, and maintained a lusty and promiscuous life with immortal and mortal women thereafter.

Graves notes the contest between Apollo and the poet Thamyris for the affection of the beautiful youth Hyacinthus. They were the first god and first man to fall in love with a member of their own sex. Apollo wins, unfairly, with the help of the Muses, but the jealous West Wind kills Hyacinth, from whose blood sprang the flower of that name. Homer mentions Dorion as the place where the Muses deprived Thamyris of his ability to sing, but the homosexual element in the legend comes from later sources. In the *Odyssey*, Odysseus, incognito, tells a swineherd a yarn about his adventures in Egypt and his encounter with a rascally Phoenician who attempts to sell him as a slave in Libya. Later the swineherd warns him against joining the court as a servant, hinting that homosexual vice is a recognized institution at such places.[47]

Greek philosophers did not perhaps regard these myths with full seriousness, nor approve the arbitrary and licentious tales that were increasingly attached to the members of the original pantheon. In the popular view it may well have been held that 'what was permitted to Zeus was also permitted to the ox' but the real reasons for the pre-occupation with homosexual love in later Greece are to be found elsewhere.[48]

(c) THE GREEK ACCEPTANCE OF PEDERASTY

Several related and overlapping concepts of male relationships are to be found in the literature of classical Greece, broadly from the sixth to the fourth century BCE. This is the period of the historian Herodotus, the dramatist Aristophanes, and the philosophers Socrates, Plato, and Aristotle. Their writings provide ample evidence that the Athenians regarded love between males as superior to heterosexual love, which was often dismissed as little more than the basic sexual drive for the preservation of the species. Homosexual attraction was described as a means towards intellectual companionship and the search for ultimate truth, notably in the thought of Socrates and Plato, though this does not seem to mean that physical expression was excluded; it was accepted as an interim expression on the way to maturity. But there were also more sensual exploitive and commercial aspects in which the notional tolerance for an educational process between older and younger men enabled pederasts to pursue homosexual lust for younger boys, despite the largely ineffective prohibitions of the law. It is probably right to stress the emphasis on education, and the particular sense that the Greeks had of affectionate friendship as the means to learning, while recognizing that passion and eroticism and expression of love and desire were not inappropriate components of such relationships, as they would have been in Jewish and did become in the Christian tradition. But this recognition of vigorous homosexual love has to be balanced by the other evidence, perhaps more clearly provided in their poetry, art, and decorative pottery, that the Greeks also knew heterosexual romantic love, and, of course, the lusts for which the brothels and prostitutes provided. The category of women known as the *hetairae*, educated, musical, and cultured, served as courtesans or mistresses and were welcomed to male social life while wives languished at home. It is possible, therefore, for modern commentators to emphasize either the excessive preoccupation with male partners, or the normality in heterosexual terms of Greek social life. The surviving literature certainly stresses the former, though even then, what Aristophanes can praise at supper with Plato, he can also mock on the stage, confident of a roar of approval from the public at large. Although Socrates was probably sentenced to death for political reasons, among the charges laid on him was that he corrupted youth.

Some signficant factors in the emergence of an attitude of toleration to homosexual behaviour can be identified. Wives were secluded in Athenian domestic life and provided with guards or companions when shopping; they were seldom educated, though Plato recommended that they should be. Intellectual companionship was usually all male, discussion at dinner parties a favourite occasion for it, and when women were admitted to these, they were the *hetairae*. Younger men were expected to gain sexual experience with commercial prostitutes or at brothels. The development of sports and gymnasia and in Sparta the military training camps, tended to separate the sexes and marriages were arranged for dynastic or financial reasons, romance and courtship being hardly possible. The Greek preoccupation with physical beauty provided the opportunity for mature males to seek young partners at the games and in the changing rooms of the gymnasia, and part of a young man's development was expected to take place in the close companionship and guidance of an older friend. Taken together, these factors could be seen to make homosexual behaviour more likely, though of course it seems at this distance something of a chicken and egg situation. In Greek culture the position of women was inferior and homosexual love was exalted. By contrast, in Jewish culture women were hardly more respected, but homosexual behaviour was considered abominable.

(d) PLATO

Perhaps the best analysis of the Greek understanding of love is to be found in Plato's *Symposium*. This takes the form of a dinner party in which the dialogue puts various points of view until Socrates, pretending to defer to a fictitious woman Diotima, draws out from her a final definition of love in terms which are in a sense comparable with the beatific vision of Christian spirituality. Before quoting from this crucial passage, it is of interest to note in the speech of Aristophanes a different form of the androgynous myth. He argues that the original constitution of man was a rounded whole with four hands, legs and other sets of organs. They had three sexes, male, female, and hermaphrodite, but Zeus modified this original man by splitting each sexual type in two, and moving the genital organs forward so that intercourse between males and females become possible. From then onwards, the separated halves spent their lives seeking each other and this is how love began. Where male and female halves joined, procreation occurred. Where female halves met they were lesbians; where males met they were manly, virile, and public spirited, the desire for intercourse being incidentally satiated.

As the dinner proceeds what we might call the higher philosophy of love is progressively set out until Diotima sums up the conclusion:

> When a man, starting from this sensible world and making his way upward by a right use of his feeling of love for boys, begins to catch sight of that beauty, he is very near his goal. This is the right way of approaching or being initiated into the mysteries of love, to begin with examples of beauty in this world, and using them as steps to ascend continually with that absolute beauty as one's aim . . . from physical beauty to moral beauty, and from moral beauty to the beauty of knowledge, until from knowledge of various kinds one arrives at the supreme knowledge whose sole object is that absolute beauty, and knows at last what absolute beauty is. . . . What may we suppose

to be the felicity of the man who sees absolute beauty in its essence, pure and unalloyed, who, instead of a beauty tainted by human flesh and colour and a mass of perishable rubbish, is able to apprehend divine beauty where it exists apart and alone? . . . Do you not see that in that region alone where he sees beauty with the faculty capable of seeing it, will he be able to bring forth not merely reflected images of goodness but true goodness, because he will be in contact not with a reflection but with the truth? And having brought forth and nurtured true goodness he will have the privilege of being beloved of God, and becoming, if ever a man can, immortal himself. (Plato, *The Symposium*)[49]

How far Plato intends to use the dialogue at the Symposium to reflect accurately what he learned from Socrates and how far it also includes his own thought is not known. Socrates died in 399 BCE, and this dialogue was probably written some fourteen years later, and is in that sense fictitious, though its participants were real people and had no doubt often shared such parties. Perhaps the development of the examination of love into higher realms from a somewhat prosaic set of observations by early participants has to be accepted on its merits as a superb piece of writing, its conclusions certainly being approved by Plato if not fully original to him. It is not perhaps irrelevant to mention that Socrates, an ugly man, married late, and although his wife Xanthippe cared for him and struggled for his reprieve, the relationship was somewhat stormy. Plato remained unmarried.

In Plato's later works, the institution of homosexual love is swept away in his vision of the ideal society. Thus, in the *Republic*, a more spartan system of education for the Guardians is envisaged, and the state will take responsibility instead of private tutors. Women will share in the training, be admitted to the gymnasia, naked like the men, and breeding will be controlled. Marriage, however, becomes a temporary arrangement for this purpose, and sexual activity thereafter promiscuous, though unwanted male or female offspring will be exposed.

Plato's final work, *The Laws*, reflects the ideals of the *Republic* in more practical and everyday terms, in the form of the regulations to govern the proposed small city state of Magnesia. In Book 8, paragraph 14 deals with the problems of sexual conduct. Plato, speaking as the Athenian in the dialogue, recognizes that in his co-educational system, passions and lust will not be eliminated automatically. He therefore proposes two alternative laws to encourage self-control:

God willing, perhaps we'll succeed in imposing one or other of two standards of sexual conduct.

(1) Ideally, no one will dare to have relations with any respectable citizen woman except his own wedded wife, or sow illegitimate and bastard seed in courtesans, or sterile seed in males in defiance of nature.

(2) Alternatively, while suppressing sodomy entirely, we might insist that if a man does have intercourse with any woman (hired or procured in some other way) except the wife he wed in holy marriage with the blessing of the Gods, he must do so without any other man or woman getting to know about it.
Plato, *Laws*, Book 8, Para. 14)[50]

The whole dialogue leading to these conclusions is cast in totally different terms from that in the *Symposium*. Friendship rather than love is the underlying concept, and the restraint of physical passion is to be imposed by regulation, and not seen as a desired consequence of ascetic maturity. To justify the regulations Plato claims the example of nature; animals are sexually inactive apart from the breeding season, he holds, and claims this is in accordance with natural law for humans also. As a sanction, religious beliefs are to be emphasized, for 'these acts are unholy, an absolute abomination in the sight of the Gods'. Subsidiary themes are the advantage of sexual abstinence for training, and self-discipline, and the sense of decency.

In a striking way, this first regulation from Plato's *Laws* matches exactly that of the Christian tradition regarding sexual morality, and the reasons given are similar. The obvious difference between this view and that of the *Symposium* reflects, no doubt, Plato's age (the *Laws* were published posthumously) and his wish to provide a new system of government to restore the ancient glories of Greece. There is a hint in the discussion that he has come to regret the acceptance of homosexual culture and looks back to a previous age when it was not so.[51]

(e) ARISTOTLE

Aristotle, the last of the three great Greek philosophers, includes homosexuality among men as one of the categories of 'bestiality' by which he means unnatural pleasures in general and not sexual activity with animals. Thus such themes as devouring a foetus, child sacrifice, eating charcoal, and biting one's nails are lumped together in a general list and their origins are said to be perversion or mental disease. All such things are contrary to the principle of virtue.[52] He holds that the virtues of temperance and continence apply to the human condition and in that sense not to animals, hence the term bestiality is used to label actions that are animal-like in their irrationality.[53]

Aristotle does not, however, repudiate the notion of homosexual love, which he mentions approvingly in a later section of the *Ethics*, defining friendship. The whole of Books 8 and 9 are concerned with this examination of *philia* and it includes a good deal of common sense and ordinary observation, including references to friendship between spouses and with their children. Of key importance is the love for each other's character and desire for their well-being, and thus, if a lad's beauty wanes, so does love for him, unless, as Aristotle seems to hope, 'the bonds of intimate friendship are based more substantially than on physical attraction or material gain'.[54]

(f) SUMMARY

Homosexuality among the Greeks is well attested by the fifth-century philosophers as a normal and valuable relationship, chiefly associated with private tuition, and their concepts of friendship. Commercial exploitation and pederasty especially among older men and immature boys was disapproved. By Aristotle's time, perhaps reflecting the argument of the *Laws*, heterosexual marriage reasserts itself as the predominant human aspiration; probably it never ceased to be outside Sparta and the Academies.

(g) ROME

The surviving literature of the Roman civilization presents an even greater problem than that of Greece in terms of establishing briefly attitudes to homosexual behaviour. Ancient patrician Rome was strict in its marriage law and custom, deeply committed to the preservation of the family under the *potestas* of the father, and the protection of the household deity. The Roman pantheon borrowed from the Olympian, but there was less sense of direct interference by the gods in ordinary life apart from the ineluctable 'Fates'. The records of imperial Rome are more detailed, of course, than those from Greece—we know more of Caesar's campaigns than Alexander's, but the descriptions of decadence come chiefly from such satirical writers as Petronius and Juvenal. Martial is a fairly explicit if good-natured observer, and the historians Tacitus and Suetonius do not hesitate to describe the sexual mores of their times and leading personalities.[55]

Several of the Roman Emperors, whose reigns covered the period of the early Church and the composition of the major books of the New Testament, were renowned for their sexual licence and cruelty, and the impression left by these Roman authors of the rich and idle citizens conniving at adultery and sodomy is no doubt accurate for that section of Roman society. These seems little point is quoting examples from them, except perhaps those of Julius Caesar and Nero.

Julius became catamite to King Nicomedes of Bithynia at an early stage in his career. The story was used by his political enemies and cited in ribald songs by his troops.[56]

On 15 July AD 64 a vast fire destroyed a major part of the city of Rome. The blaze began after an extravagant banquet, and suspicion fell on the Emperor Nero himself who might have planned it as a means of clearing the city for rebuilding. Nero blamed it on the

Christians, who were then killed in large numbers. Tacitus records that Nero went through a wedding ceremony

> with one of a perverted gang called Pythagoras. The Emperor, in the presence of witnesses, put on the bridal veil. Dowry, marriage bed, wedding torches, all were there. Indeed, everything was public which even at a natural union is veiled by night.

Tacitus hints that the fire might have been divine retribution for the Emperor's criminal act.[57]

Although there is, understandably enough, no direct mention of this verdict in the later New Testament writings, nor in the early sub-apostolic writers, it was in the subsequent persecution that Peter and Paul lost their lives. The Christians might well have agreed with Tacitus that Nero brought destruction on the city by this 'marriage', and it would have added point to their own denunciation of such practices.

From the third century BCE, homosexual behaviour had been prohibited by the *Lex Scantinia*, but it seems that it was only invoked occasionally for political purposes.[58] It may be concluded that compared with the Greeks the more pragmatic Romans did not develop in imperial times a philosophy of temperance to replace the originally strict obligations of family life. It was not until after the conversion of Constantine, and eventually the legal reform of Justinian, that the Christian ethic became predominant. That development is considered later.

PART C

An Historical Survey of Christian Attitudes

Introduction

The Christian attitude to homosexual behaviour has been remarkably consistent throughout church history. From the middle of the second century to the end of the nineteenth, the records show that homosexual offences were always declared sinful and those who were found guilty of them rigorously punished. The views expressed by St Paul in his major epistles are matched or reiterated by the early church fathers both in their commentaries on his writings and in their own pastoral works, and conciliar decrees confirm their judgement. With the rise of monasticism, and the development of more detailed regulations for the Christian life, a range of specific offences and appropriate penances is formulated, notably in the penitentials, and this ecclesiastical discipline is matched in many respects by the secular law under the Christian emperors, Justinian's codification providing the pattern on which mediaeval Europe was to depend until the Reformation. This consistency is not perhaps surprising, for it is equally clear that the Christian Church has seldom modified the ethical traditions it inherited from Judaism, and the major precepts of the decalogue concerning marriage and sexual problems generally have been adopted as biblical. Only for divorce and the status of women has much significant change been made, and that mostly in the twentieth century, under the twin pressures of secularism and modern understandings of sexuality.

The historical survey of attitudes to homosexual behaviour provided in this section is therefore selective, concentrating most attention on the period of change in recent years. Sufficient evidence is provided from the early and mediaeval Church to show that the problem of homosexual behaviour was never absent and required periodic denunciation.

As Europe's off-shore island, England inherited and maintained this attitude, enforcing it first by church and later by state law from Henry VIII onwards. In Victorian times the harshness of the law was mitigated, until apparently unintentionally, by a carelessly worded amendment to an Act of 1885 intended to protect young people from sexual exploitation, private homosexual practices among consenting males were made an offence. This led to a series of 'monstrous martyrdoms' of which Oscar Wilde was the first and Lord Montagu of Beaulieu was the last in a series of famous victims.

The public disquiet at Montagu's conviction in 1954 obliged the government to set up the Wolfenden Committee, which recommended the repeal of the 1885 amendment. This was supported by representative Christian bodies, and after a long campaign to create a sympathetic public opinion, the recommendation was put into effect by Parliament in the Sexual Offences Act of 1967. By that time the majority of European countries had amended legislation in the same way, but most of the American States still retained the old prohibitions.

In this survey church and state law, the private lives of famous people, discussions in Parliament and others behind the closed doors of church committee rooms are intermingled, though some coherence is attempted by dividing the period into three chapters, from the first century to 1885, from then to 1949 in terms of victims and welfare work, and then finally, in chapter 8, from 1952 to 1967. Each of these chapters has two sections: chapter 6 starts with the record of the Christian attitude to the time of the Reformation, and in the second section deals with the church and state law in England until the Labouchère amendment was included in the 1885 Sexual Offences Act. Chapter 7 takes Oscar Wilde, Charles Vaughan, Stewart Headlam and Roger Casement as examples of the many in all ages whose private life affected their public standing in tragic ways. Headlam was not officially identified as homosexual but for all four, recent studies have made a fresh assessment of their lives relevant. In the second section of this chapter, the virtually forgotten work of the White Cross League from 1883 to 1932 is recalled. Although on a small scale, the White Cross League attempted to provide rescue work for boy prostitutes in London, chiefly at the Shelter Home on Clapham Common. This makes an interesting contrast to the scandals of the famous, but it also serves as a reminder that Christian attitudes were not only negative and repressive. The first part of chapter 8 concentrates on the discussions in Parliament which finally led to the removal of the Labouchère Clause, and the second section traces the highly significant but discreet part played by Dr Sherwin Bailey and his colleagues in the Church of England Moral Welfare Council in pressing the Government to set up the Wolfenden Committee and explaining why the Christian Churches, while continuing to regard homosexual behaviour as sinful, nevertheless thought it an inappropriate matter to be dealt with by the criminal law as far as consenting male adults were concerned. The advice of a Roman Catholic group and of the B.M.A. to the same effect is noted.

To cover all these matters at reasonable length requires compression, and even so, the reports on the Parliamentary debates and the Moral Welfare Council's publications may seem over-detailed. They are included because they show how much careful work and thought was put into this long campaign by those of high motive in public and Christian service. Many of them are still alive and much remains confidential, but their story deserves telling. Further supplementary material is reserved for five additional notes: these are, perhaps, more specialist matters, but extend the scope of the survey.

6 Chastity Enforced

A The Early Church Period

As Christianity spread round the Mediterranean, its local communities began to establish a separate identity. Just as the Jewish Diaspora had resisted uncompromisingly, at least in principle, the life-style of the Greeks and Romans, so the Christians found themselves in opposition to much of the contemporary conventional morality. In particular, the sexual ethics advocated by St Paul and the sub-apostolic writers were clearly incompatible with those of the declining Empire, and yet, like the gospel itself, they needed formulation in a more logical and coherent way if they were to be successfully commended to the new converts. An early example of how this was attempted is given in the *Didache*, a manual of instruction on Christian morals and church order ascribed to the Twelve Apostles, but best dated early in the second century and probably earlier than the Apocryphal New Testament books quoted in the previous chapter.

The manual begins by describing the two love commandments as the way of life, and then follows a rather arbitrary selection of sayings of Jesus from the Sermon on the Mount and other sources. The second chapter of the manual starts with a household code in the decalogue form similar to those in the New Testament, introduced as 'The second commandment of the Teaching'. It continues:

> Do not murder; do not commit adultery; do not corrupt boys; do not fornicate; do not steal; do not practise magic. . . .[1]

In chapter three, reasons are given for obeying these precepts; lust, foul language, and leering are said to lead to fornication and adultery, but pederasty is not mentioned again.

One of the most attractive early Christian authors, Justin Martyr from Shechem in Samaria, wrote an *Apology* for the Christians addressed to the Emperor Antoninus Pius. Composed about 155 CE, after an appeal for respect for the truth against ancient customs, Justin argues that in following the truth of Christ, Christian moral standards are worthy of more respect than the contemporary mores, and takes as an example the custom of exposing children and giving them away for prostitution, even to the extent of mutilating them for 'the purpose of sodomy'. Such brutalities are done 'in the name of the mother of the gods' and so the defence of the superiority of Christian morals is used as an argument against the pagan deities.[2] Parallel with the Christian denunciation of pagan sexual vice, the early Christian writers frequency appeal for stable monogamous marriage among the

Christians, and the avoidance of fornication, adultery, and all forms of unchastity. A typical example is given by Clement of Alexandria, a Greek contemporary of Justin, who advises all Christians, young and old, to 'hasten to accomplish marriage', the remedy for temptation to adultery.[3]

In their attempt to explain Christian ethical training, the Apologists also found the Neo-Platonist teaching of Philo and his followers useful. This teaching laid strong emphasis on ascetic attitudes to the body, and Christian teaching tended to coalesce with it in stressing the moral superiority of the unmarried and the chaste. Philo's attitude to homosexual practices has already been noted (chapter 4), and it was reiterated by the church Fathers with a vehemence which suggests that they preferred his view of the matter to the caution of the New Testament.

A notable early example of their rigorous view is provided by Tertullian, the Carthaginian lawyer converted in Rome in 195 CE. One of his later treatises concerns modesty, *De Pudicitia*, written about 217 CE, and this demonstrates the determination of church authorities to achieve strict control of the sexual behaviour of its members. Thus, in chapter four, he links together adultery and fornication, forbids secret marriage, insists widows should remain inviolate and concludes with a general denunciation which seems to include homosexual behaviour:

> All the other frenzies of passions—impious both towards the bodies and towards the sexes—beyond the laws of nature, we banish not only from the threshold, but from all shelter of the church, because they are not sins, but monstrosities.[4]

Tertullian wrote this after he had become a Montanist. Montanism was an ascetic movement within the second-century Church, seeking to distinguish the spirit-filled community from the worldly forms of Roman Christianity, and was eventually condemned for unorthodoxy. This movement was only one form of Christian reaction against the difficulties of living in the conditions of Roman society, and the search for holiness through separation led eventually to the courageous but sometimes excessive mortification practised by the Desert Fathers. World negation could not, however, be the whole answer and the bishops eventually found themselves responsible for dioceses of largely nominal Christians, after Constantine had tipped the scales towards making the Empire Christian by the Edict of Milan in 313 CE.

(a) THE CHRISTIAN EMPIRE

In the Church of the East, early in the fourth century CE, the Cappadocian brothers, Basil and Gregory of Nyssa, both record disciplinary regulations for those who practise homosexuality, assessing the gravity of the offence as similar to adultery, rather than fornication, with penances between four and fifteen years, though full repentance would mitigate this. In the same period, the Councils of Elvira in Spain, and Ancyra (Ankara in Turkey) included regulations prohibiting homosexual behaviour. In the first case, bestiality and sodomy are treated together, a reflection of Leviticus, and in the second the specific point is the refusal of communion to unrepentant pederasts.

The struggle with pagan cults continues to occupy the theologians of the now officially recognized Church, and Arnobius and his pupil Lactantius, later tutor to Constantine's son Crispus, continue the now familiar challenge that the sexual frenzies associated with the old deities are repugnant. Not only are incest, child exposure, and subsequent prostitution mentioned, but the phallic symbolism in statue and art associated with Bacchus is described as an example of the false religion of those who unjustly accuse the Christians.[5]

A good conspectus of the development of church discipline by the end of the fourth century is provided by the *Apostolic Constitutions*, a collection of ecclesiastical laws compiled by the Church in Syria. Book Seven of the *Constitutions* is an expanded version of the *Didache*, conflating the clauses of the Decalogue with dominical sayings from the New Testament and references from the Old Testament. The commandment against adultery is amplified as follows:

> Thou shalt not commit adultery, for thou dividest one flesh into two. They two shall be one flesh, for the husband and wife are one in nature, in consent, in union, in disposition, and the conduct of life; but they are separated in sex and number. Thou shalt not corrupt boys; for this wickedness is contrary to nature, and arose from Sodom, which was therefore entirely consumed with fire sent from God. Let such a one be accursed, and all the people shall say 'So be it'.[6]

The biblical references to support this instruction are given as Genesis 2.24; Leviticus 18.20; and Genesis 19; and it is interesting that St Paul's Epistles are not referred to here, though they are in other sections. The instructions are set in a form which permits liturgical use with a congregational response inserted at appropriate points.

Full consideration of the problem of homosexual behaviour is given by St John Chrysostom in his commentaries on the relevant passages in Romans. Chrysostom, originally a lawyer and monk, became Patriarch of Constantinople in 398 CE, and was nicknamed 'Golden mouth' because of his accomplished preaching. His commentaries were probably written while he was still at Antioch and are in the form of a series of *Homilies*. Homily four on Romans is concerned only with chap. 1.26 and 27, and although he has little to say about homosexual behaviour in commenting on 1 Corinthians 6 or 1

Timothy 1, he returns to the same theme as part of an examination of lust in reference to Titus 1.6, where 1 Corinthians 6.9 is examined in more detail as an illustration. Homily four on Romans extends to some 3,500 words almost entirely concerned with homosexual behaviour, and although Chrysostom is a somewhat prolix writer, he clearly intends here to set out full arguments against it, and not merely reiterate the standard condemnation of the easily criticized pagan institution of pederasty.

He begins by arguing that both the men and the women to whom Paul refers have chosen this deliberately, as there is no suggestion that heterosexual activity was not available. They refused the pleasures of natural sex as a consequence of their decision not to obey what they knew of God's will by natural reason, and therefore God withdrew from them and they became dominated by Satan. The women are the more disgraceful as they should have a stronger sense of shame. The men who make themselves mad in this way are of less use than animals or eunuchs, and deserve to be driven from the society of the Church and stoned. The Epistle of Jude and the destruction of Sodom are cited for those who doubt that the punishment of hell awaits them, and the moral is drawn that all this depravity is the consequence of turning away from God and enjoying a life of luxury. Chrysostom here combines New Testament and Rabbinic teaching.[7]

St Augustine of Hippo, who had been a Manichaean, and then a Neo-Platonist before his baptism in 387 CE, writes about homosexual practices in his *Confessions*—*c.* 400 CE, and the reference occurs in parenthesis in Book 3 where Augustine is describing his Manichaean period, and is considering afresh the presupposition that it might be possible for the Christian duties to love God and his neighbour, to clash with man-made regulations. If they do, he concludes that God must be obeyed, but often human customs agree with God's commands, and a Christian may not opt out at his own whim. He takes Sodom as an example:

> There are those foul offences which be against nature, to be everywhere and at all times detested and punished; such as were those of the men of Sodom: which should all nations commit, they should all stand guilty of the same crime, by the law of God, which hath not so made men, that they should so abuse one another. For even that intercourse which should be between God and us is violated, when that same nature, of which he is Author, is polluted by the perversity of lust.[8]

This passage shows greater restraint than that from Chrysostom, and while firmly identifying the sin of Sodom, echoes Paul's two reasons for condemning homosexual practices—they are contrary to nature, and a lustful perversion which interferes with men's relationship with God.

One of the standard criticisms of the traditional Christian attitude to sexual behaviour is that, under the influence of monasticism and Augustine, a largely negative view of sexual activity became firmly established, love-making in particular being a sign of mankind's dominance by the sinful lusts of the flesh, redeemed only by the concession of God in the act of conception. There is no doubt a sense in which this is irrefutable, the preference for virginity already noted in the Pseudo-Epistle of Titus is a recurrent theme in the writings of the church Fathers, Latin as well as Greek. But apart from those who became monks and took the vow of celibacy, there were some Christian leaders who experienced happy marriage and were prepared to defend it on more positive grounds. Clement of Alexandria, for example, was one of these; Tertullian also was married; and Augustine himself cohabited for some fifteen years with a woman who bore him a son and shared a contented domestic life within the then accepted bounds of concubinage. Only after his move to Rome did Augustine abandon her, and she probably became a good catholic 'widow' of whom he writes tenderly later in the *Confessions*. Augustine, then, was no stranger to sexual desire and his often expressed embarrassment at the force of this fire in his loins was not a particularly Christian sentiment. In the patrician Roman tradition, a similar austerity is often expressed together with a sharp rebuke to any woman who expressed sexual feelings. There is one section in his *City of God* where Augustine writes with heavy irony and sarcasm about the Roman customs of invoking a group of lustful deities to assist the initial union of marriage. The note of derision takes much of its force from Augustine's suggestion that a healthy male needs no such assistance to perform his sexual duty.[9]

In later life, Augustine is involved in controversy with a younger man, Julian, bishop of Eclanum, who takes a markedly liberal view of the rights of married people to make love day or night when it pleases them. Although Augustine disapproves, he argues with an explicitness which shows him to be, like Luther, no stranger to sexual vigour.[10]

Since his 'marriage' started when he was eighteen years old, and he was clearly markedly heterosexual, it is perhaps not surprising that he deals with homosexuality only very cursorily. He does lament in one of his sermons that his pastoral work gives him too much evidence of adultery, far too little of chastity.

(b) THE MEDIAEVAL CHURCH

Once the Benedictine rule becomes established as the supreme guide to Christian holiness for the mediaeval Church, regulations controlling sleeping arrangements in both monasteries and nunneries clearly reduce opportunities for sexual licence and the third Lateran Council of 1179 condemns incontinence against nature. By this time of course, the Corpus of Canon Law governs Church life throughout Europe and is applied in England. Further evidence of the need to suppress homosexual behaviour is found in the *Penitentials*, regulations originating in the Celtic Church.

In line with the attitudes of the mediaeval scholastics and the decision of the church councils, there are many examples in the *Penitentials* of how seriously the various manifestations are to be punished, notably, of course, in religious communities. These handbooks for confessors developed systematic regulations to govern all aspects of human sinfulness as a practical expression in specific cases of the general principles of the Western councils and Canon Law. A wide range of homosexual offences was recognized with appropriate penances according to the gravity of the act. Sodomy was the most serious offence, and the penalty for it could be death, but this penalty had to be carried out by secular authorities, and the Church was seldom willing to ask for this extreme punishment. Among the lesser homosexual offences were various forms of physical contact, ranging from those intended to induce orgasm to mere kissing. Lesbianism among lay people was punished with a three-year penance, or seven years for nuns. Boys under twenty were treated more leniently according to age.[11]

(c) SCHOLASTIC TEACHING

It is difficult to know how widespread homosexual offences were in the Middle Ages, but the existence of these regulations, and their application to secular as well as monastic communities, show their continued existence. There seem to have been periodic outbursts of scandal and indignation when a notable ecclesiastical or civil personality was convicted, and this would be followed by a reissue of the regulations and solemn exhortations to discourage future offenders.

As early as 744 CE, Boniface writes to the King of Mercia that 'the people of England have been living a shameful life, despising lawful marriages, committing adultery, and lusting after the fashion of the people of Sodom', but there is no certain evidence that the English were exceptional in their sexual licence, and a fierce and detailed attack on homosexual behaviour is offered by Peter Damian, abbot of Fonte Avellana in his *Liber Gomorrhianus* of 1051 CE. He finds the regulations of the *Penitentials*, of which there were many continental versions as well as the Celtic, far too liberal in the penances they required, and he lists three degrees of male homosexual offence, mutual masturbation, inter-femoral connection, and sodomy. For all three, he argues, monks and clergy must be removed from their orders, but this severity was received with protest, and eventually the Pope, Leo IX, decreed that only those who were persistent in sodomy should be thus degraded.[12]

In the later mediaeval period detailed consideration of homosexuality is given by St Thomas Aquinas in the *Summa Theologica* II.II.QQ.153, 154 where he lists homosexual practices among the six species of lust. The others are fornication, adultery, incest, seduction, and rape, and all of them are condemned as contrary to the natural order of the venereal act which right reason shows to be for the preservation of the human race. Among the species of lust, homosexual practices are the most grievous form of sin because they corrupt this principle most directly. The *Summa* is a comprehensive conflation of ideas taken from the Bible, Aristotle, and Augustine, and it is interesting that Aquinas deals carefully with Aristotle's teaching that homosexual practices are a form of behaviour which belongs to the animal order rather than the human; Aristotle had argued that it is a species of bestiality rather than of lust because of its irrationality. Aristotle based this on his observation of homosexual behaviour among animals when deprived of their natural mates. Aquinas regarded Aristotle, of course, as 'The Philosopher whom it was impertinent for most people to criticize', and whose teaching represented the fullest expression of that natural theology on which Aquinas' own system was partially built.

Since the teaching of Aquinas has remained in many respects the dominant influence in the theology of the Western Catholic Church, his argument that homosexual behaviour is not only contrary to reason but also contrary to the natural order for human sexuality has proved to be the definitive ground for all subsequent rejection of homosexual behaviour by the Catholic Church. The most recent authoritative reiteration appeared in the Vatican 'Declaration on Certain Questions concerning Sexual Ethics', approved by Pope Paul on 6 November 1975, where it is stated that Scripture attests 'to the fact that homosexual acts are intrinsically disordered and can in no case be approved of.[13] The Declaration refers in a footnote to the Romans, Corinthians, and Timothy Epistles, but the phraseology of the text itself is Thomist. In response to the query that homosexual acts are less sinful than adultery, seduction, and rape, which injure another, Thomas argues that this breach of the divine law injures God, himself the creator of it. This argument is not, of course, conclusive, for heterosexual breaches of the divine law have the same effect as well as harming other humans, but in Thomas' appreciation, of course, the offence against God is the more serious matter.

The vigour of mediaeval poetry expresses on occasion the fascination with, and difficulty of controlling, the lusts of the flesh:

some of Chaucer's tales are examples. The story of Sodom was sometimes used as a morality, as it had been even in the time of Tertullian, when an anonymous poem amplifying the biblical narrative was attributed to him, probably falsely. An anonymous fourteenth-century English poet, comparable with Chaucer, but known chiefly for the legend of Sir Gawain and the Green Knight, also wrote a long poem based on the three biblical epics of the deluge, the destruction of Sodom, and the death of Belshazzar. It illustrates the theme of God's attitude to sins of the flesh and commends purity. The title of the work is *Cleanness* and in modern translation the incident at Sodom is described thus:

The men uttered these words in a loud fierce shout;
If you value your life in these parts, Lot, push out
those young men who went in a little while ago,
so we can teach them about love as our pleasure requires,
as the custom of Sodom is to men who pass by.[14]

After a narrative section, Lot replies:

I shall teach you a better device in accordance with nature. I have a treasure in my house, my two lovely daughters, unspoiled by any man. Though I say it myself, there are no ladies more beautiful in Sodom. It is a better pleasure to join naturally with them.[15]

The poem takes the Genesis narrative literally and suggests that it was assumed at this time that heterosexual behaviour should have been accepted as a more agreeable alternative. This was without doubt the standard ecclesiastical opinion. The early English legal treatises *Fleta* and *Britton*, which date from this period, make sodomy a capital crime, going beyond the French Councils of Paris and Rouen which maintained the traditional punishments of degradation and penance. Presumably this was intended as a deterrent in principle, and in practice the actual discipline of the Church was expressed in refusal of the sacraments, or in an extreme case, as with William Rufus, the withholding of funeral rites.

(d) THE REFORMATION

The political and religious upheaval of the Reformation broke for ever the Catholic unity of Europe and the penitential theology of the Reformed Churches revived the ancient Christian understanding of the full freedom of God's grace for the individual, in many ways a radical release from the oppressive and legalistic casuistry of the later mediaeval Church. Luther could cry 'simul peccator, simul justus' without intending thereby to proclaim antinomianism, but in sexual ethics the re-enhanced primacy of the Scriptures ensured that there was no great change. The crucial issue of the time was the freedom to marry for those who as monks and nuns of the old dispensation had vowed celibacy, and to some extent the opportunity for divorce under local ecclesiastical authority replaced the old procedure of papal annulment of marriage. The condemnation of homosexuality continued.

Reference has been made earlier to Calvin's interpretation of the story of Sodom's destruction in his commentary on Genesis (see p. 33). Although Calvin suggested the townspeople used subtlety in the ambiguous wording of the demand 'to know' the visitors, he concludes that they were, in fact, determined on a crime 'the atrocity of which would not suffer the destruction of the place to be any longer deferred'.[16] In similar vein, his commentary on Romans 1.27 makes clear that he has no doubt about the sinfulness of 'that which even the brute beasts abhor', but he is not drawn into further particular comment, preferring to emphasize in a typical way the general sinfulness of all men.[17] His comment on 1 Corinthians 6.9 makes the same point.

Before turning to Luther, whose writings on the conflict between flesh and spirit are voluminous but who seems to have been quite uninterested in the problem of homosexuality, it is important to recall the developments in biblical studies that preceded the Reformation proper in the later stages of the mediaeval period. The French Jewish biblical commentator, Rashi, already quoted in the previous section, had revived a style of commentary on the biblical texts which avoided elaborate allegorizing and concentrated on the clarification of basic meanings in the original Old Testament commentaries. His work was widely circulated, and despite the persecution of the Jews and the burning of their sacred books in the fourteenth century, particularly in France, Judaism continued to be regarded officially by the Church as the one heresy God allowed. The Jews were not to be forcibly converted nor subjected to inquisition, and their centres of learning and libraries, particularly in Eastern Europe, were available to Christian scholars. The best equipped biblical scholar of the later middle ages was Nicholas of Lyra, himself a converted Jew who became a Franciscan and a doctor of the Sorbonne in Paris. His commentary on the Bible, written soon after 1300 CE, was very popular and refers frequently to Rashi, whose Hebrew he, of course, understood. Nicholas' biblical commentary was one of the first to be printed, its precision widely admired among the Reformers, William Tyndale's friend, John Purvey, for example, suggesting that copies be made available in England.[18] This was done, and many English Cathedrals still have them among their collections of incunabula. The Vulgate Bible, printed in Basle in 1498, had the Jerome text surrounded by the *Glosses* of Anselm and the *Commentary* of

Nicholas. Martin Luther used this extensively, and in his lectures on Romans, quotes and comments on Nicholas' work.[19]

Since the Lyra commentary won such approval from the Reformers for its stress on the 'sensus literalis historicus' and was in effect one of the standard biblical commentaries available to them, the best since Jerome, the interpretation given to the Sodom, Gibeah, and Leviticus passages deserves mention at this point. Nicholas comments on Genesis 19.6:

> Lot went out to them lest they should enter his house for nefarious intercourse and assault his guests.

Then, in an extended note on verse 7 he considers the problem whether or not Lot was justified to offer his daughters to prevent the greater evil, the vice against nature. His argment proceeds in a scholastic style, first suggesting that although natural law requires protection of guests, and a lesser evil may be used to prevent a greater, nevertheless, as Augustine has argued, chastity is ordered, and therefore Lot was not in his right mind in making this offer. Nicholas concludes that even though human law permits prostitution and hence fornication, leaving the punishment to God's judgement, fornication must not be encouraged, and Lot should not have attempted to safeguard his guests by unlawful means. The distinction between natural law and human law is standard scholastic teaching.

This comment shows that Nicholas interprets 'ut cognoscamus eos' as clearly sexual in meaning, the vice against nature, and illustrates the systematic tidiness looked for in the biblical text as to the moral motivation of its characters—Lot is declared 'confused' to avoid the text becoming an argument for the end justifying the means.[20]

When Nicholas comes to the rape at Gibeah in Judges 19, he observes that most commentators maintain that sodomitical intercourse is intended, but he then quotes Josephus, apparently with approval, to suggest that they were really looking for the woman and made the homosexual demand only to force her to be surrendered. He repeats the conclusion that it would have been mortally sinful to surrender the daughter, referring back to the Sodom comment, and concludes that the Levite's woman was actually his wife.

For Leviticus 18.22 Nicholas comments briefly:

> Such intercourse is contrary to nature and is called the sodomitical vice after the city of Sodom, which is recorded to have been utterly destroyed on account of such wickedness.[21]

It is clear from these comments that Nicholas has no doubt of the literal meaning of the Sodom story, but has detected the ambiguity in the event at Gibeah. The mental picture of God's wrath expressed in fire and brimstone had a strong hold on the mediaeval mind and was vividly illustrated at the time by a painting by Dürer entitled 'Lot and his daughters', which is now in the National Gallery of Art, Washington. The whole town is depicted engulfed in flame as the three of them look on appalled.

Few people would have seen Dürer's painting at the time, but the effect of engravings in early printed books was, of course, widespread and important. One of the best engravers of the sixteenth century was Theodore de Bry who worked in Frankfurt and specialized in providing illustrations for the very popular histories of the exploration of America. One of these engravings, perhaps to be dated 1593, shows Balboa throwing 'some Indians who have committed the terrible sin of sodomy' to the dogs to be torn to pieces.

Bry never crossed the Atlantic himself, and the brutalities he depicts are offensive to modern eyes, but would not have surprised European readers of the time who were accustomed to cruel death for much less serious crimes.[22]

Luther delivered his *Lectures on Romans* in 1515 and 1516 at the University of Wittenberg while he was still an Augustinian monk of the Catholic Church, but also Professor of Biblical Theology at the University. His lecture notes, preserved by his son, found their way to the Royal Library in Berlin where they were overlooked until the present century. In considering the closing verses of Romans 1, Luther is reticent about the particular categories of sins, at least as far as his notes show, and he observed that the glory of the body lies in chastity and continence and its disgrace consists in unnatural abuse. Bodies are ordained to an honourable marriage, and to chastity which is still more honourable (this is some years before he married Katherine von Bora and he inverts the order in his comment on the fruits of the Spirit in Galatians 5). Among the humiliations of the body more disgraceful than adultery and unchastity, is the 'pollution of an even worse turpitude'. He then details various forms of uncleanness or effeminacy, such as lascivious thoughts, petting, especially of a woman's body, rubbing of the hands, and obscene movements. He also refers to nocturnal emissions and distinguishes these from sexual intercourse with a person of the same or other sex. At this point he asserts that God can forgive all such sin, or harden the sinner in it and condemn him, as he chooses. Although he is not explicit, it seems likely that homosexual behaviour is being implied in the comment about sexual intercourse with a person of the same sex, but these are lecture notes which he could amplify in delivery. The same reticence is shown in his lecture notes on Galatians, where he describes lust as various 'species libidinis' and notes that he has defined these in detail before and does not need to interpret them further, his purpose now being to concentrate on explaining justification. It is, of course, characteristic of Luther's theology to take a somewhat negative view of human nature outside grace, and therefore not to mention the old argument of unnaturalness, universally stressed by previous mediaeval authors and, in fact, Nicholas of Lyra. Luther's comment on Genesis 19 also shows his characteristic widening of interpretation to include heterosexual vice and general corruption of society. God had to destroy Sodom because it became ungovernable through these consequences of idolatry, and the Church takes the same risk—hence the need for reformation.

The post-Reformation situation in England was one in which the old Catholic moral theology was, in many respects, retained in the Anglican tradition, though the new Canons were a greatly simplified summary for the administration of the new established Church. State law took over jurisdiction in homosexual offences and this survey can be concluded by noting that Bishop Jeremy Taylor, in his *Holy Living*, refers briefly to these as contrary to the order of nature in his exposition of chastity.[23]

B Church and State

(a) CHURCH AND STATE ATTITUDES IN ENGLAND

The Laws of King Alfred, dated about 890 CE, begin with the decalogue and extracts from the Pentateuch, but are, of course, largely a modification and codification of Saxon customary law. The laws were administered by the sheriff and bishop sitting together in court, but when the Normans arrived, William I separated the secular and ecclesiastical jurisdictions. This change was not motivated by anti-clericalism, for William was a sincere churchman and a great collaborator with Lanfranc, Archbishop of Canterbury, in bringing canonical order to the Church in England, but he retained the common law tradition of England, under the control of his own judges. The discipline of the clergy, matrimonial causes, and offences against sexual morality, however, continued to be within the jurisdiction of the ecclesiastical courts. William resisted the demands of Pope Gregory VII, Hildebrand, to surrender to him the appointment of bishops, but the King's appointments were sensible, good Normans taking over, apart from Wulfstan, who retained his see of Worcester.

The Western Canon Law developed rapidly at this time and was finally codified by Gratian as the *Concordantia Discordantium Canonum* of around 1140 CE and this was, in effect, also the Canon Law of England though subject in principle to the king's approval and in practice to local variation in minor respects among the dioceses.[24] The traditional prohibitions of homosexual behaviour from the early councils and papal decretals were maintained in the canons.

There seems little doubt that the next English king, William Rufus, was justly accused of homosexual behaviour, and his successor Henry I held a Council in London to pass extra canons for the reform of clerical and moral abuses, including one (28) in which 'those who commit the shameful sin of sodomy, and especially those who take pleasure in doing so' were condemned by a weighty anathema, until by penitence and confession they should show themselves worthy of absolution. Clerics guilty of this crime were not to be promoted, but deposed, and laymen deprived of legal status. Only a bishop could absolve, except for monks.[25] The next royal scandal concerned Edward II, brutally murdered at Berkeley Castle in 1327.

Reformation theology in its continental form advocated a separation between church and state law—the left and right hand of God's rule as Luther saw it. Support for this view was readily found among the European princes in the wake of the Holy Roman Empire, the growing sense of nationalism, and the independence needed for commercial expansion. The English solution was a compromise.

(b) THE ACT OF 1553

As part of Henry VIII's policy of asserting the royal supremacy over ecclesiastical matters, he caused an Act to be passed in 1553 which transferred jurisdiction 'for the detestable and abominable vice of buggery committed with mankind or beast' to the royal courts. The preamble to the Act complained that 'there was not yet sufficient punishment' for the crime, and this suggests that the church courts were very reluctant to pass a death penalty. Sodomy was thus made a felony, for which hanging, mutilation, or deportation were the usual punishments.[26]

The Act related only to sodomy, and jurisdiction in other homosexual offences remained with the Church, though Sir Edward Coke observes in the *Institutes* of 1628 that a woman who made herself pregnant from a baboon was condemned under this Act. Henry's original Act was limited in operation 'until the last day of the next Parliament', but was reintroduced three times in his reign, temporarily repealed by Edward VI in 1547, restored by him the next year, repealed again by Mary in 1553 with the probable intention of reviving the ecclesiastical court's jurisdiction, and finally became a permanent part of English law when it was re-enacted by Elizabeth I in 1563, the preamble stating that since the repeal 'divers ill disposed persons have been the more bold to commit the said most horrible and detestable vice of buggery aforesaid, to the high displeasure of Almighty God'.[27]

This new law was enforced only occasionally in the next two hundred and seventy-five years as far as public records indicate, but these would, of course, only report the more notorious cases. Among the earliest is that of the Revd Nicholas Udall, headmaster of Eton and author of the early English comedy *Ralph Roister Doister*. He was examined by the Privy Council in 1541, found guilty of homosexual and sadistic practices with two of his boys and a servant, dismissed from Eton, and sent to prison for a few months. But he was subsequently allowed to continue as a parish priest, and then became headmaster of Westminster School and was honourably buried in St Margaret's, Westminster. Among others convicted were the Earl of Castlehaven, tried by his Peers in 1631, the Bishop of Waterford in 1640, the Revd Robert Thislethwayte of Wadham College, Oxford, for assaulting one of his pupils in 1739, Samuel Forte, the actor, in 1742, and a woman, Mistress Clap, for keeping a 'sodomitical house' in Holborn in 1742.[28]

(c) CAPITAL OFFENCES

Judge Tudor Rees wrote in 1955 that he was unable to come across a recorded instance of the extreme penalty of death or life imprisonment being imposed,[29] but, in fact, such punishments were occasionally inflicted.[30] The death penalty was still being exacted in the nineteenth century, examples of which were an army trooper, caught with the Irish Bishop of Clogher 1822, and two labourers in Bristol whose execution the local newspaper reported in 1800 without any further comment. But as Blackstone observed[31] this was still the usual punishment for all felonies. The bishop escaped to Scotland and died there in 1843.

The problem of proof, also referred to by Blackstone, caused anxiety, especially when public opinion began to move against the great number of crimes that incurred capital punishment. Sodomy has sometimes been interpreted to cover a wider range of offences than anal intercourse, and by a court decision of 1781, both penetration and emission of seed were required to be proved. By the eighteen-twenties, with the establishment of a regular police force, more than a hundred crimes ceased to be capital, but Sir Robert Peel reinstated the old rule that only penetration was needed for sodomy, and this offence remained capital despite an attempt by Lord John Russell to gain Parliamentary support for a change. The armed forces had their own disciplinary rules, and all forms of homosexual offence were harshly punished, four members of H.M.S. Africaine being hanged for buggery in 1816. The army had similar punishments, though, as A. J. Symonds and others have recorded, male prostitutes from the Brigade of Guards were a familiar sight in the London parks that adjoined their barracks. Despite that tolerance, the Cambridge criminologist, Sir L. Radzinovitz has noted that in London in 1826 there were more death sentences for sodomy than for murder.[32]

The death penalty was finally removed in 1861, when the punishment of penal servitude for life was substituted. To establish the crime it was necessary to prove only anal penetration and not seminal emission. At this time the jurisdiction of the ecclesiastical courts was substantially curtailed. All matrimonial causes were transferred to a division of the High Court, and church courts ceased to be concerned with sexual offences except where clergymen were involved, and not always then. The civil courts had, meanwhile, come to deal with indecent assault as one of the types of 'offences against the person' and, under this heading, homosexual practices other than sodomy could be included where a complaint was made. The 1861 Act laid down a maximum of ten years for attempts to commit sodomy, or for indecent assault, and thus the viciousness of the old law was mitigated.

(d) THE CRIMINAL LAW AMENDMENT ACT OF 1885

The result of the 1861 Act was that homosexuals who kept their physical activities private among themselves were left tolerably free from legal prosecution, but in 1885 a Bill was introduced into Parliament 'to make further provision for the protection of women and girls, the suppression of brothels and other purposes'. At a late stage of the Bill's passage through Parliament an extra clause was added which provided that:

> any male person who in public, or private, commits or is a party to the commission of, or procures or attempts to procure the commission by any male person, of any act of gross indecency with another male person, shall be guilty of a misdemeanour. . . .

The briefly stated reason for adding the extra clause was that it would provide for the protection of men and boys, as well as women and girls, from assault, the main object of the Act, and this reasoning may well have been justifiable as there were numbers of male prostitutes and boy catamites to be found in the parks of London at this time. If that was the intention, it was unfortunate that the clause was a late addition and so escaped any serious examination, for it apparently unintentionally made a much wider change in the law. Gross indecency in private could include a range of activity far short of sodomy, and the clause was quickly dubbed 'The blackmailer's charter'.

The extra clause is commonly known as the 'Labouchère Amendment' because Henry Labouchère, a Liberal-Radical M.P. and editor of the journal *Truth*, was the author of it. The original bill had passed all stages in the Lords and was being considered by the Commons in a committee of the whole House when Labouchère moved his amendment. It was a late session, between 11.30 p.m. and 2.55 a.m. the next day in a series of late night sittings, with a handful of members present, and one of them immediately intervened to ask the Speaker if the new clause was within the scope of the Bill as it dealt with a totally different class of offence. The Speaker ruled that at this stage of the Bill anything could be introduced by leave of the House, and the Attorney-General, Sir Henry James, said that the government accepted the amendment, asking successfully at the same time that the punishment should be a maximum of two years' imprisonment.

A close inspection of the *Hansard* Commons report for Thursday 6 August 1885 makes it plain how vague the proceedings were. Labouchère, the Member for Northampton, said the meaning of his amendment

> was that at present any person on whom an assault of the kind here dealt with was committed must be under the age of thirteen, and the object with which he brought forward this clause was to make the law applicable to any person whether under the age of thirteen or over that age.

He went on to say that he didn't think it necessary to discuss the amendment at any length as he understood the government was willing to accept it.[33] In view of the Speaker's ruling, no one else discussed it either, and Hansard continues:

> New Clause (Outrages on Public Decency) Mr Labouchère, brought up and read a first and second time.

It is extremely difficult to establish from this short report exactly what Mr Labouchère intended his clause to achieve, and maybe he didn't know himself. Whoever it was who affixed a title to the new clause seems to have supposed it was dealing with a public offence, at least primarily. Earlier in the debate a clause had been passed raising the age of consent for girls from thirteen to sixteen, and it seems logical to suppose that Labouchère was trying to extend this ordinary legal protection to boys as well, without wanting to fix an age limit of sixteen. His clause, in fact, had no age limit at all.

Four days later, on 10 August, the Bill, which had originated in the House of Lords, and had been several times considered by the Commons, was sent back to the Lords for final approval, which it received, and became law on 1 January 1886. In this final Lords Debate, several people regretted the amendments as ill considered, but accepted them on the principle that the Bill as a whole would do good. (Clause eleven was never specifically mentioned.) Opinion was divided between those who thought that the Bill demonstrated the ability of the Lords to lead public opinion, and those who thought it was a belated response to the facts revealed in recent newspaper articles. The summer recess beckoned, and no one was inclined to pick the Bill to pieces again, and so the last words for it were spoken by the bishop of Winchester:

The Bishops were interested in this question as the natural guardians of the morals of the people. He was speaking for all his Revd. Brethren (*sic*) when he said they were most anxious that the Bill should pass their Lordships' House, and he believed, whatever faults might be in the Bill, it was calculated to do a great deal of good, and it would be a great strength to the country. It was said, truly, that you could not make people moral or chaste by Act of Parliament, but a great deal might be done to prevent things which were immoral and unchaste.... Living in a Diocese in which there were more naval and military stations than in any other part of the country, he happened to know how terrible were the conditions of the streets of those places, especially in connection with this prostitution of infants. Unless they took some steps to prevent the continuation of the evil, this country which had hitherto prided itself upon being more moral than any other country in Europe, would expose itself to the taunts of the civilised world.

(e) CHILD PROSTITUTION

The bishop's sentiments no doubt reflected the general wish of the House that the Bill would help to clean up the streets and protect the young. The contrast between public attitudes and private practices in Victorian times needs no reiteration, but the Act of 1885 was prompted by causes much more serious than moral posturing. A most unpleasant feature of the later Victorian scene was the commercial exploitation of the young for both heterosexual and homosexual gratification. The main clauses of the 1885 Act were the direct consequence of an investigation carried out by W. H. Stead, the editor of the *Pall Mall Gazette*, into the traffic in procuring young girls for prostitution. His horrifying discoveries were published in his newspaper, and a government Commission, chaired by the Archbishop of Canterbury (Benson), with Cardinal Manning and the Bishop of London (Temple) as two of the other four members, was set up to enquire into the report and confirmed its truth in July 1885.

Labouchère's motives in adding the extra clause, have been scrutinized in recent years by Montgomery Hyde[34] and F. B. Smith.[35] The relevant factors can be briefly summarized. One may have been government's wish to take a firm line following the trial for homosexual behaviour of certain officials in Dublin the previous year. The session was nearly at its end, with an election pending, and the pressure of the Purity Society and Josephine Butler and her associates to achieve the main object of the Bill was probably irresistible even when Clause 11 was added. Labouchère himself probably disapproved of the Bill in general terms as loosely drawn and likely to interfere overmuch with personal liberty. Some years later, explaining his motives during the trial of Oscar Wilde, he suggested that he wished to prevent the government passing such a Bill after their successful attempts to prevent the prosecution of certain highly placed persons implicated in the Cleveland Street scandal. But, as Smith suggests, this justification rests on a mis-remembered dating for that event, and Labouchère's claim that he was following the Code Napoléon was also a confusion between Clause 11 and a previous amendment to which this was relevant. Perhaps all that can be safely said is that it was an opportunist intervention in an attempt to delay the Bill and embarrass the government which failed of its purpose and, in fact, led to the monstrous martyrdoms of which Wilde was the most famous victim. The loosely drafted clause should have been scrutinized by Parliament at more leisure or restrictively interpreted by a Court of Appeal, but this never happened.[36]

Close attention to the reports by Stead and the progress of the 1885 Act through Parliament was given by *The Guardian* newspaper, an influential church weekly journal of the time, which included in its many pages full reports on Parliamentary proceedings with a good deal of national news and detailed accounts of church events. In a series of leading articles from July to December 1885, Stead was rebuked for his sensationalism and failure to report the steady rescue work being carried on from no less than thirty-three hostels provided by the Church of England. In the first leading article for the issue of 12 August, two days after the House of Lords had approved the Commons amendments to the Act, including the one concerning gross indecency among males, the Archbishop of Canterbury is rebuked for not having spoken in the House along the lines he had already expressed to the Purity Society.[37]

The leading article notes as the most important amendments the provision for unsworn statements to be made by young children, the requirement of corroborating evidence, and the removal of a clause which would have provided a defence of poverty as justification for a number of people using the same bed. At no point in this issue, or in the many column inches devoted to the Bill in the Parliamentary reports, the editorials or correspondence throughout the whole of the year, does the Guardian ever mention indecency among males. By comparing the relevant *Hansards* with the pages of *The Guardian*, it seems clear that the staff of the paper were far too well-informed to be unaware of the precise subject matter of the amendment, so it was presumably editorial policy to report somewhat ambiguously in the 'business done' column:

> Mr. Labouchère moved and passed a clause dealing with outrages on decency.[38]

In the context, most readers would probably have assumed that some aspects of prostitution were being referred to, but there was also disquiet about pornographic publications.

The activities of homosexuals were less vicious than those associated with the procurers of young women described by Stead, and probably little changed from earlier times. Clubs for pederasts had been known in London since the eighteenth century and Restoration comedies often made fun of them. Bloch has shown the public interest in stories of sodomy which were published and as avidly read as were the lurid details of the trials for 'Criminal Conversation'. Before divorce became generally available, this offence was a popular means for enabling a cuckolded husband to recover damages from his wife's seducer, and unexpurgated reports of the graphic details of the cases given in court were printed in the many volumes of the 'Crim. Con.'. These reports were, in effect, a widely read form of pornography and they frequently included details of homosexual offences as well.[39]

The commercial trade in male prostitution was recognized and apparently tolerated by the police. By 1881, however, pederasty in London was beginning to be thought a public nuisance. Hotels near Charing Cross had notices in their windows which read 'Beware of pederasts', and in Holborn, Leicester Square, Fleet Street, Marble Arch, and the Strand, 'Mary Anns' as the young prostitutes were called, flaunted their invitations with graphic gestures as openly as their female counterparts.[40] It is not surprising, therefore, that Labouchère was able to carry his amendment without demur; it would have seemed to many people a sensible attempt to clean up the streets of London. It failed to do anything about the root of the problem which lay in the poverty and bad working conditions from which the young prostitutes could escape into the gaiety and warmth of the clubs, restaurants, and flats of their patrons.

One of the most interesting comments on this change of the law has been made by Sir Travers Humphreys, a distinguished criminal lawyer and High Court Judge, who acted as a junior counsel in the three trials of Oscar Wilde in 1895. Writing in the introduction to H. M. Hyde's *The Trials of Oscar Wilde*,[41] Humphreys describes how the amendment was passed, and concludes

> It is doubtful whether the House fully appreciated that the words 'in public or private' in the new clause had completely altered the law.

However, Judge Tudor Rees doubted that the government had been trapped, because the Law Offices had been consulted beforehand, and could have delayed the Bill if they so wished.[42]

7 Victims and Rescue Work

A Some Famous Victims

(a) OSCAR WILDE

The most famous victim of the extension of the law by Clause Eleven of the Act of 1885 was, of course, Oscar Wilde, son of an Irish surgeon, Sir William Wilde, who became notorious through a libel case concerning a child born to him by Jane Travers, the daughter of a professor at Trinity College, Dublin. As Hesketh Pearson drily observed in his biography of Oscar, 'William had done his full share in raising the birth rate of Ireland.'[1] Oscar's early years were lived among the reverberations of this affair, but he arrived at Oxford as an undergraduate physically strong, intellectually stimulating and sociable, so that his flamboyance led to no suspicion of his later bi-sexuality.

Wilde became well-known first to the public as the leader of the 'aesthetic' style of life, which he elaborated in London, and was sharply caricatured in the operetta *Patience* by Gilbert and Sullivan, which played to packed houses in London and New York in 1881.

Wilde married two years later, and settled happily with his wife Constance, the daughter of an Irish barrister. As his fame as a satirical and perceptive writer grew, so he moved into the life of London's society as an always welcome guest and conversationalist. Constance and Oscar were apparently deeply in love, and enjoyed normal sexual relations. Two sons were born to them. The emergence of Wilde's homosexual disposition has been studied by scholars in recent years, and much of the data is conveniently collected in *The Trials of Oscar Wilde*.[2] Although his childhood and Oxford experiences may have had some predisposing influence, he seems to have grown up and married with normal heterosexual characteristics. While at Oxford, he contracted syphilis from a prostitute. An attempted cure was made with mercury, and before his marriage a doctor examined him and assured him that the treatment had been successful. Two years after his marriage the symptoms reappeared and he ceased intercourse with his wife. By 1886 his intellectual curiosity in homosexual practices was matched by his participation in them.

At first, all this was carefully concealed, and the first hint to the general public of his homosexual interests was probably given in his novel *The Picture of Dorian Gray*, serialized in the *Monthly Magazine* in 1890, and published as a book in the following year. From then on, he was a marked man, and public opinion on the whole swung against him. Two leading Christian newspapers, however, reviewed it favourably—*The Christian Leader* and the *Christian World* described it as 'an Ethical Parable'.[3] The fatal meeting between Wilde and Lord Alfred Douglas took place in 1891. Douglas was the third son of the Marquess of Queensberry, budding poet and physically beautiful. Wilde found the combination irresistible and they were quickly obsessed with each other. Their attraction was not, however, merely platonic. Douglas was a practising pederast, and one of Wilde's first actions on his behalf was to travel down to Oxford and pay off a blackmailer who was threatening Douglas with exposure.

Furious at the friendship, Queensberry publicly accused Wilde of 'posing as a sodomite', and Wilde had no alternative but to prosecute him for criminal libel. In the subsequent trial, 3 April 1895, the defending lawyers knew they were able to produce sufficient evidence of Wilde's relationship with other men to substantiate their plea that the description of posing was justified. On the third day of the trial it was clear to Sir Edward Clarke, chief prosecutor for Wilde, that the men's evidence, together with the attitude taken by the court to certain passages in *The Picture of Dorian Gray*, and to extravagant expressions of love in several letters of Wilde to Douglas, quoted by the defence, showed that the longer the trial continued, the more Wilde would be exposed. He therefore asked leave to discontinue the action, which the judge granted.

The facts about Wilde revealed in the trial made it inevitable that Wilde would be, in his turn, prosecuted for gross indecency under the 1885 Act. The initiative was taken by Queensberry's solicitors, who sent copies of the evidence of their witnesses against Wilde to the Director of Public Prosecutions.

The Director and the police acted very quickly. When the defeated Wilde left the Old Bailey in the middle of the morning of 5 April, his friends urged him to leave for Paris to avoid the public reaction against him, but he was arrested in Douglas' room in the Cadogan Hotel at 6.30 p.m. that day. Wilde was refused bail and sent to trial for gross indecency under the 1885 Act on 26 April. Partly because the witnesses against him were all admitted accomplices, partly because of Wilde's own moving speech in defence 'of the love that dares not speak its name', partly because of Clarke's advocacy and partly because of the judge's impartiality, the jury disagreed, and Wilde was discharged. The jury's disagreement in this trial did not amount to an acquittal, and the Crown were free to bring Wilde into court again on the same charges. Some attempts were made to persuade the officers to let the case rest, but it was decided that Wilde must be tried again a second time with a new judge and jury.

Wilde might have escaped again but for three new factors. The first of these was a kind of inbuilt class sense of outrage. Much was made of the fact that Wilde associated with people of the 'lower orders'. Secondly, two emotional letters Wilde had written to Lord Alfred

Douglas were produced in court, renewing the revulsion sparked off by *The Picture of Dorian Gray*. Thirdly, Wilde's own demeanour had changed. Six weeks in prison without bail had made him listless and even more unattractive in appearance. His sparkle and resistance were gone. The judge summed up impartially, the jury found Wilde guilty of several acts of gross indecency after a retirement of three hours. The judge sentenced him to the maximum penalty under the 1885 Act—two years' imprisonment with hard labour. On release from prison Wilde went to France.

Two days before Wilde died in Paris, Fr Cuthbert Dunne, an Irish Priest attached to the Passionist church in Paris, was called to Wilde and conditionally baptized him. He received Holy Unction the next day and died very early on 30 November 1900, aged 46. He was buried eventually in the cemetery of Père Lachaise, alongside Balzac, Bizet, and Chopin, and a massive and controversial tombstome was made for him by Jacob Epstein.[4]

Of the two people who contributed most to his destruction, Lord Alfred Douglas attended the funeral and retained his affection for Wilde until he, too, joined the Catholic Church in 1911 and subsequently denounced his past. He survived until 1945. W. T. Stead, of the *Pall Mall Gazette*, whose revelations had led to the 1885 Act, wrote in the *Review of Reviews*, that:

> The trial and the sentence bring into very clear relief the ridiculous disparity there is between the punishment meted out to those who corrupt girls and those who corrupt boys. If Oscar Wilde, instead of indulging in dirty tricks of indecent familiarity with boys and men, had ruined the lives of half a dozen innocent simpletons of girls, or had broken up the home of his friend by corrupting his friend's wife, no one could have laid a finger upon him. The male is sacrosanct: the female is fair game. To have burdened society with a dozen bastards, to have destroyed a happy home by his lawless lust—of these things the criminal law takes no account. But let him act indecently to a young rascal who is very well able to take care of himself, and who can by no possibility bring a child into the world as a result of his corruption, then judges can hardly contain themselves from indignation when inflicting the maximum sentence the law allows. Another contrast, almost as remarkable as that which sends Oscar Wilde to hard labour and places Sir Charles Dilke in the House of Commons, is that between the universal execration heaped upon Oscar Wilde and the tacit universal acquiescence of the very same public in the same kind of vice in our public schools. If all persons guilty of Oscar Wilde's offences were to be clapped into gaol, there would be a very surprising exodus from Eton and Harrow, Rugby and Winchester, to Pentonville and Holloway.[5]

(b) SCHOOLS AND COLLEGES

Boys' Public Schools and University colleges proliferated in the latter part of the nineteenth century, and one of the standard criticisms of these one-sex institutions has been that they encouraged homosexuality, not of course by intention, but by their style of life in which proximity and lack of supervision gave particular opportunities for some masters and older boys to prey upon the young. Since the evidence for this criticism is widely documented, and fully listed in some of the books already referred to in this chapter, it is not further pursued here. In any case it is now widely recognized that homosexuality among immature boys or girls occurs frequently in all societies and cultures, but is seldom if ever determinative of their adult sexual orientation unless other factors are present.

However, as an illustration of the Victorian Church dealing discreetly with clergymen who, in the first case certainly and in the second case probably, were homosexually orientated, the careers of Charles Vaughan and Stewart Headlam are of interest. Headlam knew Wilde, and Archbishop Randall Davidson during his long tenure of Lambeth helped Headlam, respected the advice of Vaughan, and was later to plead for the reprieve of Roger Casement. It is a little realized facet of the Archbishop's life that he had this sympathy for the predicament of homosexual people, shared by his wife, and the record of it conveniently takes the story well into the twentieth century.

(c) CHARLES VAUGHAN

Vaughan was born in 1816 and died in 1897. Educated at Rugby under Arnold, he was Headmaster of Harrow, Vicar of Doncaster, Master of the Temple, and finally Dean of Llandaff, and a founder of University College, Cardiff. In the *Oxford Dictionary of the Christian Church*, in Bell's *Life of Randall Davidson*, in Moorman's *History of the Church of England*, Vaughan is regarded as something of a saint, and a brilliant pioneer in the training of ordination candidates. On leaving Harrow, Vaughan was offered the Bishopric of Rochester, but declined it, and the reason for this strange decision and for his relative lack of preferment thereafter is given by Symonds in his unpublished biography.

Vaughan practised pederasty at Harrow, and Symonds learned of this from a fellow pupil and friend who was a victim. He told his father, a doctor in Bristol, who threatened Vaughan with exposure unless he resigned and threatened him again by telegram when he heard that he was about to accept the Bishopric.[6] Bishop Wilberforce of Oxford learnt of this, and passed it on to the Prime Minister (Palmerston) and the Archbishop of Canterbury (Longley). This information must have been handled with discretion by those who knew of it. Vaughan continued to be consulted about ecclesiastical matters by church leaders, and Randall Davidson as Archbishop cites his opinion frequently in his papers, clearly regarding his views and advice as widely respected and reliable.[7]

(d) STEWART HEADLAM

Headlam was trained for ordination by Vaughan, as one of his 'doves' as the students who studied with him at the Temple were called, and became a much publicized Tractarian priest of the period in East London. Much influenced by the writings of F. D. Maurice, Headlam became, for his time, markedly left wing politically, urging for example, closer co-operation between Church and Trade Union leaders, and pioneering educational work for the deprived children of his parish. His pastoral zeal extended to the younger members of the theatrical profession who were subject to immoral exploitation, and he founded the Guild of St Matthew, originally a young communicants' fellowship, but later developed by Headlam as a pressure group for Christian socialist principles.[8]

Headlam was somewhat outspoken, and Frederick Temple, Bishop of London, deprived him of his curate's licence for eleven years. Davidson first came to know him as one of a group of young clergy for whom he was responsible as Archbishop's Chaplain at Lambeth and felt strong sympathy for his particular concerns. Eventually Davidson, as Archbishop, persuaded the next Bishop to reinstate him. Although ostensibly dismissed from his Bethnal Green curacy for praising the charms of the Gaiety Theatre girls in a public lecture, it was his outspoken identification of socialism with the gospel that irked the ecclesiastical authorities of the time. Headlam's enthusiasm and vigorous advocacy of these causes hardly seems sufficient reason for withholding preferment throughout his life, and maybe both his Bishop and vicar had private anxieties and suspicions which they could not voice.

On the other hand, Headlam's own statements and actions suggest that he felt sympathy for the difficulties of homosexuals rather than that he shared them. At the time of the *Pall Mall Gazette* 'revelations' and the passing of the 1885 Act, the Guild of St Matthew resolved that it was the duty of all churchmen to support the Criminal Law Amendment Bill as far as the age of consent for girls was concerned, to allow women to vote, and to promote all such measures of social reform 'as tend to get rid of the tyranny of wealth over poverty, which is the main cause of the special crimes now brought to light'.[9] No mention was made of the Labouchère amendment.

Headlam was almost certainly a natural celibate, and although nothing specifically homosexual is attributed to him in his biography by Bettany,[10] his life style was all of a piece with that of the Tractarian leaders described by Geoffrey Faber in *Oxford Apostles*. Unconscious of it they may have been, but Faber, with hindsight, has no difficulty in establishing, as he puts it, that 'their emphasis on virginity and their great involvement in masculine emotional friendships pointed unmistakably to a homosexual disposition'.[11] Headlam lived with his wife for only a few months and Bettany, with the reticence common at the time, dismisses the whole affair in a brief embarrassed paragraph, not even mentioning the wife's name and describing the marriage as a failure which was followed by a legal separation within a few years. Headlam apparently left letters describing the causes of the breakdown, but Bettany withheld their evidence as likely to cause pain to people still alive.[12]

When Alex Waugh published *The Loom of Youth*, a description of life at a fictional school called 'Fernhurst' but assumed to represent Sherborne, Headlam commented that he had seen very little of it in his time at school and thought Waugh's description much exaggerated.[13] Headlam was in later years a member of the anti-puritan league, and as such supported Wilde at his trial, particularly by providing bail at the third trial and accompanying him to the court each day. He did not, however, know Wilde well, having met him only twice before. He explained that he thought Wilde's case was being prejudged, and added 'I was a surety not for his character but for his appearance in Court. I had very little personal knowledge of him at the time.'

Headlam promised Wilde to meet him when he was released from prison, and did so, bringing him in a private brougham to his Bloomsbury house where Wilde met his friends before he left for Paris. Wilde has reservations about Headlam's help, writing to a friend the day before he was released, 'I do not like the idea of going to Stewart Headlam's at all. I don't know him very well and I am afraid of strangers.'[14] Headlam, in his own life, had experienced the force of rejection and misunderstanding. However, Davidson maintained his friendship with Headlam to the end, writing a final affectionate letter as Headlam lay dying in October 1924.[15]

Headlam had been for a time a fringe member of the Bloomsbury group, though not entirely trusted by them. Some aspects of the group's life and their writings would be marginally relevant at this point, but the links of most of the members with organized Christianity at the time were minimal, and in any case their lives and influence have been increasingly documented in recent publications.[16]

(e) SIR ROGER CASEMENT

Casement was arrested on Good Friday, 21 April 1916, at McKenna's Fort near Tralee, on the south-west coast of Ireland. He had landed from a German submarine, and was eventually charged with high treason and found guilty. His appeal was dismissed on 18 July by the Court of Criminal Appeal, and his execution was fixed for 3 August.

Casement had two chances for a reprieve. The first came with the possibility of an appeal to the House of Lords on a technical point of the law of treason. This appeal needed the sanction of the Attorney General, then F. E. Smith, afterwards Lord Birkenhead, who refused it. The second chance lay with the Home Secretary, who could advise the King to exercise the prerogative of mercy. He did not.

At this point in the story, Casement's personal diaries became important. They had been taken by the police at the time of his arrest, and showed he was an active pederast. In preparation for his biography of Asquith, published in 1964, Roy Jenkins was allowed access to the Prime Minister's private papers which showed that the Home Secretary had, unusually but understandably in this case, referred the use of his discretion to the Cabinet. They discussed the matter fully at four meetings. When the members saw the diaries they sent a copy to an alienist (i.e. a psychiatrist) who was asked to advise them if they showed Casement could be regarded as insane. When the Cabinet received the report of the alienist, the members noted that it declared Casement 'to be abnormal, but not certifiably insane', and therefore Asquith advised the King that it was the unanimous decision of the Cabinet that Casement should be hanged. The King himself had also seen a copy of the diaries.

What effect the diaries had on Casement's fate is hard to judge. Asquith recorded his own view that it would be better to reprieve him if possible, and keep him in confinement as a criminal lunatic rather than that he should be canonized as a martyr both in Ireland and America. This may be defended as a sound political judgement, but psychological knowledge of homosexuality had advanced sufficiently by this time for it to be really impossible to equate pederasty with such a measure of insanity as would justify Casement being regarded as not responsible for his treason. Casement knew perfectly well what he was doing. However, the fact that the Cabinet hoped to use the diaries as an excuse for reprieving Casement is not generally known, and it is commonly supposed that their discovery made his execution certain.

It was alleged in a BBC Television programme in 1970 that the Archbishop of Canterbury withdrew his support for a reprieve when he learned of the diaries but this was inaccurate. What actually happened was this. Archbishop Randall Davidson had known Casement in connection with his earlier excellent work in the Congo. He refused, with the Bishop of Durham, to sign any of the public petitions (Free Church and Roman Catholic ministers of prominence did so) but he wrote privately to the Home Secretary on 14 July and to the Lord Chancellor on 1 August urging a reprieve, and the later letter was considered by the Cabinet at their final meeting on 2 August, which reaffirmed their earlier decision. The Archbishop argued for Casement in both letters on the same grounds as Asquith had—that it would mollify the Americans and the Irish, and would take account of the fact that although, 'according to the experts he is not out of his mind, he is shown to have been mentally and morally unhinged'. Continuing his letter to the Lord Chancellor, the Archbishop shows, albeit in rather stilted language, that he is familiar with the problems of homosexuals. He writes:

> I have purposely not dwelt upon all the complexities of immoral morbidities, about which I have so much unpleasing experience every month of my life. Though my experience is abundant and varied, we must in the main be guided, in that field, by professional mental experts. In the main, but not to the exclusion of the unprofessional but solid experience of actual facts which is possessed by some of us, and forms an element, no more, in our consideration of the question.[17]

Although Casement's homosexuality is still commonly regarded as a factor which weighed against him in the final decision to execute him, this private evidence from Asquith and Randall Davidson shows that the opposite was, in fact, the case. Although it could not save him, the discovery of this propensity was seen by the authorities as offering a possible ground for mitigation, and therefore Casement's case can be regarded as one of the earliest indications that a gradual change of attitude to homosexuality among both senior politicians and churchmen was taking place.

B Rescue Work

(a) THE WHITE CROSS LEAGUE

The opportunism of Labouchère in adding Clause Eleven to the Criminal Law Amendment Act of 1885 has to be set in the context of the long campaign by Josephine Butler, Ellice Hopkins, General Booth of the Salvation Army, together with several bishops and lay readers, to improve the conditions of women at the time, of which the many hostels for rescued prostitutes were probably the most substantial achievement. Attempts to change the age of consent and to tackle the problem of venereal disease by legislation had been made in the years preceding the 1885 Act, not always successfully. By comparison the incidence of boy prostitution in London and other major cities was regarded by the church organizations as, no doubt, degrading but less urgent. However, the Victorian conscience was keenly aware of the double standard, and it was realized that women's ultimate safety depended upon a change of attitude among men and this educational task was begun as the rescue work and legal reform gathered momentum. Although the educational task was seen as primarily to commend purity among men towards women, by implication this included some steps towards discouraging homosexual behaviour, though the records of this are scanty and the work was always on a small scale.

Following a meeting arranged by Bishop Lightfoot at Bishop Auckland in 1883, and addressed by Ellice Hopkins, there gradually emerged a new group, the White Cross Society, directly concerned with the task of encouraging Christian men to purity of living and speech. The Society was an immediate success, becoming international and inter-denominational, with local secretaries in every diocese in England. Conferences were held and a large publishing programme of pamphlets was undertaken, but after Lightfoot's death the initial momentum was not sustained, and there were some uncertainties as to the League's role in relation to other similar organizations, so it merged with the Purity Society in 1891, becoming the White Cross League.[18]

Despite the merger of the original Society with the C.E.P.S., the League did not have the field of moral welfare work to itself. From 1890 onwards, dioceses gradually set up their own organizations for rescue work among women, and by 1918, due largely to the initiative of Mrs Randall Davidson, wife of the Archbishop, a new central co-ordinating organization was set up, called the 'Archbishop's Advisory Board for Spiritual and Moral Welfare Work'. This Board, meeting regularly at Lambeth, was in close liaison with governmental committees on such problems as sexual offences against young people, and attempted, for example, to arrange protection for women and girls at the Wembley Exhibition in 1926 (Advisory Board Minutes, 12 March 1926), and gave advice to the Government about the clauses of the 1927 Street Offences Bill. These were accepted. (Advisory Board Minutes, 15 July 1927.) They also recommended to the Central Advisory Council for the Training of the Ministry that the paper on Moral Theology in the General Ordination Examination should always include obligatory questions on 'preventive' and 'rescue work' and also on 'sex psychology'.

The subsequent history of moral welfare work in the Church of England lies with the Council of that name and eventually with the Board of Social Responsibility which operates now within the Synodical structure. The Council and its Executive Committee took a leading part in preparing the Church of England's submission to the Wolfenden Committee, and the Board has appointed two working parties in recent years to study the moral questions concerning homosexual behaviour. The work of the Council and the Board is considered later, but the virtually unknown attempts of the White Cross League to provide rescue work for the boy prostitutes of London at their Shelter Home on Clapham Common is described below, after a brief mention of the League's most famous publication—*The Blanco Book*. The discreet rescue work of the League through the years from the 1885 Act to the end of the First World War is an example of local Christian compassion to be set alongside Archbishop Davidson and his wife's influence in the corridors of power.

(b) THE BLANCO BOOK

Many of the early pamphlets of the White Cross League, which sold in hundreds of thousands, were written by Ellice Hopkins, and these continued to sell well in the Edwardian era. The start of the war meant that the conscripts in France were exposed to strong moral temptation in their brief spells away from the trenches, and so *The Blanco Book* was designed for them, and commended by the generals. It cost one shilling. It warns against the evils of prostitution and veneral disease and speaks realistically about masturbation which it admits to being a very common practice learned from other children or 'servants'. Belief in God is assumed to be common among the readers of *The Blanco Book*, biblical texts are occasionally quoted, and marriage commended, but it is national and masculine pride, the presence of the White Cross of purity as a constituent element of the Union Jack, as Ellice Hopkins puts it, which is used as the chief argument for chastity.[19] The strongest secondary argument is an appeal to recognize the plight of the women who in their innocence have been seduced by wicked men, and who now find themselves able to earn much more as prostitutes than by honest but poorly paid work. Encouragement is frequently given to those who have already been impure to seek forgiveness and to recommence prayer, Bible-reading, and attendance at Holy Communion that 'your sinful body may be made clean by His Body and your soul washed through His most precious Blood'—a quotation from the Prayer of Humble Access in the Book of Common Prayer Communion Service of 1662.

(c) THE SHELTER HOME

The Shelter Home, established by the White Cross League, was not the first nor the only attempt by church welfare organizations to care for boy prostitutes, but the Diocese of London was probably unique in having its own organization for rescue work among men and boys, and for the purpose established a Council, an office near Charing Cross, and a Secretary. He took an advertisement in the White Cross League Pamphlet for 1866 to say that his help was available for 'Young men and lads arriving in London, to find them suitable lodgings, contact with local clergy, a friendly welcome and recreational clubs'.

The White Cross League executive committee was approached in June 1911 by a Mr R. C. Bridger who asked permission to act as an authorized agent for the League for rescue work among boys. The League declined this offer, and set up their own sub-committee 'to obtain information and make suggestions concerning matters connected with boys, especially with regard to particular phases of vice'. On 16 November the sub-committee reported, and recommendations were made to carry out rescue work by providing a home and a refuge worker, by asking the Home Secretary to strengthen existing legislation, by sending a cautionary letter to institutions for boys warning them of the dangers of sodomy, by seeking to prohibit street selling by boys of school age, and by urging the police and sanitary authorities to carry out careful inspections of public urinals.

The first of these recommendations was implemented by the appointment of Mr Pritchard, an ex-police constable from Hastings, as the rescue officer for a month. His salary was two pounds a week and he began work on 1 January 1912. With letters of encouragement from both Archbishops, the committee went ahead in the ensuing months with their plans to provide a shelter home; funds were raised from private donors, a house for the purpose was obtained at No. 9 Clapham Common on 26 June, and Mr Pritchard moved there with a permanent appointment, quickly joined by Mr and Mrs Pittaway as housekeepers. On 19 September 1912, the house was blessed by Bishop Priestley, and the Revd L. E. Parsons was appointed honorary chaplain. The committee suggested that boys should be brought to the home for a short time, and then 'placed in situations or emigrated'.

Mr Pritchard's diary shows that he divided his time during the week between tours of inspection of the main areas in London where 'boy sodomites' were soliciting, in the hope of persuading them to come back with him to the shelter home, and in making arrangements with local employers for his resident boys to be given work. A typical day's entry is this for 28 August 1912:

> Engaged at the home until 11 a.m., then went to 7 Dean's Yard with the two boys Galvin and Gladwell to see the Revd. G. F. Cartwright (The Clerical Secretary of the White Cross League). Also received wages, etc. Then, as directed by Mr. Cartwright, went to a second-hand shop and bought a pair of boots for 2/6d. for the boy Galvin. Returned to the Home. Saw Harry Blake who said he had lost his wife, and had been sent to me by the Revd. Cartwright as he thought she may have been decoyed away for the White Slave traffic. I told Mr. Blake he had better leave it in the hands of the police. Then made enquiries with a view to finding work for the above two boys. Also went to Victoria and kept further observation re sodomites and saw a boy named William Noonan, aged 16, who I have known as a sodomite for six months. He said he would like to come into this Home, and would be a better boy if I allowed him to come in. I told him that I would do my best to get him some work first. I returned to the Home at 9.45 p.m. where I saw the boy Galvin who said that his friend Gladwell was not coming back to the

Home, as he was going down in Kent, hop-picking. Prayers were 'red' (*sic*) at 10 p.m.

In future entries it appears that Galvin continued to be co-operative, but Noonan was lazy and dirty, had to be de-infested of vermin on 21 September, and was turned out of the Home as a 'hopeless case' the following day for stealing money. Pritchard made contact with the families of the boys when he could and records enough of their circumstances and comments to show that most of the boys came from broken homes, or unstable backgrounds of various kinds. He worked in close co-operation with the police and courts and was sometimes able to take a boy given a prison sentence for soliciting, and keep him at the Home instead. His methods of rehabilitation were simple. He hoped that by providing shelter and employment, compulsory church-going on Sundays, and a generally caring atmosphere, he would be able to encourage the boys to abandon their prostitution.

The results of the first year's work at the Hostel were encouraging. The committee heard in July 1913 that 32 boys had been admitted, their average age was 17.1 years, and the average stay about a month. The prospect for 15 boys was hopeful, and for three was doubtful. The Home Office were paying six shillings a week towards the cost of accommodating boys referred to the Home by magistrates, and a further three shillings and sixpence for education in appropriate cases. The committee began to make plans for another home, in the country, where it was hoped boys could be accommodated for up to a year, as it was felt that the short periods at Clapham Common were often insufficient. Mr Pritchard reported that he worked in co-operation with the Roman Catholic home of a similar nature, St George's House, Westminister Bridge Road, and was sending boys he found of the Catholic Faith to the Superintendent there. He also worked in conjunction with Miss Clarke, who was the Lady Visitor of the Actor's Church Union, chiefly concerned with protecting young stage girls from the white slave traffic.

The work of the Warden and the Home continued in this style during the next year, and then as the war intervened, the number of boys admitted grew less, their age was younger, and they stayed longer. In 1915 only four were admitted during the first quarter, and there were also financial difficulties. Hopes of establishing another permanent home were abandoned. As the year proceeded, the committee noted that the number of prosecutions for soliciting had dropped sharply, and then Mr Pritchard, whose family lived in Margate, was appointed a special constable and resigned. The housekeepers had left also, part of the building collapsed and on 16 December the committee decided to close the Home for the duration of the war. In the three years of its existence, 65 boys had been dealt with, 34 of them with hopeful results, 12 were considered failures, and 19 doubtful. Some £300 of the original fund for the Home remained, and after the war the committee made several attempts to re-start the Home in new premises, but these were unsuccessful, and the money was eventually given to the Anglican Franciscan Order who agreed to take some boys at one of their houses at Hook, Dorset.

(d) LATER HISTORY OF THE WHITE CROSS LEAGUE

The final attempt by the White Cross League Executive Committee to continue work among boys is recorded in their minutes for 1929 and 1930. At this time Canon Pym was Chairman, later to become a Canon of Bristol.[20] The committee took an interest in an experimental home at Sudbury, Middlesex, operated by a Mr Scott. Ten lads were housed there, and Mr Scott described his method of dealing with them:

> The treatment was based on the recognition that in each case there was a physical, a mental and a spiritual factor. On the physical side the aim was to ensure bodily health by proper diet, regular sleep and exercise. As regards the mental and spiritual sides, the moral factor was not overlooked. At the same time, most of the lads entered the Hostel in a condition of mental or moral disease and the aim was to find out the cause of the trouble and to treat each case according to its special need. The main lines of the treatment were:
>
> (1) To induce the lads to face up to their responsibilities.
>
> (2) To encourage the right use of prayer and sacraments.
>
> (3) To find healthy channels for the expression of excessive sex energies.
>
> (4) To keep the lads as far as possible in touch with normal life by attending church services, social clubs connected with the church, sports and evening classes and so far as possible to allow them to have social intercourse with normal boys and members of the opposite sex.
>
> (5) Corporal punishment to be used only when absolutely necessary to keep discipline, never as a punishment for impurity.

Eventually the committee decided, after some debate, to take financial responsibility for the Hostel in part, but unfortunately Mr Scott himself had a nervous breakdown and the whole affair had to be wound up. There is a gap in the League's minute books in Church House from 1932 until 1949, and thereafter the records available only show how the League was finally reduced to no more than the small committee necessary to administer the remaining funds under a scheme approved by the Charity Commissioners. The Committee still makes grants for research each year.[21]

The problem of boy prostitution did not re-appear in an obvious way between the wars,[22] at least as far as the stations and parks of London were concerned, and perhaps opinions were changing as to the fundamental basis of rescue work. Canon Pym himself, who had been Chaplain of Balliol and became a Canon of Bristol, wrote rather cautiously about homosexuality in several of his books on Pastoralia. The understanding of homosexuality and the treatment proposed in Mr Scott's Hostel at Sudbury were hardly compatible with the by now widely available writings of Freud and the sexologists. These publications were taken seriously in the Archbishop's Advisory Board, and the trustees of the League began to set more hopes on research and education.

8 Reforming the Law

A Discussions in Parliament

(a) 1921: A LAW AGAINST LESBIANISM?

Between the wars, the British Parliament had two further opportunities for discussing homosexuality. The first of these took place in 1921, when a new Criminal Law Amendment Bill was being passed with the general aim of further protection for young people. Mr Frederick Macquisten, a Scottish Conservative lawyer and the son of a minister, representing one of the Glasgow divisions, moved the following new clause under the heading of 'Acts of indecency by females':

> Any act of gross indecency between female persons shall be a misdemeanour and punishable in the same manner as any such act committed by male persons under section eleven of the Criminal Law Amendment Act 1885.

Macquisten told the House that he knew of sad cases in which marriages and homes had been ruined by the intervention of abandoned females who pursued the wife concerned, and he thought it was high time 'this horrid grossness of homosexual immorality' was grappled with by the lawgivers. He thought lesbianism was sapping the highest and best in civilization now as it had previously to a large extent caused the destruction of the early Grecian civilization, and was still more the cause of the downfall of the Roman Empire. A fellow lawyer and future judge, Sir Ernest Wild, spoke in somewhat similar terms, managing to indicate that from conversations with doctors he had evidence of lesbian practices too shocking to reveal. All the same he gave lurid hints of the 'asylums largely peopled by nymphomaniacs', the streams of people with nervous breakdowns resulting from being tampered with by their own sex, and the imminent decline of the race because the lesbians were refusing to have children.

Fortunately, there were some members of the Commons who refused to be persuaded by this misreading of ancient history and confused exaggeration of the present scene. Colonel Josiah Wedgwood, afterwards Lord Wedgwood, pointed out that people could not be made moral by Act of Parliament, and warned that for every conviction under the clause there would be endless opportunities for blackmail. Colonel J. Moore-Brabazon, afterwards Lord Brabazon of Tara, suggested that this was not a matter for the criminal law, but for an investigation into how far it was wise for the law to attempt to deal with mental cases and 'abnormalities of the brain'. However, time was again pressing, and just before midnight on 4 August the House passed the clause by 148 votes to 53. Among those voting against it were Viscountess Astor, the only woman in the House at that time, and also Stanley Baldwin and Winston Churchill. For it were Austen and Neville Chamberlain and Lord Robert Cecil, the then leading lay spokesman for the Church.[1]

On 15 August the amended Bill came to the House of Lords, and the Earl of Malmesbury moved that the 'lesbian' clause be removed. His arguments for doing this were chiefly that it was a considerable change in the law which ought not to be passed as a subsidiary addition to a Bill about other matters without further discussion, and the taking into account of the experience of the police and law officers. He suggested that women were naturally more gregarious than men, and it could not be assumed that if they shared a room they were necessarily committing an offence. He had noted that when a large number of women shared the same premises, they preferred to live together rather than have separate bedrooms, to combat fear and loneliness, while when a shooting party was arranged, the first thing that had to be cleared was that all the men in it could be assured of their own private bedrooms. His speech was followed by one from Lord Desart, formerly the Director of Public Prosecutions who had started the proceedings against Wilde, and he thought that the clause would, in fact, encourage many women who before had no idea of these practices to start them.

The Lord Chancellor, Lord Birkenhead, declared from the Woolsack that he was bold enough to say that of every thousand women, taken as a whole, nine hundred and ninety-nine had never even heard of these practices. As a necessary consequence of the shortage of small houses, they had to have the same bedroom, and even sleep together in the same beds. It would be wrong, therefore, for the legislature by such a clause to impute the horrible suspicion of such a vice to such people, without a scintilla of evidence that it was widely practised. The Bishop of Norwich, who was standing in for the Bishop of London (rather inadequately, it was suggested by one noble Lord), and who had introduced the clause for discussion, said he was convinced by the arguments of its opponents, and so the clause was abandoned without a vote. The Commons did not seek to reintroduce it.[2]

(b) 1937 A GROUND FOR DIVORCE?

Homosexuality was again discussed in the House of Lords in 1937, as a rather unexpected digression when its members were considering the A. P. Herbert Bill to amend the Divorce Law. Herbert's Bill laid down four matrimonial offences for which the courts should grant a divorce, namely adultery, desertion, cruelty, and intervening incurable insanity. Lord Dawson of Penn moved a series of amendments to add three new offences. These were the practices of homosexuality, of habitual drunkenness, and drug addiction. Lord Dawson said of homosexuality:

I am not at all sure that in the future it may not be regarded as an insufficiency disease, and although it is true that the law must take cognizance of it and punish it in order to act as a preventive to potential offenders, the more reasonable view is gradually being adopted that it at any rate has one foot in the realm of disease and is not wholly in the realm of crime.[3]

The very distinguished judge, Lord Atkin, however, who had been one of the judges hearing Casement's appeal, opposed the amendment. He said that his judicial experience had shown that while Dawson's description was part of the truth, there was also an element of wickedness in homosexual cases. Like other wicked impulses, it was capable of being controlled, and checked by advice and resolution. He therefore thought that homosexual practices should not be used as a justification for divorce. A majority agreed with him, including the Archbishop of Canterbury,[4] who intervened in the debate to ask what was the precise significance of 'practices'—did this mean an occasional act or a regular habit?—and he clearly thought the distinction was material.

In both the debates of 1921 and 1937, it is clear that some of the views expressed anticipated the more liberal views that Parliament was eventually to accept in the passing of the 1967 Act, particularly in defining the relationship between sin and crime. The Lords' refusal to proscribe lesbian behaviour was prompted by a mixture of pragmatic wisdom and the traditional attitude that homosexual behaviour among women was less offensive.

(c) 1952–4 AN ENQUIRY NEEDED?

During, and immediately after, the Second World War, there was a rapid increase in the number of homosexual offences known to the police. The Wolfenden Committee Report of 1957 showed that between 1931 and 1955 the increase had been from 622 to 6,644. Of these, 390 and 2,504, respectively, had been proceeded against in the courts.[5] Among the causes for this increase, it has been suggested that the most important was a change of police policy at the highest level, and followed by junior police officers seeking promotion. Offences of this kind, particularly in the public lavatories of London, were relatively easy to detect.

Montgomery Hyde has noted that the defection of Guy Burgess and Donald Maclean to the Soviet Union in March 1951 seemed to have led to increased police activity in this respect. Both men were reputedly homosexuals, and in America particularly there was anxiety about security, homosexuals being assumed to be prone to blackmail.[6] He also suggests that the Home Secretaries, Herbert Morrison, followed by Sir David Maxwell Fyfe, together with the newly appointed Metropolitan Police Commissioner, Sir John Nott-Bower, and the Director of Public Prosecutions, Sir Theobald Mathew, pursued a common policy of encouraging the police to step up the number of arrests for homosexual offences. Corroboration of this 'new drive against male vice' announced at the time by the Home Office is suggested by Peter Wildeblood, a journalist on the staff of the *Daily Mail* who was convicted of homosexual offences in the same trial as Lord Montagu in 1954.[7]

The increase in prosecutions was, however, so large that increased police activity seems an inadequate explanation, and while the growth in population and the social disturbance of the war and its aftermath may have been other contributing factors, there does seem to have been a heightened awareness of homosexual behaviour in England in the 1950s, as there had been in the later Victorian period, and seems to be at the present time as a consequence of the Gay Liberation Movement. As to the prosecutions, there is some evidence that confessions by known homosexuals enabled the police to charge associates with this and other crimes, on the understanding that the informant would not be brought to court. More broadly, Jeffrey Weeks suggests that changes in the pattern of family life and an increased emphasis on sexual pleasure between men and women which began at this time, made it inevitable that the homosexual stood out in society as a more obvious aberration. They were either accused of a quaint virginity or had to 'come out' and defend an alternative sexual pattern of their own.[8]

However, the immediate situation was marked by a polarization between those who were critical of the rise in prosecutions and those who felt that these were a symbol of a new malaise in society that had to be resisted firmly. The popular papers tended towards ridicule and caricature.[9] Early critical reaction to the rise in prosecutions was expressed in the correspondence columns of the *New Statesman*. Kingsley Martin, the then editor, was in strong sympathy with a move to change the law, and subsequently gave support to the Homosexual Law Reform Society. A young Anglican ordinand, Mr Graham Dowell, wrote a letter to the periodical *Theology* suggesting this was a matter for Christian concern and this led to a vigorous educational programme by the Church of England Moral Welfare Council.[10]

The issue was raised in Parliament at the end of the year. At question time in the Commons on 3 December Mr Shepherd asked the Home Secretary, Sir D. Maxwell Fyfe, what were the numbers of cases involving male perversion in 1938 and 1952 respectively, and what complaints he had received from the police as to their lack of power to deal with these cases. It was obviously an expected question, and Fyfe replied with figures showing a similar increase to those already quoted from the later Wolfenden Report. The figures given were for combined cases of sodomy and bestiality and 'unnatural offences' in general, so they are not strictly comparable with those in the Wolfenden Report, but they undoubtedly registered a dramatic increase for the period. The Home Secretary also said that he had received no complaints from the police and then reminded the House that:

> The present maximum penalties for those offences were—for sodomy and bestiality, life imprisonment; for attempts to commit unnatural offences and indecent assault, ten years' and for gross indecency two years' imprisonment. He thought these penalties were adequate.

In the discussion that followed these answers, Sir Robert Boothby and Mr Desmond Donnelly argued that there was a good deal of evidence now to hand to show that psychiatric problems led people to commit these offences and that it was utterly inappropriate to commit those convicted to prison. The overcrowding in prisons made it often necessary for three prisoners to be kept in the same cell, which encouraged the continuation of these practices, and prison warders shared in them. As one member put it, 'to make men live in monasteries without the will to be monks' was futile.

Two weeks after this Commons debate, Lord Montagu of Beaulieu was tried at Winchester Assizes on charges of committing an unnatural offence and of indecent assault. He was acquitted on the first charge, but the jury disagreed on the second and the Director of Public Prosecutions decided he should be charged again, with three others, at the next sessions in March 1954. At the second trial, on 25 March, he was found guilty and sent to prison for twelve months. The prosecution evidence was largely provided by two R.A.F. men, who had both been practising homosexuals for some years, but acted as police witnesses in this case and were themselves never charged.[11]

The Montagu verdict was the final goad to action among those who had become increasingly dissatisfied with the police procedures and harsh court sentences associated with the series of similar trials in the past three years. There were immediate protests in the newspapers and on radio, and leading articles in the *Sunday Times* (28 March 1954) and the *New Statesman* (10 April 1954) pressed for a public enquiry into police methods and for a committee to consider changing the law. On 28 April Mr Desmond Donnelly raised the matter again in an adjournment debate in the Commons as follows:

> I wish to raise the question of a Royal Commission to investigate the law relating to and the medical treatment of homosexuality

and he explained that he only wished to criticize the laws in so far as they applied to people over the age of consent. He then quoted from the preface by Sir Travers Humphreys to Montgomery Hyde's book on the *Trials of Oscar Wilde* to remind the House of the unsatisfactory way the Labouchère amendment had originally been effected. (Hyde was at this time a Member of Parliament for Belfast North. His book was originally published in 1948.) Donnelly's speech included four main points:

(1) The present law contained several anomalies, not least in that it did not apply to women.

(2) Prison was the worst possible place to treat adult homosexuals.

(3) Police methods of dealing with homosexual offenders were unsatisfactory. This was particularly so when accomplices were employed as agents provocateurs, or when people were vaguely charged with conspiracy to commit the crime, which might mean anything, rather than the crime itself—for which more precise evidence was needed.

(4) The law should not interfere in a moral issue of this kind.

He thought this point was well made in the Church of England Moral Welfare Council Report, which he quoted:

In no other department of life does the State hold itself competent to interfere with the private actions of consenting adults. A man and a woman may commit the grave sin of fornication with legal impunity, but a corresponding act between man and man is liable to life imprisonment, and not infrequently is punished by very long prison sentences.[12]

Sir Robert Boothby spoke second, and referred to the prejudice against homosexuals, their persecution by the police, the happy field for blackmail provided by the present law, and the distress felt in the country about recent cases. Delving into history he continued:

The basic laws dealing with the problems are enshrined in the ecclesiastical doctrines of the Middle Ages, and are really derived directly from the Jewish Law, with the inevitable emphasis on reproduction of a race struggling for survival many centuries ago. Solomon could have a thousand wives, but homosexuality was punishable by death. It is significant that no laws, however savage, have in fact succeeded in stamping out homosexuality. In France where they have the Napoleonic Code, which is far less severe than the laws in this country, there can be no doubt at all that the problem of homosexuality is far less intense than in this country. All the laws relating to this subject were enacted before any of the discoveries of modern psychology. I do not rate modern psychology too high, but I think it has significance. I am not sure that with all his bias and with all his defects, Professor Freud will not go down in history as a considerable figure. . . . The duty of the State, as I see it, is to protect youth from corruption, and the public from indecency and nuisance. What consenting adults do in privacy may be a moral issue between them and their Maker, but in my submission it is not a legal issue between them and the State. . . . To send confirmed adult homosexuals to prison for long sentences is in my opinion not only dangerous, but madness.

Boothby then quoted from a British Medical Journal paper by Dr S. Jones who wrote,

It is as futile from the point of view of treatment as to hope to rehabilitate a chronic alcoholic by giving him occupational therapy in a brewery.

Replying for the Government, Sir Hugh Lucas Tooth, the joint Parliamentary Under-Secretary at the Home Office, announced that the Home Secretary, along with the Secretary of State for Scotland, agreed to the appointment of a departmental committee to examine and report on the law of homosexual offences and the parallel problem of the law relating to prostitution. In answering other points in the debate, the Under-Secretary took a much more optimistic view of the amount of psychiatric help available in prisons to those convicted than anyone with specialist knowledge at the time was inclined to think the facts warranted. He assured the House that one of the difficulties was the refusal by many prisoners of the help that could be offered.[13] The official announcement of the composition of the 'Wolfenden Committee' as it has since been usually called, was made on 26 August 1954.[14]

Following the Commons debate, a rather fuller discussion of the problem of the current law and the incidence of homosexual offences took place in the House of Lords on 19 May. This was introduced by the Earl of Winterton, who had been born in 1883, two years before the passing of the Act now under attack. Lord Winterton began by saying that the whispering campaign against the police was unjustified. He hoped that the law would not be changed, and he strongly disagreed with the views expressed in the Moral Welfare Council Report, that the social consequences of homosexual practices were less serious than those from pre-marital and extra-marital sexual activity. He said:

I contest the view that they are more evil and more harmful to the country than the filthy unnatural disgusting vice of homosexuality. I think that the particular sentence from the report which I have quoted is an astonishing doctrine to emanate from an organization of the Church of England.

Later in the debate Lord Brabazon of Tara was to agree with the views expressed by Donnelly and Boothby 'in another place', and to admit he was agreeably surprised by and supported the attitude taken in the Moral Welfare Council Report. Lord Jowitt, the Lord Chancellor, also expressed some agreement with the Report, and told the House of his surprise when appointed Attorney General some years before, after a legal practice mostly concerned with commercial cases, that ninety-five per cent of the many blackmail cases he had to deal with concerned allegations of homosexual offences. The Bishop of Southwell spoke for the bench of Bishops:

English Law, as it stands at present, regards these offences with quite exceptional severity.... I am sure that it is a highly debatable question whether sin could, or should, rightly be equated with crime. There are many sins of which clearly the law cannot possibly take cognisance: it is impossible to send a man to prison for unclean thoughts, for envy, for hatred, for malice or for uncharitableness. On the other hand, there may be things for which a man may be sent to prison which are not in any real sense sins at all. I venture to think, without any suggestion of condoning these offences, that we may have to ask ourselves seriously whether making this particular kind of moral wrong-doing a crime may not be only aggravating the total problem. And, in the present state of public opinion we are on very dangerous ground there, because one of the results of the immense volume of social legislation in recent years is that the popular mind tends to equate right and wrong with legal and illegal. People tend to say: 'The law does not forbid it, so it is all right'. It would be most disastrous if it could ever be said: 'You see, after all, there never was any harm in it, for the Government have now said that it is not illegal any longer and even the Church seems to think it all right.'

On the other hand, I think it is a big question whether the moral welfare of society is rightly served by making this particular kind of sexual offence a matter of criminal procedure for the law.... If the law is going to take cognisance of these offences between consenting parties, what is the ground for differentiating between male and female perverts?... If the law protects a boy from assault by a man, why does it do nothing to protect a girl from assault by a woman? Obviously in all these cases the offender must be restrained and punished, and, if possible, reformed. Almost nowhere, I think in the whole field, is the relation between retribution and rehabilitation so difficult and so delicate as at this point.

... we must not allow our judgement to be clouded by passion on this subject, and heaven forbid that I should in any way seem to minimise the gravity of the problem before us! But further medical and psychological knowledge may lead us to a more enlightened or, at any rate, to a different approach to the whole question, and to yield to a clamour for vindictive action or for even harsher punitive measures may easily defeat our ends.

We have to disinfect our minds of the idea that the state of being a homosexual or an invert is necessarily, in itself, something morally reprehensible. It is something which happens to a man, like colour-blindness or paralysis or anything else.... Rather does it make a demand from us for sympathy and understanding; and society through all its agencies, ought to be co-operative in trying to help people so frustrated and so conditioned, whether men or women.

Certainly the Church, like nearly everyone else, would vehemently repudiate what I might call the 'behaviourist' plea—the suggestion that a man in this condition is not a free and responsible moral agent, so that he simply says: 'I am made that way: I cannot help it'. And here the specifically religious contribution, surely, is the reminder that, by the Grace of God, a man can triumph over his disabilities and turn even the most crippling limitations into achievement. These forms of unnatural association are, of course, morally evil and sinful in the highest degree, because they are a violation of natural law, or, as the Christian would say, of the purpose of the Creator also, who, when he created man in his own image, created them male and female.[15]

The Bishop of Southwell had reminded the House in an earlier part of his speech that:

As St Paul said about this point a long time ago, once the creature is confused with the Creator, once people cease to believe in God and, therefore in ultimate moral obligations, everything begins to go bad on us, and natural instincts and affections become unnatural and perverted.

This speech in toto was an early indication of the attitude the Church of England would consistently take in the ten year long battle to implement the main recommendations of the Wolfenden Committee. Homosexual behaviour was still thought to be sinful by the Church: Romans 1 still stood, but should not be the concern of the criminal law. Although the Bishop of Southwell could claim to be one of the more learned of the bishops in the House of Lords at this time, it was and is the practice for bishops who are acting as chief church spokesmen in such debates to be briefed by either the appropriate department in Church House or from the secretariat at Lambeth Palace. It is clear that in this speech, the points made by Southwell were much in line with the recommendations of the Moral Welfare Council.[16]

The Parliamentary debates of 1953 and 1954 were only the preliminary skirmishes, but in them can be detected the main lines of the debate that continued up till the passing of the Sexual Offences Act of 1967 itself. Until the Wolfenden Committee reported, the supporters of reform like Donnelly and Boothby had to rely on the general public disquiet and a widespread awareness that prison sentences were an inappropriate remedy for homosexual practices among consenting adults. Although the Christians could not be accused of being responsible for Clause 11 and the 1885 Act, their initiative in urging its repeal probably disturbed a good deal of moral complacency among members of Parliament, and this was perhaps as important in opening the way for reform as the more obvious impact of the Montagu trial.

(d) 1957–67 THE WOLFENDEN RECOMMENDATION IMPLEMENTED

The Wolfenden Committee deliberated for three years, holding sixty-two meetings and taking evidence from over two hundred witnesses, of which many were expert in the field, and many were, in fact, representing public and professional bodies with carefully prepared memoranda. Christian opinion in a direct sense was expressed by the Church Commissioners, the Church of England Moral Welfare Council, and by the Roman Catholic Advisory Committee set up for the purpose, but neither the British Council of Churches, nor any of the Free Churches, nor any other religious body was apparently officially consulted. Among the judges called was Mr Justice Devlin, who was later to write that his appearance before the Committee started the train of thought which led him eventually to take his stand for the principle that the law should sometimes be used to enforce morality.[17] The Wolfenden Report's chief recommendation on homosexuality was the abolition of the law relating to private homosexual acts between consenting adults on the ground that it was not 'proper for the law to concern itself with what a man does in private unless it can be shown to be so contrary to the public good that the law ought to intervene in its function as the guardian of that public good'.[18]

The Report was received with wide approval, but it was clear that the Conservative Government was by no means eager to implement its proposals with legislation as the then Home Secretary, Mr R. A. Butler, explained. However, Lord Pakenham, a Roman Catholic, and later to become the Earl of Longford, moved a debate in the Lords on the Report in December 1957 supporting the principal recommendation of the Committee.[19] The Archbishop of Canterbury (Fisher) agreed with him, as did Lord Brabazon, who had spoken in the earlier debates and was incidentally a friend of Montagu's father. Lord Kilmuir (previously Sir David Maxwell Fyfe), Earl Winterton and several others spoke against the motion, and Pakenham withdrew it.[20] No time was provided by the government for a Commons debate, but outside Parliament steps were being taken to bring pressure to bear. Among the most important of these was the formation of the Homosexual Law Reform Society, started by Mr A. E. Dyson, then a lecturer in English in the University of Wales, and a young Anglican curate from Birmingham, the Revd Andrew Hallidie Smith. Dyson and Smith had seen one of their fellow students at Pembroke College, Cambridge, commit suicide, probably in connection with anxieties about homosexuality.

The Homosexual Law Reform Society began with Kenneth Walker as chairman, Hallidie Smith as secretary, and A. J. Ayer as president. In March 1958 a letter was printed in *The Times* to enlist support for the reform, and this was signed by an impressive list of thirty-three distinguished supporters, among whom were Lord Attlee, the Bishops of Birmingham and Exeter, A. J. Ayer, Isaiah Berlin, Sir Robert

Boothby, J. B. Priestley, Bertrand Russell and Barbara Wootton. The letter began:

The present law is clearly no longer representative of either Christian or liberal opinion in this country and now that there are widespread doubts about both its justice and its efficacy, we believe that its continued enforcement will do more harm than good to the health of the community as a whole.

The case for reform has already been accepted by most of the responsible newspapers and journals, by the two Archbishops, the Church Assembly, a Roman Catholic committee, a number of Non-Conformist spokesmen, and many other organs of informed public opinion.

In view of this, and of the conclusions which the Wolfenden Committee itself agreed upon after a prolonged study of the evidence, we should like to see the Government introduce legislation to give effect to the proposed reform at an early date and are confident that if it does it will deserve the widest support from humane men of all parties.[21]

In November 1958, over a year after the Wolfenden Committee Report had been published, the House of Commons was allowed to discuss it for the first time. Mr R. A. Butler, the Home Secretary, moved 'That this House take note of the Report' and stressed his opinion that 'there is at present a very large section of the population who strongly repudiate homosexual conduct, and whose moral sense would be offended by an alteration in the law which would seem to imply approval or tolerance of what they regard as a great social evil'. Montgomery Hyde spoke third in the debate, in favour of the Report's implementation, but Butler was probably right in his political judgement that the country was not yet ready to accept a change in the law, and Hyde found himself refused re-adoption by his local constituency committee in Belfast for the 1959 election because 'we cannot have as our Member one who condones unnatural vice'.[22]

After a large public meeting organized by the Homosexual Law Reform Society on 12 May 1960, at which the Bishop of Exeter described the present law as a 'monstrous injustice', and Mr Kingsley Martin moved a resolution asking the government to implement the Wolfenden recommendation without delay (carried unanimously by over a thousand people present), Mr Kenneth Robinson, a member of the society's executive committee, a Labour M.P. and future Minister of Health, introduced the matter again in the Commons. No effective progress was made, and despite the opportunity of a free vote, it became clear that the issue was polarizing, at least temporarily on party lines. All the Labour speakers but one were in favour of the motion, none of the Conservative speakers were, and the voting showed the following division: For the motion: 75 Labour members,

22 Conservatives and 4 Liberals—a total of 101. Against the motion: 178 Conservatives, 37 Labour—a total of 215. Amongst those voting for the motion was Mr Enoch Powell.[23]

Twenty-one months later the Welsh solicitor and Labour M.P., Mr Leo Abse, was successful in the ballot for Private Members' Bills, and introduced his first Sexual Offenders Bill into the Commons with the very limited aims of assisting uniformity in the application of the law by having all prosecutions authorized by the Director of Public Prosecutions, minimizing opportunities for blackmail by requiring all charges to be brought within a year of the alleged offence, and insisting that for all first offenders the court must have a psychiatrist's report. Unfortunately, less than an hour was available for the debate and the Bill was 'talked out' without a vote being taken.[24]

In the autumn of 1962 the trial of the Admiralty clerk William Vassal for spying was followed by an enquiry which revealed that he had been blackmailed by the Russians because of his homosexual activities. This was followed by the Profumo affair, and shortly afterwards Mr Macmillan resigned as Prime Minister in favour of Sir Alec Douglas-Home. Lord Arran, a Liberal peer, wrote to the new Prime Minister to ask if there would now be government backing if he introduced a Bill into the House of Lords to bring forward the main Wolfenden recommendations. On 4 March 1964, Sir Alec advised him 'to leave it over to the next Parliament and see what you think of the chances then'. Mr Henry Brooke, the successor to Mr Butler, told the Commons on 16 April 1964, that he had no evidence of any material change in the balance of opinion since the debate four years previously. In October, a Labour government with a small majority was elected.

Lord Arran, with the help of the Reform Society, put down a motion in the Lords for 12 May 1965 'to call attention to the recommendations of the Wolfenden Committee on homosexual offences'. He was supported by another letter in *The Times*, published the day before the debate, signed by five bishops (Birmingham, Bristol, Exeter, London, and St Albans) and by leading peers from the fields of medicine (Lord Brain), law (Lord Devlin), and education (Lord Robins). Of the eight signatories, that of Devlin was perhaps the most surprising in view of his earlier doubts. In the debate itself, it was soon obvious that Lord Arran's plea 'as an ordinary man who is privileged to be a member of your Lordships' House and as a Christian' gained wide approval, with sixteen of the following speeches supporting him, including those by the Archbishops of Canterbury and York, and only three against.[25]

Twelve days later he was able to move the first and second readings of a simple Bill designed to protect consenting adults. The voting was

94 in favour and 49 against on the second reading, and the debate was enlivened by the opposition of the Chief Scout, Lord Rowallan, and of the ex Lord Chief Justice, Lord Goddard, who coined the memorable phrase 'the buggers' charter' to describe the Bill. Among those in favour was the Marquess of Queensberry, the great grandson of Wilde's persecutor.

Mr Abse attempted to bring in a similar Bill in the Commons two days later on 26 May, but was defeated by the narrow margin of 19 votes. From then onwards, Parliamentary procedures and another General Election could do no more than delay the long overdue reform, and the Commons finally accepted it by a majority of 85 in the early morning of 4 July 1967. The Lords voted again, as they were bound to do in order to fulfil the requirement that a Bill must pass both Houses in the same session, and gave the new Bill a majority of 63 on 13 July. As the 'Sexual Offences Act of 1967' it received the Royal Assent on 27 July 1967.

The effect of the Act has been, of course, only to remove the threat of prosecution from consenting adults who share homosexual practices in private. Minors are still protected, and people in special categories like members of the Armed Forces are still liable to prosecution, and the word 'private' is interpreted strictly so that an offence would be committed if any third person were present, even as an observer. Thus, the ill-drafted amendment, so casually moved by Mr Labouchère in a fifteen-minute debate, took more than a hundred hours of busy Parliamentary time to modify eighty-two years later. The English law is now similar to that of the Code Napoléon, which Labouchère said he had in mind.[26]

Although a number of Christian laymen and bishops spoke in the series of debates, generally in favour of reform, probably the most substantial Christian view was expressed in the following words by the Archbishop of Canterbury in the Lords debate on 12 May 1965:

> I want to make clear the moral standpoint from which I approach this question. I believe that homosexual acts are always wrong in the sense that they use in a wrong way human organs for which the right use is intercourse between men and women within marriage. Amidst the modern talk about the 'new morality' I would uphold the belief that just as fornication is always wrong, so homosexual acts are always wrong. At the same time, wrong acts in this case as in others can have various degrees of culpability attached to them. In this case, there are not only degrees of culpability, but also varieties of causes of the trouble and categories of the trouble, psychological and sociological.... The case for altering the law in respect of homosexual acts between consenting adults in private rests, I believe, on reason and justice and on considerations of the good of the community. I think there is a real cogency in the plea of the Wolfenden Report that not all sins are properly

given the status of crimes, not even such sins as the adulterous conduct of a man or a woman, which can smash up the life of a family and bring misery to a whole family of children. If a line can reasonably be drawn anywhere, homosexual acts in private between consenting adults fall properly on the same side of the line as fornication.[27]

In the same debate Lord Arran reminded the House:

It cannot be mere accident that the Wolfenden Committee's recommendations on homosexuality have been supported by the Church Assembly, the Church of England Moral Welfare Council, the Roman Catholic Advisory Committee set up by the late Cardinal Griffin, the Methodist Conference and an influential group of Quakers. These are great bodies and their views cannot be taken lightly.[28]

B Church Initiatives

(a) MR DOWELL'S LETTER

1952 was the year in which the increased police activity against known homosexuals began to produce a public reaction. Mr Graham Dowell, an ordinand at Ely Theological College, noticed the correspondence in *The New Statesman* and during the Christmas vacation wrote from his home address to the influential Anglican magazine *Theology*, then being edited by Dr Alec Vidler, Dean of King's College, Cambridge.[29] His letter, entitled 'The Church and Homosexuals', questioned the wisdom of using penal measures to punish homosexual practices, and asked what the Christian conscience had to say to those homosexuals who wished to be active and healthy members of the Christian community.

Dr Vidler knew Dr Sherwin Bailey had just become lecturer to the Moral Welfare Council after some years as Chaplain at Edinburgh University. Bailey had become interested in the problems homosexual people faced through his chaplaincy work,[30] and so when Vidler asked him to provide a reply to Dowell's letter, he was able to respond quickly, and his article 'The problem of Sexual Inversion' appeared in the February number of *Theology*.

(b) BAILEY'S ESSAY IN *Theology*

The article welcomes Dowell's initiative in asking for a long overdue discussion. English Law, writes Bailey, in common with other legal systems, penalizes male homosexual activity only, although it is a common phenomenon among females, and the Kinsey Report shows that homosexual experience among men is widespread. A distinction is to be drawn between the 'invert' and the 'pervert', only the latter choosing his condition, but these categories are not exhaustive, and when they are defined and extended, they only serve to show that the complexity of the problem prohibits an indiscriminate moral judgement. Bailey is clear that society must demand of the invert the same restraint in sexual matters as it demands of the heterosexual, protecting the young, and all from assault, nuisance and indecency, but he thinks that the English law, by intruding into the privacy of the invert's sexual life, is grossly unfair and conducive to crime. 'It is, without doubt, a Christian duty to press for the removal of this anomalous and shameful injustice, which has done untold harm, and has achieved no good whatever, and it is to be hoped that those who look to the Church for a lead in this matter will not be disappointed.'

Bailey then turns to the question of homosexual 'marriage' and other forms of institutionalized homosexual union which could be considered. Here, he is reluctant to concede any real similarity between homosexual and heterosexual relationships. He repeats briefly the major theme of his book, *The Mystery of Love and Marriage*, that the heterosexual relationship is based on *henosis*, the one flesh relationship, primarily expressed in sexual intercourse. While recognizing that those who define marriage primarily as a means of generation can never accept homosexual marriage, nor, he holds, can those who share his *henosis* definition. For him this point is decisive, and of more weight than the biblical prohibition on sodomy, which he suggests probably alludes to perversion only. He concludes by observing that a reform of the law and a change of public attitude would make it easier for an invert to accept his condition and take advantage of psychiatric treatment.[31]

(c) ACTION BY THE CHURCH OF ENGLAND MORAL WELFARE COUNCIL

This article, Bailey records,[32] evoked such a response by way of private correspondence as to make it clear that many in the Church were concerned about the present law and its administration, and anxious to know what help could be given to the invert. He therefore asked the Moral Welfare Council to consider a study of homosexuality (Council meeting of 29 April 1952), and the Council's education committee approved the calling together of a small group of clergymen, doctors, and lawyers to undertake, unofficially and privately, a full investigation of the problem. Canon Hugh Warner, Education Secretary to the Council, reported to a meeting of the Council's Executive Committee on 3 December 1953, that the group had been meeting for a year, and that 'in view of the recent wide and unexpected interest in the subject, a draft *interim* report had been prepared, and would be considered by the group next week'. In the meantime, the Home Secretary had indicated that he would be interested to read the report.

The Council meeting of 3 December 1953 took place at the Diocesan House in St Albans. The same evening in the House of Commons the Home Secretary was asked about the increase of prosecutions for male perversion between 1938 and 1952. After stating that there had been a five-fold increase over these years, Sir David Maxwell Fyfe added 'Homosexuals in general are exhibitionists and proselytisers, and a danger to others, especially the young. So long as I hold the office of Home Secretary, I shall give no countenance to the view that they should not be prevented from being such a danger.'[33]

Having expressed himself in this way, the Home Secretary may have been surprised to see how widely the Council's views diverged from his own. At the 3 December meeting of the Executive Committee it was resolved that a letter should be sent to him containing the following resolution and stating that the report of the *ad hoc* group on homosexuality would follow. The text of the resolution was:

> That the executive committee of the Church of England Moral Welfare Council asks the Home Secretary to set up an official enquiry into the whole subject of homosexuality and proposes that the following aspects should be included in such an examination:
>
> (a) the penalties to which a homosexual is liable and the wide diversities of penalties actually imposed for identical offences;
>
> (b) the implications of new psychological knowledge in assessing guilt and imposing punishment;
>
> (c) the adequacy of treatment available in prison and the effect of normal prison regime upon the homosexual prisoner;
>
> (d) the validity of the right given to the State to take cognisance of the moral private actions between adult male homosexuals while no such right is given in cases of female homosexuals or in cases of heterosexual immorality between adults. The duty of the State to protect the young people is self-evident.
>
> (e) the effect of this right of State interference on the whole question of blackmail;
>
> (f) the factors contributing to some forms of inversion which are due to wrong attitudes developed in childhood and the responsibility of parents and teachers for the emotional, moral and spiritual development of their children in this respect.

It was agreed that the Dioceses be informed of this decision and that the Church Information Board be asked to release the statement to the press as soon as possible, saying that the Council would welcome the expression of support from other organizations.

(d) THE INTERIM REPORT

The Interim Report was quickly printed, entitled *The Problem of Homosexuality* and on the front cover marked in red print 'Private, not for publication'. The Report covers twenty-seven pages, with four tables of relevant criminal statistics from 1926 to 1952 at the end. Although written by Sherwin Bailey, this is not acknowledged; there is a foreword by the Bishop of St Albans, stressing that the group who produced the Report are alone responsible for the views expressed, and asking that comments should be sent to Canon Warner.

The first chapter of the Report, entitled 'Variations in the Homosexual Pattern', reiterates with more precision the points made about this in Bailey's *Theology* article. The second chapter deals with 'causes of inversion', and sets out briefly what were thought to be the chief causes, namely an ineffective or absent father, a clinging or dominating mother, a broken family. Other contributory causes mentioned are a congenital factor, the influence of school friends, and the accidental lack of female company.

The third chapter, 'The Moral and Religious Aspects', is the main section of the Report, and in effect offers a refutation of the argument that for an invert, homosexual love-making is as natural as heterosexual intercourse is between men and women. This refutation is cast in orthodox terms. Heterosexual love, it is argued, is *sui generis*, connected with God's purpose in creating man as a male–female duality, and his establishment of an ordinance towards which sexual activity is directed, namely, union in 'one flesh', in the specific context of marriage. A homosexual 'union' cannot be in terms of 'one flesh', and an invert is not a female with a male appearance; he is a man with many male characteristics, but lacking heterosexual desire. This last point is substantiated by reference to Dr Kinsey's report that a male invert responds to the same sexual stimuli as a normal male, his reactions being characteristic of the man, not of the woman. Further, the chapter continues, homosexual physical expression has and can have no relation to procreation and the family whereas, between man and woman, it always has at least implicitly this relation. Even some types of caress are immoral for homosexuals, which are morally legitimate for heterosexuals 'within marriage'.

Having made this rather sharp distinction between the significance of homosexual and heterosexual physical activity, the chapter then deals with the situation faced by a homosexual, and a pastoral rather than judgemental attitude is taken. Homosexuals are said to be like normal unmarried women who can learn to live with only transitory friendships and a prospect of eventual loneliness. They can accept their situation and sublimate their sexual lives and achieve personal fulfilment in various socially useful ways. 'Homosexual marriage' would not solve the problem any more than extra-marital concubinage does for a woman. Repentance of post sin, forgiveness and grace, especially through Holy Communion, are the means of liberation for the invert; he will still have his old instincts, but will have power to avoid 'occasions of sin', in brackets defined as 'association with perverts'. Priests are asked to offer the ministry of reconciliation, and to work with psychiatrists sympathetic to Christian understandings, and the public are asked to help by strengthening the moral foundation of society, supporting the law in defence of the young and of public decency, and by insisting on justice for the homosexual.

The fourth and final chapter of the Interim Report is entitled 'The Law and the Male Homosexual'. The law as it then was is reviewed, with a preliminary point that it is the State's duty to protect the young from seduction and assault, and therefore any change in the law should not endanger the welfare of young people. The influence of the Code Napoléon in removing private homosexual acts between consenting adults from the cognisance of the Criminal Law is noted, and then attention is drawn to the difference of treatment accorded to males and females in relation to homosexual practices in English Law. Section 52 of the Offences against the Person Act of 1861 made an assault against a woman an offence without specifying the sex of the assailant, so it would be possible theoretically to charge a woman with this offence, but it does not seem to have been done. The much more serious legal anomaly, however, is that in no other department of life does the State hold itself competent to interfere with the private action of consenting adults. A footnote suggests that the law against incest is concerned with the biological and domestically anti-social aspects of such behaviour. The Report then argues that fornication and adultery present much clearer evidence than private homosexual practices of consequent damage to society; the risk of illegitimate children from the former and the risk of the break-up of the family unit from the latter are clearly apparent, but the law does not punish fornicators or adulterers as criminals. The individual aggrieved (father or spouse) may bring a civil action for damages. It is also noted at this point that the penalties for soliciting are far more severe for male prostitutes than for females.

The chapter then deals with subsidiary considerations which point towards a change in the law. As it stands, the law encourages blackmail, encourages adult homosexuals to seek young companions who will not report them, discourages normal friends who run the risk of being assumed to be homosexuals themselves, provides an undesirable opportunity for the police to use *agents provocateurs*, and prevents homosexuals from seeking psychiatric help because they risk prosecution if they reveal their activities. A final note in the chapter recommends that the age of consent in a new law be retained at twenty-one. Although for heterosexual intercourse this is only sixteen, homosexual intercourse as an unnatural activity involves a different principle, and no risk should be taken of precipitating an unnecessary life-long inversion by participation too young. Retaining the age at twenty-one would also continue to give protection to young National Service men.

The Report was printed in January 1954, and the Executive Committee decided at their meeting on 9 February to set aside five hundred copies for free distribution, and to make it available at a reduced rate to clergy and students at theological colleges. At the full meeting of the Moral Welfare Council six weeks later, on 31 March 1954, it was decided to send free copies of the Report to all diocesan bishops, to certain members of the House of Commons and the House of Lords, to Principals of theological colleges, to the head Chaplains of the three Services, to the Law Society, the British Medical Association, the Chief Scout, and to newspapers and periodicals 'read by responsible people'. In fact it had already been sent to and favourably commented on in the columns of *The Times*, *The Spectator*, the *New Statesman* and the *Lancet*. Canon Fenton Morley reported that he had taken part in the pre-recording of a BBC programme on homosexuality soon to be broadcast. Within these first two months of publication, some three thousand copies of the Report had been issued, the Council was told. Under normal circumstances, this could be considered a startling circulation for a Report that was not on sale to the public generally, but the trials of Lord Montagu and Peter Wildeblood were taking place through this period. In fact, two anonymous donations of £100 each made it possible to distribute the Report to all members of both Houses of Parliament before the debates in the spring, though this was not reported to the Council until their meeting in November. By then one thousand five hundred and seventy comments and case histories had been received in response to the Report and these were being collated. The Council agreed that the Report should not be sent to members of the Church Assembly, but that Council members would be briefed beforehand in case questions were asked about it.

(e) ANGLICAN EVIDENCE TO THE WOLFENDEN COMMITTEE

At the Adjournment debate in the House of Commons on 28 April 1954 it was announced that the government would set up a departmental committee, and this was formally constituted on 26 August. Without doubt, the Interim Report, so rapidly and widely circulated, played an important part in persuading the government to consider the problem seriously. Once that decision was taken, the

Moral Welfare Council abandoned its intention to produce a second fuller report, taking account of the mass of new data available in response to the Interim Report. The main objective, setting in motion a process for reforming the law, had been achieved. The next task was to prepare evidence for the departmental committee. Following the death of Canon Hugh Warner, the major responsibility for this fell to Dr Sherwin Bailey. This was a busy period for Bailey, for his own much expanded study *Homosexuality and the Western Tradition* was published the next month, and he also contributed to the volume of Essays, *They Stand Apart*, both highly significant books of the time. The latter also contained an essay by Viscount Hailsham, better known once perhaps as Mr Quintin Hogg, on the social aspects, in which he disagreed with Bailey on the need for changing the law. Bailey submitted his full book to the Wolfenden Committee as a piece of private evidence; it is surprisingly not listed in the Report's index of individually submitted memoranda, perhaps because it was taken as part of the Welfare Council's material.

The Wolfenden Committee interviewed the representatives of the Moral Welfare Council on 30 March 1955. With Dr Bailey were the Venerable E. N. Millard (Archdeacon of Oakham), and Dr F. G. Macdonald. No record of what was said is available, but Bailey recollects that although he was not a member of the Wolfenden Committee, he was constantly in consultation behind the scenes, and in correspondence with the secretary, Mr W. C. Roberts of the Home Office.[34] The written evidence submitted by the Council consisted of three parts (in addition to Bailey's own text of 'The Western Christian Tradition'), and was subsequently published by the Moral Welfare Council with additional material in the pamphlet *Sexual Offenders and Social Punishment*.[35]

The first part of the evidence is a brief introduction, referring to the Interim Report, and the evidence collected in response to it. Sections 1, 2, and 4 of the Report are submitted as part of the evidence to the Committee, but section 3, 'The Moral and Religious Aspect', is omitted. This section is, of course, covered more fully in the text of 'The Western Christian Tradition', but the Council had decided it was inappropriate to offer the Wolfenden Committee information on this aspect because its terms of reference excluded any consideration of the moral aspects of homosexuality. The second section of the evidence is specially written for the Committee by Bailey and is, in effect, a summary of some of the points that have emerged in comments on the Interim Report. Stronger emphasis is given to the Kinsey Report; the classification of types of sexual condition is modified; the causes of inversion are made less specific and more contextual; homosexual practices are described as not necessarily including sodomy which many homosexuals find distasteful; the possibility of loving relationships between homosexuals is stressed, and there is more hesitancy about the possibility of cure for definite inverts.

Part three of the evidence makes general and specific recommendations. The general recommendation is that the objectionable terminology of the old law be replaced by the less emotive term 'homosexual acts' to include everything previously described in the four terms 'buggery', 'indecency', 'carnal knowledge', and 'unnatural offences'. The reason for this recommendation is not embarrassment at the language, but the conviction that the 'gravity of a homosexual offence should not be determined arbitrarily by the nature of the act involved, but each case should be judged according to its specific circumstances'. The specific recommendations are the repeal of the various nineteenth-century laws concerned with homosexual acts, and their replacement by a new law which penalizes any male or female person who commits any homosexual act with a person under the legal age of consent, or in circumstances constituting a public nuisance or infringing public decency, or involving assault, violence, fraud, or duress. It is further recommended that better facilities be provided for those charged under the new law to receive treatment by specialists, and the age of consent is suggested as seventeen years.[36]

When the evidence submitted to the Wolfenden Committee was published the following year in the booklet *Sexual Offences and Social Punishment*, four appendices were added. The first of these was a reprint of Bailey's essay from *They Stand Apart*, and the second was a new article by him entitled 'The Pastor and the Homosexual'. In a foreword to the booklet, the Bishop of St Albans paid tribute to Canon Warner, and to Bailey's scholarship, and in the introduction Bailey himself explained how the series of documents had been produced during the past three years, and what had been the main policy considerations in providing evidence to the Wolfenden Committee in the form it was actually given.

One further aspect of the production of the evidence for the Wolfenden Committee deserves mention. Early in 1955 a typewritten draft of the evidence was sent to the Archbishop of Canterbury (Fisher), and the executive committee noted at their meeting on 8 February that year that he had replied saying there were points on which he would wish to comment when he had had time to study it. In fact, the Archbishop wrote to the Bishop of St Albans on 3 March a confidential letter in which he makes clear his objections, and the Bishop sent a copy to Bailey on 5 March with comments. Bailey replied in somewhat vigorous terms.[37] The Archbishop's comments are chiefly concerned to make two points: first that only the practising homosexual is identifiable (Bailey disagrees with this) and second that both the Interim Report and the evidence are misguided to suggest that private acts between homosexuals have no social consequences. In support of this the Archbishop cites his own knowledge of highly organized groups of inverts who maintain links with similar groups in other places and actively seek new members. From other (unquotable) sources, it has been strongly suggested that clergy, and particularly curates, were involved or enticed into such groups at this time, and that it was the discovery of this, and the responsibility for dealing with the ensuing pastoral problems, which made the Archbishop become increasingly anxious that the Moral Welfare Council should not be seen to be supporting a lenient line. However, two years later, when Lord Pakenham introduced a debate on the Wolfenden Committee's recommendations in the House of Lords on 4 December 1957, the Archbishop supported him in pressing for the change in the law.

(f) ROMAN CATHOLIC EVIDENCE TO THE WOLFENDEN COMMITTEE

Apart from the Anglicans, the Roman Catholic Church was the only other religious body asked as such to give evidence to the Wolfenden Committee. This was done through a special advisory group formed for the purpose under the leadership of the Very Revd Monsignor G. A. Tomlinson, at that time Roman Catholic Chaplain to the University of London. The report of the Catholic Committee was printed in full in the *Dublin Review* for summer 1956, with a three-page introductory comment by Mr N. St John Stevas, the then editor of the *Review*.[38] The report is short and concise, with three sections, headed:

(1) Catholic teaching on homosexual offences
(2) The nature of sex inversion
(3) Summary of conclusions and recommendations.

Section one begins by stating firmly that 'Homosexual activities and desires to which the informed will give full consent involve grave sin.' On the basis of various Papal statements, it is made clear that the Church does not officially recognize any theory about the causes of homosexual tendencies, but emphasizes the significance of original sin, and the freedom of the human will, informed by grace, to overcome instinctual forces. While sympathy must be shown to homosexual people, they must not be led to believe they are doing no wrong when they commit homosexual acts. It is the business of the State to defend the common good, and this will include the protection of the immature, but sin as such is not the concern of the State. Penal sanctions are not justified for the purpose of attempting to restrain sins against sexual morality committed in private by responsible adults.

The present law should be discontinued because it is ineffectual, inequitable, disproportionate in severity to the offence committed, and gives scope for blackmail. The law should, therefore, be amended to restrict penal sanctions for homosexual offences to prevent the corruption of youth, offences against public decency, and the exploitation of vice for gain.

Section two is written in a far more tentative style. It distinguishes homosexuality from sex inversion by describing the former as the phase through which children and adolescents pass, consciously or unconsciously, while the latter, it is suggested, should be applied to a sexual impulse which appears to be congenitally and ineradicably homosexual. Various causes for sex inversion are mentioned, and its occurrence 'from the dawn of human history' is noted. Along with the usual kinds of reference to pederasty in Hellas and Islam, the romantic relationship between the adult Samurai and their pages in feudal Japan is mentioned.

In the concluding section the recommendations for changing the law are repeated, and among the other suggestions, the committee wished to retain the age of consent at twenty-one, they approved the use of drugs to suppress sexual desire and activity when other remedies proved ineffectual, but they regarded castration, which they believed to be practised in Denmark, with abhorrence.

In his comment on the report Mr St John Stevas implies that he is aware of the course the discussions followed, and it is, therefore, interesting to see how firmly he argues for a separation between law and morality at this point. For example, he writes 'The witness of the history of certain Puritan States is sufficient warning against the idea that individuals can be made morally good by Acts of Parliament.' He continues by stressing the undesirable system of police espionage needed for applying the present law, and the anomalies implicit in the fact that neither adultery nor lesbian activities are illegal. These points are not made in the text of the report, but when the report and the comments are taken together, it seems clear that Stevas was disposed to strengthen the Committee's report with considerations of his own. That he was aware of the dilemma between what he called 'traditional Catholicism' and 'English liberalism' emerges from his subsequent book *Life, Death and the Law*[39] in which he also records his debt to Sherwin Bailey for material included in his chapter on homosexuality.

To summarize, the Catholic evidence of the Wolfenden Committee is cast in a traditional mode of thought as to its moral theology: it is somewhat markedly separatist in its attitude to the law by comparison with the usual Thomist approach, and it is clearly hesitant about the proper implications to be drawn from the medical and psychological data provided. In effect, the clear conclusion for the Wolfenden

Committee was the same as that from the Anglican Committee; both Churches wanted the law changed in respect of homosexual behaviour between consenting adults over twenty-one.

(g) EVIDENCE FROM THE BRITISH MEDICAL ASSOCIATION SUBMITTED TO THE WOLFENDEN COMMITTEE

Although the British Medical Association has no religious affiliations, the evidence on its behalf, prepared by a special committee, is relevant to this chapter in three ways. First, the special committee invited both Dr Bailey and Dr F. G. Macdonald to advise them in preparing their evidence; Dr Macdonald was one of the trio from the Moral Welfare Council who appeared before the Wolfenden Committee. The B.M.A. committee quote with approval a passage from the Moral Welfare Council evidence, which they had seen, and there was clearly a full exchange of views.

Secondly, the B.M.A. evidence cautiously recommends that adult private homosexual behaviour may not be contrary to public order. It avoids specifically suggesting a change in the law, but indicates that the social consequences of such a change are, on balance, likely to be beneficial. The membership of the committee was a highly qualified one, with a good representation of prison and police doctors, and the evidence includes a detailed consideration of lesbianism (offering cogent reasons for its relative unimportance), and also a careful examination of the alleged increase in homosexual behaviour in recent years. The committee did not feel convinced from these data that there was necessarily proved to be an actual increase in homosexual practices.

Thirdly, in an Appendix to the evidence, the secretary of the committee, Dr E. E. Claxton, provided at the committee's request a memorandum on religious conversion and the homosexual, an aspect of the subject in which he had clearly a special interest. He gives fourteen case histories, five of the individuals concerned being known to him personally, and the details of the others being supplied by medical colleagues. Ten of the histories concern men, including a magistrate, a Royal Air Force Chaplain, a Salvation Army sergeant-major and several school teachers; all of them seem to have been helped towards abandoning homosexual practices by experiences of conversion.[40]

ADDITIONAL NOTE 1

Statute of Henry VIII against Sodomy

The original in the House of Lords Record Office reads:

The Act of 25 Henry VIII Chapter 6

Forasmuch as there is not yet sufficient and Condyne punishment apoynted and limited by the due course of the Lawes of this Realme for the detestable and abominable Vice of Buggery committed with mankind or beast ... that the same offence be from henceforth adjudged felony and such order and form of process therein to be used agaynst the offenders as in cases of felony at the Common Lawe. And that the offenders being hereof convict by verdict confession or outlawry shall suffer such paynes of death and losses and penalties of their goods chattels debts lands tenements and hereditaments as felons being accustomed to do accordynge to the order of the Common Lawes of this Realme....

Sir William Blackstone, first Vinerian Professor of Law in the University of Oxford, began his four volume *Commentary on the Laws of England* in 1753, and this was to become a most influential source book for law, not only in England but also in the American Colonies. Book IV concerns public wrongs, and in chapter 15, entitled 'Offences against the persons of individuals', he deals with mayhem, abduction, rape, sodomy, and then five inferior offences as he thinks them to be namely: assaults, batteries, wounding, false imprisonment and kidnapping. After some cautious advice about the need for substantial evidence to justify a conviction for rape (which has a modern ring in view of recent deliberations by the House of Lords and the Law Revision Committee) Blackstone continues with the following linking sentence:

IV What has been here observed, especially with regard to the manner of proof, which ought to be the more clear in proportion as the crime is the more detestable, may be applied to another offence, of a still deeper malignity; the infamous crime against nature, committed either with man or beast. A crime, which ought to be strictly and impartially proved, and then as strictly and impartially punished. But it is an offence of so dark a nature, so easily charged, and the negative so difficult to be proved, that the accusation should be clearly made out: for, if false, it deserves a punishment inferior only to that of the crime itself.

I will not act so disagreeable a part, to my readers as well as myself, as to dwell any longer upon a subject, the very mention of which is a disgrace to human nature. It will be more eligible to imitate in this respect the delicacy of our English law, which treats it, in its very indictments as a crime not fit to be named; 'peccatum illud horribile, inter christianos non nominandum'. Which leads me to add a word concerning its punishment.

This, the voice of nature and reason, and the express law of God (Levit. XX 13, 15), determined to be capital. Of which we have a signal instance, long before the Jewish dispensation, by the destruction of two cities by fire from heaven; so that this is an universal, not merely a provincial, precept. And our ancient law in some degree imitated this punishment, by commanding such miscreants to be burnt to death; though Fleta says they should be buried alive: either of which punishments was indifferently used for this crime among the ancient Goths. But now the general punishment of all felonies is the same, namely by hanging: and this offence (being in the times of popery only subject to ecclesiastical censures) was made felony without benefit of clergy by statute 25 Hen. VIII c. 6 revived and confirmed by 5 Eliz. c. 17. And the rule of law herein is, that if both are arrived at years of discretion, agentes et consentientes pari poena plectantur.

(Quoted from W. Blackstone. Commentaries on the Laws of England, 14th edn, Book IV, chapter 15, Section 216 printed in London 1803 by A. Strahan. This edition contains the last corrections by Blackstone himself and was prepared for publication by Edward Christian, Downing Professor of Law in the University of Cambridge.)

The early English legal treatise *Fleta* and the nearly contemporary subsequent treatise *Britton* gives burying and burning as the appropriate punishments, but scholars doubt if these late thirteenth-century authorities are correct as to punishments actually given in England at this time. Blackstone may indirectly offer the true explanation, that the Goths used this barbarity. In any case by the time of Henry VIII, church authorities could not administer capital punishments themselves.

ADDITIONAL NOTE 2

Wilde's opinions of Homosexuality and Christianity

(a) Wilde's moral views were of an intuitive rather than rational kind. Although he was often at pains to voice epigrams which were intended to outrage conventional moral opinions, his chief concern was to contend for artistic freedom, and he was not in a general sense radical in either his political or social aims. In his very long letter written to Lord Alfred Douglas early in 1897 from H.M. Prison, Reading, he writes:

Morality does not help me. I am a born antinomian. I am one of those who are made for exceptions, not for laws. But while I see that there is nothing wrong in what one does, I see there is something wrong in what one becomes. It is well to have learned that. (*The Letters of Oscar Wilde*, ed. Rupert Hart-Davis, London 1962)

This is, of course, part of the famous letter earlier published in abbreviated form as 'De Profundis'. The original typescript was given to the British Museum in 1909 on the condition that no one be allowed to see it for fifty years. Rupert Hart-Davis has produced a definitive edition in his complete volume of Wilde's letters, 1962.

Wilde clearly regrets the ruin his life has become as a result of his trials, and his letter shows that he despises himself for allowing his 'unintellectual friendship' with Douglas to have dominated his life. But it is Douglas, not pederasty, that he is repudiating, as his subsequent conduct in Paris shows, and he seems to have remained convinced that, for him, the physical expression of the 'love that dare not speak its name' was not only a strange shameful excitement, but also morally justified in his exceptional case. His most explicit recorded defence of homosexual love appears in the transcript of his second trial, when prosecuting counsel cross-examines him about the meaning of one of Douglas' poems published in *The Chameleon*. The poem is called 'Two Loves' and depicts an encounter between the two, in which the first (heterosexual) claims to be the true love, and accuses the other of being a lying impostor whose name is 'shame':

> Then sighing said the other, 'Have thy will, I am the Love that dare not speak its name.'

Having read this, Counsel then asks 'Is it not clear that the love described related to natural love and unnatural love?' Wilde replies, 'No', and then produces his famous, apparently unprepared defence, which probably ensured his subsequent acquittal:

> What is the 'Love that dare not speak its name'?—'The Love that dare not speak its name' in this century is such a great affection of an elder for a younger man as there was between David and Jonathan, such as Plato made the very basis of his philosophy, and such as you find in the sonnets of Michelangelo and Shakespeare. It is that deep, spiritual affection that is as pure as it is perfect. It dictates and pervades great works of art like those of Shakespeare and Michelangelo, and those two letters of mine, such as they are. It is in this century misunderstood, so much misunderstood that it may be described as the 'Love that dare not speak its name', and on account of it I am placed where I am now. It is beautiful, it is fine, it is the noblest form of affection. There is nothing unnatural about it. It is intellectual, and it repeatedly exists between an elder and a younger man, when the elder man has intellect, and the younger man has all the joy, hope and glamour of life before him. That it should be so the world does not understand. The world mocks at it and sometimes puts one in the pillory for it. (Quoted from Hyde *Trials*, op. cit., p. 236)

As described, with great stress on the emotion and intellect, Wilde is endowing homosexual love with an heroic character, but as far as his own life was concerned, the majority of his homosexual associations were of a brief and sordid kind with men who were, in effect, male prostitutes, and this speech, for all its effectiveness in court, must be taken as what Wilde hoped for rather than what he achieved.

(b) Wilde's death-bed conversion to Catholicism was not forced upon him by a well-meaning friend, but a planned decision of his own.

It was at Oxford and in Reading Gaol that Wilde seems to have thought most carefully about religion. Oxford of the seventies was preoccupied with the Tractarians, and Wilde knew some of them. Several of his friends became Catholics, and he records in his letters his own attraction to the 'Scarlet Woman'. There were influences on the Anglican side; his uncle was a rector in Lincoln, and he often stayed there and in other clerical households. He paid two visits to Italy, receiving a personal blessing by the Pope at the second of these, and began conversations with a Catholic priest in Oxford who observed that 'the finger of God has not yet touched him'. Wilde said that it was the fear that his father would disinherit him which kept him from taking the step, and he found that a legacy of £3,000 from another relative was cut to £100 because of his known attraction to Catholicism. He sent a fairly orthodox poem on 'The Resurrection' to Gladstone, then Prime Minister, who received it courteously.

At this time Wilde seems to have been a believing Christian, not only attending services, but reading the Psalms, and quoting from them in a way that indicates personal faith (Letter of 26 July 1876, Hart-Davis, op. cit., p. 20). His father died just before Oscar heard that he had gained a First, and he writes of this to a friend as follows:

> My poor mother is in great delight and I was overwhelmed with telegrams on Thursday from everyone I know. My father would have been so pleased about it. I think God has dealt very hardly with us. It has robbed me of any real pleasure in my First, and I have not sufficient faith in providence to believe it is all for the best—I know it is not. . . . I heard the Cardinal (Manning) at the Pro-Cathedral preach a charity sermon. He is more fascinating than ever. (Letter of 10 July 1876, Hart-Davis, op. cit., p. 15)

By the end of the summer of 1877, however, on his return from Greece, Wilde shows clearly in his letters that he has decided to remain free from the Church as an institution. Twenty years later, in his letter to Lord Alfred Douglas from Reading, Wilde devotes a fifth of it, some 12,000 words, to the character of Jesus, whom he clearly admires. He begins by showing why religion does not help him:

> Religion does not help me. The faith that others give to what is unseen, I give to what one can touch and look at. My Gods dwell in temples made with hands, and within the circle of actual experience is my creed made perfect and complete: too complete it may be, for like many or all of those who have placed their Heaven in this earth, I have found in it not merely the beauty of Heaven, but the horror of Hell also. When I think about Religion at all, I feel as if I would like to found an order for those who cannot believe: the Confraternity of the Fatherless one might call it. . . . (Letter to Douglas, Hart-Davis, p. 468)

With this quotation may be contrasted:

> Christ's place indeed is with the poets. His whole conception of Humanity sprang right out of the imagination and can only be realised by it. . . . He was the first to conceive the divided races as a unity. . . . There is still something to me almost incredible in the idea of a young Galilean peasant imagining that he could bear on his own shoulders the burden of the entire world; all that had been already done and suffered, and all that was yet to be done and

suffered . . . the suffering of those whose name is Legion and whose dwelling is among the tombs, oppressed nationalities, factory children, thieves, people in prison, outcasts, those who are dumb under oppression and whose silence is heard only of God: and not merely imagining this but actually achieving it, so that at the present moment all who come in contact with his personality, even though they may neither bow to his altar nor kneel before his priest, yet somehow find that the ugliness of their sins is taken away and the beauty of their sorrow revealed to them. (p. 477)

As the letter goes on, Wilde seems to be describing his own attempt to find acceptance from Christ, and he expresses it in terms which are a fascinating mixture of orthodoxy and interpretations of his own:

But it is when he deals with the Sinner that he is most romantic, in the sense of most real. The world had always loved the Saint as being the nearest possible approach to the perfection of God. Christ, through some divine instinct in him, seems to have always loved the sinner as being the nearest possible approach to the perfection of man. . . .

Of course the sinner must repent. But why? Simply because otherwise he would be unable to realise what he had done. The moment of repentance is the moment of initiation. More than that. It is the means by which one alters one's past. The Greeks thought that impossible. They often say in their gnomic aphorisms 'Even the Gods cannot alter the past'. Christ showed that the commonest sinner could do it. . . . It is difficult for most people to grasp the idea. I dare say one has to go to prison to understand it. If so, it may be worth while going to prison.

There is something so unique about Christ. Of course, just as there are false dawns before the dawn itself, and winter-days so full of sudden sunshine that they will cheat the wise crocus into squandering its gold before its time, and make some foolish bird call to its mate to build on barren boughs, so there were Christians before Christ. For that we should be grateful. The unfortunate thing is that there have been none since. I make one exception, St. Francis of Assisi. . . . He understood Christ and so he became like him. We do not require the *Liber Conformitatium* to teach us that the life of St. Francis was the true *Imitatio Christi*: a poem compared to which the book that bears the name is merely prose. Indeed, that is the charm about Christ, when all is said. He is just like a work of art himself. He does not really teach one anything, but by being brought into his presence one becomes something. And everybody is predestined to his presence. Once at least in his life each man walks with Christ to Emmaus. (Hart-Davis, *The Letters of Oscar Wilde*, pp. 486–7)

It is interesting that Malcolm Muggeridge, who in recent years has discovered his own faith by walking the road to Emmaus with a television camera team, used Wilde's last sentence to introduce the programme.

In his middle years, when asked what his religion was, Wilde replied, 'Well, you know, I don't think I have any. I am an Irish

Protestant', but he gives a rather more positive answer in a letter to Charles Leyland, 1882:

> Prayer is a compliment, a spiritual courtesy, which one may surely hope is appreciated in the proper place. But it must never be answered: if it is, it ceases to be prayer and becomes a correspondence. (Letters, op. cit., p. 186)

From these hints and fragments, it is only possible to say that Wilde was in his own way keenly alert to the fundamentals of religion, but it was part of his whole understanding of himself that he should remain uncommitted to its conventional expression. There is no reason to doubt the genuineness of his final decision, and it seems that, apart from the oblique reference to David and Jonathan, he was not interested in the biblical texts about homosexuality, having satisfied himself that Christ in the end would accept him as he was.

ADDITIONAL NOTE 3

John Addington Symonds

J. A. Symonds was a wellknown nineteenth-century Essayist, whose ability as a writer was less than that of Oscar Wilde or Lytton Strachey, and who would, therefore, have passed by now into obscurity if he had not been a homosexual who left a large number of letters recording his inner conflict. These letters have been largely collected in a trunk bequeathed to the University of Bristol Library, and they have been put in order and published in three volumes by two American scholars, H. M. Schueller and R. L. Peters. In 1964 a biography of Symonds by Phillis Grosskurth appeared, which includes references to these letters, and to his unpublished autobiography. Montgomery Hyde has also been allowed to read the autobiography and quotes from it indirectly in his section on Symonds (*The Other Love*, op. cit., pp. 101–7). The revival of interest in Symonds is certainly due to the general concern about homosexual problems in the sixties.

Symonds was born on 5 October 1840, the son of a wellknown Bristol doctor. He went to Harrow in 1854 and to Balliol College, Oxford, in 1858, becoming a Fellow of Magdelen College in 1862, and marrying Miss Catherine North in 1864. His frail health prevented him from continuing to teach and, after a short period at the Temple, he divided his time between Italy and Switzerland, writing and lecturing intermittently. He published privately for restricted circulation two monographs on the ethical problems associated with homosexuality, the first *A Problem in Greek Ethics* in 1883, and the second *A Problem in Modern Ethics* in 1891. In the last years of his life he worked on a biography of Michelangelo whom he was convinced was a homosexual (letter to Edmund Gosse, 18 September 1891) and in June 1892 he began a correspondence with Havelock Ellis (letter in Bristol University Library no. 1984) which led to their co-operation in writing the second volume of *The studies in the Psychology of Sex* concerned with sexual inversion. Symonds died on 19 April 1893 in Rome.

In the preface to the essay on *Greek Ethics*, Symonds notes that it was originally written in 1873, and was several times read to special audiences as a lecture, but is now published in a limited way for the first time. The essay is concerned with *paiderastia* which he describes as the Greek institution of 'boy love'. (Published in London 1901—a hundred limited copies, of which the University of Bristol has No. 9 from which these quotes are taken.)

He argues that the institution is not mentioned in Homer or other early Greek literature, but when it does appear later it is regarded as a 'heroic' relationship, akin to the Christian idea of chivalry, an ideal rather than a reality. Among the explanations of the origins of 'boy love' he quotes the myth of the Rape of Ganymede, and he is anxious all through the essay to distinguish between the 'heroic' and 'vulgar' strands of thought about this, as he says the Greeks always distinguished the two. 'The one' [he writes, pp. 30–1] 'was chivalrous and martial and received a formal organization in the Dorian states; the other, sensual and lustful, though localized to some extent at Crete, came to pervade the Greek cities like a vice.'

Later in the essay (p. 43) he refers to the public brothels for males established in Athens in the fifth century BC, provided by the State which derived part of its revenues from them. It was in one of these that Socrates first saw Phaedo, who became his pupil. The effect of the approval of paiderastia was the debasement of women (p. 54), but even so lesbianism among them was not approved, and was regarded by the men of Athens in the same way as men in England now think of homosexuals.

In his final paragraphs, Symonds describes how he understands the original Christian reaction to the vicious forms of 'boy love' and male prostitution prevalent in the Mediterranean cities (p. 32):

> In the first century of the Roman Empire, Christianity began its work of reformation. When we estimate the effect of Christianity, we must bear in mind that the early Christians found paganism disorganised, and humanity veering to a precipice of ruin. The first efforts were then directed towards checking the sensuality of Corinth, Athens, Rome, the capitals of Syria and Egypt. Christian asceticism, in the corruption of the pagan system, led logically to the cloister and the hermitage. . . . To the impassioned followers of Christ, nothing was left but the separation from nature which had become unbearable in its mastery of men. But the convent was a mutual

abandonment of social problems. Not in escape, but in the fellow-service of men and women must be found the solution of social problems.

Between the first and second essay, the 1885 Act was passed and Symonds refers to it critically a number of times in letters of this period. He also asks Wilde to send him a copy of *Dorian Gray*, which he describes as having 'a morbid and perfumed manner of treating such psychological subjects. It seems calculated to confirm the prejudices of the vulgar.' (Letter No. 1810, 22 July 1890.) In the second essay, he summarizes his arguments against the Labouchère amendment:

The points suggested for consideration are whether England is still justified in restricting the freedom of adult persons, and rendering certain abnormal forms of sexuality criminal, by any real dangers to society: after it has been shown,

(1) that abnormal inclinations are congenital, natural and ineradicable in a large percentage of individuals;
(2) that we tolerate sterile intercourse of various types between the two sexes;
(3) that our legislation has not suppressed the immorality in question;
(4) that the operation of the Code Napoléon for nearly a century has not increased this immorality in France;
(4) that Italy, with the experience of the Code Napoléon to guide her, adopted its principles in 1889;
(6) that the English penalties are rarely inflicted to their full extent;
(7) that their existence encourages blackmailing, and agitation;
(8) that our higher education is in open contradiction to the spirit of our laws.

Elaborating on the last of these points, Symonds suggested that higher education

still rests on the study of the Greek and Latin classics, a literature impregnated with paiderastia. It is carried on at public schools, where young men are kept apart from females and where homosexual vices are frequent. The best minds of our youth are therefore exposed to the influence of a paiderastic literature, at the same time that they acquire the knowledge and experience of unnatural practices. Nor is any trouble taken to correct these adverse influences by physiological instruction in the laws of sex. (Quoted from H. M. Hyde, *The Other Love*, pp. 102–3. For a fuller assessment of Symonds and his Essays see Weeks, *Coming Out*, op. cit., chap. 4).

ADDITIONAL NOTE 4

Legal Prohibitions in other countries

Roman Law prohibited male homosexual practices long before the Christian era, by the Lex Scantinia of *c.* 226 BCE, but the law was infrequently invoked and then mostly for political purposes. By the middle of the third century CE homosexual prostitution, which before had been tolerated and taxed as a useful source of state income, became proscribed, and minors were protected from homosexual assault. The Christian emperors increased the penalties for these offences, and by a new law of 390 CE, active sodomites, or perhaps procurers of boys for prostitution, could incur the penalty of death by burning. The greatest Roman legal reformer, Justinian, issued two edicts concerning homosexual practices in 538 and 544 CE. Neither of these edicts changed the law nor the severe punishments associated with it, but concentrated chiefly on exhorting those guilty of these offences to repentance and forgiveness as a better way than risking conviction. Justinian clearly accepts the interpretation of the Sodom story which explains its destruction as an act of divine vengeance for homosexual practices, and is anxious to preserve his own empire from a similar fate.

In Europe generally, this teaching was followed and penalties of burning or castration were continued, both under Charlemagne, and in the later German states. Some church leaders, and notably Pius V in the sixteenth century, discouraged severe punishments, especially for those who indulged in homosexual acts only occasionally, but pederasts were still being burned in France in 1750. Lesbians were also punished, and Ellis quotes a story taken from Montaigne's *Journal* of a French girl who married another woman and was hanged in Vitry le Francois 'for using illicit inventions for supplying the defects of her sex' (Ellis, op cit., p. 259). (Some centuries earlier, the only charge actually proved against Joan of Arc was that she wore male clothing.) After the French Revolution, the new Code Napoléon of 1810 made a clear distinction between civil crimes and moral and religious offences, concerning itself only with the former. Private homosexual practices between two consenting adults were not punishable under the Code, unless there was public outrage, or lack of consent by force or through minority.

In more recent times, among the European countries, Austria, Holland, Switzerland, Greece, Denmark, and Sweden have made similar provisions to the French, while Norway does not enforce the old law except in protection of young people. In Germany homosexual acts were statutory offences and a recommendation of a committee in 1927 to limit the application of the law to offences 'in aggravated circumstances' was defeated by Nazi legislation in 1935, which also provided for increased prison sentences. Since 1967, homosexual acts between males over 21 have ceased to be criminal in West Germany and in East Germany the law is the same but the age of consent is 18 years. The age of consent now varies in Europe between 16 and 21, and several legislatures are considering the argument for lowering them. The Russian Penal Code of 1926 ignored homosexual offences, but in line with the general reversal of policy in sexual matters, a decreee of 1934 made homosexual practices among males a 'social crime' to be punished by imprisonment for between three and five years. Other Eastern bloc countries tend to be more liberal, primarily concerned to protect minors and prevent commercial exploitation.

Beyond Europe, Moslem countries tend to respect the condemnation in the Koran. Morocco, for example, revived the ancient prohibition after independence, and recent newspaper reports from Iran indicate that capital punishment has been in fact carried out for adult homosexuals. Among African countries, gross indecency among males is punished by imprisonment in Ghana and Nigeria, and the laws of the Australian State and New Zealand remain as the English law before 1967. South African law imposes heavier sentences. Japan does not prohibit homosexual behaviour where there is consent, but children of either sex under 13 years are held unable to give it.

In America, the situation is too complex to record here in detail, partly because it is a matter for State and not Federal Law, and partly because there has been considerable pressure towards liberalization in recent years. It is probable, at the time of writing, that more than half the States continue to punish homosexual behaviour among male adults with a range of punishments severe or trivial. In 1973, the American Bar Association adopted a resolution calling for 'the repeal of all State Laws which classify as criminal non-commercial sex between consenting adults', but as West observes, American public opinion and politicians are not yet ready for the change. The situation is similar to that in England in the early sixties. (West, *Homosexuality re-examined*, op. cit., p. 291, chap. 10 contains an up-to-date summary of present law. Dr Hammelmann's essay in *They Stand Apart*, op. cit., Part 3, gives a very full description of the legal situation in other countries as it was in 1955. A few years later Norman St John Stevas covered the American situation fully in *Life, Death and the Law* (Eyre & Spottiswoode 1961), pp. 310ff. The research for this book was done at Harvard.)

ADDITIONAL NOTE 5

Letter to 'Theology', January 1952, from Mr Graham Dowell, headed

The Church and Homosexuals

To the Editor of Theology:

Dear Sir,

A recent correspondence in the columns of the New Statesman and Nation has exposed not only the anomalies latent in our civil laws for the punishment of homosexual practices, but also a widespread doubt as to the wisdom of any penal measures whatsoever. Yet, although this vexed question must be judged to come within the domain of faith and morals, and so under the judgement of the Church, no Christian comment is to be found. It is with the hope that some Christian re-statement of the problem may be evoked that I trust it is neither inappropriate nor untimely for a layman to raise it in your columns: to ask, in fact, what the Christian conscience, acting under the charity and humanity as under the discipline and wisdom of the Church, has to say to the homosexual, who wishes to be an active and healthy member of the Christian community.

I venture to think that this is a pressing pastoral and ethical problem. Is homosexual concubinage to be treated purely and simply as an unio illicita, like fornication, and are those who practise it to be judged as 'living in sin' and to be deprived of the sacraments of the Church? If so, what are we to say to those who profess to be congenitally homosexual? There are some who say, though this seems to be doubted by some psychiatrists, that the state is incurable: and others who think that it is not the homosexual who needs to be 'cured' but those who think he should be. At any rate, there are many who, desiring adjustment and seeking psychiatric and medical treatment, have found no cure: and some of these, who would otherwise be unhappy, neurotic and ineffective members of society, have found not only solace but opportunity for service through accepting what would appear to be their 'natural' state. This is no place to assess the contribution of homosexuals to the cultural, social and even religious well-being of, to mention no others, our European heritage: this is surely indisputable. What is needed is a Christian judgement of our English treatment of the homosexual, dictated as it is by a penal code and a public opinion sadly lagging behind those of our neighbours.

We are still lamentably accustomed to raising this question in hushed and embarrassed tones: if it is raised it is either side-tracked or, to invert a saying of Charles Williams from your columns, 'the hungry sheep look up for morals and are given metaphysics'. Is it too much to hope that the light and fresh air admitted, perhaps too freely during the last fifty years, to the problems of sexual morality in general may be extended during the next fifty, and as soon as possible, to the particular problems of the homosexual? It should be emphasized that a distinctively Christian approach need not be quixotic or romantic: that would rightly be construed as open approval of the relationship and an invitation to licence. Neither need it merely find 'gross indecency' where many have found great beauty. The Christian conscience should distinguish between promiscuity and fidelity, between, in fact, the invert and the pervert: it should then examine both the justice and the expediency of a penal code which, far from curing or deterring the homosexual, has so often led to crime (particularly in the form of blackmail), to bravado, or to the tragedy of wrecked lives.

49 Frognal, Hampstead,
London N.W.3

Yours faithfully,
GRAHAM DOWELL

PART D
Old Morality or New

Introduction
The Dilemma For Pastors And Moral Theologians

One effect of the passing of the 1967 Sexual Offences Act has been a greater freedom among homosexual people to discuss their condition and problems with others, including Christian pastors, and the pastors in their turn have had some need of reliable guidance as to what the Christian attitude now is.

If they look around extensively for that guidance, they will find, in fact, a wide range of attitudes and very little which pretends to be authoritative, except among those who reiterate the traditional teaching of the Bible or the Church. Herein lies the dilemma of the pastor. Traditionalists claim that the moral teaching is clear and should be maintained against all attacks from our pluralist and increasingly secular society. Those who feel obliged to take seriously the implications for Christian morality of the data we now have about human sexuality speak less decisively, sometimes suggesting that homosexual friendships are acceptable but physical activities are not, while some accept these provided they take place within the context of a stable relationship.

The question as to whether it is permissible for a pastor to 'bless' a homosexual relationship which both partners intend to be permanent is no longer merely a theoretical one. The pastor finds himself therefore under pressure from both sides, reluctant to reject the homosexual who seeks his help, reluctant to depart fully from the tradition of the institution he represents.

The moral theologian, from whom the pastor might expect clear guidance, experiences the same dilemma. If he merely restates the tradition, he may convince only traditionalists. If he attempts to come to terms with the new knowledge, he will find that agreed facts with which to work are somewhat elusive, and he still has to decide how this information is to be used. To what extent has there to be a distinctive 'givenness' about Christian ethics; to what extent can it be an empirical science; to what extent can it be situational, seeking only to inject the spiritual perception of agapaistic love to the facts of a case discovered as fully as rational investigation permits?

The dilemma of the pastor has not, of course, arisen only with homosexual problems, but in the whole range of sexual life among adults and young people. The so-called trend towards permissiveness needs no elaboration here, but that is only a symptom of a more fundamental and long-term change which is clearly seen in twentieth-century society, the progress towards equality for women. Insofar as it is possible to identify any underlying theological causes for a progress which has seemed to be inevitable, these may be traced back to the Reformation. Whereas Luther regarded the sexual aspects of marriage as *medicina libidinis*, God's provision to release fallen mankind from lust, Calvin and later Protestant ethicists increasingly emphasized the relational aspect of marriage. Calvin, for example, castigated Jerome for branding as unclean what Christ had honoured as his symbol of the union of the Church.[1]

The obvious examples of women's liberation have been her acceptance as a partner at work away from home, and as an equal in higher education. Whereas the Christian sexual ethic was based on the family unit in a stable society, hierarchical, static, and locally based, in which the regulation of marriage ceremonies and the control of consanguinity were the chief effective constraints, once women and men found themselves meeting at work and leisure and not only at home in the evenings and weekends in a private domestic setting, the traditional teachings about fidelity, continence, and chastity lost their social and economic buttressing. The development of cheap and readily available contraceptives was encouraged by the desire for family limitation and freedom for women to share the less domestically fixed life-style of men, rather than as the deliberate encouragement of safe fornication, though the church bodies between the wars who feared that consequence were not mistaken.

However, once men and women and particularly young people became free to share daily life, and perhaps often experience partnerships outside the home in which their joint skills and insights were fully engaged, physical desires would inevitably also arise. Not only in the office liaison, but more starkly in the creative professions sexual intimacy could become an assumed concomitant of working together. The pastor's appeal to maintain marital fidelity lost cogency in such situations where home life became the secondary relationship, and children a weekend hobby. Parliament had little choice but to respond to this new situation by progressively removing the legal barriers to divorce and providing social security for one-parent families. Once heterosexual coupling outside marriage had become a matter of individual choice and conscience, insistently advocated by a flood of permissive films, novels, and magazines, it was to be expected that intelligent and reflective homosexual people would begin to seek the same freedom. And so the pastoral dilemma presented by heterosexual freedom has re-occurred for homosexual relationships.

The next two chapters trace from Victorian times until 1979 the Christian attempts to resolve this dilemma. Those who hoped to preserve the old tradition maintained that chastity and sympathetic pastoral care should be the policy. Those who were more influenced by the New Morality Movement and the demand to end discrimination against homosexual people by the Churches, explored the possibilities of consent within limits. A Church of England Board of Social Responsibility working party, which reported in 1970 that it was divided on this issue, conveniently marks a midpoint in the discussion.

9 Chastity and Pastoral Care

A Chastity maintained in the 1920s

The Evangelical revival and the Tractarian movement have left an abiding legacy in terms of the present constituency of the Church of England, but in Victorian times their contribution to moral theology was marked more by a vigorous study of their theological forebears than by fresh or different insights of their own. Perhaps that is a dangerous simplification, but some evidence for it can be found in the publishing policy of the two groups. Calvin's commentaries and those of Matthew Henry were reproduced on the one side, while the other concentrated on the works of the Early Church Fathers.

Henry, like Calvin, has little to say about the relevant biblical texts beyond affirming the traditional view, and the Fathers, as we have seen, were unanimous in their condemnation of homosexual behaviour. These works were readily available in the theological college libraries and perhaps on the shelves of the more learned clergymen of the nineteen-twenties. Jeremy Taylor's *Holy Living* would also be available to confirm this view. More forthright was Henry Liddon, a friend of Pusey, and the Ireland Professor of Exegesis at Oxford University from 1870 to 1882. His commentary on Romans was published in 1893, posthumously. On the relevant verses Liddon writes that the heathen lose their natural knowledge of God by their indifference to him, and this leads to 'fetichism' and abandonment to the moral consequences of this unfaithfulness. It is clear from the context that by fetichism he means idolatry, but this neglect of the creator leads on to sensual degradation which assumes unnatural forms in both sexes. He then cites the usual Latin and Greek authors to remind his readers of the 'well-known shame' which characterized pagan society of that time.[1]

It would be unfair, however, to limit the action of the Church at that time on the question of homosexuality in the early nineteen-hundreds to a reiteration of these statements by the biblical exegetes. The educational work of the Archbishop's Advisory Board has already been noted, but there was also within the Anglo-Catholic tradition the ministry of spiritual counsel to penitents, revived by Pusey and adopted in High Church parishes. The chief guide book for those priests who wished to learn this ministry was Pusey's abridgement of the classic *Le Manuel de Confesseurs* by the Roman Catholic Abbé J. J. Gaume, first published in 1837, often reprinted in France, and in Pusey's version well known in England. In the original, Gaume suggests questions on each of the Ten Commandments which could be used to examine penitents. It is noteworthy that Pusey reproduced all the questions, except those arising from the seventh commandment, which he excludes entirely, with the observation that in sexual matters, great harm can be done by specifying sins to those who may have previously been unaware that such practices existed. This reticence will also be found in a more recent Roman Catholic manual. Examples of later Anglican teaching for use by confessors confronted with homosexual behaviour will also be referred to when these occur chronologically.

Two other books of this period deserve mention. The first is *The Manual for Confessors* by F. G. Belton, originally published by Mowbrays in 1916, several times revised, and still on sale in the late sixties. In the third revised edition of 1936, Belton notes in his preface that he has included additional sections on subjects which have come into prominence in recent years, including the relation of psycho-analytical practice to the method of the confessional, which he believed had been seriously misunderstood, and he has provided a revised bibliography which, at that date, included works by the Anglican moral theologians, Kirk and Mortimer, as well as references to the new cheap and full edition of the *Summa Theologica* of St Thomas Aquinas made by the fathers of the English Dominican Province.

Belton does not deal with the question of homosexuality specifically, (even in the 1949 revision) but takes all forms of sexual sin together, including fornication and masturbation and all forms of impurity as did Gaume, recommending confessors to take a strict line and refuse absolution unless the penitent promises to abandon them.

Writing for a more general public, the popular preacher Canon Peter Green, who was in many respects liberal for his time, took a firmly traditional line on sexual ethics in his *The Problem of Right Conduct* of 1931. Although in his historical assessment of the waning incidence of homosexuality in the Christian era, and the explanation he offers for its causes, he writes as someone doing little more than offering the conventional Christian opinions of his time, it is also true that he identifies the main issues that will be debated thirty years later concerning law reform and gay liberation. His mention of 'The New Morality' and the governmental provision of V.D. clinics also shows that some issues are perennial.

In chapter 10 entitled 'Ethics of a social being', Green includes a short comment on unnatural vice, having in the previous paragraphs dismissed the teaching of the new morality school that fornication is permissible as sinful indulgence, wrongly encouraged by the government's recent provision of V.D. clinics.

It is impossible, in a book on Christian ethics altogether to ignore the subject of unnatural vice. As a matter of history, it cannot be denied that one of the moral triumphs of Christianity was the cleansing of society from unnatural vice such as disgraced society in Imperial Rome, and such as still disgraces China and India. But today, in Western Europe and in America, there is a disquieting tendency among a small but determined minority to reverse the judgement of history and to represent the men and women addicted to these practices as more to be pitied than to be blamed, and as so constituted by nature that they have a right to 'live their own lives' and 'develop their own natural instincts', untrammelled by laws made by men unaffected by these special desires.[2]

Green continues the passage by discussing the prevalence of this 'perversion', which he thinks may amount to two per cent in sophisticated states, but is virtually unknown in simple society, proving its unnaturalness. He thinks that the isolation of boys and girls in separate schools is the chief cause, and that the use of Confession and consultation with mental pathologists are the best lines of treatment. He concludes:

That the law should be so modified that unnatural offences should no longer be punished is not to be thought of. It may be wise to treat the matter as one of insanity—as we should treat a homicidal maniac, or a klepto-maniac, by treatment rather than by punishment rightly so-called—rather than of wilful crime. But the good of society and the protection of innocent third parties must be the first consideration.

Belton referred to Kenneth Kirk, Professor of Moral and Pastoral Theology at the time, and later Bishop of Oxford. Kirk was the leading Anglican moral theologian of this period and describes the task of Christian ethics in his *Some Principles of Moral Theology* of 1921.

The standing problem of all ethics is the reconciliation of two apparently opposed principles, which may be called respectively the principles of law and liberty, or of authority and individualism. Particularly is this the case with Christian ethics. A society which has its roots in divine revelation once given (however much expanded under the later guidance of the Spirit)—a society moreover of which it is a fundamental principle that no member lives to himself alone—cannot dispense with authority and law. Limits must be set to the freedom of the individual. Yet they must not interfere with his *true* freedom: he must be free to develop every part of his personality to its utmost in the service of God and his neighbour. Christian theology then, above all other thought, is called to the task of solving this problem—the reconciliation of authority with freedom.

Later in the Preface, Kirk describes his own view of the value of modern psychology:

One purpose of this book is to indicate in general terms the extent of agreement which exists between modern psychological practice and the 'ascetic' principles of the Church. It is sometimes urged, on insufficient grounds, that Catholic methods of dealing with souls are antiquated or mistaken, and it is consequently important to recognise that, so far from this being the case, there is a quite extraordinary degree of identity between the methods on the one hand of Scaramelli and Jeremy Taylor, and on the other of Starbuck, James, Welton and their colleagues. The great Catholic directors of souls based their practice, no doubt, on experience rather than on scientific knowledge. But they brought to bear upon their experience an insight and power of criticism of exceptional truth and acuteness; and psychology is daily vindicating the accuracy of their teaching.

B Charitable questionings in the 1930s

Kenneth Kirk's abiding contribution from his Oxford period, and notably in his Bampton Lectures, published as *The Vision of God* in 1931 was the affirmation that Christian morality was academically respectable and had nothing to fear from the new sciences provided it combined flexibility with a thorough knowledge of the basic truths given in the past. Despite this confidence, in fact the study of Christian ethics suffered something of an eclipse as the Second World War approached, and remained a cinderella subject right through to the later fifties, a sad fact exemplified by the abandonment of the paper from the General Ordination Examination for a number of years.

This eclipse was due in part to the dissociation between theology and philosophy that followed the concern with biblical studies by the theologians and the search for new methods among the philosophers, of which logical positivism was the dominant school. As Ayer argued in his famous *Language, Truth and Logic* of 1936, ethical statements could not be verified analytically nor empirically and were therefore expressions of emotion. Perhaps the statement 'It's wrong to steal' had the same effect as the command 'Don't steal' for most hearers, but nevertheless it was readily concluded that the claims of morality had lost some of their status. In consequence, Christian morality was expressed in terms of training the individual conscience within the Church, and most books of the period concentrated on personal obligation and individual decisions, apart from the notable insistence of William Temple and his colleagues in the early ecumenical movement to press for a social order that resisted fascism and exploitive capitalism. Apart from R. H. Tawney, Reinhold Niebuhr was a lone voice with his *Moral Man and Immoral Society*—also published in 1936. If the perplexed pastor of the thirties had searched the religious book shops for suitable works to advise him about homosexuality, he would have found precious little, and what there was seldom included that word in the index.

Notable exceptions to this reticence were Herbert Gray in a book written with students in mind, and Leslie Weatherhead who had early seen that psychological studies were important for the pastor. Writing for clergy and ordinands, Pym, Dewar, and Hudson were the forerunners in offering psychological information, integrated as far as was possible at the time with the traditional Christian ascetic tradition. Although the brief quotations set out below obviously cannot do justice to the conscientious and pioneering work of these authors, they do give a glimpse of the typical counsel of the period. It was not without sympathy.

(a) H. GRAY, *Men, Women and God*

Gray's advice is rather moralistic in tone, commending daily cold baths for males, and a bracing life as the best means of resisting sexual temptations, reminiscent in some ways of the earlier days of the White Cross League. In chapter 8, entitled 'A girl's early days' he warns against the dangers of the grand passion for older women: 'inexorable developments take the bloom off it'. He goes on to make a direct appeal to all men and women who are involved in passionate relationships with members of their own sex:

> Do act before things have gone any further. Though you drifted into your present condition, and do not feel that any one time you did anything you felt to be wrong, do wake up and take hold of your life with both hands . . . face the plain facts openly together, and by common consent refuse to travel any further on a road which can only bring you acute pain and much loss of true usefulness.

He adds a footnote:

> I find a certain amount of talk going on in some quarters which assumes that some people are of the homosexual type, and that it is natural and right for them to express themselves in this way. But this seems to be a complete and serious mistake.[3]

(b) L. WEATHERHEAD, *The Mastery of Sex*

In describing homosexuality, Weatherhead distinguishes between innate and acquired kinds, the first being a congenital abnormality which cannot be called a vice. He suggests that a realization of this fact alone is of great comfort to innate inverts, whose mental torture is sometimes distressing. He then describes some pastoral problems with lesbian relationships, taking the view that younger partners are always in danger, and that for older women, the fact that they may be past child-bearing does not relieve them from anxieties of conscience. He accepts that cuddling among women in bed may be common, but warns that this supposedly harmless custom can lead to the arousing of sexual desires which have to remain unsatisfied.

While stressing that a cure is never easy, Weatherhead writes that analysis has sometimes given good results and that he has used hypnosis with success, and concludes:

The most that can be done in many cases is the removal of morbid emotion and self-loathing, the reduction of sexual hyperaesthesia, the fear that inversion is a sign of mental deficiency, and the strengthening of the patient's spiritual life, so that he may not cause others to acquire the perversion or endanger their well-being.[4]

(c) T. PYM, *Our Personal Ministry*

A young man aged twenty-five came to see me . . . the subject upon which he needed help was that of homosexuality. Now the first thing to note is that most clergy would feel rather awkward and not know what to say. Some would even require a translation of the word before they could understand it. Understanding it, many would regard it as a very peculiar and rather disgraceful thing, so peculiar indeed as not to fall within the clerical scope at all. This is just not true. Homosexual tendencies in bi-sexual people, both men and women, are common enough to fall within the scope of the shepherd of souls. Habitual adult inverts or perverts are common enough to require that a shepherd of souls should know enough of the subject to be able at least to start dealing with them. Yet it is unlikely that many, if any, theological colleges so much as mention the subject. It is hard to imagine a course of lectures for clergy on moral theology that would contain any reference to the subject at all.[5]

(d) DEWAR AND HUDSON, *Manual of Pastoral Psychology*

Homosexuality is referred to in this book a number of times. The first mention, oblique and in a footnote to the chapter on Clerical Failings, arises from an analysis of vanity, to which the clergy are said to be prone, and which, it is suggested, conceals a sense of inferiority and inadequacy, particularly in condemning sins in others to which they themselves are tempted. The footnote reads:

It seems not impossible for example, that the heavy legal penalties attached to homosexual vice represent an unconscious over-compensation for the lax standard of the community as a whole in regard to heterosexual sin—at least on the part of men.[6]

The main discussions of homosexuality occur in an additional note to chapter 5, 'Individual types' and in chapter 7 'Individual Treatments'. In the first reference a distinction is drawn between inversion, perversion, and bi-sexuality, with footnote references to Havelock Ellis, and these are defined:

A pervert is grossly immoral and bluntly described in Romans I:27. A bi-sexual person has a weak homosexual impulse eclipsed by the presence of a heterosexual object, and the invert is by contrast one whose sexual feelings are evoked solely and *exclusively* by members of his own sex.

Normal people are said to find incredible the fundamental fact that inverts regard sexual relations with the other sex abhorrent and unnatural and that the same abnormality is found in women as with men.[7]

On the subject of treatment, it is suggested that bi-sexual people may be helped towards normal sexual behaviour; but for true inverts, sympathy, help to accept his condition, and consultation with a psychoanalyst, where this can be afforded, are the rather cautious recommendations. A priest's advice might be:

It should be carefully pointed out to him (the true invert) that there is nothing in his condition of which he need be ashamed, and, in fact, that, until and unless God wills him to be changed, it is his vocation to be an invert. He should be shown how his peculiar temperament affords him various opportunities of service which are denied to his more normal brethren. Inverts, it has been well said, occupy a position in the middle of the road. This gives them a special advantage as advisers, and it is perhaps the secret of their undoubted gift of friendship which leads others naturally to turn to them for help. If the invert be a man, he should be shown that his position is not essentially different from that of many normally constituted women. For his real privation and trial is that he must cut out the possibility of marriage from his life; and this is the case with many normal heterosexual women.[8]

C Pre-War Roman Catholic Teaching

A standard Catholic manual of moral and pastoral theology for Roman Catholic priests in English available in this period was that of the Jesuit Priest, Henry Davis, S.J., originally published by Sheed and Ward in 1935 and reaching a final revised edition in 1946. Some Anglican clergy also used it. Davis, in his preface, explains that he aims to present for the clergy the common teaching of modern Catholic authors on moral and pastoral theology with reference to the Canons of the Codex Juris, and the recent decrees issued by the Sacred Roman Congregations, and he also acknowledges his debt to the English Dominicans for permission to use their English version of the *Summa Theologica*, published in 1921.

By comparing Aquinas' treatises on temperance, in which he includes consideration of chastity, modesty, and lust,[9] with the seventh chapter of Davis' second volume, entitled 'The Sixth and Ninth Commandments', it is clear that the same subject matter is being treated and with much the same teaching given, although Davis does not follow the 'question and answer' style of St Thomas. The last two sections of this chapter are written in Latin. As the rest of the whole work is in English, apart from some references, it seems that these must be intended mostly for priests or other readers able to translate it, the topics being thought unsuitable for ordinary laity to whom reticence is owed.

Section 7
is entitled 'De Peccatis externis contra Castitatem' with sub-divisions:
1. De Peccatis juxta Naturam
2. De Peccatis contra Naturam

Section 8

is entitled 'De Actibus Impudicitiae in Specie' with sub-divisions:

1. De Tactibus
2. De Aspectibus

The external sins against chastity according to nature are, fornication, adultery, incest, rape, and abduction; and those against nature are, masturbation, sodomy, and bestiality. Sodomy (*sodomia*) is defined as 'concubitus usque ad pollutionem inter personas ejusdem sexus per aliquam conjunctionem corporum'. After some further explanation of what is meant, and the inclusion of heterosexual sodomy, Davis continues:

> Essentia sodomiae consistit in affectu ad eundum sexum. Hoc peccatum est gravissimum, id quod patet ex eo quod est maxime contra naturam, et ex poenis gravissimis in jure antiquo et ab ipso Deo ob illud inflictis, et ex verbis S. Pauli (Rom. 1.26–28.)

With this may be compared Aquinas, Question 154, article 12 in the 1920 Dominican version:

> Since by the unnatural vices man transgresses that which has been determined by nature with regard to the use of venereal actions, it follows that in this matter this sin is gravest of all.

And he goes on to quote Augustine: *Conf.* 3.8:

> Those foul offences that are against nature should be everywhere and at all times detested and punished, such as were those of the people of Sodom, by the law of God, which hath not so made man that they should so abuse one another. For even that very intercourse which should be between God and us is violated, when that same nature, of which He is the Author, is polluted by the perversity of lust.

While it is clear from these quotations that Davis is in no degree departing from the ancient tradition as he had found it to be, nevertheless his work has a clarity and specific detail in the advice he gives to the clergy which many of them, no doubt, found more helpful than the reticence and hesitancy of the similar guidance offered to pastors in other books, and Davis urges on other pages the duty of the priest to be patient and sympathetic, lest by judgemental attitudes he frightens penitents away.

D The Church Assembly's Consideration of the Wolfenden Report

By the early summer of 1957 the Report of the Wolfenden Committee was being prepared for printing, and its main recommendations were known. At the Assembly's autumn session the whole of 14 November was given to debating the Report.

Since the Wolfenden Committee's recommendations covered both homosexuality and prostitution, the motion for the Assembly was framed to take account of both topics, together with the underlying principles, as follows:

That this Assembly generally approves the principles on which the criminal law concerned with sex behaviour should be based, as stated by the Wolfenden Committee, and also its recommendations relating to homosexuality; but it is unable to accept all its recommendations relating to prostitution.

The motion thus contained three substantial parts, and although the speakers mostly confined themselves to one of them, there was some risk of confusion in attempting to debate them all together, especially as the third was negative. It soon became clear that the recommendations concerning prostitution needed more study and the motion was split up into three for voting. The first part, referring to the principles, was accepted on a show of hands without exact numbers being counted. The second part, approving the recommendations relating to homosexuality, was also accepted narrowly, after a division, the count showing 155 votes in favour, 138 votes against. The majority was only 17, and the total vote cast, 293, was less than half of the Assembly's total membership. Abstentions were not recorded. The Assembly preferred to agree to a changed wording for the third part of the motion, and voted without a division 'that the recommendations relating to prostitution require further study'.

In opening the debate, the Bishop of Exeter was chiefly concerned with the principles that lay behind the Committee's recommendations, rather than with the details. The criminal law existed to protect both the rights of the individual and the community, but where neither was infringed, this law had no place. In mediaeval Christendom, it had been assumed that the purpose of the criminal law was also to enforce the observance of a particular moral code, but he thought this was inconsistent with Christian ethics. He supported the view of the Wolfenden Committee that morality was a matter of free choice and responsibility; the work of the Church in training souls was to dispense with coercion and establish a position in which acts were freely chosen because, and only because, of their rightness.

The Bishop then considered other examples of human behaviour, where the distinction between sins and crimes was already commonly accepted. Among them, he cited fornication, adultery, drunkenness, gluttony, heavy gambling, and homosexual behaviour among consenting women in private. But the law was not wholly consistent in the matter, and there were traces still of the older mediaeval conception in the treatment of homosexual practices between adult males. Incest he regarded as a special case, where the interests of the family needed protection. He also believed that the proposed change in the law, while not removing the risk of blackmail, would lessen it. Few things had horrified him so much as the evidence given in the Report of the attitude of certain chief constables, who had issued an instruction that the police were not to prosecute the blackmailer, but both of them for their homosexual activities. He thought that there was a certain robust objectivity about the Committee's Report. The Committee had denied that it considered homosexual practices to be necessarily symptoms of disease, or that it thought homosexuals necessarily suffered from diminished responsibility. And they were rightly careful to protect the young and mentally defective from exploitation. In conclusion, he rested his case on the manifest injustice of the present law in selecting one particular form of sexual behaviour for treatment as a criminal offence while others were left outside the law. The law could not make people chaste, but only seek to prevent the exposure of the immature to temptation, and try to create conditions in which it was difficult and not easy to be immoral. The task of teaching chastity and strengthening character belonged to the Church, and he did not think any researches into the etiology (*sic*) of homosexuality would add anything to what the Church knew already about the desperately sick heart of man, and the restorative powers of the grace of God.

The Bishop of St Albans seconded the motion, concentrating on the section concerning prostitution, and the rest of the morning was taken up with speeches by laymen. The first of these, Mr O. H. W. Clark, a Church Commissioner and member of the Assembly Standing Committee, hoped for a middle position, between the re-creation of a Calvinist position in which all sexual offences were regarded as crimes, and a total separation between sin and crime. Whatever the moral theologians said, he believed that the public at large did ascribe to the law a moral force so that if an action was not forbidden by law it was not wrong in their judgement. He hoped that no decision would be made until public opinion had time to be convinced.

After lunch the speeches were shorter. The Revd Kenneth Ross, Vicar of All Saints, Margaret Street, quoted figures from the Kinsey Report which seemed to him to justify the conclusion that over five hundred thousand men in the British Isles over sixteen years old were habitually committing homosexual acts which under the present law could lead to imprisonment. The magnitude of the problem was such that perhaps two million people were occasionally committing homosexual acts, but in 1955 only two thousand of them were proceeded against. It was inequitable to maintain the present law. Chancellor Garth Moore, a senior canon lawyer, took the view that morality and the law could not be completely dissociated, but that in this particular matter, over which the law had no effective control, it would be better to remove it to the realms of morality; the motion would not be licensing vice, but upholding a true morality which was not to be enforced by coercive measures.

It was left to two lay members of the Assembly to quote Scripture. The first, Major-General D. R. D. Fisher, from Salisbury, referred to the 'cities of the plain', and the second, Mr Goyder from Oxford, read the relevant passage from Romans chapter 1, and drew the conclusion that in this respect the old law was not wholly abrogated. 'This was a crime worthy of death because it was contrary to God's whole order, and undermined the whole order of humanity.' There was some reluctance to press the debate to a vote, but after some adroit chairmanship from the Archbishop of Canterbury (Fisher), the three motions were finally carried. In all, six bishops, eleven laymen, four clergymen, and two women contributed to the debate, all but four of them coming from the southern province.

In his concluding remarks, the Archbishop of Canterbury told the House that the bishops would soon have to speak on behalf of the Church in the House of Lords, and it would be helpful to them to know what the Assembly thought. Taken as a whole, the mood of the debate was a little sombre, as if the Assembly sensed that any forceful expression of opinion would be out of place. They had, in fact of course, been presented with a 'fait accompli'. The Moral Welfare Council had not sought their opinion before presenting their evidence to the Wolfenden Committee, yet nothing could now be gained by publicly repudiating it. On the narrow point of the injustice of the present criminal law, the Bishop of Exeter's case was strong; on the wider issue of the relationship between sin, morality, public opinion, and the law, the Bishop's view might well have been challenged by other theologians. In the event, it was left to Mr Goyder, a well-known industrialist of evangelical persuasion, to argue the opposite case strongly.[10]

E Action by the Methodist Church

Apart from the pastoral concern of individual ministers, the Methodist Church does not seem to have taken any direct corporate action until the announcement was made of the setting up of the Wolfenden Committee. At that stage, the Church's Citizenship Department co-operated with the Public Morality Council in preparing and submitting evidence to the Committee.[11]

After the Wolfenden Committee Report was published the Citizenship Department set up a working party to examine its detailed recommendations relating to homosexual offences, and the working party's Report was used as the basis of the Department's lengthy statement to the Methodist Conference in 1958. The most important part of this statement reads as follows:

The Department registers the judgement that the Wolfenden Report is a sane and responsible approach to the difficult questions with which it deals. We are generally agreed that the functions of the law, at any rate in relation to sexual behaviour is, as the Report states, the preservation of public order and decency and the protection of the citizen, particularly the young and vulnerable citizen. It is not the function of the law to interfere with private behaviour unless it can be shown that such behaviour is detrimental to the public good in an extraordinary degree. Thus, adultery, fornication and prostitution, though they are grievous sins, are not offences for which a person can be punished by the criminal law. Sin and crime are not synonymous terms.

The Department agrees with the recommendation that homosexual behaviour between consenting adults be no longer a criminal offence. We considered with the utmost care the arguments of those who oppose this Recommendation and who fear that the removal of the ban of illegality would lead to an increase in homosexual behaviour. We believe that this possibility has been exaggerated and that there are weighty reasons why this suggested alteration in the law should be accepted. Such alteration would remove the anomaly which discriminates between male and female homosexuals; it would mitigate the evil practice of blackmail; and we believe it would help towards the creation of a healthier attitude on sex questions generally. The elimination in this field of ignorance and false emotionalism is of paramount importance.

The Department is in general agreement with the remaining Recommendations relating to Homosexuality and particularly with the suggestion that research be instituted into the aetiology of homosexuality and the effect of various forms of treatment.

The Methodist Conference considered the statement and endorsed a resolution approving the Wolfenden Committee recommendations.

F Church of Scotland Attitudes

The law in Scotland is in some respects distinct from that in England,[12] particularly in regard to procedure. Although the Wolfenden Committee heard evidence from Scotland, and its assistant secretary was an official of the Scottish Home Department, the Church of Scotland did not provide official evidence itself. The Wolfenden Committee noted:

that the number of men prosecuted in Scotland for homosexual offences committed in private with consenting adult partners is infinitesimal in comparison with the number so prosecuted in England and Wales. From our examination of Scottish witnesses, including the police and legal and medical witnesses, we are led to believe that homosexuality and homosexual behaviour are about as prevalent in different parts of Scotland as in comparable districts in the rest of Great Britain, and it seems to us that the disparity in the number of prosecutions is due to some fundamental difference in criminal procedures.[13]

In effect, the crucial difference of procedure is that in Scotland prosecutions are initiated by a public prosecutor when he is satisfied that to do so would be 'in the public interest'. It seems to have been tacitly assumed by the Scottish prosecutors that the public interest was very seldom served by prosecuting adult homosexuals.

The Church of Scotland set up a special sub-committee of their Church and Nation Committee in 1955 to study the subject, and this sub-committee reported to the main committee that it agreed with the conclusions of the Wolfenden Committee. The majority of the main committee did not, however, agree with the findings of its own sub-committee, and the result was that in 1958 the General Assembly of the Church of Scotland adopted the following deliverance:

The General Assembly, while recognising the great importance of the Report of the Wolfenden Committee on Homosexual Offences and Prostitution, and its thorough and fair-minded exposition of two complex social problems, do not feel able to support the recommendations of the Report with regard to removing from the sphere of Criminal Law certain forms of homosexual behaviour. The General Assembly would regard such changes as inopportune, as liable to serious misunderstanding and misinterpretation, and as calculated to increase rather than diminish this grave evil.

At the same time the General Assembly believe that a much more sympathetic understanding of the difficulties and handicaps of those suffering from homosexual tendencies is required throughout the community; that where necessary both psychiatric and medical treatment should be made available; and in particular that ministers should regard those so handicapped as having a special claim upon their pastoral concern and care.[14]

This meant that the Church of Scotland was the only one of the major Churches in the United Kingdom which did not accept the Wolfenden Committee recommendations. The law of Scotland was not changed by the 1967 Act, and the old law remains in force, although, in fact, the practice of the Lord Advocate's Department is not to prosecute consenting adults who commit homosexual acts in private. Undoubtedly, the paucity of prosecutions up till 1958, and their absence in recent years, has made the need for legal reform in Scotland appear less urgent than in England and Wales, and has reduced pressure on the Church of Scotland to make an independent stand. In 1966, the General Assembly was advised:

that adequate protection for the individual already existed (in Scotland) and no amending legislation was required.

Despite this advice, the impending enactment of the 1967 Bill in the English Parliament led the General Assembly Committee on Temperance and Moral Welfare to set up a working party to reconsider the matter, which reported to the Assembly in 1967 and 1968, and has since kept the matter under review, also providing a 'Care and Counselling' unit for homosexual people.

Following two reports of the working party, in 1968 the Assembly's deliverance was as follows:

The General Assembly, whilst not condoning or approving homosexual acts, urge:

(i) that a more sympathetic understanding of the difficulties and handicaps of those suffering from homosexual tendencies is required throughout the community, and regret the comparative lack of psychiatric and medical treatment available;

(ii) that ministers show special pastoral concern and care of those suffering from such tendencies, so that they may know that the Gospel of Redemption through Jesus Christ is for all;

(iii) that Her Majesty's Government consider whether homosexual acts between consenting adults in private should continue to be an offence under the Law of Scotland.

So far the law in Scotland has not been changed.

G The Church Assembly Questionnaire of 1969

As a consequence of the Life and Liberty movement led by William Temple, the ancient Church of England system of government through Convocation was modified in 1920 by the formation of the Church Assembly which included diocesan bishops and elected clergy and laity from both Provinces. The Assembly was to be replaced by the General Synod of 1970 and so it seemed in 1969 that an opportunity existed to test the attitudes of these senior and representative church people to homosexuality, many of whom had been members of the Assembly at the time of the Wolfenden Report debate of 1957. Perhaps in the intervening years there had been a shift of opinion concerning the legal question, for less than half of the membership of the Assembly had voted in the debate and the approval given was by the small margin of 17 votes. The 1967 Act had been in force for a brief period. The moral question had not been debated in 1957 and so it might be possible, and certainly valuable, to elicit information about that. The 1957 vote had been of the Assembly as a whole and there might be a significant difference in attitude taken by members of the three Houses of Bishops, Clergy, and Laity, and even between the Provinces or individual dioceses.

Clearly such an enquiry would not be welcome to all members, but for statistical reasons and because it was a public body with a published membership, the proper way to test opinions and reactions was to send a questionnaire with a wide range of questions to everyone on the official membership list, it being made clear that obviously there was no obligation to respond.

Included in the sixty questions were some preliminary ones concerning books and publications which members might have read, about how interested they were in the subject and how they became aware of it, their attitude to biblical references, the change in the law, their acquaintance with homosexual men or women, and their attitude to the sinfulness or otherwise of homosexual behaviour.[15]

When the enquiry was conducted, the Assembly consisted of 736 members, and of these 41 per cent replied, either by completing the questionnaire or answering some of its questions by letter. Some disquiet was expressed by Assembly officials at the nature of the enquiry and after a note to this effect was circulated to members, the response rate dwindled. Of those replying, the highest proportion were bishops, the lowest laity, and there was a significantly better response from Canterbury Province than from York, and from urban rather than country dioceses.

The answers showed that adolescence was the time when most members became interested in the subject of homosexuality and clergy were more interested than laity. A total of 145 different books were listed, Bailey and Lake being most frequent, and among biblical references, Romans 1 was most quoted, four times as often as Genesis 19. Only nine members mentioned Leviticus and none referred to Judges. Seventy-five per cent of the members found biblical references helpful. Only 30 per cent of members had read the Wolfenden Report but 90 per cent had read summaries and 68 per cent of the members responding agreed with its recommendation concerning consenting adults. This was a much higher proportion than in the 1957 debate, but the figure must be treated with caution since neither for the debate nor the questionnaire was the full membership's opinion expressed, and those attending or responding may well have been among members more sympathetic to the Recommendations.

The most exacting questions concerned members' acquaintance with homosexual people and their attitude to the sinfulness of homosexual behaviour. The responses showed that over 80 per cent of members knew people whom they thought to be homosexual; that the clergy had far more direct knowledge of them than the laity did, arising from their pastoral work; and that they knew twice as many male homosexuals in comparison with female homosexuals. In reply to the question, 'Do you think homosexual behaviour between consenting male adults is always sinful?', 51 per cent of the members answering voted 'Yes', 34 per cent said 'No' and 15 per cent were undecided. For a similar question concerning adult females, the answers were 50 per cent 'Yes', 34 per cent 'No' and 16 per cent undecided; in effect, not significantly different. The results of these questions that the 'Noes' and 'undecideds' virtually match the 'Yes's' may seem surprising, but the caution previously expressed about response from those sympathetic applies here also.

Among other interesting results from questions, most members agreed that the church attitudes to people with homosexual tendencies had changed since 1957 and the change was thought to be towards tolerance and understanding of the condition. From replies to a question addressed to clergy only about pastoral training at theological colleges concerning homosexual problems, it was clear that only a few colleges are remembered as having included the subject in their syllabus and these were in the Anglo-Catholic tradition.

The questionnaire was subsequently sent, under the same conditions of confidentiality, to a smaller group of junior clergy. The average age of Assembly members had been 57, and this group was all under 40 and mostly recently ordained. The differences in the answers from the junior clergy showed that while they mostly agreed with the change in the law, and placed greater emphasis on the need to interpret Scripture in the light of modern knowledge, they lacked pastoral experience of counselling homosexual people, despite being well acquainted with them. They were less convinced of changes in the Christian attitude, suggesting this was more apparent than real with regard to homosexual behaviour. In their period of training, which was after the Wolfenden Report, about half the theological colleges had included teaching about homosexuality.

The results of the enquiry showed few unexpected features. In statistical terms the response was quite encouraging for such a subject addressed to such a body, and although a few strong expressions of moral disapproval were received, the predominant note was sympathetic caution. If a personal expression of opinion is permissible at this stage, it seemed to me that there was more acquaintance with homosexual people and evidence of non-judgemental counselling than I had expected, particularly from clergy and laity living in the South and East of England, and this probably reflects the composition of the Assembly, its clergy being on the whole experienced pastors, and its laity very often from the caring, legal, or teaching professions. The statistical studies showed no obvious correlation between churchmanship and the kinds of answer provided, and pastoral experience seemed to have a greater effect on clergy attitudes than the books they remembered reading.[16]

H The Board of Social Responsibility Working Party Report of 1970

The nineteen-sixties were a period of transition in which the various official church bodies assimilated the consequences of the Wolfenden Report while supporting the proposal to be implemented by the Act of 1967. For some people, the most disturbing consequence was that in this area of human life, the law would no longer enforce morality. This anxiety was clearly expressed by Sir Patrick Devlin in his Maccabaean Lecture to the British Academy in March 1959. There was an immediate response by H. L. A. Hart, the Oxford Professor of Jurisprudence and the discussion was maintained in a number of books in the next few years.[17]

While this discussion of the philosophical and religious issues continued, some observers saw the implementation of the Wolfenden Report as a further demonstration of the success of the movement towards sexual liberty, for which the slogans, 'the permissive society' or 'the new morality' were often used. Actual changes in patterns of sexual behaviour at particular times are, of course, very difficult to determine, and whatever may be concluded about the trend, there was an immense liberalization of discussion. To some this was a threat, to others it was welcome. As one critic of Devlin's lecture expressed it,

> The real solvent of social morality is not the failure of the law to endorse its restrictions with legal punishment, but free critical discussion.[18]

Devlin had spoken in his lecture of the 'Shift in the limits of Tolerance' by the public towards homosexual behaviour, though his own attitude moved the other way. Whereas in giving evidence to the Wolfenden Commitee he was in favour of modifying the law, he later concluded that the law should not reflect this shift too quickly. When it, in fact, occurred, other Christians responded by advocating that increased resources should be provided for the treatment and reform of homosexual people.

At its meeting in September 1967, the Church of England Board of Social Responsibility discussed a paper by Captain Smith of the Church Army concerning a suggestion originally made by the Bishop of London in the House of Lords Debate on the Sexual Offences Bill of 1967 that provisions should be made 'for the reformation and recovery, if it can be, of those who become victims of homosexuality'. The Board then agreed to establish a working party 'to review the situation concerning both male and female homosexuality and to report to the Board', the Board intending to present the report to the Archbishop of Canterbury, for subsequent publication only if he so directed.

The working party included a diocesan bishop, a doctor, a psychiatrist (Roman Catholic), a clergyman and two senior members of the Metropolitan Police Force. Given this composition, it is perhaps not surprising that when the group reported in July 1970 it was not in all respects unanimous. In particular, two views were expressed about the sinfulness of homosexual behaviour with a settled partner. Although that had not been an issue the Group was asked to decide, they found in their discussions that any recommendations they could offer for pastoral care were affected by it. If the traditional view was followed, the Church must ask homosexual people to do without any physical expression. The second view was expressed as follows:

> Although homosexual relationship could never be as fully human—as satisfactory for a human being—as a heterosexual relationship, nevertheless it may be the best relationship that is possible for a person of an exclusive and fixed homosexual disposition. In such a case, a homosexual relationship is not 'sinful'; it may be a right relationship for the parties concerned if it is the best they can achieve. There is no evidence that such relationships are socially harmful and only the people concerned can judge whether or not their relationship is the best of which they are capable, and therefore right or wrong for them. Those who hold this view hold that the first view cannot be reconciled with modern psychiatric insights into human behaviour problems.

Probably because of this lack of unanimity in the Report, it was given only limited circulation and marked 'Confidential—not for general release'.

10 Consent within Limits

A Introduction

In the previous chapter, the dilemma for pastors and theologians following the publication of the Wolfenden Committee Report in 1957 was discussed in a somewhat retrospective context. Since the old books were still available in revised editions, and the official church bodies concentrated on approving the legal changes and pressing for more pastoral care of homosexual people, the resilience of the old moral tradition was demonstrated, and reservations towards it seldom expressed by quasi-official groups until the 1970 working party reported. Perhaps church leaders expected that homosexual Christians would remain obedient to the traditional rule that genital activity was excluded for them. But the movement for Gay Liberation was steadily gathering strength and confidence as Parliament and public opinion swung towards the acceptance of the removal of penalties among consenting adults. In this chapter, therefore, an attempt is made to outline the main issues debated in the past twenty years between the various Christian groups who have tried to work out what response the Churches should now make to the challenge that homosexual behaviour is not contrary to God's will.

The debate has been world-wide, involving all denominations and the trans-denominational theological loyalties which makes it difficult to review what has been said in neat categories. Publishers' willingness to undertake translation, and the now common practice of simultaneous publication in English-speaking countries, notably between the Commonwealth and America, means there has been a wide international participation in the debate, notwithstanding the different legal, social, and ecclesiological situations obtaining where they were originally written.

The spate of books and pamphlets from Christian authors has been matched of course by those in the medical and psychiatric field, and by many popular works advocating a policy of general sexual liberation. Since the days of the Homosexual Law Reform Society, concerned Christians, some but by no means all of them homosexual themselves, have maintained contact with the Gay Liberation movement and been active in its specifically Christian counterpart. Records of counselling services are now available, and if they may be so described without offence, the strident views of the National Festival of Light and the Gay Liberation Front have been made available in leaflets and magazines, some of them short-lived. Never since the publication of Peter Damian's *Liber Gomorrhianus* in 1051 CE has so much been said in so short a time about homosexuality.

Apart from full length books, many writers on Christian ethics have felt obliged to devote a chapter to the subject instead of the paragraph and footnotes which were considered sufficient before 1955.

Recording the major aspects of this debate over the past twenty years at reasonable length creates obvious problems. If justice were to be done to the many authors who have made significant contributions, full quotations would be needed. That cannot be, but most of these works are still in print and can be consulted direct.[1]

A simple division between the views expressed could be achieved by separating conservative, liberal, and radical views by a test such as, 'Is homosexual behaviour condemned, left to private conscience, or accepted?' and such a division would seem to correspond in a loose way with the general theological stances of the sections of the Churches so identified. But all such labels would be in some sense libels, and possibly do less than justice to the independence of mind of the various writers, and indeed, since the terms are somewhat emotive, to the objectivity of the reviewer.

One such classification is offered by J. B. Nelson who suggests that four types of attitude can be identified, which he calls: 'Rejecting punitive': 'rejecting non-punitive': 'qualified acceptance': and 'full acceptance'.[2]

Nelson states that his own attitude has moved steadily towards the last of these positions, but other commentators might well not accept as appropriate Nelson's placing Karl Barth, for example, as among those whose views are 'rejecting punitive'. While it is true that all Christians 'see through a glass darkly', every study adds to our data.

Certainly, for some Christians, guarding the long-established meaning of the biblical texts and the teaching of the Church has seemed a major obligation, however much they respected the case for removing discrimination against homosexual people, and wished to extend to them full acceptance as members of their fellowship, provided genital activities were abandoned. Catholics and Evangelicals have stated this position with clarity, but many Christians who in general terms would not identify with these loyalties, seem to think that the present time of anxiety about sexual ethics is not an appropriate one for relaxing the teaching against homosexual behaviour. Other Christians have found that the present emphasis on the quality of relationships is a positive development that the Churches should welcome, allowing the full truth of the gospel to be expressed in sexual matters, freed at last from the fears of the body and the passions which have so long distorted the Church's witness to God's design for human love and sexuality.

An element of confusion has been introduced into the debate by the pace and variety of medical and psychological research into the aetiology of the homosexual condition and the possibilities of treatment.[3] Since few moral theologians could claim competence in the medical field, the information they provide is often second-hand, and lays them open to criticism by a later writer. To some extent this difficulty is losing its force as the early confidence about causes and cures is found to be unjustified, but it remains true that markedly different accounts are given in the books of the period. It has been estimated by one commentator that no less than seventy-seven variables may be included in aetiologies popularly advanced in up-to-date psychiatric literature and therefore any Christian commentator who offers explanations of the causes of homosexuality, and many of them do, runs the risk of selecting only those variables which 'fit' the ethical stance he is advocating.[4]

Given the complexity of the debate, and the various factors involved, all that is attempted in this chapter is to provide some indication of the various views expressed, distinguished rather arbitrarily, in two sections. At some risk of imposing conclusions at this stage, before the evidence is presented, but to sketch out the main lines of the argument, the following pattern may help:

VIEW 'A' argues that the model of heterosexual marriage is determinant. This is expressed in two forms:

(1) procreation is the primary 'end' or reason for marriage

or

(2) heterosexual relationship is the primary end, of which procreation is a normal fulfilment for most people, but not essential to a complete marriage.

For both forms of View 'A', the homosexual condition need not be a bar to marriage, but is likely to impose stress on the partners. Homosexual behaviour is regarded in View 'A' as not criminal among consenting adults, but sinful, and at best incomplete, and at worst perverse. It is not to be accepted among Christians, so homosexuals are asked to obey the rule of abstinence.

VIEW 'B' argues that the quality of the relationship is determinant. Heterosexual marriage is the opportunity for most people to learn, develop, and express the quality of the relationship, but, for those constituted homosexual, a stable bond with a person of the same sex provides a similar opportunity. It follows from View 'B', that the ethical and pastoral guidance the Church offers to homosexuals includes:

(1) helping homosexuals to accept themselves, accept God's approval of them, and experience acceptance also within the fellowship of the Church,

(2) encouragement of homosexual partners to explore friendship, selflessness, and fidelity similar to that available to heterosexual partners.

It should be noted that View 'B' is often qualified by the realization that heterosexual marriage, as an institution buttressed by society, cannot be reduplicated by homosexual partners in all respects, of which parenthood is one but not the only one. However, the quality of the relationship is not determined in either heterosexual marriage or homosexual partnership by the presence or absence of children, as some proponents of View 'A' would agree.

Obviously this pattern is only devised to indicate in advance some of the central issues implicit in the various contributions to the debate.

A further complication to be noticed is that the views expressed about homosexual behaviour do not stand in isolation from the more general appraisal of the character of Christian morality and its application to rules about marriage and chastity. This was, of course, equally true for the biblical writers, and therefore it is often necessary to understand what position is taken about, for example, the significance of natural law, or the relationship between rules and love with regard to human sexual activity *in toto* to represent fairly why homosexual behaviour is approved or rejected. These are perennial problems and require, even in this last chapter, occasional reference back to the earlier periods of Church history. The emergence of the notion of courtly love, and its consequence in terms of entrenching the insistence on romance ever since, is an illustration. Perhaps that should have been referred to in an earlier chapter, but in fact, its exposition by C. S. Lewis properly belongs in this period.

Perhaps it is fair to reiterate that placing a particular view in the first section, 'Guarding the tradition', or in the second, 'The pressure for Gay Liberation', does not imply that the views of any author are adequately represented by these titles. The encouraging feature of the considerable attention Christians have given to the problem of homosexuality in this period, is the evidence that there is much more common ground and understanding than there was twenty years ago.

The course of change in any large institution is bound to be slow and only a later historical judgement can identify what proved to be decisive steps along the way. Whether or not the Christian Churches are now on course to change their traditional hostility to homosexual behaviour in any marked way is at the moment not clear, but it may be so. If they are, it will not happen without some forceful restatement of the tradition and the Vatican Declaration may be such a restatement. The third section of this chapter concerns the reports of three working parties, Catholic, Anglican, and Methodist, whose membership could be in no clear sense identified with either the traditional or liberal protagonisms. All three working parties recommend the acceptance of homosexual behaviour within limits, for those homosexuals whose orientation is apparently fixed.

B Guarding the Tradition

(a) ROMAN CATHOLIC TEACHING

During the period under review, official Roman Catholic Church teaching has maintained that sexual activity must be confined within heterosexual marriage, and this necessarily inhibits any form of homosexual behaviour. Individual catholic writers in Europe have not questioned this. The English Anglo-Catholic writers tend to take the same position, but as shown later, some American Roman Catholics have recently suggested alternative views, not always without criticism from their own authorities.

In the Pastoral Constitution on the Church in the Modern World, one of the official documents produced by the Second Vatican Council in 1965 and known as *Gaudium et Spes* from its opening words in Latin, one of the specially urgent problems considered was 'fostering the nobility of marriage and the family'. The text apparently owes something to the arguments of Cardinal Suenens and others who pressed that the Church's teaching about marriage should be cast in positive form. This theme is firmly struck in paragraph 49 which speaks of conjugal love 'which is uniquely expressed and perfected through the marital act'. The whole paragraph seems careful not to represent the ends of marriage in terms of procreation first, followed by affection in the traditional way, though, of course, adultery, divorce, and contraception are forbidden elsewhere in the Constitution.[5]

If the Constitution *Gaudium et Spes* was taken to indicate a developing approach to human sexuality within the authoritative teaching of the Catholic Church, the Encyclical letter of Pope Paul VI, *Humanae Vitae*, published two years later, showed that it had not entirely replaced the old teaching. The Encyclical reaffirmed the prohibition of artificial birth control, and in the preceding paragraphs referred to sexual activity between husband and wife as 'honourable and good as the recent Council recalled', but also observes that

> the Church, nevertheless, in urging men to the observance of the precepts of the natural law, which it interprets by its constant doctrine, teaches as absolutely required that any use whatever of marriage must retain its natural potential to procreate human life.[6]

The footnotes to Paragraph 11 of the Encyclical give references to *Gaudium et Spes* in the first example and to the Encyclical of Pius XI, *Casti Connubii* of 1930, for the second. The stress Pope Paul puts on the natural law argument that procreation is the primary end of marital sex is, in effect, a reversion to the doctrine as it stood before Vatican Two. It is also noteworthy that the Church's position as interpreter of the natural law implies that without such guidance, natural man may be mistaken, which perhaps deliberately weakens the status of natural law as that was scholastically understood as God's way of enlightening the conscience of every man.

Neither in *Gaudium et Spes*, nor in *Humanae Vitae* is any direct reference made to homosexuality, though their emphasis on conjugal love and procreation were clearly directed only to heterosexual expression. The American edition of the *New Catholic Encyclopedia* of 1967 left no doubt:

> The homosexual act by its very essence excludes all possibility of transmission of life: such an act cannot fulfil the procreative purpose of the sexual faculty, and is therefore an inordinate goal of human nature, it is a grave transgression of the divine will.[7]

In the European Catholic encyclopedia of theology, *Sacramentum Mundi*, of 1970 edited by Karl Rahner, S.J., a more ecumenical attitude is expressed in the whole article on Sex. Although clearly influenced by *Gaudium et Spes*, it quotes also from Thielicke and other German Protestants. Homosexuality is described as a defective form of sexual behaviour, calling for some form of satisfactory 'pastoral solution'. St Paul's condemnation is said to have referred to the time of pederasty, and homosexual people are capable of entering permanent and total relationships 'seeking the totality of the other person, missing however, the Christian form of encounter with the neighbour'.[8]

Although this Encyclopedia was given an *Imprimatur* for its English translation, it has, of course, no authority beyond that of its distinguished authors. The Vatican *Declaration on Sexual Ethics* of 1975, already briefly referred to in chapter 6, is an authoritative rejoinder to any Catholic who might think the old teaching can be disregarded, but appears to be chiefly prompted by a continued anxiety in the Vatican that

> the corruption of morals has increased and one of the most serious indications of this corruption is the unbridled exaltation of sex.[9]

In paragraph 4 of the *Declaration*, the norms of natural law and sacred Scripture are defended as immutable against the assertion that they reflect a particular culture at a certain moment of history, and in paragraph 7 the doctrine is affirmed that every genital act must be within the framework of marriage. In paragraph 8, the transitory and incurable categories of homosexuality are distinguished, and of the second the *Declaration* states:

In regard to this second category of subjects, some people conclude that their tendency is so natural that it justifies in their case homosexual relations within a sincere communion of life and love analogous to marriage, in so far as such homosexuals feel incapable of enduring a solitary life.

In the pastoral field, these homosexuals must certainly be treated with understanding and sustained in the hope of overcoming their personal difficulties and their inability to fit into society. Their culpability will be judged with prudence. But no pastoral method can be employed which would give moral justification to these acts on the grounds that they would be consonant with the condition of such people. For according to the objective moral order, homosexual relations are acts which lack an essential and indispensable finality. In Sacred Scripture they are condemned as a serious depravity and even presented as the sad consequence of rejecting God (18). This judgement of Scripture does not, of course, permit us to conclude that all those who suffer from this anomaly are personally responsible for it, but it does attest to the fact that homosexual acts are intrinsically disordered and can in no case be approved of.[10]

The official Roman Catholic teaching therefore remains clear, and the strong emphasis in *Gaudium et Spes* on conjugal love has provided no opportunity for any parallel recognition of the value of love between homosexuals. An English Catholic priest, Fr M. J. Buckley, anticipated the danger of separating the two 'ends' of marriage in his *Morality and the Homosexual* of 1959.[11] He describes the purpose of sexual intercourse as conceptional and relational, the former destined for the procreation of children, and the latter for the establishment of the 'one flesh union' (*henosis*). These purposes must never be separated so that the one would exclude the other entirely and permanently. The use of the sexual organs therefore is significantly limited to an exclusive and lifelong relationship within the married state.

Buckley criticizes some modern theories about homosexuality and writes that:

A priest should not be deterred by the false claim that homosexuality is essentially a medical or psychiatric problem. Modern scientific theories are but mists which some moralists use in their attempts to obscure the teaching of the true Church.

He concludes that pastoral guidance towards reorientation to heterosexuality is the main task in all cases, but where this is not possible, the individual must instead make 'an adjustment to his condition in the only way acceptable to Catholic moral theology—a life of chastity'.

(b) SOME ANGLICAN VIEWS

Among High Church Anglicans, Lindsey Dewar, once settled as vicar of the Hertfordshire village of Much Hadham, had time to reassess the new situation for moral theology and the empirical sciences, and he deals with the problem of homosexuality briefly. He reiterates the basic descriptions of the condition given in his earlier book of the '30s, and adds footnote reference to Bailey, but his conclusion is much as before:

> We have no ground for questioning the truth of St Paul's argument that homosexual practices lead men not nearer to God but away from Him. It is certainly going much too far to claim that it has been shown empirically that the Christian tradition which has consistently condemned homosexual practices as evil and degrading has been mistaken. It is quite possible to adhere firmly to the Christian tradition here and at the same time to deny that homosexual practices should, in general, be treated as criminal.[12]

In another book of 1964, which covers much the same ground as Dewar's but has a wider perspective, Canon H. Waddams of Canterbury shows he is aware of the writings of Thielicke, and some of the American moral theologians. His *New Introduction to Moral Theology* was based on lectures he gave at the Montreal Theological College before he returned to England. When he deals with homosexuality he notes that:

> There has been some change in the climate of British opinion, but homosexuals still arouse feelings of revulsion on the grounds that they are 'unnatural'. In one sense of the word, homosexuality is 'unnatural' and in another it is not. Clearly the sexual powers are by nature designed for the propagation of the species, and this is the only truly natural use of them or of the emotions associated with them. But a born homosexual is 'natural' in the sense that to him or her the homosexuality is not artificial.

He continues by stating that homosexuals who are born with this innate characteristic can have no moral blame attached to their innate tendencies, but

> there are others who have resorted to homosexual practices in order to gratify their general sexual desires, who are not truly homosexuals at all, and moral blame is attached to their homosexual emotions because they have been deliberately chosen, and they are therefore a revolt against the natural purposes of God in the world generally and in their own natures particularly.

Having taken this attitude to homosexual emotions, Waddams continues by asserting that any indulgence in homosexual practices is gravely sinful 'both those which are mildly erotic, and still more those that involve the sexual organs'. He concludes by agreeing with the

Wolfenden proposals for consenting adults, and suggesting that homosexuals can play a most useful part in society, provided 'they rise above their selfish physical desires'.[13]

Awareness of the complexity of the issues in the light of new findings about human sexuality is shown by F. R. Barry, formerly Bishop of Southwell, in his *Christian Ethics and Secular Society.*[14] In chapter 8 entitled 'Charity and Chastity' Barry enumerates the new facts not known or recognized by biblical authors which have 'far-reaching moral implications', and make it no more sensible to send 'inverts to prison than alcoholics to a brewery'. He thinks the intense disgust and horror aroused in men, especially of the Public School type, by male forms of perversion is one more reminder that our sexual ethic is almost exclusively masculine in origin, whereas the female appears to excite no such indignation, and lesbianism seems to be regarded in the popular mind as a social curiosity rather than as a 'sink' of moral corruption. Barry will have heard some of the debates in the House of Lords, and he acknowledges his debt to Sherwin Bailey in what he writes, but he concludes that Christians will judge perversion among men and women as deflecting the laws of creation from their course, and subjecting human beings to degradation and, therefore, grievously sinful in the sight of God. He is firmly in favour of the implementation of the Wolfenden Committee recommendations.[15]

The development in the Anglican tradition of the practice of sacramental confession with emphasis on the priest's counselling role has been noted earlier. This ministry is primarily exercised by the parish priest for his own people. Some priests, of course, develop a much wider ministry among penitents, and two examples of how to counsel homosexual people from the writings of notable 'pardoners' are now considered, one of whom travelled a great deal, while the other worked mostly from a famous London church.

The author of *A Guide for Spiritual Directors* was, in fact, an Anglican priest, W. Somerset Ward, though his book was published anonymously.[16] The third part of the book consists in twelve exercises which set out example confessions, and instructions on how to give counsel in such cases. Exercise 2 postulates a man aged 38, a well-dressed journalist with an intellectual face, who confesses laziness about getting up in the morning, cynical attitudes to good people, inadequate prayer life and 'serious acts of impurity with boys'. Questioning elicits that the man has been a homosexual from school days, was expelled from school for this reason, had found in religion the only means of resisting this tendency and had fallen again and been afraid to have anything further to do with religion until a narrow escape from prosecution had brought him back to God.

The diagnosis and suggestions for advice and penance given in the rest of the exercise lay emphasis on helping the penitent to reject the idea that he is abnormal in his orientation, but misusing his gift of love in selfish ways. He should try to join a tennis club and get games on Saturdays, and a heavy rule of prayer each day is to be laid down. If the penitent is in Holy Orders, he is to be warned that a requisite sign of repentance before absolution is the acceptance of the necessity of informing a bishop. The reasons for the advice suggested are given as:

(1) removal of the feeling that he is abnormal and cannot be helped.
(2) If he really wants to love God, he can prove this by accepting the conditions and penance—not being voluntarily alone with a boy for a year.
(3) To learn that there is a plentiful outlet and use for his sex instinct if he will search for it.
(4) To lessen the power of temptation by attacking its starting point.

Kenneth Ross was the Vicar of All Saints, Margaret Street, for a number of years, moving in 1970 to a Canonry at Wells, but dying shortly after. He was a prolific writer of popular theology, and left at his death a nearly complete manuscript on *Hearing Confessions*.[17] In chapter 7 of this book, on special problems, he writes about the

> doubts which may be thought to arise in the absolution of practising homosexuals. They often accuse themselves of sexual sin with members of their own sex, and promise to try to steer clear of these sins in the future. But there are those who are living together in a relationship not of lust, but of love, and who declare that they do not and cannot regard it as wrong to express their mutual love in bodily intercourse. What is the confessor to say? Those who regard 'good faith' as the crucial test would presumably give absolution, together with any priests who dissented from the traditional teaching of the Church in this matter. But the majority of confessors would be unwilling in general to push the plea of good faith so far, and would decline to agree that 'there is nothing good or bad but that thinking makes it so'. What are the limits of conscientious refusal to accept the Church's teaching? Here it should be noted that there is no such substantial body of informed opinion to justify a departure from traditional teaching, nor have any who would urge such a departure given an adequate rationale to justify it.[18]

Ross refers then to unacknowledged uneasiness among those who claim a clear conscience in this matter, and agrees that conscientious divergence from the teaching of the Church should be respected by the confessor on matters of secondary importance, but if there is a divergence on first principles the confessor cannot condone it. As to whether homosexual practices are in conflict with first principles or are only secondary, Ross does not commit himself but observes:

He who is rigorist by conviction will tend to expand the former category, and he who is more liberal will tend to expand the latter. Only the study of competent books on Moral Theology will enable the Confessor to proceed as he should in his ministry on behalf of Christ and his Church.[19]

(c) POST-WAR EUROPEAN PROTESTANT THEOLOGIANS

The influence of German and Swiss Protestant theologians on the Churches of England in this century has been most marked in relation to doctrinal and biblical studies. Since the Protestant Churches lack a common Canon Law tradition and Church–State relationships vary to some extent among the nations, the ethical systems are rather more particularized, except where confessional or ecumenical consultations cause assimilation. While books about homosexuality of American origin abound in England, this is unusual for German and Swiss works. However, the writings of Barth, Thielicke, and Bovet are well known in England and each of them deals with homosexuality to some extent.

K. Barth

Whereas much theological assessment of homosexual behaviour is expressed in terms of departure from the heterosexual norm, either as disobedience to biblical precepts or as a breach of natural law, a quite different approach is possible when human sexuality is understood as a command to develop relationships with other people. This approach is characteristically employed by Karl Barth who based what he had to say about homosexuality on the premise that, as God calls man to himself, he also directs him to his fellow man, in particular through the man–woman relationship, but also to that between parents and children and near and distant neighbours, thus expressing honour to each other and themselves. Barth works out the consequences of this in a long section of his *Church Dogmatics*, entitled 'Man and Woman'. When he comes to homosexuality, in an extended footnote he argues that since men and women are on an equal footing in Christ, 'related and directed to each other', any attempt at seclusion, except temporarily as an emergency measure, is disobedience. The comradeship of soldiers is respected but the formation of one-sex communities, secular or religious, is not. No doubt Barth can recall his experience in the Confessing Church and the Nazi encouragement and then destruction of homosexual circles for political ends, but he is remarkably fierce on clubs and women's circles where men or women meet apart from each other: 'What commands or permits them to run away from each other?' he demands, and warns that such artificially induced isolation may well be the first steps of 'the malady called homosexuality'.

The footnote ends severely:

This is the place of protest, warning and conversion. The command of God shows him irrefutably—in clear contradiction to his own theories—that as a man he can only genuinely be human with a woman, or as a woman with man. In proportion as he accepts this insight, homosexuality can have no place in his life whether in its more refined or cruder forms.[20]

Barth bases this footnote in the *Dogmatics* on Romans 1.25–7 which he quotes, and this is a far more extensive expression of his views than he gives in either the longer or shorter versions of his *Commentary* on the Epistles. In the first of these, dating back to 1918 but revised several times, he notes:

What is at first merely open to suspicion moves inexorably on to what is positively absurd. Everything then becomes Libido: life becomes totally erotic. When the frontier between God and man, the last inexorable barrier and obstacle, is not closed, the barrier between what is normal and what is perverse is opened.[21]

Bonhoeffer

Barth's view of human nature is somewhat sombre and for a more positive attitude to human sexuality by another major theologian associated with the Confessing Church in Germany this example from the uncompleted *Ethics* of Dietrich Bonhoeffer may be compared:

The life of the body is an end in itself. Sex is not only the means of reproduction, but independently of this defined purpose, it brings with it its own joy, in married life, in the love of two human beings for one another. . . . The meaning of bodily life never lies solely in its subordination to its final purpose. The life of the body assumes its full significance only with the fulfilment of its inherent claim to joy.[22]

Thielicke

Helmut Thielicke, also a German Lutheran, devotes a chapter to the problem of homosexuality in *The Ethics of Sex* published in English translation in 1964.[23] In his opening section on homosexuality, Thielicke critically reviews the literature of Protestant theology and finds it seldom noticed therein nor understood. Only the Swedish bishops for their report in 1951 approving the removal of criminal sanctions against adults, and the work of Bailey, and of the Wolfenden Committee, are thought satisfactory, and Barth's footnote is singled out for particular criticism, mostly on the point that his advice is useless to an adult who is already fully settled in his disposition, a kind of person Thielicke suggests Barth could never have met.

In the second section Thielicke considers the biblical evidence. With regard to the Old Testament texts, he agrees with Bailey's exegesis, and Von Rad's commentary on Genesis, concluding that on the evidence of Leviticus 18 and 20 only, and not elsewhere, the Old Testament regarded homosexuality and pederasty as crimes punishable by death, but he asks:

> To what extent the Old Testament cultic law can be binding upon those who are under the Gospel . . . ? Even the non-theologian can see the scope of this problem when it is realised that in the Old Testament the prohibition of divination, the drinking of blood, sexual intercourse with a menstruating woman, and many other things are put on the same level with the capital offence of homosexuality. It would never occur to anyone to wrench these laws of cultic purification from their concrete situation and give them the kind of normative authority that the Decalogue, for example, has.

He goes on to consider the New Testament texts, arguing that while there is no doubt that St Paul regards homosexuality as a sin and a perversion of the order of human existence willed by God, its inclusion in a catalogue along with adultery and fornication may mean that certain kinds of homosexual behaviour are offensive because, like the heterosexual sins listed, they result from 'libido-conditioned disregard for one's neighbour'. He then observes that Jesus in the synoptic Gospels is represented as taking a lenient view of sensuous sins in comparison with sins of the spirit and cupidity. There follows an examination of Romans 1.26 in which he makes the standard point that disorder in the vertical dimension is matched by perversion on the horizontal level.

The next step in Thielicke's argument is to assert that Christians, thinking biblically, cannot regard homosexuality as having no ethical significance, as if it were a 'sport' of nature. Since the Fall, creation is disordered, and the homosexual potentiality as such is to be no more strongly deprecated than the status of existence which we all share, but like all other disorders it looks for healing when considered in the eschatological perspective. Therefore, the homosexual person should be willing to consult a physician, and be receptive to pastoral care. But Thielicke does not expect the constitutional homosexual to be changed, and so raises what he calls 'the most ticklish question of all'. In the light of the findings of medical research, the problem as alien to the New Testament as is the problem of authority in modern democracies must be argued afresh. And the conclusions he offers are that the constitutional homosexual can be asked whether,

> Within the co-ordinating system of his constitution, he is willing to structure the man–man relationship in an ethically responsible way. Thus the ethical question meets him on the basis, which he did not enter intentionally, but which is where he actually finds himself, into which as Heidegger would say, he has been 'thrown'. We may assume that the homosexual has to realise his optimal ethical potentialities on the basis of his irreversible situation . . . the question of how the homosexual can achieve sexual self-realisation.

At this point in his argument, Thielicke leaves this final question without specific answer. He does say that celibacy is not the solution, and that the Christian pastor will have to be concerned primarily with helping the person to sublimate his homosexual urge and to see the potentialities in his abnormal existence which

> may be found in the actual danger zones of pedagogical eros, because this is where the 'charism' of the homosexual is presented with appropriate tasks,

but he adds that these opportunities may only be recommended

> to homosexuals who indicate that they are ready for sublimination and evidence their stability.[24]

Whereas Thielicke's theology of sexuality reflects Barth's general principles, in the biblical exegesis he is clearly more influenced by Bailey, and in his pastoral advice follows the Swiss doctor T. Bovet.

Bovet

Bovet considers homosexuality, which he prefers to call 'homophilia' in *That They May Have Life*, one of several of his books published in English.[25] He takes the view that homophilia is not a perversion but a different state of being, constitutionally conditioned, for which psycho-therapy may help if a neurotic infantile element is strong, but otherwise no change may be expected. Therefore, since marriage must usually be ruled out, and minors protected (though homophilia must be sharply distinguished from pederasty) homophiliacs must be encouraged to form permanent friendships at the physical and spiritual level, and follow professions which encourage sublimation through contact with people of the same sex, a process called 'ergotherapy', that is healing through work. Such contact should not be abused as an opportunity for sexual relations, and among the list of suitable work, barmen, masseurs, male nurses, psychologists, and pastors are included.

(d) EVANGELICAL VIEWS

Advice to Young People

An important feature of the work of Christian student unions has always been their provision of cheap paper-backs and pamphlets, together with various kinds of Bible study notes, to build up the faith of the newly converted and provide a basic core of evangelical teaching on issues of the day as they are encountered at student level. These publications paralleled those of the S.C.M. in the early days of both movements, but Christian Union membership has far outstripped the S.C.M. in recent years. One of the long-running I.V.F. books by Capper and Williams crisply expressed the traditional view. This was *Towards Christian Marriage* and in later editions, in the chapter entitled 'Disorder', reference is made to 'homosexual practices'. These are said to be strictly forbidden in Scripture as being unnatural, and strongly condemned, for males and, by analogy, for females also. The cause is described as failure to switch into the heterosexual phase in adolescence, and over-attachment to mother and a harsh and disinterested father are associated factors. A Christian doctor with some psychological experience should be consulted, normal associations with the opposite sex should be cultivated and physical intimacies with one's own should be strictly avoided.[26]

Once the Gay Liberation Movement became a force to be reckoned with in the greatly expanded student scene of the seventies, the Christian societies had to make a more comprehensive response. The S.C.M. at the time kept contact with the Gay Rights organization and their participation is referred to later. The I.V.F. provided in 1970 a guide to counselling homosexual students in the form of a series of letters entitled *The Returns of Love*,[27] where the author, Alex Davidson (a pseudonym) advises a fellow homosexual how to sublimate his homosexuality and move towards heterosexual marriage. This approach has been criticized as failing to take account of the fixed direction of the adult homosexual, but it can also be said that among young students this may still, in fact, be at a flexible stage, easily pulled in either direction at a time of personal uncertainty. The strong influence of a supporting Christian fellowship and the enhanced sense of the love of God experienced through 'conversion' at the beginning of adult life may well, for some people, shift the sexual orientation towards an enduring heterosexual preference despite previous short-lived experience of homosexual arousal and behaviour.

In 1977 a Christian psychiatrist Roger Moss wrote *Christians and Homosexuality*,[28] and while this pamphlet concludes from a brief review of the biblical texts that its witness stands firmly against the homosexual act, it contains sufficient references from psychiatric sources, and no doubt Dr Moss's own professional experience, to encourage a marked sympathetic tone to the experience of rejection and isolation young homosexual people may suffer. Homosexual relationships are to be discouraged at an early stage lest they diminish the chance of other relationships, create guilt later and cause insecurity, since a great deal of maturity is required to stick to a homosexual partnership through thick and thin, lacking a social support structure. Moss finds in the David and Jonathan story no hint of a sexual component, and commends this kind of friendship, loyalty, and mutual support as a helpful model for some homosexuals. He also sets out a set of six ethical principles, in effect practical guidelines for 'exercising responsibility' which are loosely similar to those of Pittenger[29] as he acknowledges 'though for reasons, I hope clear by now, I do not go as far as he does'.

The National Festival of Light

Anxieties of a more general kind about the British scene led to the formation of the National Festival of Light in 1971, attracting a good deal of attention from the media for its London rallies, but also publishing a series of pamphlets on moral issues. This movement was supported by a wide spectrum of well-known Christians, and many young people, but its publications usually reflected a traditional and evangelical viewpoint. Homosexuality was part of their concern when submitting evidence to the Home Office Criminal Law Revision Committee on the question of reducing the age of consent, which they opposed.[30]

Together with the evidence for the Home Office Committee, the Festival of Light also published a pamphlet *The Truth in Love* in 1975.[31] In the preface the author distinguishes child gregariousness and adolescent friendship from the temptations to homosexual practices (which should be resisted) and sodomy which is condemned in Scripture. These latter two categories of sin are being encouraged by propaganda, the pamphlet suggests, notably by the Campaign for Homosexual Equality, on the basis that 'homosexual activity is a natural and acceptable sexual attitude'. But this is said to be a lie, for

> Homosexual activity is unnatural, found nowhere in Nature, except in a sexually stunted human being and in certain animals under conditions of extreme stress.[32]

In the second main section, the pamphlet quotes the biblical texts from Genesis and Leviticus and the New Testament Epistles as 'a standing reminder to Christians of the judgement of God upon homosexual practices', and later hopes that most men and women of good will, even if they cannot share the Christian certainties just stated, will agree that there are good reasons for 'deploring the spread of homosexual practices and propaganda in our society'.[33] Apart from its teaching programme, the National Festival of Light hoped at one stage to establish a rehabilitation home for homosexuals, reminiscent perhaps of the Shelter Home at Clapham Common of 1912. This project was later reported to be in abeyance, but it appears probable that the telephone counselling service for homosexuals in Bournemouth was established in 1976 with financial help from the National Festival of Light and similar arrangements were made in other cities soon after.

The Biblical Witness

The tendency of modern biblical translations and paraphrases from evangelical scholars to remove any ambiguity in their renderings of the various texts referring to homosexual behaviour in Scripture has been noted at the relevant points in Part B of this book. The texts had been rescrutinized in the light of Bailey's exegesis and the challenge of the radicals, but in effect their traditional meaning was confirmed. Reference will be made in the next section to the contribution of the American Baptist, Professor Carl Henry, to *Is Gay Good.*[34] He does not quote the Bible extensively in this short essay, but does refer to Genesis:

> From the Genesis creation narrative, which Jesus made part of his own teaching, we know that God ordained a heterosexual life for mankind, and that the monogamous union of Adam and Eve as 'one flesh' is the pattern of God's intention for the whole human family. In this framework of relationships both the procreation of the race and the sexual fulfilment of the individual were ideally and naturally to be found.[35]

A thorough presentation of the Evangelical approach is to be found in *Report on Homosexuality* from the Anglican Diocese of Sydney 1973. This calls on homosexuals to cease from practising homosexual acts, to seek help from qualified counsellors, and to see whether a sexual reorientation can be achieved. It is also somewhat unusual in advocating the retention of legal penalties for homosexual activity among adults in Australian State law, the chief ground for this in the report's text being given as the risk to both the concept and stability of heterosexual marriage if an alternative homosexual pattern is permitted by the law.

The report was produced by a local committee of doctors and clergymen who obviously took care to research widely. The appendices are as long as the report and deal with biblical texts, the aetiology of homosexuality and the Australian State laws dealing with indecency, buggery, and the age of consent. In the report itself careful but critical note is taken of the views of Bailey, Thielicke, and Kimball-Jones. The report makes clear the confidence of its writers that the real solution for homosexual problems is to be found in religious conversion:

> From the Church the homosexual should expect to find understanding and sympathy for human weakness and he should also expect to find support and encouragement to live the kind of life which God requires. He will not expect to be blamed or shunned for his homosexual propensity (regardless of its causes) but, on the other hand, he will not expect to be received if he does not intend to abide by God's word and stop his homosexual acts, and seek to achieve, with God's help, such sexual re-orientation as may be open to him. Despite his own history of failure he will take seriously the words of Jesus, 'with God all things are possible', and the testimony of his apostle, 'I can do all things in Him who strengthens me'.[36]

In appendices on the biblical texts, the Sodom narrative is reconsidered in the light of Bailey's interpretation, the Leviticus texts having already been used to establish the biblical prohibition, and the hospitality argument is rejected, the verb 'to know' being taken in the context to have its sexual connotation. The event is treated as historical and described as 'the most vivid historical illustration' of God's attitude to homosexuality. Commenting on Romans 1 the appendix has:

In Romans 1, homosexuality (like idolatry) is a gross distortion of how human beings should behave.... It is true that Romans 1 does not distinguish between so-called 'bi-sexual' and the 'invert', but this is not because the Apostle is insensitive to different kinds (or degrees) of homosexuality, but because he saw its justification and indulgence in any circumstances as a sign of human folly and divine judgement.... It is possible that in Romans 1, St. Paul offers a broad and general description of the signs of decadence in the ancient Graeco-Roman civilisation and that in verses 24–27 he has his eyes on the well-known vices of leading public figures in the Imperial capital and other centres of wealth and affluence. But, as we have already observed, the Apostle's list is a very comprehensive one and he regarded unrighteous behaviour at every level and for any reason as inconsistent with the will of God and membership of His Kingdom (cf. 1 Cor. 6.9–10).... More particularly, St. Paul's attitude to homosexuality in Romans 1 was not simply a reaction to experimental homosexuality practised in high places, but reflects a permanent aversion to all homosexual behaviour. Such an aversion was clearly grounded on the Old Testament revelation, and formed part of the tradition of ethical tuition associated with the Gospel.[37]

The impetus to prepare this report seems to have been the anxiety caused by the emergence of Gay Liberation in Australia and pressure on the Australian Government to relax the law, admitted to have been somewhat confused by State differences. Noting the dangers of the English law with regard to police, provocation, and public prosecution, the report suggests a special private tribunal should deal with these offences in the first instance, and the government should provide qualified psychological help for those who seek rehabilitation.[38] The report was made available in England through the National Festival of Light movement.

The range of opinions in America among those claiming to be evangelical can be seen by contrasting two recent books, now available in England. The first, written by two married women, Letha Scanzoni and Virginia Mollencott, *Is the Homosexual my neighbour?* uses this question to argue against the rejection of homosexual people by Evangelical Church groups. The evidence they quote of children banished from home, of Gay bars filled with youths who once accepted Christ but found they had not become heterosexual in consequence, and therefore felt excluded from his body, and of cars in the Dade county area carrying bumper stickers with the motto 'Kill a Queer for Christ', reflect the extreme antagonism stirred in some quarters by the strident Gay Liberation Movement in that country. But their plea to the Evangelical and Pentecostal churches to accept the facts of homosexuality is powerfully made, and supported by an exposition of the biblical texts which owes much to Bailey, Thielicke, and McNeil. Whether or not this acceptance should include permitting genital behaviour is not stated, but the authors quote a suggestion of the Christian Association for Psychological Studies that

> a loving committed permanent relationship between two persons of the same sex . . . is not condemned by Scripture

and observe that

> this alternative to the traditional view is worth exploring in greater depth.[39]

The second recent American book *Homosexuality and the Church* by R. Lovelace[40] also shows the degree of polarization between conservative and liberal views in America at the present time, though his own position is one of firm resistance to any compromise. After a brief review of the tradition in early and mediaeval Christianity, the statements from the Reformers Luther and Calvin are given much weight. Barth and Thielicke are also approved, though the latter with some caution—he is said to move up to the barrier of affirming active homosexuality, but not to cross it. Lovelace's own exposition of the biblical texts, disagreeing with Bailey but taking his arguments seriously, concludes that neither homosexual behaviour nor homophobia are permitted to Christians. Lovelace finds the reported action of some American churches in ordaining publicly confessing homosexual men and women to their ministries deeply disturbing, and thinks this should be confined to the Metropolitan Church which is specially concerned to provide a fellowship for Gay people. The other Churches should only ordain homosexuals who declare they intend to observe celibacy, for this would restore to the main Churches their integrity in terms of social witness.

Commending practising homosexuals to the Metropolitan Church does not, however, mean that Lovelace approves of that Church, nor that he has no expectation that the condition of homosexuality can be changed. At this point, a doctrine of the personal work of the Holy Spirit is set out in terms of a personal recognition of his indwelling. This is not the same as charismatic speaking in tongues, which Lovelace notes is experienced among Metropolitan Church members, but he suggests 'Where there is a genuine walk in the Spirit, both homophobia and homosexuality melt away'.[41] It is impossible to do justice to this very recent book here. Professor Lovelace is a Presbyterian teaching at the Gordon Cornwell Seminary. His book reflects the American situation and may not correspond entirely with contemporary English Evangelical views.

The need to censure homophobic reactions to homosexuality is also expressed in *The Homosexual Way*, by David Field, the latest I.V.F. publication on the subject.[42] Field notes that the distinction between invert and pervert is important, and that any condemnation of the homosexual must make it plain whether it is addressed to the person or the behaviour, or both. Anxiety about adolescent students is also expressed—these may need protection while their sexual orientation is finely balanced. The biblical evidence is carefully reviewed, including, untypically, Judges 19, and the conclusion is that the mobs at Sodom and Gibeah were bent on homosexual assault. The New Testament references are set in context, in both literary and theological terms, and the possible limitation of St Paul's remarks to perverts is considered but found mistaken. In God's plan from creation to the coming of his Kingdom, homosexual behaviour has no place.[43] The situationist argument is said to be unfaithful to the New Testament teaching, because love's vision is blurred in the individual. God's moral law is crystallized in the Decalogue and applied by the Holy Spirit. In the final pages of the pamphlet and in the personal postscript to homosexual people, Field lays much stress on the Christian's duty of acceptance, both in terms of accepting the Gay person in the fellowship and the Gay person's acceptance of his nature. Although this is a sensitive book, always conscious of the arguments put in recent years for Gay Liberation, it does in fact come to the same conclusions as most of the Catholic and Evangelical authors quoted in this section—the biblical teaching and the Church's tradition stand unassailed.

In the Autumn of 1979, the National Festival of Light responded to the publication of the Church of England Board for Social Responsibility Discussion paper 'Homosexual Relationships' by issuing together the appendix of Professor Lovelace's book with a summary of the 1975 Vatican *Declaration on Sexual Ethics*. The convergence of Catholic and Evangelical views is further demonstrated in another pamphlet published in anticipation of the Board for Social Responsibility Report, *Homosexuals in the Christian Fellowships*, by D. J. Atkinson (Latimer House 1979). This contains a substantial criticism of Bailey's exegesis of the biblical and inter-testamental texts and a medical view by Dr A. W. Steinbeck of the University of New South Wales which suggests a Christian may 'will' an alteration in his sexual disposition.

C The Pressure for Gay Liberation

(a) THE NEED FOR MORE INFORMATION

Anthony Grey, the Director of the Albany Trust, has described the passing of the 1967 Act as 'opening the floodgates', in terms of people seeking advice about homosexuality and other sexual problems.[44] Publications about homosexuality, however, increased steadily in the preceding years. The original reports from the Church of England's Moral Welfare Council, and Bailey's own full length study[45] were all published between 1954 and 1956 and were highly influential in central church and parliamentary circles, but were necessarily circumspect and concentrated on the immediate purpose, to explain why the Churches favoured a change in the law. Their readership was limited. While the government hesitated, the anticipation that the Wolfenden recommendation would eventually be implemented set in motion a steady movement towards freedom in society generally and among the Churches to discuss homosexual behaviour, and straightforward information was needed at a popular level.

There had been in existence before the war several organizations concerned with sex psychology and the World League for Sexual Reform, but these movements and their leading personalities clashed with European Fascist ideals, and the war itself prevented any significant action in England, though the books of Norman Haire, one of the notable pioneers, remained available.[46] In the fifties and sixties education in sexual matters was provided in a number of popular books by doctors and psychiatrists, and these were informative and generally non-polemical, quite often appearing under the Penguin or Pelican imprints. *Sex in Society* by Alex Comfort argued in support of the Wolfenden recommendations and by 1970 Eustace Chesser allocated fifty-two pages of *The Human Aspects of Sexual Deviation* to case histories and information about female and male homosexuality. Anthony Storr's *Sexual Deviation* had covered some of the same ground more briefly in 1964, and Brian Magee had written a full length non-technical account of his research into male and female homosexuality for two BBC Television programmes in 1966. There was, therefore, no longer any need for the general reader who wished to inform himself about homosexuality to struggle with medical or psychiatric textbooks, or seek out the 'erotica' section of specialist booksellers.[47]

(b) HOMOPHILE ORGANIZATIONS

Magee and others drew attention to the presence in other European countries of recognized and open organizations, notably in Holland, where homosexual people were able to meet socially. In England, homophile societies such as the Minorities Research Group for Lesbians became active at this time.

For men, the Gay sub-culture which had long been confined to certain clubs and pubs, began to form its own societies and produce magazines to exchange views and reduce the sense of isolation that had been one of the great disadvantages for homosexual people until the spread of tolerance allowed them to come out. Police vigilance was, of course, maintained and some pubs had their licences revoked. Some Gay magazines were prosecuted for advertisements which appeared to be encouraging homosexual prostitution and were therefore 'conspiring to corrupt public morals'.[48]

The emergence of the Gay scene, at one stage partially identified with political radicalism and the advocacy of an alternative society, but now calmer and more concerned with counselling services and reducing confrontation with heterosexuals, cannot be followed in detail here, though one sad feature of it was the occasional antipathy between the early groups such as the Albany Trust, largely supported by Christians, and the Gay Liberation Front. It was, perhaps, inevitable that the former, guided by Anthony Grey, would remain sensitive to public opinion and establishment tolerance lest there be a backlash, while some left-wing members of the new groups regarded these as their chief enemies. Universities become one arena where the right to have Gay societies was fought for, opposition coming more from conservatives, and Student Christian Unions, anxious to preserve the traditional biblical teaching, than from the student leaders of the Unions themselves, for whom this sometimes became a convenient issue for demonstrating their radicalism.[49] Lesbians were fully involved in the Gay Liberation campaigns, though there was an area of conflict here, the problem of male domination within the movement symbolizing the entrenched resistance to women's rights within society.

An extensive collection of case histories recording the difficulties faced by men and women who found themselves homosexual has been provided by Jack Babuscio, a London lecturer who, for a time, organized counselling services for homosexuals associated with the Campaign for Homosexual Equality. Babuscio writes:

> It is as a direct result of society's failure to accept homosexuality as a legitimate variation of the sexual drive that the Gay person's principal problem becomes one of finding an acceptable identity within an hostile environment. Yet this search for a satisfying self-image is often thwarted by a barrier of demeaning myths and stereotypes which still surround the issue of homosexuality.

He then asks us to consider the case of 'Claude':

You can't name a book that I didn't consult. And in each of them the message rang out loud and clear. You're a criminal. And your crime is against God, nature, society and yourself.[50]

The names of the persons quoted in this book have been altered. Chapter 5 has poignant examples of people whose discovery of their homosexuality has caused acute anxiety, their situation seeming to be in conflict with their knowledge of church and scriptural teaching. Babuscio gives his own brief account of this teaching and suggests that the Jewish position tends to fall somewhere between the Catholics and the Protestants, though he assumes that all the latter take a modern liberal view of Scripture. He also suggests that it is

the worrying possibility of an extension of the subject into a much broader area of Christian sexual ethics which may well pose the principal obstacle to full acceptance by the Churches of several million homosexuals.[51]

A sign of the measure of tolerance of Gay people now achieved has been the peaceful march of some thousands of Gay men and women through London streets to a carnival in Hyde Park which took place on 30 June 1979 as part of International Gay Pride Week. Drama, films, and workshops exemplifying Gay culture were also included in the week's programme. However, it would be premature to assume that opposition to the Gay Rights Movement has been permanently silenced and this very brief account of its history may be concluded by quotations from a recent statement *Towards a Charter of Homosexual Rights* published by the Campaign for Reason in 1978. Among the one hundred and seventy-four listed sponsors of this statement are forty-five ministers of religion, many of whom hold senior positions in the major English denominational churches.

A Beliefs:

1. We believe that fear or hatred of homosexuals is a social evil, akin to anti-semitism, racism, slavery, and with the same evil consequences. It harms both the victimised individuals, and the society which tolerates it.

B Causes of the Phobia:

1. It seems clear that the fear or hatred of homosexuality which still exists and which sometimes emerges in the form of prejudice in conversation and occasionally in journalism, is still tolerated by many people, including some who very strongly disagree with it. Often, it is allowed to masquerade as respectable or even 'Christian' morality. The basis is irrational, and the tone may be manifestly uninformed and unloving, yet it seldom earns official rebuke. Clearly fear and ignorance have still a disproportionate power to inhibit knowledge, and humanity.
2. In the past, even the Christian church condoned the evils of slavery, racism, anti-semitism, heresy-hunting—so strong is the power of social conditioning, before it has been successfully challenged, even over the followers of a religion proclaiming universal love and acceptance.

Nowadays, these evils are recognised for what they are, and no one perpetuating them could expect to do so either in the name of ordinary socially accepted morality, or in the name of the Christian church.

3. We appreciate that certain features of the homosexual sub-culture disturb many otherwise well-disposed people, but think that two factors should be kept in mind.
First, the heterosexual world also has its unpleasing side, but no one imagines that life-long marriage and genuine love are to be equated with (say) prostitution or rape. Again, most people accept that heterosexuals are free to make their own adult sexual choices, as long as these harm no one but themselves.
Second, it should be recognised that the homosexual sub-culture is largely *caused* by social hostility and persecution in the first place. Many homosexuals find themselves forced into it, as an only alternative to celibacy, for lack of social acceptance for their own love, and partnerships, by the world at large. The church, which should be specially helpful, has failed to be—a glaring fault in the religion of love.[52]

(c) GAY CHRISTIAN MOVEMENTS

For some Gay people within the Liberation Movement, the Christian Churches have seemed to be one of the most intransigent obstacles to their aspirations. This is not because the Churches have in any official way attempted since 1957 to impose their own moral teaching on non-members, except in the very limited sense of occasional protests in Student Unions, and some polemical rallies, but because, in a secular period, the Church can easily be made a scapegoat for a majority homophobic view in society. It is also the case that official declarations from the Vatican are widely reported and confirm, apparently, that theirs is the universal Christian attitude. Conversely, since many of those who have been most active in various parts of the Gay Liberation Movement are themselves university teachers or post-graduates, or more loosely members of the academic and political circles, the initiative of the Churches in encouraging legal change is well known.

From the early days of the Homosexual Law Reform Society to the present sponsors of the Charter of Homosexual Rights, leading Christians have been deeply involved. That support may have been in part a reflection of the preoccupation of the Churches with human rights generally, their anxiety about discrimination in any form, and the emphasis on the social gospel in the last two decades, though it is interesting that Edward Norman excludes sexual politics from his all-embracing criticism of these priorities in his Reith Lectures for 1978. However that may be, there has been no iron curtain between Gay Liberation in general and the specifically Christian movements. These movements have tended to be ecumenical in character, largely run by enthusiasts in a part-time capacity with little financial support.

In consequence, there has been flexibility but also some short-lived organizations.

At the time of writing, the two largest ecumenical groups seem to be The Open Church Group, and the Gay Christian Movement. There are also groups with clear denominational affiliations such as Quest (for Roman Catholics); The Friends Homosexual Fellowship; The Jewish Gay Group; and the Metropolitan Church which was founded in America by Troy Perry particularly for Gay people and Christians in sympathy, and now has several English Congregations. Other special interest Gay groups provide for particular professions or regional support, and there are telephone counselling services in major cities. The history and publications of these movements is not further considered here, but some of the points made by the publications of the Gay Christian Movement and in the Reports from the S.C.M. Conference 'Towards a Theology of Gay Liberation', are noted later. The convictions and aims of the G.C.M. are as follows:

Statement of Conviction

It is the conviction of the members of the Gay Christian Movement that human sexuality in all its richness is a gift of God gladly to be accepted, enjoyed and honoured as a way of both expressing and growing in love, in accordance with the life and teaching of Jesus Christ; therefore it is their conviction that it is entirely compatible with the Christian faith not only to love another person of the same sex but also to express that love fully in a personal sexual relationship.

Aims

The aims of the Gay Christian Movement are:

(1) To encourage fellowship, friendship, and support among individual gay Christians through prayer, study and action, wherever possible in local groups, and especially to support those gay Christians subjected to discrimination.

(2) To help the whole Church re-examine its understanding of human sexuality and to work for a positive acceptance of gay relationships within the framework outlined in the Statement of Conviction above, so that all homosexuals may be able to contribute fully to the life and ministry of the Church.

(3) To encourage members to witness to their Christian faith and experience within the gay community, and to witness to their convictions about human sexuality within the Church.

(4) To maintain and strengthen links with other gay Christian groups both in Britain and elsewhere.

(d) THE QUAKER REPORT

A small group from the Society of Friends was among the first to express a firmly liberal Christian point of view. The pamphlet *Towards a Quaker View of Sex* published for them by the Literature

Committee of the Friends Home Service Committee in 1963, was in fact largely concerned with homosexuality, the response to a request for guidance from Quaker students faced with difficulties of this kind. Although in no sense an official statement of the Society of Friends, it caused some anxiety in drawing attention to the normality of adolescent masturbation, the steady increase in physical familiarity casually allowed, and the suggestion that

> light-hearted and loving casual contacts can be known without profound damage or 'moral degeneracy' being the result to either partner.[53]

Turning to homosexuality, but 'without alacrity' the report observed that although a homosexual orientation is usual among boys in the 11–17 age group, and a boy's first love will be for another boy, this could be far from casual, and if it be denounced, the shock might make it harder for him to reach a satisfactory sexual adjustment later. Female homosexuality is then discussed in the context of its greater social acceptance, but the emotional dangers for young women in such relationships, and the stresses of older women who seek in female partners what could only be provided by a male, are described more critically.[54]

After a quotation from a sermon by Bishop John Robinson about our 'utterly mediaeval treatment of Homosexuals'[55] the report challenges the traditional condemnation of homosexuality in direct terms:

> It is the nature and quality of a relationship that matters: one must not judge it by its outward appearance but by its inner worth. Homosexual affection can be as selfless as heterosexual affection, and therefore we cannot see that it is in some way morally worse. Homosexual affection may, of course, be an emotion which some find aesthetically disgusting, but one cannot base Christian morality on a capacity for such disgust. Neither are we happy with the thought that all homosexual behaviour is sinful: motive and circumstances degrade or ennoble any act, and we feel that to list sexual 'sins' is to follow the letter rather than the spirit, to kill rather than to give life. Further we see no reason why the physical nature of a sexual act should be the criterion by which the question whether or not it is moral should be decided. An act which (for example) expresses true affection between two individuals and gives pleasure to them both does not seem to us to be sinful by reason alone of the fact that it is homosexual. The same criteria seem to apply to us whether a relationship is heterosexual or homosexual.[56]

In the next section of the report, headed 'A New Morality Needed' it argues for a conviction that love cannot be confined to a pattern. The group observe that it is unfortunate that sexual intercourse takes place between Adam and Eve only after expulsion from the Garden (a point surprisingly made since biblical literalism is not an obvious feature of the report elsewhere), for this provides an excuse for thinking that sexual intimacy is associated with a sinful or disobedient state. Bailey's suggestion that 'I love you' should properly be said in the context of a possible marriage, is countered by the suggestion that it is the waywardness of love in tending to leap every barrier which provides its tremendous creative power. Finally, the group, mostly teachers, doctors, and psychologists, reassure their readers that several of them have, in fact, found it possible 'to give substance to the traditional code, conscious of their debt to Christ in showing what love implies'.

The importance of this Quaker Report at the time lay partly in the high reputation the Society itself always has for moral caring responsibility and in the courage and clarity of its writing, which left no doubt as to its meaning. If the morality of heterosexual and homosexual relationships is to be tested by the same, and only rule—does it contain affection, pleasure and selflessness?—then the old formulations are redundant, and even Mill's check—avoiding harm to others—seems negative by comparison.

Beguilingly expressed as the report's suggestions are, they are open to various interpretations. For example, selflessness and affection might only be fully expressed within the permanency of monogamous marriage, as Bailey argued; or conversely, giving temporary pleasure to another through sexual intercourse might be considered selfless and a sign of affection, however transient. The report was, therefore, quickly glossed with such interpretations by different Christian commentators, but there is little doubt that its abiding influence has been to articulate the basis of a liberal case. The cogency of the case as this group of Friends put it was their

> concern with homosexuals who say to each other 'I love you' in the hopeless and bitter awareness of a hostile criminal code and hypocritical public opinion.[57]

(e) THE STATUS OF HOMOSEXUAL LOVE

The concept of love is notoriously difficult to define. It can include a great range of human feelings and motives, from lust through passion, affection, and friendship to romance, self-denial, and heroic altruism. While it has been habitual for Christians nurtured on the hymn to charity in 1 Corinthians and the events of Good Friday to feel confident they have little to learn from unbelievers in this regard, it has also been a standard accusation of homosexual people that the Christian Church has obscured the many meanings of human love by its emphasis on spiritual love and fear of the body. Nietzsche's sharp comment may be recalled:

> Christianity gave Eros, the god of love, poison to drink: he did not die of it, it is true, but he degenerated to vice.

Oscar Wilde's attempt to explain romantic love between males fell on deaf Victorian ears and this aspect of the relationships between some members of the Bloomsbury Group was represented as friendly affection at the time. Love among women had been recognized as an eccentricity in the eighteenth-century example of the domestic retirement together of Lady Eleanor Butler and Miss Sarah Ponsonby—the Ladies of Llangollen as they were called. But when Radcliffe Hall and Lady Una Troubridge set up house together in London, and the former wrote an almost autobiographical novel about lesbianism, *The Well of Loneliness*, in 1928, she and her publisher were successfully prosecuted for an obscene libel, despite the advocacy of Sir Norman Birkett for the defence. Explicitness was dangerous, and other novels of the time included the subject more parenthetically.

With the heightened perceptiveness to evidence of a homosexual disposition developing in the fifties, a kind of literary equivalent to the search for 'Reds under the bed' of Senator McCarthy began. Biographers of famous people who had remained unmarried added dark hints about unsatisfactory relationships to mothers, absent fathers, and other well recognized signals that their subject might have been homosexual, and in some cases they were probably right. The lines of A. E. Housman, quoted in the Quaker Report, 'curse the God that made him for the colour of his hair' were perceived to have a new and poignant significance. Ten years ago it would have been possible to provide some astonishment and confirm some suspicions by listing perhaps twenty recent biographies in which such dark hints were being made, but perhaps it is a sign of further maturity that the present style is to be explicit where that is justified, as, for example, with Lytton Strachey, Somerset Maugham, and E. M. Forster, and otherwise make no imputation of homosexuality unless the subject of the biography has chosen to 'come out'. Many have, but not always in a style of writing that has enhanced the homosexual's substantial case for fair recognition.

The changing styles in biographical investigation can be well illustrated through the succession of 'lives' of T. E. Lawrence and R. F. Scott, both originally regarded as heroic figures. Lawrence's own account of the homosexual assault imposed on him by the Turkish soldiers at Deraa is restrained, but the phrase with which he ends his account in *The Seven Pillars of Wisdom*

> that night the citadel of my integrity had been irrevocably lost[58]

has led to a good deal of investigation of his own sexual orientation. Since his letters have become available, it seems probably that masochism rather than homosexuality was the disturbing discovery he made of himself at that time. It is not clear what allegations about Captain Scott, if any, are likely to prove well founded but for both these men some rehabilitation of their reputations may well be deserved.

A helpful example of a well-handled progress towards explicitness is provided by the story of the marriage between Harold Nicolson and Victoria Sackville-West. One of Victoria's friends was Virginia Woolf, and both of them wrote novels which hinted at lesbianism obliquely. These were, *Mrs Dalloway* (1925); *To the Lighthouse* (1927); and *Orlando* (1928); all written by Virginia Woolf and, with hindsight, it is easy to identify the setting of the last of these with the Sackville-West family seat, a great Elizabethan house at Knole in Kent. Victoria Nicolson wrote *The Dark Island* in 1934.

Thirty years later their son Nigel began editing Harold Nicolson's diaries and letters for publication, which appeared in 1966–7.[59] Nigel Nicolson hints in the introduction to these volumes that his mother had a private and masculine aspect to her personality. She had died, in fact, in 1962, and it fell to him as executor, to go through her personal papers. Among these, in a locked case, he found his mother's account of her affection for another woman, Violet Trefusis. By 1973 he judged it appropriate to publish details of this in *Portrait of a Marriage* where he describes the forty-nine years during which both his parents had a sequence of homosexual affairs. He assesses the marriage thus in his introduction:

> It is the story of two people who married for love and whose love deepened with every passing year, although each was constantly and by mutual consent unfaithful to the other. Their marriage not only survived infidelity, sexual incompatibility and long absences, but became stronger and finer as a result.[60]

Perhaps it needs to be said that Harold Nicolson died in 1968, and Violet in 1972, so confidentiality was preserved in their lifetime, as Victoria intended. It is also true that Nigel Nicolson's parents must be considered by ordinary standards, as remarkable people, and it cannot be assumed that most marriages would endure and thrive in such circumstances. However, the story as finally told shows something of the lives of these authors when they wrote their pre-war novels.[61]

When the negro author James Baldwin addressed the World Council of Churches Assembly in Uppsala, Sweden, in 1968 on the problem of Racism, he startled that well-disposed audience, crowded on a hot evening into the University Auditorium, with the words: 'I am one of God's creatures the Christian Church has most betrayed.' In his novel *Giovanni's Room*, Baldwin describes the emotional pain of being a homosexual.[62] The story is a simple one of a man's discovery of his homosexuality through an intensifying experience with a waiter, Giovanni, while he struggles to maintain a full relationship with his woman Hella. It ends, of course, in tragedy and loneliness but the strength of the book is the description of the dawning desperate realization that the homosexual love could not be denied.

(f) HOMOPHOBIA

Perhaps the hardest frustration of those who find themselves homosexual has been to convince heterosexuals that homosexual love is capable of just the same integrity, selflessness and total commitments as heterosexual love can show at its best: the David and Jonathan 'archetype' is often called in aid. The difficulties are formidable, not only because there is very little awareness in society of profound and permanent homosexual relationships, a consequence it would be alleged of the prevailing antipathy towards them by the heterosexual majority, but also for a more profound reason in that love in its self-giving always involves risk and self-abandonment, so that even those who are happily fulfilled in a heterosexual relationship find it difficult to accept that another, and to them alien, form can be as genuine.

Perhaps the roots of homophobia lie here. In his searching study, *Freedom in Love*, A. E. Dyson, a joint-founder of the Homosexual Law Reform Society, and now chairman of the Open Church Group, records how fear of this alien form of love can create hatred.

> In the armoury of hell few weapons are stronger than vices masquerading as virtues, or than hatred set up as a respected opponent of love. Envy of the loving by the unloving, the daring by the cowardly, the joyful by the joyless—these are the social virtues fostered in hell. There are some people who gladly vent on adulterers, homosexuals, or any other accepted scapegoats the hatred they would secretly like to vent on creation itself. When campaigning for homosexual law reform I sometimes felt that though there will be neither marriage nor giving in marriage in heaven (where love is apotheosized) there will be permanent laws against sex, and love, in hell.[63]

One of Dyson's colleagues on the staff of the University of Essex has devoted more than half of his book *Sexual Stigma* to the case of male homosexuality. In contrast to Dyson's literary style (he is in the English Department), Plummer uses the vocabulary of the social scientist, but with the same force. He begins his description of the inter-actional problems of the homosexual thus:

> Homosexuality in this culture is a stigma label. To be called a 'homosexual' is to be degraded, denounced, devalued, or treated as different. It may well mean shame, ostracism, discrimination, exclusion or physical attack. It may simply mean that one becomes 'an interesting curiosity of permissiveness'.

But always, in this culture, the costs of being a homosexual must be high. It is the knowledge of the cost of being publicly recognised as a homosexual that leads many people to conceal their sexual identity. A central fact of the experience thus becomes the necessity for the homosexual to manage a discreditable identity; to present a suitable non-sexual front; to play down the homosexual self; to 'pass'.[64]

(g) CHRISTIAN MEANINGS OF LOVE

The Christian Churches had not, of course, ignored the problem of the many meanings of love. Over the years, they had debated the relationship between the three Greek words: *eros: philia:* and *agape*, and distinguished the first from *porneia*. Erotic love between married partners was acceptable, if given muted attention by comparison with friendship and selfless love. Lust meant sexual exploitation, the misuse of the sexual drive outside marriage, and this omnibus term covered all that the Bible included in *porneia*. There was some risk of confusion over the meaning of the word *libido*, the original Latin word implying sexual desire or impulse. In Lutheran theology, the libido tended to corrupt unless redeemed, but in Freudian terminology it meant the sexual drive in essence, not its misuse. Pornography, writing about *porneia*, 'doing dirt on sex' as D. H. Lawrence called it, became a related issue in the permissive sixties, and the Christian theologians did not find it easy to explain that erotic literature might be an appropriate stimulant to sexual activity among married people, while pornography proper degraded both sexuality and women.

The meaning of love in the Christian tradition was, perhaps, best expressed at this time by C. S. Lewis. After his conversion, Lewis thought his way deeply into Christian orthodoxy and used his academic knowledge and mastery of English to write not only popular apologetics, but also the famous Narnia tales for children together with major works on mediaeval literature. On sexual morality, he was clear that the Christian rule is 'Either marriage with complete faithfulness to your partner, or else total abstinence'. But he was always alert to the inward realities and could add 'A cold, self-righteous prig who goes to church regularly may be far nearer to hell than a prostitute; but, of course, it is better to be neither.'[65]

Lewis was well aware of the need to rehabilitate the Christian doctrines of marriage and sexuality against the accusation that the Church had made a mess of them. In this same broadcast he argues:

> I know that some muddle-headed Christians have talked as if Christianity thought that sex, or the body, or pleasure were bad in themselves. But they were wrong. Christianity is almost the only one of the great religions which thoroughly approves of the body—which believes that matter is good, that God Himself once took on a human body, that some kind of body is going to be given us even in Heaven, and is going to be an essential part of our

happiness, our beauty and our energy. Christianity has glorified marriage more than any other religion; and nearly all the greatest love poetry in the world has been produced by Christians.[66]

Few more recent commentators on the Christian tradition have felt as confident as Lewis here seems to be, but Lewis knew the case against him, and dealt with it in his longer works.

A typical example is this passage from his chapter on Charity in *The Four Loves*. He is commenting on Augustine's description of the death of his friend Nebridus, and the desolation he felt (*Confessions*, IV.10). Augustine writes:

All human beings pass away. Do not let your happiness depend on something you may lose. If love is to be a blessing, not a misery, it must be for the only Beloved who will not pass away.

Lewis comments:

I think that this passage in the Confessions is less a part of Augustine's Christendom than a hangover from the high-minded Pagan philosophies in which he grew up. It is closer to Stoic 'apathy' or neo-Platonic mysticism than to charity. We follow one who wept over Jerusalem and at the Grave of Lazarus, and loving all, had one disciple whom, in a special sense, he 'loved'. There is no escape along the lines St. Augustine suggests. Nor along any other lines. There is no safe investment. To love at all is to be vulnerable. Love anything and your heart will certainly be wrung and possibly be broken.[67]

Lewis had personal experience of the brokenness love might bring through his friendship with Joy Davidman in his later years, and their subsequent brief marriage. She was stricken with cancer from the beginning, and he supported her for four years until she died suddenly in 1960.[68] Lewis also knew from his studies of mediaeval literature that in the development of courtly love, the Church had been presented with an opportunity which, for reasons strong at the time, was missed. Eroticism and friendship had been well understood in the classical world, but faced with their degeneracy into vice, the early Christians had no alternative but to turn towards asceticism and press for the recognition of selfless love, of which Christ himself was the archetype. Notions of romantic love were relatively undeveloped by the Greeks and Romans and remained so in Christendom. The one canonical book which dealt with this, the Song of Songs, was usually intepreted as an allegory of the love between Christ and his Church. The present-day popularity of the story of Abelard and Heloise reflects, in the Christian tradition, the longing for a romantic myth, similar to that of Romeo and Juliet, or the original Tristan and Iseult.

Lewis devoted one of his major studies to the allegorical love poetry of the Middle Ages. He sets out the challenge of courtly love to the concepts of sex held by the Church and secular world of the time, showing that in Christian teaching the act of intercourse itself could never be called sinful within marriage, but the passion and desire that led to it often was. Passion was suspect because it was irrational, as we have already seen in the *Summa* of Aquinas, but friendship between spouses and God's provision of a partner to man 'made it possible for mediaeval theory to find room for innocent sexuality'. While mediaeval marriage was arranged to further political or financial policies and could be dissolved if these failed, the context of married life within feudalism meant that in the castle community, ruled by 'my lord and my lady', there often existed unattached males, knights without property. In this setting and probably because of it, the doctrine of courtly love was conceived.

From its small beginning in Provence, Lewis traces the whole concept of romantic love, taken for granted today, and assumed to be immemorial and universal. He sharpens his point by suggesting that it would have been impossible to explain romantic love to Aristotle or St Paul. In so far as modern Christian people expect to find it in marriage, even Plato would be baffled, for in the *Symposium*, progress towards divine love implies a firm abandonment of boy love and then woman love.[69]

It can be easily but superficially said that the ideas of courtly love were a proper correction to the emotional barrenness of marriage relationships as they were taught and practised in the Middle Ages, and one can easily see the present day stress on romantic love—the *sine qua non* of heterosexual and homosexual relationships—as the same corrective in modern dress. But courtly love had a serious defect from the Christian viewpoint and therefore it could never be baptized. Had it not been for this defect—the exclusion of marriage—the Christian tradition would have been stronger in emphasizing love and especially its joy and lightness, and therefore better able to defend itself against the continual attack that Christians are afraid of sexuality.

It was essential to courtly love that the lover remained the abject suppliant to an often totally unattainable beloved, and if sexual union were achieved, it was in circumstances of fornication or adultery. The achievement of straightforward matrimonial bliss and domesticity would have destroyed the point of the enterprise, which required every risk to be accepted gladly in the name of chivalry, except the ultimate one of permanent and public commitment.

In a most perceptive analysis of the primary myth of unattainable love, the romance of Tristan and Iseult, Dennis de Rougemont records not only the reaction of the mediaeval Church to the threat of courtly love, but also its perpetuation in films and novels of our own day. The

Church responded at the time with the alternative of the mystical union between Christ and the believer to be achieved in Heaven and for which prayer and contemplation now would be a foretaste. The description of the Virgin Mary as the Queen of Heaven, a spiritualized alternative to Iseult perhaps, was first promulgated at this time. And the paradox of much modern romance is that the pursuit of the beloved, unhappily married to another, ends at the point of divorce and remarriage. We are not told exactly how the new couple live happily ever after, and so the cynical public wonder, rightly, if 'marrying Iseult' will ever be successful. Rougement writes:

> Iseult is for ever a stranger, the very essence of what is strange in woman and of all that is eternally fugitive, vanishing and almost hostile in a fellow-being, that indeed which incites to pursuit and rouses in the heart of a man who has fallen prey to the myth an avidity for possession so much more delightful than possession itself. She is the woman-from-whom-one is parted; to possess her is to lose her.[70]

(h) HOMOSEXUAL BEHAVIOUR APPROVED?

Recalling from the past the notion of courtly love, and noting the suggestion of Lewis and de Rougemont that this was the origin of the modern idea of romantic love, leads on to a possible new way of thinking about homosexual relationships. Since it seems to be generally held that heterosexual behaviour derives some of its morality from the presence of romantic love between the partners, might not this test also be applied to homosexual relationships? Few, if any, Christian commentators nowadays would deny that homosexuals can love each other sincerely. Has the opportunity to 'baptize' this other love now arisen for the Churches? Even if marriage is too firmly located in the heterosexual institution for this to be the appropriate model, could not some form of 'blessing' be provided for those homosexuals who seek grace in support of an intended permanent relationship?

Those authors, often American, who have discussed these questions have tended to avoid explicitness about genital activity within the permanent homosexual relationship. The long-accepted pattern of shared domestic life and enduring friendship among women, with the assumption of separate bedrooms and a goodnight 'peck', could no doubt be paralleled among men, and probably often was. But once sexual activity became advocated as an essential part of being fully human, not just a liberation of the libido, but a proper matching of the body to the emotions, then the assumption of genital chastity could not be made so readily. There is therefore a detectable reticence or hesitation in describing exactly what is permitted to homosexual partners in a permanent relationship in many of the more liberal writings. Perhaps out of caution on the printed page, perhaps because the consistent Christian tradition could not be challenged directly, it has become necessary to read between the lines.

H. Kimball-Jones was Methodist pastor of the American Protestant Church of Antwerp when his *Towards a Christian Understanding of the Homosexual* was published in England, but he seems to have written it the previous year in America, having the American scene mainly in mind, and a good knowledge of what had recently been happening in England.[71] His book is a concise review of the situation as it stood in 1966, first as to the prevalence, types, and causes, then how Christian thinkers were pondering the effects on their tradition, and finally on the possible ways forward.

In his third section, Kimball-Jones seeks to re-evaluate the traditional Christian attitude toward the homosexual and to arrive at a responsible Christian ethic which is valid for the time in which we are living. He suggests that:

> the Church must be willing to make the difficult but necessary step of recognising the validity of mature sexual relationships, encouraging the absolute invert to maintain a fidelity to one partner when his only other choice would be to lead a promiscuous life filled with guilt and fear. This would by no means be an endorsement of homosexuality by the Church. Rather it would simply be a realistic, and thus responsible, solution to an otherwise insoluble problem, for there is really no other practicable answer for those homosexuals who cannot change.[72]

The caution of the last sentence quoted is amplified in a succeeding paragraph:

> Such an acceptance is not an idealisation of the homosexual way of life. . . . Thus we could not go along with the proposal that the Church perform marriages between homosexuals. . . .
>
> It is one thing to say that a homosexual relationship, though necessarily falling short of the will of God, can be an occasion for mutual love and devotion. But it is quite another thing to say that the Church should offer formal sanction of such a relationship. . . . A mature homosexual relationship may be recognised as a valid way of life, a maximum possibility within a given context, but it cannot be recognised as meeting the standards of Christian marriage. However creative and fulfilling it may be, it nevertheless remains an unnatural expression of human sexuality.

The remainder of the book is concerned with practical action already proceeding or recommended among the American Churches, irrelevant here, but Kimball-Jones does have one final attempt to be positive, pleading that:

> we should accept the homosexual as a child of God and recognise his way of life as a potentially creative expression of human sexuality, even encouraging homosexual relationships when necessary

but he still warns that these relationships are doomed by their very nature

to never pass beyond a certain point.[73]

Probably the best known advocate for the homosexual case in England in the seventies has been Dr Norman Pittenger, formerly Professor of Christian Apologetics at the General Theological Seminary of New York, and now settled as a senior fellow at King's College, Cambridge. Pittenger is primarily a dogmatic theologian, associated with such modern movements as Process Theology, but in 1967 he wrote a brief piece entitled 'Time for Consent', published in the *New Christian* magazine and relating to the final stages of the passing of the Sexual Offences Act. He received many letters about the article, most of them encouraging him to expand his views, which he did, first in an S.C.M. broadsheet, and then in a book of 1970, further enlarged in a 1976 edition.[74]

Since this is a highly influential book, it may be best to observe first that its treatment of the biblical material at the beginning of chapter 9 is its weakest point, not much more than a short reiteration of Bailey's position. Its strength lies in its calm presentation of the case for homosexual behaviour in chapter 5. Since it is so carefully written, brief quotations can scarcely do justice to Pittenger's argument, but his main points are expressed as follows:

> What a homosexual person is seeking is love; in this respect he is like all human beings. I do not mean simply love which is given to him. I also mean love which he can give. (p. 46)

> We shall do well to recognise that very few human beings are called to the celibate life. . . . For most of us the expression of our created nature as lovers 'in the making' will be by loving another person, and with this there will go the desire for sexual expression of love in physical contacts of various kinds. (p. 46)

> It remains true that if the homosexual person is to be accepted, he is expected by religious leaders to refrain from any physical acts which give external expression to his impulses. . . . The attitude which demands of the homosexual no physical expression of his love seems to be inhuman, unjust and above all, unchristian. I do not understand it, nor can I find any reason to support it. (p. 48)

Pittenger then describes the kinds of physical contact in which homosexual men and women are likely to engage, and notes that none of them are in themselves peculiarly homosexual, for they are also practised by many heterosexuals, though some may find particular acts distasteful.

For homosexual men and women, only through such acts can they manifest in the fullest way the love which is deepest in their personalities.
Let us put it this way. A man who is committed to another who wishes to have with the other the mutuality which is giving and receiving, who feels tenderness towards the other, who wishes to give himself in faithful and hopeful union with the other, will almost inevitably desire to express this. He will seek an expression which is so total, so much the whole of him, that it will include physical contacts of one sort or another. To fail in this, he thinks, would be to hold back something of himself. It would not be the kind of love which is all-inclusive of himself, either as the giver or the recipient.[75]

In the hope that these quotations sufficiently represent the main points of his argument, we can move on to another question that Pittenger faces squarely, the realistic expectations of stability and fidelity for a homosexual partnership. Since there can be no natural children of the couple, some adopt successfully,[76] but it is recognized that the relationship must be based on the love of the partners for each other. Pittenger recognizes that such partnerships break up, often through jealously, when one partner has a brief affair with someone else, and both partners have to decide whether or not such freedom is likely to be acceptable. Open or closed situations are possible, as they are in heterosexual marriage.

Pittenger hopes that counsellors will prepare homosexuals for disappointments of this kind, and assist them to establish relations 'which will be by intention as permanent and faithful as can be possibly managed' (p. 90).

In his final chapter, entitled 'An Ethic for Homosexuals', six suggestions are made of a practical kind; these may be summarized as:

(1) do not accept one's homosexuality without questioning it, testing one's capacity for relationship with the other sex and taking advice;
(2) accept the fact once established as 'given', without shame;
(3) remember that God loves the homosexual just as he is—that is the whole point of the Christian gospel;
(4) a homosexual should be a responsible person; it is bad manners and irresponsible to attempt the seduction of others;
(5) a homosexual should try to develop close friendships with people he esteems and likes;
(6) if a homosexual does find a person whom he loves and who loves him in return, he must decide whether or not physical contacts are permissible.

Pittenger himself concludes they could be, provided that they are

expressive of his total self, that they are genuinely desired by his friend, and that they promote increasing love between them.

For behaviour in the past that has not reached these standards, Pittenger affirms that God forgives, and God still loves: this is the assurance of Christian faith.[77] Pittenger's seemingly rather cursory treatment of the biblical texts reflects the situation ethic approch which was widely discussed at the time of his original article in *New Christian.* Although this discussion concerned the fundamental principles for making moral decisions generally, sexual ethics became a particularly controversial aspect of it. Apart from the New Testament statements about the primacy of love, this school could appeal to the dictum of Augustine, 'Dilige et quod vis fac',[78] loosely translated as 'Love and then what you will, do'.

In the views of the situationists, this could become 'nothing is prescribed in advance but love', and a chief exponent of this view was Joseph Fletcher, Professor of Social Ethics at the Episcopal Theological School, Cambridge, Mass. He owes his familiarity among British Christian circles to John Robinson's references to him in *Honest to God*,[79] and the subsequent popularity of two lively books in which, *inter alia*, Fletcher identified himself with those who approved premarital sexual intercourse in some circumstances. Fletcher has been described by the American philosopher, W. Frankena, as an act-agapaist, that is, one for whom the normative theory in ethics is one in which no appeal is made to rules:

> We are to tell what we should do in a particular situation simply by getting clear about the facts of that situation and then asking what is the loving or the most loving thing to do in it. In other words, we are to apply the law of love directly and separately in each case with which we are confronted.[80]

Certainly, there is a kind of instantness about the ethical decisions with which Fletcher sprinkled his more popular writings, and a good example of his style is the way he deals with the New Testament teaching on fornication:

> The Bible clearly affirms sex as a high order value, at the same time sanctioning marriage (although not always monogamy) but any claim that the Bible requires that sex be expressed solely within marriage is only an inference. There is nothing explicitly forbidding premarital acts. Only extra-marital acts, i.e. adultery, are forbidden. Those Christians who are situational, refusing to absolutize any moral principle except 'love thy neighbour', cannot absolutize St. Paul's 'one flesh' (*henosis*) theory of marriage in 1 Cor. Chap. 6.[81]

Taking remarks of this kind in context, it is clear that Fletcher was much concerned with the confused situation in the American States about legal penalties for various kinds of sexual behaviour, and the difficulties of the Christian pastor faced with the sexual mores of the university campus, and this is also clear in his occasional references to homosexuality. Thus, addressing the Duke University School of Law in 1960, he points out that for male homosexual acts, the punishment in New York will be one day in prison, while in Nevada it will be life imprisonment. He thought it vital for American jurists to keep abreast of British developments, and he agreed with the Wolfenden Committee recommendations and Bailey's advocacy in the Anglican evidence submitted to the Committee.

In 1971 the Presbyterian Westminster Press in America published a book of essays with the crisp title *Is Gay Good?*[82] This was a collection of essays by Christians of various denominations including essays by Kimball-Jones, Pittenger and Anthony Grey. It begins with an essay by Professor J. Von Rohr, an American Lutheran of the Pacific School of Religion and the Graduate Theological Union, Berkeley, and the other authors react and comment. Von Rohr's position is cautious, describing the situation in a familiar way (the essay was originally written in 1965 in a longer version) and offering the contribution in theological terms that the homosexual is entitled to look for 'redemption' within the Church, which might include any or all of the following: acceptance within the fellowship, treatment, and progress towards expressing his own love in more faithful and selfless terms. Among the reactions to this essay in the book, one by Carl F. Henry, Professor of Theology at the Eastern Baptist Theological Seminary, Philadelphia, quotes Frank Lake among others in support of the view that only conversion in the Christian sense offers hope and cure 'for a condition that Christianity has long declared as wicked'. In his view the meaning of the biblical passages is quite clear, Jesus and the New Testament reserve some of their stringent moral condemnations for sexual infractions, and the word of God must not be subverted by a pagan trans-valuation of its norms.

Henry then sets out how he sees the Christian gospel applied to homosexuals, and the following quotation can perhaps be regarded as an orthodox American Baptist view:

> It is true indeed that divine redemption alone can lift the universally broken life of sex to an approximation of the ideal. But in the one case, that of heterosexuality and marriage, redemption renews and perfects human sexual relationships, while in the other instance, that of homosexuality, it brings such relationships to a halt, and shapes a kind of interest in the divine order of creation and in the expression of deep and abiding personal love in ways the Scriptures encourage. . . . The healing of homosexuality is possible by the same method whereby Christ makes all men whole who come to Him, by opening their beggarly lives to the realities of the spiritual world. The new birth inaugurates a new series of relationships with God and man, one in which we are fully accepted in Christ, while we are on the way to a wholly new selfhood. The Holy Spirit then triggers the human ego with a new sensitivity to the possibilities of decision for good and evil, enhances the sense of responsibility and love for other persons, and undergirds the determination to do right.[83]

In the next chapter there follows a short forceful challenge to this interpretation by Troy Perry, a minister trained at the Moody Bible Institute, founder and pastor of the first congregation for predominantly homosexual people in the U.S.A., the Metropolitan Community Church of Los Angeles. Perry in one sense accepts the text of the Bible in a literal and conservative way, as might be expected from his place of training, but then accuses the Christian Church of inconsistency in deciding which bits it will obey. Thus, the Sodom story is used as a justification for condemning homosexuals, but no one remembers that Lot's daughters committed incest with him, and they were not and are not condemned. In Christian theology, no attention is any longer paid to Paul's injunctions against women speaking in Church, or not wearing hats, or the command of slaves to obey their masters.

Perry then turns to the interesting question of the sexual orientation of Jesus and his silence on the question of homosexuality:

In fact, if Jesus lived in our day and age, he would probably have been labelled a homosexual. Let me say I am not calling Christ a homosexual: I am merely stating a fact. When you have a man in our society who is raised by a mother with no father (Mary's husband Joseph is last heard of in the Scriptures when Jesus was twelve years old), who never marries, who is constantly in the company of twelve men, who allows one of them to have bodily contact with him (John 13.21–26) and who is taken into custody by the police after another male kisses him—you would have, according to many Christians, a homosexual on your hands. Again, let me state that I am not calling Christ a homosexual: many others would.

Troy then states his own position in relation to conversion:

I believe in the fundamentalist doctrine of being 'born again' of the spirit and the water. I know that I am a 'born again' child of God. I also know that I am a homosexual. Can this change my relationship with my Lord? No, never! Jesus said 'Come unto me, all ye that labour and are heavy laden, and I will give you rest'. Not once do I read Jesus saying in the Gospels, 'Come unto me, all you heterosexuals, who if you have sex or intercourse, must have it in the missionary position with another heterosexual, and I will accept you as the only true believers'. No, Jesus, my Lord, sent the invitation to all, whosoever will.[84]

In another essay, putting the defence for the Catholic tradition, J. F. Harvey, president of De Sales Hall of Theology, Maryland, stresses the difference between Von Rohr's understanding of 'natural' and his own. The point is of importance because, in Lutheran terms, man's corruption by original sin is so deep that

all men sin in their expression of sexuality. Even in marriage, man gathers within himself the impulses of both lust and love. Since all humans have a common ground of sinfulness, there is no need for the heterosexuals to cast stones at the homosexuals.

Against this, Harvey sets a doctrine of natural law as that in human nature which indicates what is normative. God's grace helps us to live up to these norms. In practical terms in counselling homosexuals, therefore, Harvey cannot agree with Von Rohr's suggestion that a marriage-like state may be suitable for some homosexuals, but instead a discipline of prayer, attendance at Mass and Confession, and habitual involvement in works of charity should be advised.

Not all American Roman Catholics have felt able to reiterate this traditional style of teaching without question. The Jesuit, John McNeil, prepared a full scale study of the moral and pastoral issues of homosexuality in 1972, and after a cautious review by his superiors in Rome, he was allowed to publish it in 1976 as *The Church and the Homosexual.*[85] It would not be derogatory to describe this book as an updated American Catholic version of Bailey's original study, the biblical material and the Church's tradition being considered in much the same way, but with a thorough knowledge of more recent psychological and ethical studies added, especially in the latter case from the Protestant theologians, Thielicke and Kimball-Jones.

At two points in his book, McNeil comes close to approving homosexual behaviour, but given the scrutiny to which the text was subjected, his reticence is understandable. The first is in his consideration of 'homosexual activity and creation' (pp. 100–1) where he draws attention to what he calls a relatively overlooked section of the 1930 Encyclical 'Casti Connubii' where the mutual inward moulding of husband and wife is said to be the chief reason and purpose of matrimony ('primaria matrimonii causa et ratio'). He notes that the Church continues to condemn any voluntary separation of the co-equal purposes of sexual behaviour, procreation and mutual love, but since the homosexual is not free to choose heterosexual relationships, his situation is more comparable factually with that of the infertile than of those who use contraception. McNeil, therefore, suggests that there is evidence that

> homosexuals who have limited their sexual expression in an ethically responsible way have by that means achieved what Pius XI indicates as the chief reason and purpose of sexual love within marriage looked at in a wider context.

That Pius XI intended the logic of his argument to be extended in this way is unlikely.

The second reference which gives an indication of McNeil's own attitude to homosexual behaviour is to be found in a footnote to a section on 'Moral Norms and the Homosexual' in Part 3 of the book, generally concerned with pastoral ministry. In this section, the Quaker Report and Pittenger's *Time for Consent*, (1970 edition) are quoted to support the possibility that homosexuals may grow in selfless love by their friendships, and the footnote to this section reads:

> That there can be a morally good sexual relationship between two homosexuals who love each other is my personal conviction. Once again, I call the attention of my readers to the fact that this conviction contradicts the traditional teaching of the Church in this matter. It is not my intention to attempt to supplant the magisterium, but rather to invite a public debate and discussion of this issue in the hope that the Church will listen and reconsider its position.[86]

McNeil was formerly a professor of Moral Theology at Fordham University, and a founder member of Dignity, a Roman Catholic organization for homosexuals. His book was published about the same time as the Vatican Declaration on Sexual Ethics early in 1976, but he includes references to it in the later English edition, observing that it is an authoritative pronouncement but not an infallible teaching.[87]

(i) GAY CHRISTIAN PUBLICATIONS

It is impossible to do any kind of justice to the range of books and pamphlets that merit inclusion here. The Gay Christian Movement as such, since its foundation in 1976 has produced a series of pamphlets and a quarterly bulletin, but there have been also notable pieces by authors associated with other earlier organizations from the early days of the Albany Trust publications onwards. Discernible in this literature is a progressive assurance. David Blamires from Manchester University, a Quaker who wrote *Homosexuality from the inside* in 1973, as an up-dating to the 1963 Report, and those who, eminent in many spheres, joined A. E. Dyson in contributing to a special issue of the magazine *Christian*, published by the Institute of Christian Studies associated with All Saints Church, Margaret Street, London, deserve recognition. On the whole, a chief contribution to the debate by G.C.M. has been its ability to widen the dimensions of the Christian understanding of love in an inclusive way so that a heterosexual Christian will find what is being said illuminates the Christian teaching for him and enhances his own capacity in love and relationships, not only in marriage, but also in friendship. It seems that the formative years of the Gay Christian Movement made special demands on those who joined it, in terms of the risk of social ostracism and ecclesiastical censure, and only with this deepening of awareness was it possible for those concerned to support each other. A sensitive advocate of this mature love is Kennedy Thom in his Harding Memorial Address,

Liberation through Love, of 1978. He quotes as an illustration some words of Bishop John Taylor of Winchester:

> To say that a person is loving or just is actually meaningless until that person is committed in particular acts of love and justice. It is by acting truly and consistently at moments when the opposite is a real option that one comes to be truthful and reliable. Action creates being: not the other way round.[88]

This somewhat existentialist approach expressed in terms of emergence from moral chaos towards order and harmony is explored by Sara Coggin, a teacher and one of the two women members of the G.C.M. Committee, in fact its secretary in 1978–9. In the pamphlet *Sexual Expression and Moral Chaos*[89] the chaos is thought of in two ways: first, that represented by Gay Liberation in the mind of some Festival of Light spokesman, and second, the primeval chaos on which God's creative love was brought to bear. In terms of morals, the static view is exemplified by, for example, Savonarola who preached that the Florentines might escape the impending French invasion if they joined the Ark of Salvation and returned to traditional moral standards. This is contrasted with the journey view, that creation is continuous, so that:

> our knowledge of continuing chaos both inside and outside ourselves demands a large awareness of God. Each of us has our own journey to make. It's not an organised hike with us all setting off from the same place and keeping more or less together. It's often a very lonely trail, though if we are lucky, we may recognise scenery that others have described or meet up with a few pilgrims on the way.

Sara Coggin also reflects on celibacy, a subject she says it has taken her a long time to get to grips with. Although at her Roman Catholic school she took it for granted among priests and nuns, part of the job, she found aggressive proclamation of it by Anglo-Catholic priests dehumanizing to women and perhaps signifying the misogyny of half-repressed male homosexuality. However, her own experience later, when separated temporarily from her partner showed her

> a little of the positive value of celibacy in being able to care more widely. The important thing to remember is that celibacy is a channelling of sexuality, not its repression.

As this quotation shows, there is some inter-changeability in the use of words such as chastity, celibacy, and virginity in contemporary speech, and this no doubt reflects uncertainty about what, if anything, is the difference, and at a deeper level about their value. To refrain from genital activity with another while the partner is away would be described in the heterosexual context as marital fidelity or marital chastity in traditional language. And virginity, so highly esteemed in the early Christian centuries is often now assumed to indicate fear or repression of one's sexuality, as Sara Coggin notes, though she does think that for some people chastity before marriage and faithfulness within it, can be a valuable way of approaching a relationship, and that there is something important about giving one's virginity as an offering of love.

The concept of celibacy, often used as an equivalent of chastity, needs some rehabilitation, and this has been most thoroughly done by Donald Georgan, an American Catholic priest of the Dominican Order in his *The Sexual Celibate.*[90] As the title suggests, Georgan's argument is that celibacy does not attempt to avoid sexuality, indeed, it is one expression of it, and this is held true for both heterosexual and homosexual couples. Georgan defines celibacy as a positive choice of the single life for the sake of Christ in response to the call of God, which is familiar enough, but his elaboration of what this means includes the recognition that friendship and tactility, that is touching, is significant for inter-personal growth, and has a proper role to play in our effective and emotional life. He notes that some Englishmen have beeen conditioned in non-tactility, and that the degree of acceptable contact varies greatly among different races. Chastity is the virtue of managing touching appropriately and is not the same as remaining virgin.

However, the particular point he makes concerning homosexual behaviour is that limitation is necessary lest it too becomes genital. The ideal of celibate love is to be pursued.

> I would say the same about homo-genital relations as about hetero-genital relations for celibates, both with respect to their unacceptability, and with respect to a healthy attitude towards oneself or another who has, or is experiencing, difficulty.[91]

An obvious polarity divides Gay Christians and Evangelical authors on the question of the biblical texts. Sometimes this can be polemically expressed, as it is by Moss, Field and Lovelace on the Evangelical side, and this brought a sharp response from G.C.M. in a review published in the *Gay Christian Bulletin* for September 1978:

> For those less ready (than Moss) to draw moral precepts for today from isolated texts of scripture, the response involves the whole person (sexual preferences and all) in a discipleship of love where, in Charles Williams's beautiful phrase: 'Eros need not for ever be on his knees to agape: he has a right to his delights: they are part of the Way.'

The Gay Christian Movement as a specific organization emerged in connection with a weekend conference held in Wick Court, near Bristol, at the end of April 1976 under the auspices of the Student Christian Movement. It was a relatively small gathering of some sixty people, but in addition to talks given at the conference, there were available some papers which had been published the previous year as a supplement to the S.C.M. magazine *Movement* and entitled *Towards a Theology of Gay Liberation*. The talks, papers and subsequent dialogues were edited by Malcolm Macourt, and published by the S.C.M. Press in 1977. This collection, therefore, represents a wide spectrum of liberal Christian views of that time. The scene is described by David Blamires, who was Chairman of the Conference, and by Malcolm Macourt who teaches Social Statistics at Durham University.

Macourt argues the Gay Liberationist case with some vigour, and offers a tantalizing illustration of the human potential for implying homophobia with the following conundrum:

> Chris and Pat are of the same sex, and are both mature adults. Both of them have had girl friends and both of them have had boy friends—both feel capable of relations with either sex. They meet, and gradually come to know and trust one another—developing their friendship into a love bond, which meets with the general approval of their families and friends; both believe that they can together, more effectively than alone, express their love for God and for their fellow human beings.

He then asks:

> What sex are Chris and Pat?

and observes that

> this question posed in this way, strips the whole gay issue of its presuppositions on both sides.

The meaning of the biblical material is discussed in the next section by Rictor Norton and James Martin, the former finding in the Judaeo-Christian tradition the roots of homophobia for which the Church should now make atonement, and the latter, a biblical theologian, sympathetic to the homophobic case but clear that Bailey and his supporters, such as Norton, cannot completely explain away the critical attitude of the Bible to homosexual practices.[92]

D Three Reconciling Reports

All the Christian Churches have to wrestle with the problem posed by their twin obligations to define orthodoxy and accept diversity. They are guardians of the faith once delivered and set down in the unchanging text of Scripture, and at the same time members of a living community ever prodded by the Spirit to see the will of God in the signs of the times. These fundamental loyalties give a debate such as the one we have been following in the past twenty years a certain dynamism, but there comes a point when the rallying has to pause and an attempt is made to reconcile differences.

If it is not, too much Christian energy is drained away in defending the various arguments, and the Church's mission to the world is blunted by preoccupation with internal dissension. By the early seventies, it seems to have become clear to church authorities that Gay Liberation had, to some extent, made a valid point. The right of a homosexual to exist, without any pressure to change and conform to heterosexual norms, was established. The medical evidence that change was seldom possible had to be taken seriously. It followed that the homosexual must be either fitted into the well-established category of the sexually inactive, namely the celibate, or that homosexual behaviour was to be allowed among loving friends in settled relationships. As we have seen, the 1975 Vatican Declaration affirmed celibacy, but many individual writers, among whom Pittenger was the most forthright, distinguished the voluntary and special vocation of celibacy from the general right to express love through genital intimacy which belonged to all human beings in good faith, heterosexuals and homosexuals alike. The Quaker *Report* had long before taken the same view.

Reconciliation between these two views would be possible if they could be seen as within the limits of diversity proper to the Christian fellowship, but not if the second view was held to be incompatible with orthodoxy. To take an example from another controversial issue of the time—the ordination of women—it could be concluded that different provinces within the same Communion might decide for themselves whether or not to extend priesthood to women, as the 1978 Lambeth Conference suggested, on the basis that there was no bar in the theological principle to this action, and such diversity was acceptable within the fellowship. But, on the other hand, if, as some members of the General Synod in England subsequently argued, the theological principle was not agreed within the whole Church, and in particular not by the Roman Catholic and Orthodox Churches, then allowing diversity was precipitate. Similarly, while no doubt some particular Churches and congregations believe in good conscience that homosexual people should be encouraged into the fellowship, and perhaps even into the official ministry, without the rule of celibacy being enforced on them, since this would be seen by other Churches as contrary to orthodoxy, any decision to do so must be delayed. Of course, where diversity is properly allowed, freedom of conscience applies not only to those who wish to depart from the old tradition, but also to those who wish to respect its continuing value.

The three Reports now to be reviewed can be regarded as offering a reconciling approach in that they do not seek to condemn the traditional teaching and replace it with a new orthodoxy but seek ways in which it can be related to new understandings. As is to be expected, none of these Reports has received official approval at the time of writing.

(a) HUMAN SEXUALITY: NEW DIRECTIONS IN CATHOLIC THOUGHT

This study was prepared by a small group for the Catholic Theological Society of America. Commissioned in 1972 the Report was finally 'received' by the Commission in October 1976, and published the next year.[93] A foreword explains that the reception of the study implies neither approval nor disapproval by the Society, who wish to make the research it contains available to members and a wider public.

This study was already in draft when the Vatican Declaration on Sexual Ethics was issued, and appears to have been revised in several places to take account of it. However, the method of the Report is to set side by side official teaching and a range of other views and then indicate the pastoral guidelines that the Committee recommend. Like McNeil therefore, the authors wish to encourage debate by placing their emphasis elsewhere than on official teaching, rather than directly challenging it. A section is devoted to homosexuality, showing the typical American awareness of Thielicke, Kimball-Jones, Bailey, McNeil, but not Pittenger. The Old Testament is taken to condemn homosexual practice with the utmost severity, but St Paul's teachings must be understood in the sense which he himself would have attached to them. Much space is given to providing pastoral guidelines.

The quasi-official report of the National Conference of Catholic Bishops is quoted and warmly commended for its understanding, but the Committee dissents from the Bishops' view that 'homosexual acts are a grave transgression of the goals of human sexuality'. Their comment is

> We see sex as including more than genitality, and the purposes of sexuality—creativity and integration—as broader than biological procreation and physical union.[94]

The committee sets out a modern understanding of homosexuality. Homosexuals are said to have the same rights as heterosexuals to love, intimacy, and relationships, and Christian sexual morality does not require a dual standard. The rights and obligations are the same. Since homosexual friendships are not sustained and supported by society, they are tempted to promiscuity and therefore a pastor may recommend close stable friendships between homosexuals, not simply as a lesser of two evils but as a positive good. Although anything approaching a sacramental celebration of a homosexual 'marriage' would be inappropriate and misleading, prayer, even communal prayer for two people striving to live Christian lives, incarnating the values of fidelity, truth, and love, is not beyond the pastoral possibilities of a Church whose ritual tradition includes a rich variety of blessings. The advisability of such an action must be determined by pastoral prudence and consideration of all possible consequences, including social repercussions.[95]

In Guideline 7, the Committee turn to the principle of moral theology 'ubi dubium, ibi libertas'—where there is doubt, there is freedom. Since the complexities, ambiguities, and uncertainties of homosexuality have only recently come to light, this principle should be applied in administering absolution and giving communion to homosexuals. The same principle allows counsellors and confessors to leave homosexuals a freedom of conscience, and this leads to the conclusion that

> A homosexual engaging in homosexual acts in good conscience has the same rights of conscience and the same rights to the sacraments as a married couple practising birth control in good conscience.

What then does the Committee say about birth control? The subject is treated at length[96] and stresses the teaching of *Gaudium et spes*, although the Encyclical *Humanae vitae* is obviously not ignored. The conclusion is that a pastor must explain what the Encyclical teaches, what other views are to be taken into consideration, and then leave the couple to make their own mature responsible judgement. The effect of the guidelines, therefore, is that this study recommends that the laity, having educated consciences, should make their own decision about the morality of both contraception and homosexual behaviour. The case of priests is also considered, and distinguished since those who have this vocation must accept celibacy. Candidates for the priesthood or religious life should therefore be confident that they can live up to the ideals and expectations of a celibate life and not enter it if they intend consistent homosexual behaviour, or are simply seeking an excape from confronting their sexuality and making it a creative force in their lives.[97]

(b) A CHRISTIAN UNDERSTANDING OF HUMAN SEXUALITY: A METHODIST REPORT

This Report was prepared by the Division of Social Responsibility and the faith and order committee for presentation to the Methodist Church Conference of 1979, where it was received and further study of some aspects of the Report requested. It is a brief report, and only Section C, some twelve paragraphs, deals with homosexuality, but earlier, the Christian sources of guidance in seeking an understanding of human sexuality are listed: these are said to be the Bible, reason, the traditional teaching of the Church, the personal and corporate experience of modern Christians, the understanding provided by the human sciences, and what may be called the spirit of the age. Applied to homosexuality these sources of guidance lead the authors of the Report to the conclusions that bear some similarity to those of the pastoral guidelines noted above, and to those of the 1963 Quaker Report. The paragraphs concerned (nos. C.9 and C.10) may be best quoted in full:

C.9 Christians affirm marriage because they believe that within it the creative, procreative and relational aspects of human sexuality can be expressed. Nevertheless, Christians have never asserted that marriage, procreative or not, is the only valid way of life—celibacy, for example, has at times been valued even more highly. It is recognised that marriages which have fulfilled their procreative character, have often failed in the quality of relationships which they ought to have created. It is because they set a high value on relationships within marriage that Christians ought also to argue that stable permanent relationships can be an appropriate way of expressing a homosexual orientation. This involves an acceptance of homosexual activities as not being intrinsically wrong. The quality of any homosexual relationship is thus to be assessed by the same basic criteria which have been applied to heterosexual relationships. For homosexual men and women, permanent relationships characterized by love can be an appropriate and Christian way of expressing their sexuality. This open acceptance of homosexuality will no doubt present problems at different levels in the life of the Church—it obviously removes the grounds for denying any person membership of the Church or an office in it solely because they have a particular sexual orientation.

C.10 It is the essence of the Christian Gospel to stand by and care for those in need. The Christian recognises a common humanity and a personal constraint to show concern for others. In the context of homosexuality and bisexuality this means helping those in need to discover their basic sexual orientation and enabling them to come to terms with it. It also means encouraging and supporting those whose orientation is homosexual to form stable and lasting relationships, for men and women are made for relationships and their sexuality is involved in and fulfilled by these commitments. It is the quality of these relationships which matters, not the physical expression which they may take. Christians may need to counsel and support families in which one member realises that his or her orientation is homosexual. Christians who discover themselves to be homosexual may need special support if they are to come to terms with their sexuality and to retain their faith within the Church which has a long anti-homosexual tradition.

(c) THE ANGLICAN WORKING PARTY REPORT OF 1979

This Report, entitled *Homosexual Relationships: a contribution to discussion* was prepared by a working party appointed by the Church of England General Synod Board for Social Responsibility. The Board undertakes many such studies on a variety of subjects and the decision whether they should be used to further the Board's own understanding, or made available to the Church and a wider public, rests with the Board.

The working party was appointed in 1974 following a request of the Conference of Principals of the Anglican Theological Colleges in England 'that a study should be made of the theological, social, pastoral and legal aspects of homosexuality'. At the time this request was made, the Gay Liberation movement was active in the Universities and its influence was felt in those theological colleges which had strong university links. However, since the 1970 report had not been circulated, the time was, in any case, ripe for a fresh appraisal within the Church of England, and the membership of the working party, larger than the previous one and strong in both academic scholarship and pastoral experience, was a sign that a full-scale work was intended. The Report was finished in draft in 1978, and then discussed in the Board for Social Responsibility, with some members of the working party attending. Whereas the 1970 report had presented two incompatible views, the 1978 Report was unanimous as it came from the working party, but proved contentious to the Board, who had to decide whether or not it should be published. Although some redrafting was done, any attempt to reach full agreement without long delay was thought unlikely, so the Report was eventually published, with an additional Part Two which contains the principal critical comments made during the Board's discussion.[98]

Chapter 3 considers the biblical evidence. The Sodom story is understood to contain a reference to homosexuality, but the Sodomites' crime is primarily the failure to respect the duty of hospitality. It is legend, not history, corresponding with a widely diffused folk-tale of inhospitable treatment to divine visitants whose identity was not realized. While the narrative does express abhorrence of homosexuality, that is not its main concern, and it cannot be taken to record an instance of divine action intended expressly to condemn and punish homosexual behaviour.

The Leviticus commandments are described as legal collections dealing with the family as that was known in ancient Israel. Their aim was to strengthen and preserve the family group, and homosexual behaviour was seen as a great threat to it and its social purposes. It was also described as an abomination because it broke the divinely-ordered pattern of sexual differentiation and relationship. Finally, such behaviour is seen as peculiarly characteristic of heathen religion and society, and that, in Leviticus, is the basic reason for avoiding it.

For the New Testament, Paul's argument in Romans 1 is to be read against the background of the Old Testament doctrine of the creation of men and women. Since humanity in general has departed from the knowledge of the one true God, so it fails to recognize the divine purpose in sex and hence misuses it, homosexual practices being the clearest example. What Paul means by 'unnatural' is unnatural to mankind in God's creation pattern. While it is easy to claim that Paul is reproducing the stock Jewish reaction to the Gentile world, and that not everyone behaved in this way his sweeping statements would suggest, nevertheless all the offences he lists are wrong and ought not to be found in the Christian community. Paul is primarily concerned with the sinful state of the world outside the Church in sharp distinction from the people of God. The same concern is reflected in 1 Timothy and 1 Corinthians.

The second half of this chapter considers the problems of interpreting the biblical evidence and seeks to balance factors such as cultural relevance, discontinuity between the Old Testament and the New, insignificant in this case, and the sovereignty of God over the natural world that he has made. The fact that he intervenes means that it is controlled by the purposes of a personal being and not by immutable laws. Further, for the Bible, this personal being is directly concerned with the condition and needs of every individual, a concern which the Church, as an agent of his loving care, must also exemplify. An example is given of the distinction between clean and unclean animals as a part of the order of creation. This was a serious matter for Leviticus, regarded as important for debate in the New Testament, but finally Christianity abandoned the distinction.

The fourth chapter—theological and ethical questions—distinguishes three views: the traditionalist, the libertarian, and the personalist. The traditionalist is based on Scripture and made explicit in the natural law approach. If *Humanae vitae* is right about contraception, *a fortiori* natural law also forbids homosexual practices. But the report notes the suggestion of Aquinas that natural law's content is provided by man's inclinations which include sexual intercourse and the upbringing of children, and this means that the biological function of sex, procreation, has to be supplemented by a wide range of other considerations.

The libertarian view (not the liberal view) sees no need for any morality relating specifically to sexual behaviour. Provided people do not hurt each other, in sexual or other matters, everything is permitted. It follows from this individualistic view that homosexual practices are in no way to be condemned as such, and they can be called natural in the sense that many people find them satisfying. Bestiality and paedophilia might remain immoral if this view is taken, since they lack an element of consent.

The personalist view tests what matters in sexual behaviour by the quality of personal relationships it serves to express and confirm, and this view takes two forms. In the stronger form it is anti-permissive, intercourse being an expression of profound erotic love and unacceptable where genuine love is absent. In its weaker form it can be minimally personal, even if recognizing that a more completely loving relationship would be better. The personalist view does, in fact, cover a wide range of attitudes within the two views, and a homosexual bond as permanent and exclusive as marriage usually is, could be defended from it.

In reviewing these three positions, the report finds the libertarian one inadequate, not doing justice to the social context of sexuality, and too subjective and individualistic. By contrast the personalist view is able to do justice to the conviction that sex is important if taken in its stronger sense, indicating that there is something in the nature of sex that is determinative for us. The origin of the traditionalist view in the early Church that sex was disordered is recalled, the necessity of marriage being the only possible response at that time. Although the recognition of the unitive aspect of married love has had an uneven course in Christian history, it is now generally held among Christians.

The question of homosexual marriage is fully considered in the report at this point, and it is noted that evidence the working party received from homosexual people showed little enthusiasm for it. The dominant opinion among them seemed to be that permanence and exclusiveness, necessary in a sexual relationship that is characteristically procreative, would be desirable but not in the same way necessary. In homosexual relationships, not constricted by the needs of children, fidelity has less importance and the commitment should last as long as the love lasts, but no longer. The report, therefore, reiterates heterosexual marriage as the norm, something given, which has the character of demand upon us. In a homosexual relationship, one strand, the deep biological complementarity of the partners, is lacking altogether. It would be a mistake to assess sexual relationships by grading them all alike upon a single scale of lovingness, and ignoring other morally relevant distinctions which human relationships, individual and social, require.

Having dealt with the marriage issue, the Report then comes to what, for many, has been the crucial point of decision—whether or not a Christian homosexual may make a careful and responsible decision to enter into or maintain a relationship in which genital acts will take place. The case is presented in a clear form for someone who has no choice in their sexual orientation and has found love with a partner to be the source of a wider care and concern. The conclusion of the working party, faced with the contrary appeals totally to forbid or explicitly to sanction homosexual practices, is best quoted verbatim:

We feel the force of both these appeals, contradictory though they are. But neither, to our mind, is sufficiently sensitive to the truth which the other represents. On the one hand, the celebration of homosexual erotic love as an alternative and authentic development of the living Christian tradition which ought to be accepted as such by the Church today would involve the repudiation of too much that is characteristic, and rightly characteristic of Christian teaching about sex. On the other hand, to declare that homosexuals may not in any circumstances give physical expression to their erotic love is unduly to circumscribe the area of responsible choice, to lay on individuals a burden too heavy for some to bear, and, by restricting the options open to them, to hinder their search for an appropriate way of life. In the light of some of the evidence we have received, we do not think it possible to deny that there are circumstances in which individuals may justifiably choose to enter into a homosexual relationship with the hope of enjoying a companionship and physical expression of sexual love similar to that which is to be found in marriage. For the reasons which we have given, such a relationship could not be regarded as the moral or social equivalent of marriage; it would be bound to have a private and experimental character which marriage cannot, and should not, have. Nevertheless, fidelity and permanence, although not institutionally required, would undoubtedly do much to sustain and enhance its genuinely personal commitment and aspirations.

Chapter 6 is concerned with social implications and pastoral care. The Report stresses the difference between the two principles of pastoral care, the integrity of the individual and the integrity of the community. For the individual, the question is what is God calling him or her here and now to be and to do? And in the answers a person makes, the integrity of conscience is to be respected. Also to be respected is the human need for 'a private space'. There is no hiding place from God and conscience, but reserve against human probing is as important as openness. The community principle looks to the well-being of the whole Body of Christ, and the avoidance of scandal. But scandal is a debased word; the stumbling blocks of which the New Testament speak are causing the members of the Church to lose faith, or challenging the preconceived ideas of the world. The first is to be avoided, the second endured. From these principles the working party concludes that there is no good reason, apart from scandal, for excluding from church membership and communion, those who in good conscience, have entered into a responsible homosexual union. At the same time, given the Church's character as an institution which will include those with sincere convictions that homosexual relationships are morally wrong, there will be stresses and strains in the church fellowship, especially for those who have made no secret of their relationships. The more prominent a person becomes in the Church, the more the right to privacy is limited. Such privacy should be accorded to clergy, but the domestic arrangements of parish priests will affect their standing as leaders of the congregation and examples to the flock of Christ.

It follows that

> a homosexual priest who has come out and openly acknowledges that he is living in a sexual union with another man should not expect the church to accept him as if he were married.

Considering the case of the priest in this situation, the working party concluded that such a one should offer his resignation to the bishop who, as the responsible minister for the Church in the locality could decide whether to accept it or not. With regard to ordinands, the report suggests that a bishop would not be justified in refusing to ordain an otherwise acceptable ordinand merely on the ground that he is, or is believed to be, homosexually orientated, but an ordinand would be wrong to conceal from his bishop any intention in his own mind to live openly in a homosexual union. However, ordinands should not be required to declare their sexual orientation as such; that would be an unjustifiable intrusion on the privacy of an individual. These suggestions are for those who have no choice about their sexual orientation. Those who are ambisexual, but predominantly homosexual, should not be advised to marry, and the report recognizes that there is a spectrum of sexual orientation so that mutual trust and confidence in the counselling situation and discernment are required to minimize the risk of wrong advice.

This report is, of course, much longer than either the section of the American Catholic Report concerned with homosexuality or its equivalent in the Methodist Report. However, there is a noticeable measure of agreement in the three Reports, and it seems most improbable that there had been any comparing of notes. The first was completed in 1976, the second in 1979 and the third in 1978, and care was taken about confidentiality. It would be easy to claim on these three pieces of evidence that there has been a shift towards tolerance of homosexual behaviour in the Christian community, but that might be to overstate the importance of these three reports, all of which are in the category of discussion papers, not in any sense authoritative statements of the Churches concerned. The Anglican report distinguished the position of the clergy as does the Catholic, although on different grounds—the risk of scandal for Anglicans, the rule of celibacy for Catholics.

The Anglican report is also distinctive in that the Board for Social Responsibility felt obliged to publish its own criticisms, as Part Two of the Report, thereby extending the range of the discussion to certain points which the Board felt the working party had insufficiently covered. These criticisms are directed to the third chapter on the biblical evidence, and the fourth on theological and ethical considerations.

Criticisms of the biblical evidence amount to the making of several points which have often been noticed previously in this book as held by some biblical scholars and writers on homosexuality from the Christian viewpoint. Thus abhorrence of homosexual behaviour is entrenched in the text of Genesis whether or not the ensuing disaster is held to be punitive; for Leviticus and Romans it is noted that, despite the new life offered in Christ, the condemnation of homosexual behaviour was not among those aspects of the Jewish law that Paul felt free to set aside. The point made in the report about God's sovereign intervention is taken up and it is suggested that he would, nevertheless, not act in an arbitrary fashion towards the created natural order.

The criticisms of chapter four begin with the suggestion that the demanding love of Jesus is related to the internal intention of the law, but that this does not entail superseding the moral obligation enshrined in the law by a private decision that another course was more loving. The questions of chastity and celibacy as the alternatives to marriage are then discussed and it is stated that many members of the Board believe that the right choice for those people with a homosexual condition is abstinence rather than genital love in a homosexual relationship. Some members of the Board hold the view that homosexual relationships, although objectively speaking disordered, should be viewed with differing degrees of culpability in relation to the subjective situations in which people find themselves.

The remaining chapters of the Report were more briefly dealt with. The Board offered no view on the legal questions, though some individual members dissented from the suggestion that the age of consent to homosexual behaviour should be reduced to eighteen.

Several members of the Board thought that the pastoral chapter did not sufficiently consider the objective facts of sin and the ministry of forgiveness. Anxiety was also expressed about the recommendation that a priest living in good conscience in a sexual union should offer his resignation to the bishop. If the Church believes that a practising homosexual priest should not continue in office, the Board thinks that the Church must take the responsibility of removing him and for doing so in a way which is legally and morally defensible, and must be prepared to spell out its reasons.

Since this book is intended as a survey of Christian attitudes to homosexuality, it would be inappropriate to comment at length at this stage on the differences of view expressed or implicit in Part I and Part II of this Anglican Report. The members of the working party were drawn from different traditions within the Church of England, as are the members appointed to the Board for Social Responsibility, though not in any sense of achieving a balanced 'party' representation, as the lists of members of both bodies show. No doubt the same could be said of the American Catholic and the English Methodist groups. The criterion of selection for such bodies must surely be that they have a useful contribution to make. What such bodies produce no doubt reflects a measure of adjustment towards each other's views as the study proceeds, but that does not mean that anyone involved is obliged to compromise the truth as he or she sees it. The two parts of the Board for Social Responsibility discussion paper, therefore, show two stages of this process.

Part one emerged from a group who worked together towards unanimity in recommending the acceptance of those who share a homosexual union in good conscience, allowing that genital expression of the union between the partners would not necessarily be a sign that their consciences were defective. Members of the Board, for various reasons, stressed other Christian viewpoints in Part two, many of them apparently preferring to recommend abstinence rather than genital activity, that is maintaining the Christian tradition in this matter.

Readers who have endured thus far, will not be surprised that in 1979 this divergence of views is expressed among members of the Church of England; it is difficult to name any major Christian Church where this is not so in fact, whatever official pronouncements have been made.

PART E
Conclusions

11 A Shift in the Limits of Tolerance

A Introduction

In his Maccabaean Lecture of twenty years ago, Lord Devlin observed that 'in the matter of morals, the limits of tolerance shift'. He was referring to public opinion and judged that the law should be slow to follow because in the next generation the swell of indignation may have abated, and the law be left without the strong backing which it needs.[1] Perhaps the most obvious conclusion to be drawn from this survey of Christian attitudes to homosexuality, and especially from the last part, is that if opinion among Christians has changed, the authorities of the Churches have heeded Lord Devlin's warning in not following it too quickly in respect of homosexual behaviour.

It seems to be true, however, that Christian people have shared in this shift of tolerance in the sense that the character of homosexuality and the difficulties of homosexual people in facing their own sexual nature are better understood. Any attempt to re-impose a punitive law in secular terms or to bar a Christian homosexual person from church membership would find little support. Perhaps the existence of loving and relatively stable relationships between homosexuals is also by now conceded as a reasonable provision for those whose sexual orientation would make any attempt to enter heterosexual marriage dishonest in terms of inner disposition, whatever external camouflage was attempted.

Not only those sharing the general views of the Gay Christian Movement have stressed the importance of the Church's providing pastoral care and help to homosexuals seeking to express responsible love and fidelity in a stable friendship. But the prevailing assumptions about the right to express love in sexual behaviour raise doubts and suspicions that for the Church to accept, and indeed assist in the formation of stable homosexual relationships, will imply conceding the freedom for genital intimacy where the consciences of the partners judge this appropriate to the quality of their relationship. This concession would be a departure from the prohibitions of Scripture and the consistent teaching of the Church, and could be made only if the grounds for doing so were compelling. To the minds of many Christians they are not, and any attempt by authority to declare they were, would in fact lack sufficient consensus at the present time.

Much of this book has been concerned with history, an attempt to record in one volume information which is scattered about in many sources, and, it is hoped, shows that the treatment of homosexual people by the Churches has seldom been more harsh than that of secular authority, and in some instances credit-worthy, noticeably in the nineteenth and twentieth centuries. It is a feature of the present situation that the heightened awareness of the significance of the sexual element in the life of every human being makes for explicit questioning where in the past none would have been thought necessary. The present anxiety about whether homosexual people should be admitted to communion or be accepted for ordination could scarcely have been expressed in the same terms in previous centuries. If it is accepted that the proportion of homosexuals in society changes little, then such events will have occurred innumerable times in Christian history, known only to God who searches the hearts and from whom no secrets are hid. The Church in the past took no action unless actual sin occurred, was confessed, or detected. It can be asked then how far the determination to come out and claim rights, while being an understandable reaction from homosexuals to the heterosexual claim for permissiveness, has in fact, served the best interests of the cause of Gay Liberation. This is not at all to suggest that concealment or dishonesty would be better, but merely to note the difficult paradox of social life that standing for truth can sometimes provoke scandal.

Two issues seem to be of major importance as the Churches continue their consideration of the problem posed by Gay Liberation. The first is the meaning and interpretation of the biblical texts that refer to homosexual behaviour, and the second is the apparent confrontation of the moral arguments used for and against changing the Christian teaching that such behaviour is sinful. Although the first has already been discussed at length in Part B, the main conclusions of that study may be summarized here. The moral precepts called in aid by those who have argued their differing views about homosexuality and homosexual behaviour have been reported as they occurred in the accounts of church history and the modern debates. Some clarification of the main points of difference seem advisable, though this can only be in terms of showing how they stand in relation to each other. Suggestions about compatibility can be made without developing at length a general theory of Christian ethics.

B Some conclusions about the meaning of the Biblical Texts

(a) SODOM AND GOMORRAH: GENESIS 18.16—19.29

Bailey argued that this classic text on the subject was wrongly interpreted—the 'knowing' requested was not sexual, and many writers have followed this view, though some have not. The biblical translators of the modern editions have tended to make the sexual meaning explicit: e.g. the N.E.B. version has 'bring them out so that we may have intercourse with them'. Old Testament scholars tend to regard this explicitness as a correct rendering of the original meaning.

The Old Testament generally treats the sin of Sodom as idolatry rather than a breach of hospitality, but inhospitality to the divine messengers is to be expected in heathenism, the rejection of God being the symbol and cause of all human futility. The credentials theory of Bailey is difficult to sustain against the interior logic of the narrative, and condemnation of homosexual behaviour is rightly found within it.

(b) THE RAPE AT GIBEAH: JUDGES 19.22–25

Textual problems make caution appropriate here. It may be that early stories of heterosexual and homosexual assault have been conflated to produce the text as it is found in the biblical Book of Judges. As it stands the same arguments for interpreting it as a condemnation of homosexual behaviour apply as for the Sodom narrative. If the suspected corruption of the text has theological significance, then the preference of Nicholas of Lyra for the version provided by Josephus should be considered. It is, perhaps, safest to regard the Gibeah narrative as a probable corroboration of the condemnation expressed in the Sodom story arising at a later stage of Israel's history.

(c) DAVID AND JONATHAN

No implication of a homosexual relationship in modern terms is made in the biblical narrative of the friendship between these men, nor of any genital intimacy. This argument of silence cannot be overpressed, but the Old Testament does not shrink from explicitness in sexual matters where they are relevant.

(d) THE HOLINESS CODE: LEVITICUS 18.22–23 and 20.13

These verses contain clear condemnation of male homosexual behaviour dating in their present form from the time of the return of Israel after the Babylonian captivity. There are good arguments for supposing that behind these texts lie earlier sources from Israel's criminal law for the protection of the family and those within its ambience. Similar provisions can be found in other ancient legal codes. In the Holiness Code such behaviour is taken as symbolic of false foreign religion and a justification for excommunicating such offenders from the worshipping life of post-exilic Judaism.

(e) INTER-TESTAMENTAL WRITINGS

These are of significance because some of them were included in the Septuagint version of the Old Testament used by the Church until the Reformation. In addition to the apocryphal writings, other Pseudepigrapha were known to early Christians. In these writings, the Old Testament view of the wickedness of Sodom is maintained, but in addition, cults which encouraged homosexual behaviour are associated with the sin of Sodom and condemned. This identification of the sin of Sodom with homosexuality is not of great significance if that condemnation is considered already clear in the original narrative. This, and many other, facets of the heathenism of the classical world would have horrified orthodox Jewry, and observation of the supposed site of the city, not far from Jerusalem and near Qumran, provided a well-known visual example of the destructive judgement of God on sinners.

(f) THE GOSPELS

Homosexuality as such is not mentioned, but Jesus uses the symbol of Sodom's destruction as a warning against rejecting God's messengers in terms of inhospitality to the disciples, and hypocrisy which blinds some Jews to the truth of his teaching. The group of male disciples that support him was a normal feature of the life-style of a religious leader of his time, as was some physical expression as a sign of affection in its culture. The reference he makes to those who were born or made themselves eunuchs arises in the context of heterosexual marriage.

(g) THE PAULINE EPISTLES

In Romans, Paul repudiates homosexual behaviour as a vice of the Gentiles, an indication of the idolatry which blinds both their religious and moral perceptions. Whether or not he intended to limit this condemnation to heterosexuals who chose this alternative as a perversion is uncertain, but the argument that the ancient world did not distinguish between inversion and perversion is sometimes overstated. The biblical writers recognized the vocation to celibacy, the choice of abstinence and the facts of impotence and androgyny, though their own conceptual framework of sexuality obviously cannot be compared precisely with such modern terms as a range of sexual orientation and bisexuality.

In 1 Corinthians, the offence which bars from the Kingdom should be translated as specific homosexual genital acts, and probably Paul had commercial pederasty in mind between older men and post-pubertal boys, the most common pattern of homosexual behaviour in the classical world. Although objectionable to both Jewish and Roman sensibilities, a specifically Christian case against it may be made out here on the grounds of the ontological character of chastity in which heterosexual intercourse is used as a sacramental sign of the union between Christ and his Church.

In 1 Timothy, the prohibition is expressed in a different form, the household code for Christians being similar to the Decalogue and Noachic lists of Judaism. Various considerations about the authority and interpretation of biblical texts have already been summarized in chapter 2. Whatever status is granted to them by contemporary

Christians, the texts sufficiently show that the biblical writers condemned homosexual practices.

C Some suggestions about the Moral Argument

(a) THE WITNESS TO CHASTITY

No easy disentanglement of a single major reason for the consistent hostility of the Church to homosexual behaviour can be achieved. A number of objectives, good in themselves, have contributed to this with varying force at different times in Christian history. Obviously recognizable from the beginning is the determination to hold pederasty at bay and outside the Christian community. This was part of the suppression of sexual vice and exploitation which has ever been a task of caring religious and humanist movements. The determination of the Fathers is matched by that of the nineteenth-century English social reformers and no doubt could be illustrated in most of the periods in between.

Although heterosexual prostitution has been scarcely mentioned in this book, that was, of course, also continually criticized, though it may have been more difficult to suppress directly since it has been much more socially acceptable outside committed Christian circles, and like premarital intercourse, so much the way of the world as to be in effect almost ineradicable. Homosexual behaviour, and especially pederasty, could be attacked more confidently, as ordinary homophobia and parental anxiety would lend support without necessarily being fully identified with Christian teaching about chastity and marital fidelity. The degree to which the Christian morality of sexual life has been obeyed in the Christian era is, no doubt, unascertainable, but obviously it has never been universal, even at the heights of clerical power in the Middle Ages. The notion of courtly love was not confined to the minds of the romantic poets. Whenever the challenge to the Church's witness to God's design for human sexuality is strongly pressed, the call for heterosexual chastity has to be vigorously repeated, and to concede homosexual rights has usually seemed inconsistent with that pressing and more urgent task.

(b) THE APPEAL TO NATURE

Apart from the biblical witness, one of the strongest arguments used by Christians against homosexual behaviour has always been that it is unnatural, and this merits examination. In the Bible the natural order is understood to be part of God's creative will, and not to be interfered with by man. In scholasticism this understanding is fused with, and to some extent submerged within, a more Stoic and rational doctrine of the order of nature which man can perceive as part of God's provision for all men, irrespective of the biblical revelation. It has been noted that in recent Roman Catholic statements, the biblical emphasis is more stressed, and in the Anglican report of 1979 the sovereignty of God over the natural law is mentioned, only to be questioned by members of the Board for Social Responsibility who preferred, apparently, the scholastic view. The same issue is debated between Von Rohr and John Harvey in the American publication *Is Gay Good?* Reformed theology tends to mistrust the value of natural law arguments as being not excluded from the total confusion of the original fall of man.

There is, therefore, some measure of theological sophistication required to make a good case for the 'contrary to nature' argument against homosexuality at the present time. Apart from the various emphases within the Church, there are difficulties presented by scientific and philosophical studies. Nature has become an ambiguous word for modern society. In its ordinary class-room meaning, nature means the fauna and flora of the countryside which may be seen on 'nature trails'. As that which is found to occur or exist in the world it is the continual subject of investigation by most of the modern sciences, behavioural as well as physical. Nature is simply there, and we are a part of it.

A further meaning of nature is that used to describe a primeval or primitive state of things. Nature is crude, or red in tooth and claw, and mankind's task is to tame it, use it, and develop its full potential. This meaning can be found in the Bible, particularly in the early chapters of Genesis where mankind is placed amidst nature to be its master and steward on God's behalf. Nature in this sense is meant to be changed, not merely observed or conformed to.

Another meaning of nature, also biblical, and the basis of much moral theology is indicated by the word 'teleological'; that is to say, a perceived ideal to which the present imperfect state is directed in hope or confidence of ultimate attainment. The vision of God—'then we shall know as we are known'—is one example, and it is generally posited in terms of learning to conform to our true—that is ideal—nature, or fulfil completely our destined role or character. All men are potentially the children of God in character, as they are now embryonically in faith and by baptism. It is equally possible, of course, to use a teleological concept of nature in a secular way, and give it a corporate dimension, as some humanistic and Marxist systems seem to do. There is a more jurisprudential meaning of nature which understands it as a conformity to certain immutable rules.

(c) THE NATURAL LAW ARGUMENT

The doctrine of 'natural law' moves somewhat uneasily between these two last meanings of nature. When it is teleologically understood, the possibility of change and development is obviously present. When it is understood as conformity to regulation previously fixed, failure and perhaps even guilt are indicated, depending on the degree of moral responsibility present. The idea of natural law as an indicator of moral objectives and as a yardstick for determining moral uncertainties has been subjected to massive criticism by philosophers in recent times. In one notable expression of this criticism, its precepts die the death of a thousand qualifications. While everyone can perceive the value of such a statement as 'it is wrong to kill', it is immediately clear that war, capital punishment, political assassination, and abortion cannot be assessed morally by the test of this precept without extending its meaning and qualifying its application.

All this said, what status may now be given to the moral judgement that homosexual behaviour is unnatural, or in what sense is unnatural being used here? It is clearly to be observed in nature as a biological and psychological fact alongside heterosexual nature, and in significant numbers. Given what is at present supposed about the causes of sexual orientation, both homosexuality and heterosexuality are natural in this sense of the word. Is homosexuality then nothing more than 'a sport of nature', a regrettable mutation that is biologically sterile depriving homosexual people of the right to be considered fully human? That view is universally rejected, and homosexuality is equally clearly not to be described as a primitive state. For most of Christian history the teleological view of nature has been applied to homosexuality; it is an incomplete state, a failure to develop towards heterosexuality: early psychological views were similar. Once the non-voluntary character of homosexuality was established, this incompleteness ceased to be considered immoral, though clearly defective in the sense that it inhibited procreation, a teleological objective which is itself now more questioned than it was. There are too many people already.

The teleological argument that homosexuality is unnatural in the sense of incomplete depends upon the assumption that heterosexuality is the norm psychologically as well as statistically and biologically. This assumption is, to some extent, questioned by the recognition of bi-sexuality, and the possibility that the true state of affairs is best described as a developing erotic attraction which is virtually controlled by factors which are little understood but condition a man's or woman's sexual drive quite arbitrarily. To question the notion of homosexual incompleteness is not to ignore the preponderance of heterosexuality, or to suggest sexual orientation is as random as the sexual gender fixed at conception, but to say that there can be complete homosexuals as well as complete heterosexuals in terms of the teleological understandings of nature's ideal state. There is one defect in this argument which should be considered, namely that in the heterosexual person, the anatomical, biological and psychological factors complement each other in a way that, for the homosexual, they do not, though of course, how much importance should be given to this complementarity is disputed.

(d) THE SITUATIONIST ARGUMENT

The argument that mankind's sexual behaviour must conform to certain laws of nature in the juristic sense of immutable rules is strongly put by those who conceive Christian morality in these terms. The challenge of situation ethics to this position, frequently used by Gay Liberation spokesmen against the traditional view, needs no repetition here, but it remains, of course, a crucial issue in the debate. Perhaps it is misleading to distinguish too sharply between a juristic and teleological emphasis in the doctrine of natural law. Just as secular law changes and develops in response to new insights while remaining committed to certain basic values for the society it aims to serve, so the natural law is the servant of the Church, not its master.

While natural law stands guard over certain verities, its formulation in human minds at any time is subject to the unavoidable limits of human perception, and has to be set against equally perceptive criticisms from others. The accusation of relativism and its defence may be made at this point.

To recognize the limits of our perception of natural law is not to evacuate it of useful content, nor to reduce it to vague general principles of what Hart has called the limits of human altruism. The Decalogue stands, and the axioms derived from it in the Bible and by the Church also stand unless or until found wanting. In that sense, though natural law may be declared dead, it refuses to lie down.

But the axioms are not inviolate to new reason, as the development in Catholic teaching on marriage from the insistence on procreation as the primary end of marriage to a reformulation in terms of conjugal love clearly shows. It would not, therefore, seem impossible to envisage the axiom against homosexual behaviour being re-expressed to include a measure of tolerance for homosexual partnerships.

Those who understand Christian ethical principles as not only illuminated by love, but as nothing else than the application of love to particular human situations have less difficulty in modifying the axiom of conjugal love to include partners of the same sex. Robinson has called such axioms 'the dykes of love in a loveless world' but it need not only be an act-agape theory which could envisage the acceptance of homosexual love. Within the rule-agape system also, the axiom that love must give quality to all sexual relationships could guide homosexual relationships, as it does heterosexual ones. It remains to be seen, of course, whether or not such new models for explaining the character of Christian ethics as those represented by rule-agapaism and act-agapaism will establish themselves within the Christian tradition or be found inadequate, useful but sometimes too uncertain in application for those who look for orthodoxy.

A cautionary note may be sounded about the state of medical and psychological understanding of homosexuality on which much argument for liberalization depends. Scientific findings proceed on the basis of models of thought which have an expected redundancy. No present day analytical psychologist would conduct his professional work exactly in the terms set out by Freud. The present interest in the chemical processes which are thought to affect sexual differentiation may produce important results, and if these are positive, certain ethical questions would arise in relation to homosexuals similar to those already posed about the possibilities of genetic engineering. The suggestion that sexual orientation might be changed by injection is, at the moment, purely fanciful, and there may be instead a resurgence of the importance once attached to family, social, and environmental conditioning.

In the present state of very limited and shifting knowledge, an interim ethic seems called for. Whether this should be understood as a shift in the limits of tolerance within the Christian community or a recognition of diversity which does not offer violence to underlying orthodoxies about the Christian meanings of human sexuality and the obligation to witness to God's design may not have to be finally decided in the next decade.

Perhaps the last word should be expressed in pastoral rather than theological terms. All pastoral work is attempted in hope; hope for the greater health and salvation of Christ's people. Health and salvation are virtually synonymous words in the New Testament. So then, a pastor may estimate, and critically discern as far as he is able, what makes for health and salvation of those in his care. Discrimination is his task, not condemnation, for judgement finally rests with God. No Christian judges another Christian's desert in ultimate terms, for if he did, he would not himself ''scape whipping'.

Notes

CHAPTER 1

Understanding Homosexuality

1 A. P. Bell and M. S. Weinberg, *Homosexualities* (Mitchell Beazley 1978), pp. 106ff. This is an official publication of the Institute for Sexual Research founded by A. C. Kinsey, and is intended to supplement his two reports on the sexual behaviour of males and females.

2 Standard text books on genetics generally contain sections on human sex determination, and a proper study includes reference to DNA and much new research of the past thirty years. For a simple introduction, see C. O. Carter, *Human Heredity* (Pelican 2nd edn 1977) chap. 3, or more detailed C. D. Darlington, *Genetics and Man* (Pelican 1966) pp. 294ff.

More technical are H. E. Sutton, Holt, Rinehart, and Winston, *An Introduction to Human Genetics* (1965) chaps. 5 and 6. C. Stern, *Principles of Human Genetics* (W. H. Freeman 1960) chap. 20.

A good summary is in D. J. West, *Homosexuality re-examined* (Duckworth 1977) pp. 58–65. This book is a revised and much expanded version of his earlier work, published by Penguin, and in this new edition he presents a masterly examination of the whole subject of homosexuality.

3 Such a claim was made in *The Times*, 13 March 1969, and reiterated on a BBC television documentary—*Horizon*—in May 1979.

4 See West, *Homosexuality Re-examined*, op. cit., pp. 7–74; J. A. Loraine, ed., *Understanding Homosexuality* (Medical and Technical Publishing Co. 1974), pp. 6–13. Dr Loraine has researched into the difference in hormonal levels between homosexual and heterosexual adults. Chap. 1 of this volume contains a concise account of recent work on causes of homosexuality. It concludes that they are still not determined (p. 21).

5 *Patterns of Sexual Behaviour*. Harper, New York, 1951.

6 W. Churchill, *Homosexual Behaviour among Males* (Hawthorn, New York, 1967) p. 98.

7 *Homosexualities*, op. cit., part II.

8 D. J. West, *Homosexuality Re-examined*, op. cit., pp. 1–7. Bisexuality is considered pp. 24–7. A. E. Dyson, *Freedom in Love* (SPCK 1975), p. 27, where bisexuality is said to be the predominant human type. See also C. Wolfe, *Bi-Sexuality* (Quartet Books 1977), chap. 1—based on case histories among women.

9 Henderson and Gillespie, *Textbook of Psychiatry* (Oxford 1962), p. 6.

10 Flugel, *100 Years of Psychology* (Duckworth 1953), pp. 15f.

11 D. Hume, *Treatise of Human Nature* (Oxford 1967), p. 415.

12 J. S. Mill, *On Liberty* (Fontana 1970), p. 135.

13 J. A. Symonds, son of a Bristol doctor, and author. See Part C. Add. Note 3.

14 Bailey, *Homosexuality*, op. cit., p. ix, p. 50, etc.

15 S. Freud, *Introductory Lectures* (Allen and Unwin 1949), p. 258.

16 Quoted from *S. Freud on Sexuality* (Pelican Freud Library vol. 7 1977), p. 46. This is a comprehensive Pelican Edition of Freud's writings based on the standard translation by J. Strachey, and edited by A. Richards.

17 See *infra*, p. 117.

18 S. Freud, *Leonardo* (Pelican 1963), expecially pp. 139–42.
19 O. Fenichel, *The Psycho-analytic theory of Neurosis*. Norton, New York, 1945.
20 I. Bieber *et al. Homosexuality—a Psychoanalytic Study*. Basic Books, New York, 1962.
21 Published in 1965, 1968, 1969 in the *British Journal of Psychiatry*.
22 Paper by J. Bancroft, *British Journal of Hospital Medicine* (February 1968).
23 Quoted by K. Freund in *Understanding Homosexuality*, op. cit., from an Essay by Freud. Leipzig 1926.
24 Freud, Letter (1935), Quoted in Lake, op. cit., p. 973.
25 *Wolfenden Report*, pp. 66–7.
26 *Against the Law*, op. cit., pp. 144–5.
27 *British Medical Journal* (1967), vol. 2, pp. 594–7. In *B.M.J.* 18 March, 1962, Dr B. James reported successful treatment of a male patient by aversion therapy using the drug apomorphine.
28 John Bancroft, 'Aversion Therapy of Homosexuality' in *British Journal of Psychiatry* (December 1969), pp. 1417–31.
29 F. Lake, *Clinical Theology* (Darton, Longman, and Todd 1966), pp. 930–1.
30 Lake, op. cit., p. 392.
31 Lake, op. cit., p. 392.
32 Lake's report on his one hundred clergy patients was considered by a team of psychiatrists at the Maudsley Hospital in comparison with a group of fifty-one Anglican clergy patients treated during the period 1954–64 by the team themselves or by Professor Curran (a member of the Wolfenden Committee) and it was suggested that a higher proportion of them had homosexual tendencies than Lake's findings would suggest; in fact, twice as high as a similar group of patients who were doctors, tested at the same time. There were also observations made about 'ineffective fathers' and 'dominant mothers', described quaintly as the Anglican and Catholic hypotheses respectively. M. Brook *et al.*, 'Psychiatric Illness in the Clergy' in *British Journal of Psychiatry* (1969), pp. 457f.

CHAPTER 2
Preliminary Questions

1 See the introduction to *The New English Bible*, Apocrypha section; the introduction to *The Common Bible*; Peake, *Commentary on the Bible* (Nelson 1962), pp. 73ff; *Book of Common Prayer*, Article 6. See also chap. 4, C.
2 See *The Church's Use of the Bible* (SPCK 1963) for an historical review of these presuppositions by an ecumenical team of scholars. For the Old Testament, see Hayes and Miller, *Israelite and Judean History* (S.C.M. Press 1977), Section I; and for the New Testament: C. F. D. Moule, *The Birth of the New Testament* (A. & C. Black 1962), especially chap. 10: or W. G. Kummell, *Introduction to the New Testament* (S.C.M. Press 1975). For an assessment of the contemporary problem in biblical interpretation see D. E. Nineham, *The Use and Abuse of the Bible* (Macmillan 1976). Homosexuality is referred to on pp. 229–30. For the Authority of the Bible see A. M. Ramsey in *Peake*, op. cit., pp. 1ff.
3 L. Hodgson, *For Faith and Freedom* (S.C.M. Press 1968), pp. 88–9.
4 Published by Longmans 1955 and reprinted in America by Shoestring Press 1975. At an early stage of his research, the present writer was greatly helped by Dr Bailey.

CHAPTER 3
Old Testament Texts

1 G. von Rad, *Genesis* (S.C.M. Press 1961), pp. 30–2.
2 For the abiding significance of the Moses attribution, see J. F. A. Sawyer, *From Moses to Patmos* (SPCK 1977), p. 9.
3 Most general commentaries on the Old Testament and on Genesis refer to sources of the Pentateuch.
 1. S. R. Driver, *Genesis* (Westminster Commentaries)
 2. J. Skinner, *Genesis* (International Critical Commentary)
 3. *Peake*, op. cit., article by S. H. Hooke, pp. 164ff
 4. J. Bright, *History of Israel* (S.C.M. Press 2nd end 1972) chap. 2
 5. R. de Vaux, *The early History of Israel* (Darton, Longman, and Todd 1978), vol. 1, chaps. 5 and 6
 6. J. A. Soggins, *Introduction to the Old Testament* (S.C.M. Press 1976), pp. 79–145
 7. Hayes and Miller, *Israelite and Judean History* (S.C.M. Press 1977), pp. 70–133
 8. D. A. Knight, *Tradition and Theology in the Old Testament* (SPCK 1977), chaps. 5–8
4 De Vaux, op. cit., pp. 168–9 and 219.
5 Skinner, op. cit., p. 310; Hayes and Miller, op. cit., p. 101: De Vaux, op. cit., pp. 168–9; and *Westminster Historical Atlas to the Bible* (S.C.M. Press 1946), pp. 657f.
6 Von Rad, op. cit., pp. 215–16.
7 For discussion of thc judgemcnt thcmc in this passagc, scc W. Eichrodt, *Theology of the Old Testament* (S.C.M Press 1961), vol. 1, p. 243; and D. Daube, *Studies in Biblical Law* (Cambridge 1947), pp. 154–60.
8 Von Rad, op. cit., p. 213.
9 This form is also used in the Revised Version, the Revised Standard Version and the Common Bible. The Good News Bible has 'the men of Sodom wanted to have sex with them'. Modern Roman Catholic Versions seek to make clear the homosexual implication: thus Knox refers to 'lust' and the Jerusalem Bible has 'abuse' following the original French 'que nous en abusions' with a footnote about the double offences of unnatural vice and inhospitality. The New International Version of the Bible, published 1978, has for Gen. 19.5 'So that we can have sex with them' and in v. 8 the daughters 'have never slept with a man'. In Gen. 4.1, this translation has 'Adam *lay* with his wife Eve'.
10 J. Calvin, *Commentary—Genesis*, ed. J. King (Edinburgh 1847), pp. 497–9.
11 G. A. Barton, Article on 'Sodomy', in *Encyclopaedia of Religion and Ethics*, ed. J. Hastings. T. & T. Clark 1920.
12 Op. cit., pp. 1–8.
13 As already noted biblical translations published since Bailey expressed this view, have tended to remove the ambiguity by giving a homosexual meaning, and most recent writers have treated Bailey's argument with caution. Support for Bailey is to be found in Pettinger, Kimball-Jones, Uberholtzer and Macourt. Caution is shown by McNeil, Scanzoni, West, *et al.* See Part D.
14 See *infra*, p. 54.

15 The girl is not a prostitute and has a legal status, though not that of a full wife. She was angry, not unfaithful, as the Authorized Version suggested. Modern Bibles rely on the LXX text rather than Hebrew.

16 For the period of the Judges, see J. Bright, *A History of Israel* (S.C.M. Press 2nd edn 1972), pp. 166ff; for the contrasting views on the relationship of the tribes, see J. Noth, *History of the Old Testament* (A. & C. Black 1958), chap. 2; R. de Vaux, *Early History of Israel* (Darton, Longman, and Todd 1978), chap. 23; and J. D. Martin, *Judges* (C.U.P. 1975), pp. 5–15.

17 For these chapters in Judges, see De Vaux, op. cit., chap. 22; Hayes and Miller, op. cit., p. 302; and Soggin, op. cit., pp. 180–1: Martin, op. cit., pp. 196ff: J. Gray, *Joshua, Judges and Ruth* (Nelson 1967), pp. 239–43 and 372ff.

18 See A. Phillips, *Ancient Israel's Criminal Law* (Blackwell 1970), pp. 121–2. De Vaux thinks Judges 19—21 represents a pre-monarchic tradition about Benjamin, ignored or rejected by the Deuteronomistic editors (op. cit., p. 689).

19 Disentangling the various sources was thoroughly attempted by C. A. Simpson, *Composition of the Book of Judges* (Blackwell 1957), pp. 74ff. J. Gray, op. cit., has reservations about Simpson's view (pp. 9–10) but recognizes the variant traditions in the Gibeah narrative (p. 240 and pp. 372ff). J. Martin, op. cit., pp. 205–6 agrees and identifies also elements from 1 Samuel 2 as he does for the remaining chapters of Judges. Josephus *Antiquities* describes homosexual assault at Sodom and heterosexual rape at Gibeah as quite distinct events. See *infra* p. 84.

20 The New International Version of the Bible has for Judges 19.22 'so we can have sex with him', following the Good News Bible here and in the Genesis equivalent. This is presumably thought more direct than the NEB 'have intercourse'. The Living Bible Paraphrase of 1971 has 'rape' for both verses.

21 See *supra*, p. 12.

22 Op. cit., pp. 53–5.

23 See note 19.

24 For a summary of the Deuteronomistic theory, see *Soggin*, op. cit., pp. 160–4, and for this in relation to Kings, see J. Gray, *1 and 2 Kings* (S.C.M. Press, 3rd edn 1977), pp. 1–43. A brief account of D and comparison with the Book of the Covenant is in D. L. Edwards, *A Key to the Old Testament* (Collins 1976), chap. 8, pp. 184ff.

25 1 Kings 13.34. See also 1 Kings 12.25–33.

26 For this period see B. W. Anderson, *The Living World of the Old Testament* (Longmans 2nd edn 1966), pp. 196–202, and for a description of Canaanite culture, chap. 4, pp. 99ff. Also Noth, op. cit., pp. 141ff, and De Vaux, op. cit., pp. 125ff.

27 The Hebrew masculine plural could imply females as well.

28 See comment on Leviticus *infra*, p. 47.

29 G. von Rad, *Deuteronomy* (S.C.M. Press 1966), p. 148. See also Gray, op. cit., pp. 342–3 and 349–50. Most Old Testament commentaries refer to cult prostitution and it is fully assessed in Kittel and Freidrich, *Theological Dictionary of the New Testament* (Erdmans 1973), article on 'Porneia'.

30 Bailey draws attention to the changed meaning of 'sodomy' (op. cit., pp. 48–53) but may press the case overmuch in suggesting that these texts 'have nothing whatsoever to do with homosexual practices'.

31 Soggin, op. cit., pp. 194–6.
32 For the meaning of 'Love' in the Old Testament see Kittel, op. cit., *Theological Dictionary*, vol. I, pp. 21–7. The meaning of 2 Samuel 1.26 is examined on p. 26.
33 For dating of the Holiness Code, see M. Noth, *Leviticus* (S.C.M. revised edn 1977), p. 128, and for its composition pp. 14–15. Also: J. Bright, *A History of Israel* (revised edn 1972), pp. 142 and 350. For general background of the exile, see B. W. Anderson, *The Living World of the Old Testament* (2nd edn), chap. 12, and D. Edwards, op. cit., pp. 190ff. See also *Peake's Commentary*, op. cit., for N. H. Snaith's view of dating, and his comments on the literary structure in his *Leviticus and Numbers* (Century Bible, Nelson 1967), pp. 22ff. See also Soggin, op. cit., pp. 135–45.
34 Genesis 22; Deuteronomy 12.31 and 18.10; 2 Kings 23.10; 2 Chronicles 28.3; Jeremiah 7.31; Ezekiel 16.20; 23.37. See full discussion in W. Eichrodt, *Theology of the Old Testament* (S.C.M. 1961), pp. 148–52, and also H. H. Rowley, *Worship in Ancient Israel* (SPCK 1976), pp. 24ff, and Phillips, op. cit., pp. 128–9, and Gray, *Kings*, op. cit., p. 734.
35 Phillips, op. cit., pp. 28–30 and 126–9; Eichrodt, op. cit., vol. I, p. 82.
36 Noth, op. cit., p. 134–50.
37 The New International Version has 'lie with a man as one lies with a woman; that is detestable', for Leviticus 18.22 and a similar expression for 20.13. Bestiality is called a perversion. The Good News Bible has 'Sexual relations with another man—God hates that', for chap. 18 and in 20 it is called a 'disgusting thing'. The Living Bible has 'Homosexuality is absolutely forbidden, for it is an enormous sin' for chap. 18, and for 20 'The penalty for homosexual acts is death to both parties'. The distinction between the condition and the acts is not made in the Codes.
38 For meanings of abomination in the Bible see A. Richardson ed., *A Theological Handbook of the Bible* (S.C.M. 1950), article by K. Grayston, pp. 11–12.
39 See the sin of Onan, Genesis 38.
40 Exodus 22.19–20.
41 For the meaning of *to'ebah* see Snaith, *Century Bible*, op. cit., p. 126; Bailey, op. cit., pp. 59–60. For the character of Old Testament morality, see Eichrodt, op. cit., vol. II, chap. 22 and ref. to Leviticus 18 on p. 335. For the importance of the family see J. R. Porter, *The Extended Family in the Old Testament* (Exeter University 1967); Phillips, op. cit., p. 123; and Noth, *Leviticus*, op. cit., p. 135.
42 *The Assyrian Laws* (Oxford 1955), and *Babylonian Laws* (2 vols. Oxford 1952 and 1955), both by G. R. Driver and J. C. Miles; J. B. Pritchard, *Ancient Near Eastern Texts relating to the Old Testament* (Princetown 1950, 1955 and 1966); W. Beyerlin, *Near Eastern Religious Texts relating to the Old Testament* (S.C.M. 1978).
43 *Theology of the Old Testament, vol. I*; W. Eichrodt, op. cit., sections III and IV; Soggin, op. cit., pp. 146–60; De Vaux, op. cit., pp. 241ff.
44 Hastings, *Encylopaedia*, art. on Sodomy, op. cit. The Epic of Gilgamesh is published in the Penguin Classics series, ed. N. K. Sanders (1960). Textual history is given in Bayerlin, p. 68ff; Sanders' translation says Enkidu 'jostled' with the animals—not necessarily a sexual activity.
45 Bailey, op. cit., p. 33.
46 Article on Sodomy in Hastings, *Encyclopaedia*, op. cit.

47 Beyerlin, op. cit., pp. 1ff.
48 De Vaux, op. cit., pp. 439ff.
49 Pritchard, op. cit., p. 196, paras, 189–90.
50 Driver, op. cit., pp. 66ff.
51 Driver, op. cit., p. 71. Phillips, op. cit., p. 122.
52 A. C. Bouquet, *Sacred Books of the World* (Pelican 1954), pp. 104–5.

CHAPTER 4

The Inter-Testamental Period

1 See J. Jeremias, *Jerusalem in the time of Jesus* (S.C.M. Press 1969), chap. 3; also Peake, *Commentary* op. cit., pp. 686ff.
2 For a history of the period, see for example, J. Bright, *History of Israel*, op. cit., pp. 430–67; or more briefly D. S. Russell, *Between the Testaments* (S.C.M. Press 1976), chap. 1 and Edwards, *Key to Old Testament*, op. cit., chap. 9. For a Jewish view see S. Sandmel, *A Jewish Understanding of the New Testament* (SPCK 1977), chap. 3; I. Epstein, *Judaism* (Pelican 1966), chaps. 10 and 11. For political background see E. Lohse, *The New Testament Environment* (S.C.M. 1976), pp. 15ff. A fuller treatment of the Apocryphal writings can be found in D. S. Russell, *The Method and Message of Jewish Apocalystic* (S.C.M. Press 1964), pp. 15–68 and B. M. Metzger, *An Introduction to the Apocrypha* (Oxford 1977).
3 Russell, *Between the Testaments*, op. cit., pp. 18–20.
4 In addition to what is said in the introduction to this Section, see Peake, *Commentary*, op. cit., Essays on Hebrew Wisdom by Rylaarsdam p. 386ff. and on Apocalyptic Literature: Rowley, pp. 484ff. See also J. Rhymer, ed., *The Bible in Order* (Darton, Longman, and Todd 1975), pp. 1119ff.
5 Russell, *Between the Testaments*, op. cit., pp. 58ff. See also Russell, *Method and Message*, op. cit., p. 334; J. M. Ross, 'The Status of the Apocrypha', in *Theology* 1979.
6 For the reshaping of the Jewish tradition see J. F. A. Sawyer, *From Moses to Patmos* (SPCK 1977), pp. 131ff. For the formation of the Hebrew Canon see Metzger, op. cit., pp. 7–10; cf. B. W. Anderson, *The Living World of the Old Testament* (Longman 1976), pp. 554–9.
7 See J. Snaith, Cambridge Bible Commentary: *Ecclesiasticus* (C.U.P. 1974), pp. 1–5.
8 See J. Bright, *History of Israel*, op. cit., pp. 450–3 for Angels, Intermediaries, and Demons.
9 See A. G. Clarke, *The Wisdom of Solomon* Cambridge Bible Commentary (1973) pp. 1–11.
10 Bailey scrutinized this verse at length, op. cit., pp. 45–8, noting its ambiguity, but thought the marginal references in the Authorized and Revised Versions to Romans 1.26 and hence to homosexual behaviour unjustified. I disagree.
11 Russell, *Between the Testaments*, op. cit., pp. 88ff.
12 R. H. Charles, *Apocrypha and Pseudepigrapha*, vol. 2 (Oxford 1913). For an account of the Pseudepigrapha, see D. S. Russell, *The Jews from Alexander to Herod* (Oxford 1967), pp. 180ff, and references in footnote supra; G. Vermes, *The Dead Sea Scrolls* (Collins 1977), pp. 209ff; D. S. Russell, *Between the Testaments* op. cit., pp. 85ff.

13 1 Enoch 10.11 quoted from R. H. Charles, *The Book of Enoch.* SPCK 1952. Also in Charles, *Pseudepigrapha* (Oxford 1913), op. cit., p. 194.

14 For commentary on these verses in Enoch see E. P. Sanders, *Paul and Palestinian Judaism* (SPCK 1977), pp. 348–50 and J. T. Milik, *The Books of Enoch* (Oxford 1976), pp. 336–7. Bailey suggests the link between the offence of the Watchers and Sodom on other grounds, op. cit., p. 18. For the date and structure of 1 Enoch see Russell, *Method and Message*, p. 51.

15 Milik, op. cit., pp. 107ff; Russell, *Method and Message*, p. 61, written in 1964, holds to the early date with reservations, noting the parallelism between the ethical teaching of 2 Enoch chapters 39–66 with that found in the Testaments of the XII Patriarchs.

16 Sanders, op. cit., p. 383; Russell, *Method and Message*, p. 54; G. Vermes, *The Dead Sea Scrolls* (Collins 1977), p. 210.

17 Hosea 1.1—4 and Jeremiah 2.1—3, 13.

18 See *Theological Dictionary of the New Testament*, op. cit., vol. 6, pp. 587–90 for the extension of the meaning of porneia.

19 Quoted from text in G. Vermes, *The Dead Sea Scrolls in English* (Pelican 2nd edn 1975), pp. 216–17.

20 Vermes, op. cit., p. 210; Russell, *Method and Message*, op. cit., pp. 55–7.

21 For the history of this period see M. Avi-Yonah, *The Jews of Palestine* (Blackwell 1976), chap. 3. For the Jewish writings see *Epstein*, op. cit., chaps. 12–13.

22 Mishnah, Kerithoth, 1.1; 1.2; 2.6, tr. Danby, op. cit., pp. 562, 565.

23 Danby, *Mishnah*, op. cit., p. 98. For a modern account of hermaphroditism see West, *Homosexuality re-examined*, op. cit., pp. 62–3.

24 Ed. Freedman and Simon (Soncino Press 1939), p. 338.

25 Op. cit., p. 438.

26 Op. cit., p. 438.

27 J. H. Lowe trans., *Rashi on the Pentateuch—Genesis* (London 1928), pp. 183–4.

28 *Genesis*, chaps. 3 and 9. Philo's works are published by Heinemann in the Loeb Classics Edition. Vol. 6 serves as a biographical introduction to the Laws with reference to Abraham, Joseph, and Moses, and vol. 7 contains his comments on the Decalogue and other laws. Supplementary vol. 1 deals with questions on Genesis. Quotations from Philo which follow are cited from the Loeb edition.

29 Philo, *Laws* Book 3, Section 32. Loeb vol. 7, p. 495.

30 Bailey, op. cit., p. 22; McNeil, op. cit., p. 72.

31 Philo, *De Abrahamo* (Loeb), op. cit., vol. 6, pp. 69–71,

32 Philo, *Questions and Answers on Genesis* (Loeb), Supplementary vol. 1, op. cit., pp. 311–12.

33 Epstein, *Judaism*, op. cit., pp. 106–8.

34 For Philo's allegorizing, see C. K. Barrett, *New Testament Background: Selected Documents* (SPCK 1958), pp. 180ff.

35 The Works of Josephus are translated in the Loeb edition (Heinemann 1926–65), *The Jewish War* and *The Antiquities* by H. St. J. Thackeray. Also G. A. Williams, tr., *The Jewish War* (Penguin Classics 1959 and reprints). An earlier translation of *The Antiquities* was by W. Whiston (London 1737 and reprints). Whiston was Professor of Mathematics at Cambridge. His edition

seems to be quoted by Bailey, op. cit., p. 23, and McNeill, op. cit., p. 73. The differences between Whiston and Thackeray are significant for one of the relevant texts.

36 The author visited this region in 1977.

37 Josephus, *Jewish Antiquities* (Loeb), op. cit., p. 97. Book 1, pp. 94–5.

38 The Greek word *homilia* is used by St Paul in 1 Corinthians 15.33 to mean association or companionship, and the condemnation of Sodom for inhospitality to strangers has been noted in e.g. Wisdom 19.13ff, and in Rabbinic writings. Whiston's translation of this passage has 'abused themselves with sodomitical practices', an inexplicable translation unless he worked from a corrupt text of Josephus. In quoting Whiston's translation, Bailey and McNeill make Josephus seem more explicit at this point than he intended.

39 Josephus, *Jewish Antiquities* Book 1, 199–202 (Loeb), op. cit., p. 99.

40 For analysis of influences on Josephus, including Hellenistic ones, see Lohse, *The New Testament*, op. cit., pp. 140–5. Lohse is the Lutheran Bishop of Hanover. For a Jewish viewpoint of Philo and Josephus and the inter-testamental period generally, see S. Sandmel, *Judaism and Christian beginnings* (O.U.P., New York, 1978), pp. 279–301ff.

CHAPTER 5
The New Testament

1 For New Testament dating, see any commentary, e.g. Peake. Detail in W. G. Kümmel, *Introduction to New Testament*. S.C.M. 1975. Alternative earlier dates are suggested in J. A. T. Robinson, *Re-dating the New Testament* (1976); cf. p. 5 with pp. 352–3 where the Gospels are dated earlier than the Epistles. For the process of collection see C. F. D. Moule, *The Birth of the New Testament* (A. & C. Black 1962), chap. 10. For extra-canonical sources see J. Jeremias, *Unknown sayings of Jesus* (SPCK 1964); E. Hennecke, ed., *Full Collection of New Testament Apocrypha*, 2 vols. (S.C.M. 1973–5).

2 See e.g. T. W. Manson, *Ethics and the Gospel* (S.C.M. 1960), chap. 3.

3 E. Osborn, *Ethical Patterns in early Christian Thought* (C.U.P. 1976), p. 19.

4 There is wide agreement about date, authorship, and purpose of Romans, conveniently summarized in C. E. B. Cranfield, *Romans*, I.C.C. Commentary (T. & T. Clark 1973), pp. 1–24, and many good modern commentaries available. The first in the I.C.C. series was by Sanday and Headlam (1895 and many edns). K. Barth wrote a full commentary before the war and his shorter version was published by S.C.M. in 1959. Other major commentaries include those by C. H. Dodd (Hodder 1932 and Fontana reprints); C. K. Barrett (A. & C. Black 1962); F. J. Leenhardt (Lutterworth 1964); and M. Black, New Century Bible (1973). See also Peake's *Commentary*, op. cit., article by T. W. Manson.

5 *Shorter Commentary*, op. cit., p. 29.

6 *Commentary*, op. cit., p. 38.

7 All the commentaries listed in Note 4 give this meaning, as do the older ones, following the Midrash and Rashi. Examples are given later from Chrysostom, Nicholas of Lyra, Calvin, etc. in chap. 6A(d).

8 Op. cit., p. 40.

9 C. S. C. Williams, *Acts of the Apostles* (A. & C. Black 1957), pp. 177ff.

10 For the influence of Rabbinic and Greek teaching on Paul's ethics, see W. D. Davies, *Paul and Rabbinic Judaism* (SPCK 3rd edn 1970), chap. 6 and Appendix A; also E. P. Sanders, *Paul and Palestinian Judaism* (S.C.M. 1977), pp. 206ff.

11 Commentaries on 1 Corinthians: *Robertson and Plummer* (T. & T. Clark 1911 and reprints); J. Moffat (Hodder 1938 and reprints); C. K. Barrett (A. & C. Black 1968); H. Conzelmann (Göttingen 1969), E. tr. J. W. Leitch (Fortress Press 1975). For the legend of Aphrodite's Temple at Corinth, see Conzelmann, p. 12n.

12 Compare Mark 10.19; Matthew 19.18; Luke 18.20; Romans 13.7–10.

13 *Paul and Rabbinic Judaism*, op. cit., pp. 116–7. Conzelmann also discusses this question, op. cit., p. 10 and pp. 100–2. R. Bultmann regards the codes as much more reflective of the Synagogue: see his *Theology of the New Testament*, E. tr. K. Grobel, vol. 2, chap. 8 (S.C.M. Press 1955), and particularly pp. 218ff. In contrast W. Lillie, following the arguments of Brunner, Dodd, and Ellul, stresses the emphasis on natural law. *Studies in Ethics* (*N.T.*) (Oliver and Boyd 1961), chap. 2, especially pp. 15–16.

14 See commentaries by Moffatt, p. 66; Robertson and Plummer, p. 119; and Barrett, p. 140.

15 Bailey objected to the Revised Standard Version translation on the grounds that this did not distinguish between the homosexual condition and homosexual practices, op. cit., p. 39.

16 R. Graves, *The Greek Myths* (Pelican 1955), vol. 1, p. 117.

17 Apart from the reference in Bailey, op. cit., p. 39, see J. J. McNeill, S.J., *The Church and the Homosexual* (Darton, Longman, and Todd 1977), pp. 50–3. M. Macourt, ed., *Towards a Theology of Gay Liberation* (S.C.M. Press 1977), pp. 43, 54.

18 The point is fully considered by C. K. Barrett, *First Epistle to the Corinthians* (A. & C. Black 1967), pp. 150–1.

19 D. Daube discusses the whole question in detail in *The New Testament and Rabbinic Judaism* (Athlone Press 1956), pp. 71–86.

20 For Rabbinic teaching on Divorce see *Marriage Divorce and the Church* (SPCK 1971), appendix I by H. Montefiore, where he suggests that the Rabbis regarded divorce with some disfavour. The whole appendix is relevant to this paragraph. In the later report *Marriage and the Church's Task* (C.I.O. 1978), chap. 4, all the New Testament texts from the Gospels and Paul's epistles are reviewed. It is argued on p. 145 in relation to the key passages from the Gospels that Jesus is not repudiating the old precept literally, but is doing so in effect. Conzelmann called it a 'supratemporal command', op. cit., p. 120, and Barrett notes that since this epistle pre-dates Mark's Gospel, it lends force to the view that the later Matthean exception for adultery is a gloss. Since the desire for celibacy is not the ground for divorce, adultery etc. would certainly not be in this absolutist view.

21 For a review of the problem of authorship see Peake, op. cit., pp. 1001ff; Kümmel, *Introduction to New Testament*, op. cit., pp. 366ff. Moule, op. cit., p. 220, sees links between the Pastorals and Luke-Acts. C. K. Barrett, *The Pastoral Epistles* (Oxford 1963); and Dibelius and Conzelmann, *The Pastoral Epistles*, E.

tr. (Fortress Press 1972); and A. T. Hanson, *Studies in the Pastoral Epistles* (SPCK 1968) all suggest the later date. J. Robinson, *Re-dating the New Testament* (S.C.M. Press 1976), reviews the whole subject at length pp. 67–85, and concludes a date of 55 CE and Pauline authorship. J. N. D. Kelly, *The Pastoral Epistles* (A. & C. Black 1963), Introduction, agrees Pauline authorship, but while at Rome.

22 Hanson, op. cit., p. 113; Barrett, op. cit., p. 43.

23 Robinson, *Re-dating the New Testament*, op. cit., sugests overlapping, the synoptic Gospels being complete by the time of Paul's death.

24 C. F. Evans, *The Bible and the Christian* (Mowbrays 1957), pp. 9f.

25 Some genuine sayings are, no doubt, contained in the Apocryphal Gospels; see J. Jeremias, *Unknown Sayings of Jesus* (SPCK 1964), pp. 44ff.

26 See the full discussion of this in the Synod Reports listed in Note 20.

27 Jeremias suggests Jesus showed an obvious interest in Sodom's destruction and perhaps based his apocalyptic prediction of fire and destruction on it. *Unknown Sayings of Jesus*, op. cit., p. 78; cf. Luke 9.51–5 where Elijah seems to be in mind.

28 See Nestle and Kilpatrick, *The New Testament* (British and Foreign Bible Society 1958), p. 118.

29 Paul makes a similar point in Romans 9.29, and elaborates it in 10.15–21.

30 Matthew 5.27–8 and Mark 10.17ff; Matthew 19.16ff; Luke 18.18 respectively.

31 *Christ For us Today* (S.C.M. Press 1968), pp. 108–10. The idea is not new; in the sixteenth century the dramatist C. Marlowe suggested Jesus was homosexual.

32 Well discussed in J. Knox, *The Ethics of Jesus in the Teaching of the Church* (Epworth 1962), chap. 1.

33 See C. K. Barrett, *The Gospel according to St John* (SPCK 1956), pp. 490–3; R. H. Lightfoot, ed. C. F. Evans, *St John's Gospel* (Oxford 1956), pp. 344–8; J. Marsh, *St John* (Pelican 1968), pp. 681–8.

34 In A. R. Vidler, ed., *Soundings* (Cambridge 1962), pp. 81–2.

35 Marsh, *St John*, op. cit., p. 683.

36 Kummell, op. cit., pp. 425–34; J. N. D. Kelly, *The Epistles of Peter and Jude* (A. & C. Black 1976), pp. 223–7.

37 *Re-dating*, op. cit., pp. 169–99, and particularly p. 193.

38 The passage is thoroughly discussed in Kelly, op. cit., pp. 256–66.

39 The collection used is that of E. Hennecke, *New Testament Apocrypha*, English edn of 2 vols. (S.C.M. Press 1973 and 1975).

40 Text in Hennecke, op. cit., vol. 2, p. 141ff.

41 Hennecke, op. cit., vol. 2, p. 368.

42 Hennecke, op. cit., vol. 2, p. 647.

43 Hennecke, op. cit., vol. 2, p. 693.

44 Hennecke, Book 6.20–5, op. cit., vol. 2, p. 720.

45 E.g. Penguin Classics series. See later footnotes for particular references. For Greek family life generally, see H. D. F. Kitto, *The Greeks* (Pelican 1951 and reprints), chap. 12. For Rome during the New Testament period, see J. Carcopino, *Daily Life in Ancient Rome*, E. tr. E. O. Lorimer (Routledge 1941 and edns), chap. 4.

46 E. V. Rieu, tr. *The Iliad* (Penguin Classics), p. 372.

47 Graves, *The Greek Myths*, op. cit., vol. 1, pp. 378–9; Rieu, *Iliad*, op. cit., p. 5; Rieu, *Odyssey* (Penguin Classics), pp. 222 and 238. Licht, *Sexual Life in Ancient Greece* (Routledge 1932, Panther reprint 1969), p. 398 interprets these references from the *Odyssey* as clearly implying that pederasty in the harem was known to Homer.
48 The argument for homosexual love among the ancient Greek heroes was pressed by H. Licht, op. cit., pp. 396ff, but rejected in the more recent R. Flacelière, *Love in Ancient Greece*, E. tr. J. Cleugh (Muller 1962), chaps. 1 and 3.
49 Tr. W. Hamilton (Penguin Classics edn 1951 and reprints), pp. 94–5.
50 Tr. T. J. Saunders (Penguin Classics 1975 and reprints), p. 340. The whole dialogue on sexual conduct begins at p. 332.
51 Herodotus, writing perhaps 50 years earlier, notes that the Persians learnt pederasty from the Greeks. He also describes the cult prostitution of the Babylonians at the temple of Aphrodite. He could travel as a Greek merchant to these places and is perhaps an accurate reporter. Herodotus, *The Histories*, rev. tr. A. R. Burn (Penguin Classics 1972), pp. 97 and 121–2.
52 J. A. K. Thomson, *The Ethics of Aristotle*, translation of the Nicomachean Ethics (Penguin Classics 1953 and reprints), pp. 193 and 204–5.
53 *Ethics*, op. cit., pp. 208–9. In the *Politics* Aristotle seems to think that open pederasty was practised by the Celts. W. Ellis, tr., *Politics* (Everyman edn 1947), p. 52.
54 *Ethics*, op. cit., p. 234 for male love, and p. 251ff for married love.
55 Translations of the standard works are available in the Penguin Classics series.
56 Suetonius, *The Twelve Caesars*, tr. R. Graves (Penguin Classics 1957), pp. 10 and 30–1.
57 Tacitus, *Annals* (Penguin Edition 1956), p. 351.
58 Details in Bailey, op. cit., pp. 64–7.

CHAPTER 6
Chastity Enforced

1 *The Didache:* Early Christian Fathers (S.C.M. Press 1953), p. 172.
2 *First Apology of Justin Martyr*, chap. xxvii (T. & T. Clark 1874), p. 30.
3 *Clement Homily Three*, chap. 68 (T. & T. Clark 1870), p. 86.
4 Tertullian, *De Pudicitia* (T. & T. Clark), p. 64.
5 Arnobius, *Adversus Gentes*, Book V, chap. 19; and Lactantius, *Institutes* Book V, chap. 9 (T. & T. Clark 1871).
6 *Apostolic Constitutions*, Book 7, chap. 2 (T. & T. Clark 1870).
7 Chrysostom, *Homily on Romans* (Oxford 1841), pp. 44–52.
8 *Confessions St Augustine* Tr. E. B. Pusey (Everyman edn 1939), p. 43.
9 D. Knowles, ed., *City of God* (Pelican Classics 1972), p. 245–6.
10 P. Brown, *Augustine of Hippo* (Faber 1967), chap. 32.
11 For a critical assessment of the *Penitentials* see R. C. Mortimer, *Western Canon Law* (A. & C. Black 1953), chap. 2.
12 For further details of the *Penitentials* and P. Damian, see Bailey, op. cit., pp. 100–15.
13 Quoted from text in *L'Osservatore Romano*, 22 January 1976, section 8.
14 The suggestion that the men of Sodom assaulted visitors rather than practised sodomy among themselves is first made in the Midrash.

15 Quoted from *Cleanness*, tr. D. S. Brewer (Oxford University Press reprint 1974), pp. 32–3. Another translation of this mediaeval religious epic is found in The Penguin Classics series, B. Stone 1971, which also contains 'The Owl and the Nightingale', a poem on the contest between marriage and courtly love in which the argument, of great importance in the later Middle Ages, anticipates in heterosexual terms many points now made in defence of homosexual love. See also C. S. Lewis, *The Allegory of Love* (O.U.P 1936 and reprints) and *The Four Loves*, chap. 1.

16 Calvin, *Genesis* (op. cit.), p. 498.

17 Calvin, *Romans* (Edinburgh tr. 1844).

18 B. Cottle, *The Triumph of English 1350–1400* (Blandford 1969), chap. 5, and particularly p. 223.

19 For Luther's use of Nicholas's commentary, see W. Panck, *M. Luther, Lectures on Romans* (S.C.M. 1956), Introd. p. xxvii.

20 That this point continued to exercise Roman Catholic commentators on this text is illustrated by a comment of R. Knox in his commentary on his own biblical translation where the same conclusion is repeated: *The Holy Bible* tr. Knox (Burns Oates 1957), p. 14, Note 2.

21 The *Commentary* of Nicholas of Lyra quoted from here was printed in Nuremberg in 1497. An English translation of the passages cited was specially made by Mr J. Warrington.

22 A copy of the engraving was loaned to Bristol Cathedral for an exhibition of de Bry's work in Summer 1978 by the John Judkyn Memorial Trust.

23 *Holy Living*, section 3 para 2. Many editions.

24 Gratian's 'Decretum' as it was known, was incorporated in the final collection of canon law in the Western Church—the *Corpus Iuris Canonici*—which remained valid until revised as the *Codex Iuris Canonici* in 1917. A further revision has been implemented for the Roman Catholic Church following the Second Vatican Council of 1963. A short form of Canons for the Church of England was produced in 1604 and these were replaced by a new set in 1969. Since then, under the Synodical Government measure, canonical revision has become a regular procedure. The current set of Canons do not concern themselves with particular issues of Christian morality. See *The Canon Law of the Church of England* (SPCK 1947), chaps. 2 and 3; and E. W. Kemp, *An Introduction to Canon Law in the Church of England* (Hodder & Stoughton 1957), for historical accounts.

25 See Bailey, op. cit., p. 124; and M. Hyde. *The Other Love* (Heinemann 1970), pp. 33ff for details.

26 For the text of Henry's Statute and Blackstone's commentary on it, see Additional Note 1.

27 Quoted in H. Montgomery Hyde, *The Other Love*, op. cit., p. 40.

28 See Hyde, *The Other Love*, op. cit., chaps. 2 and 3 for full details of these and similar trials during this period.

29 J. Tudor Rees, and Harley V. Usill, ed., *They Stand Apart*, symposium (New York 1955 and Longmans, London, 1955), p. 3.

30 See Norman St John Stevas, *Life Death and the Law* (Eyre & Spottiswoode 1961), p. 208; and also H. Montgomery Hyde, ed., *Trials of Oscar Wilde* (William Hodge & Co., London), Appendix F, pp. 375–84, which contains a full account.

31 See Additional Note 1.
32 Details in J. Weeks, *Coming Out* (Quartet Books 1977), chap. 14 and notes. The bibliography is comprehensive.
33 *Hansard* 1885, pp. 1379–98.
34 *The Other Love*, op. cit., pp. 134–7.
35 *University of Melbourne Historical Studies*, vol. 17 (1977), pp. 165ff.
36 For a fuller account of the various church movements and personalities, including General Booth and the Salvation Army, who conducted the campaign against child prostitution and the white slave traffic in this period, see C. J. Bristow, *Vice and Violence* (Gill & Macmillan 1977), pp. 75–121.
37 See chapter 7, section B for details of the Purity Society.
38 *The Guardian*, vol. XL, Part 2, p. 1175.
39 I. Bloch, *Sexual Life in England* (Corgi edn 1965), pp. 78ff.
40 Quoted by Bloch, op. cit., p. 345 from *The sins of the Cities of the Plain* (1881).
41 William Hodge 1948.
42 *They Stand Apart* (Heinemann 1955), p. 10.

CHAPTER 7
Victims and Rescue Work

1 *The Life of Oscar Wilde* (Penguin 1960), p. 21.
2 Montgomery Hyde, op. cit., Appendix E.
3 Letter by Oscar Wilde to the *Scots Observer*, 31 July 1890—Hart-Davis, p. 268.
4 For Wilde's own opinions of homosexuality and Christianity, see Additional Note 2.
5 Quoted from Hyde, *Trials*, op. cit., p. 359.
6 J. A. Symonds—See Additional Note 3. For the details of Symond's life at Harrow and of Vaughan's dismissal, see Phyllis Groskurth, *John Addington Symonds* (Longmans 1964), pp. 30–7.
7 See G. K. A. Bell, *Randall Davidson* (Oxford 3rd edn 1952). Index, p. 1439.
8 For Headlam's social reform see M. B. Reckitt, ed., *For Christ and the People* (SPCK 1968), pp. 61–8.
9 Details in Reckitt, op. cit., p. 83.
10 F. G. Bettany, *Stewart Headlam*. Murray 1926.
11 G. Faber, *Oxford Apostles* (Pelican 1954), p. 211. A reticent and characteristically puckish reference to the continuance of homosexual friendships and the kind of spiritual counsel that was given about them is recorded in Evelyn Waugh's *Biography of Romald Knox* (Chapman & Hall 1959), p. 125. Knox at the time, 1912, was Anglican Chaplain of Trinity, Oxford.
12 Bettany, op. cit., p. 46.
13 See also Evelyn Waugh's autobiography *A Little Loving* (Chapman and Hall 1964), p. 96.
14 Rupert Hart-Davis, *The Letters of Oscar Wilde* (1962), p. 563.
15 Bell, *Davidson*, op. cit., p. 47.
16 For example the comprehensive biography of Lytton Strachey by M. Holroyd. Penguin 1971.
17 G. K. A. Bell, *Randall Davidson* (Oxford 3rd edn 1952), pp. 787–8.

18 The history of the League can be traced through its Minute Books which are now held in the archives at Church House, Westminster. They were made available to the author in 1970 and contain a great deal of material which might prove useful to a social or church historian of the period. See also M. P. Hall and I. V. Howes, *The Church in Social Work* (Routledge and Kegan Paul 1965), chaps. 1 and 2, which trace the development of Rescue and Moral Welfare work in the late nineteenth and early twentieth centuries.
19 *The Blanco Book*, chap. 8, The National Flag, p. 167.
20 See chap. 9 for Canon Pym's writings.
21 The preliminary work from which this book stems was supported by a grant from the Trustees.
22 It has, however, re-emerged in recent years. Anthony Grey has given details of boys being importuned in cafes round Piccadilly (Taped conversation). In 1973 Policewoman Sergeant Woodeaton gave evidence in court of a man said to have ten boys aged from fourteen years upwards working for him as male prostitutes (reported in *The Times*, 17 July 1973, p. 3). Among subsequent cases, one of the most recent has been that of five men, one of them a Lloyds Underwriter, who were convicted in 1975 at the Central Criminal Court for various offences of a homosexual nature including buggery, gross indecency, indecent assault on boys under 16, procuring and persistent importuning. These offences were committed in connection with the Playland Amusement Arcade, near Piccadilly Circus, where it was said in evidence 'that a call boy racket had been operated using young boys on the run'. (Reported in *The Times*, 23 September 1975). See also West, *Homosexuality re-examined*, op. cit., pp. 220–33 where he reviews contemporary evidence in England and America. He also notes the increase of venereal diseases in England among homosexual men. Young men who offer homosexual service as prostitutes are not usually homosexuals themselves, but like their female counterparts, have a variety of motives, mostly financial, or the consequence of other problems.

CHAPTER 8
Reforming the Law

1 *Hansard, House of Commons Debates*, 1921, vol. 145, cols. 1799–1897.
2 *Hansard, House of Lords Debates*, 15 August 1921, vol. 46, cols. 567–77.
3 *Hansard, House of Lords Debates*, 7 July 1937, cols. 141–6.
4 Cosmo Gordon Lang, Archbishop of Canterbury 1928–42.
5 *Wolfenden Committee Report*, Appendix, pp. 130–1.
6 Hyde, *The Other Love*, op. cit., pp. 213ff. For background of Burgess and Maclean, see *The Climate of Treason*, A. Boyle (Hutchinson 1979), Chaps. 2 and 3.
7 P. Wildeblood, *Against the Law* (Penguin reprint 1959), pp. 50ff. In addition to his own observations of police activity, he quotes a dispatch from the London correspondent of the *Sydney Morning Telegraph* of 25 October 1953 about the 'Scotland Yard plan to smash homosexuality in London'.
8 J. Weeks, *Coming Out* (Quartet Books 1977), pp. 156ff.
9 For judicial anxiety, see introduction to *They Stand Apart*, p. vii. Mr Justice Stable was by no means a reactionary judge, but expressed fears that the spreading evil 'will corrupt the men of the Nation'. For examples of popular

journalism, see Weeks, *Coming Out*, op. cit., pp. 162–3. Thus—'Burgess sits in Moscow like a patient toad awaiting his next victim'.

10 *Theology*, January 1952. See next chapter for account of the Council's involvement in preparations for the Wolfenden Committee.

11 Peter Wildeblood has fully described his experiences as one of the defendants in the second trial in *Againt the Law*, op. cit., pp. 66–74.

12 *The Problem of Homosexuality* an Interim Report (Church Information Board), p. 20.

13 Peter Wildeblood gives an entirely contrary view of the competence and value of the help given to him by the prison doctor. *Against the Law*, op. cit., pp. 103–4.

14 For the Commons Debate, see *Hansard*, vol. 526, cols. 1745–56.

15 For the Lords Debate see *Hansard*, vol. 187, cols. 737–45.

16 Writing, after his retirement, as F. R. Barry, he acknowledges that what he has to say about homosexuality is largely based on the Report and on Bailey's later book. F. R. Barry, *Christian Ethics and Secular Society* (Hodder 1966), p. 182.

17 P. Devlin, *The Enforcement of Morals* (Oxford 1965), preface.

18 Report of the Committee on Homosexual Offences and Prostitution (HMSO Cmd. 247 1957), para. 52.

19 Lord Longford knew Lord Montagu's family and met him after his release from prison in 1955. He dates the formation of The New Bridge, a society to help ex-prisoners, from this meeting. C. H. Rolph was also involved. *Five Lives*, Lord Pakenham's autobiography (Hutchinson 1964), pp. 125–7.

20 *Hansard, House of Lords Debates*, vol. 206, cols. 733–832. Lord Fisher of Lambeth, Archbishop of Canterbury 1945–61.

21 *The Times*, 7 March 1958.

22 For the debate see *Hansard, House of Commons Debates*, 26 November 1958, vol. 596, cols. 365–508.

23 *Hansard, House of Commons Debates*, 29 June 1960, vol. 625, cols. 1453–1515.

24 *Hansard, House of Commons Debates*, 9 March 1962, vol. 655, cols. 843–60.

25 *Hansard, House of Lords Debates*, 12 May 1965, vol. 266, cols. 71–172.

26 The law in other countries is summarized in additional Note 4. The 1967 Act does not apply to Scotland or N. Ireland. Prosecutions are very rare, but attempts to bring their law in this respect to conform to England's law so far have been unsuccessful.

27 *Hansard, House of Lords Debates*, 12 May 1965, cols. 80–2.

28 *Hansard, House of Lords Debates*, 12 May 1965, col. 79.

29 *Theology*, January 1952; for text of the letter see Additional Note 5.

30 Bailey conv.

31 *Theology*, vol. LV (February 1952), pp. 47–52.

32 Sexual Offenders and Social Punishment (Church Information Office 1956), p. 9.

33 *Hansard, House of Commons Debates*, vol. 521, col. 1298.

34 Bailey conv.

35 Church Information Office (1956), pp. 120.

36 This final recommendation is a change from that made in the Interim Report, but in fact in the 1967 Act the age of consent was retained at twenty-one years. In the Draft Sexual Offences Bill of 1975 it was suggested that the age of consent should be sixteen but this Bill was not enacted.

37 The author has seen this correspondence but is not free to quote from it in detail.
38 *Dublin Review*, vol. 230, no. 471, pp. 57–65.
39 Op. cit., p. 10.
40 Information taken from *Homosexuality and Prostitution*, published B.M.A. 1955.

PART D
Introduction

1 *Calvin Institutes IV* xii, 24: Troeltsch, influenced by Weber, finds in this Protestant sex ethic the explanation of, for example, the development of women's ministry in the Presbyterian and Baptist Churches. The role of women in modern American life he sees as the result of her heightened religious status. Troeltsch, *Social Teaching of the Christian Church*, tr. O. Wyon (Allen and Unwin 1931), vol. 2, pp. 544ff, 809ff, and 987ff. For a fuller treatment see D. S. Bailey, *The Man-Woman relation in Christian Thought* (Longmans 1959), chap. 5. For the changing place of women in American culture see W. H. Chafe, *Women and Equality* (O.U.P. 1977), chaps. 2 and 5.

CHAPTER 9
Chastity and Pastoral Care

1 H. P. Liddon, *St Paul's Epistle to the Romans* (Longmans 1893), pp. 29–38.
2 P. Green, *The Problem of Right Conduct* (Longmans 1931 and subsequent edns); quotations taken from 1939 edn.
3 A. Herbert Gray, *Men Women and God* (S.C.M. Press, first publ. 1923, 11th edn 1935 from which quotations are taken), pp. 107–9.
4 L. Weatherhead, *The Mastery of Sex* (17th edn 1954), pp. 122–6.
5 T. W. Pym, *Our Personal Ministry* (S.C.M. Press 1935), p. 37.
6 L. Dewar & C. E. Hudson, *Manual of Pastoral Psychology* (Philip Allan 1932), p. 93.
7 Dewar and Hudson, op. cit., pp. 132–5.
8 Dewar and Hudson, op. cit., p. 186.
9 *Summa*, Part 2, Questions 151, 153, and 168.
10 The debate is recorded in the Church Assembly *Report of Proceedings* vol. XXXVII, no. 3, pp. 441–79.
11 The Revd K. Greet—correspondence, 29 October 1968.
12 The Sexual Offences Act of 1967 did not apply to Northern Ireland. The Protestant Churches there at present show little enthusiasm for a campaign to liberalize the law in a similar fashion. In summer 1979 the Secretary of State for Northern Ireland told the Commons that the government would not change the law to conform with that of England and Wales. A case has been submitted to the European Court of Human Rights alleging discrimination against homosexuals in Northern Ireland.
13 *Wolfenden Report*, para. 136, p. 50.
14 *Reports* (1958), p. 395.
15 The answers to the questionnaire were confidential in the sense that no individual's replies have been published or quoted. A statistical analysis of all the answers and a computer programme devised to examine their significance was

prepared and a copy of this placed in the University of Bristol Library as the University Research Regulations requires. The questionnaires themselves have been destroyed.

16 To the gratitude expressed already to his University supervisors and the White Cross League Trustees who made this survey possible, this seems the appropriate point for the author to add his public thanks to all those members of the Church Assembly who so kindly wrestled with a long questionnaire shortly before Christmas 1969. The event attracted some attention in the popular press.

17 Devlin's lecture was published by O.U.P. for the British Academy. Hart's rejoinder is printed in L. Blom-Cooper, ed., *The Law as Literature* (Bodley Head 1961). Hart's general position is in his *Concept of the Law* (O.U.P. 1961), chaps. 8 and 9, and he contrasts English and American situations in *Law Liberty and Morality* (O.U.P. 1963). Devlin expanded his views in *The Enforcement of Morality* (O.U.P. 1965). The debate is further considered in B. Mitchell, *Law Morality and Religion* (O.U.P. 1967). Mitchell is Nolloth Professor of the Philosophy of the Christian Religion at Oxford, and has been a member of the Board of Social Responsibility working party that produced the 1979 report—*infra*.

18 R. Woolheim, 'Crime, sin and Mr. Justice Devlin', *Encounter* (Nov. 1959), p. 34. A Research study for the Central Council for Health Education, *The Sexual behaviour of Young People* by M. Schofield (Longmans 1965) showed *inter alia* that sexual behaviour among teenagers was still restricted, and that the moral dilemma of the age group was approval of sex before marriage contrasted with the wish to marry a virgin. A survey in 1977 showed that 3,625 girls under 16 became pregnant that year, of whom 63 per cent had an abortion. A further 8,424 unmarried girls aged 16 became pregnant, nearly half of whom had an abortion. These figures are less than in the immediate preceding years, probably because doctors are now more willing to prescribe the pill for unmarried teenagers. These statistics have been used to support the case for abolishing the age of consent. *Pregnant at School*, National Council for one-parent families, 1979.

CHAPTER 10
Consent within Limits

1 A useful review is provided by the Quaker, D. Blaimires in M. Macourt, ed., *Towards a Theology of Gay Liberation* (S.C.M. Press 1977), chap. 2.

2 J. B. Nelson, *Embodiment* (SPCK 1979), pp. 188ff.

3 A small indication of this was given in the pages of the *British Journal of Psychiatry* which contained no less than ten major articles and much correspondence on these subjects between 1966 and 1969.

4 *Towards a Theology of Gay Liberation*, op. cit., p. 29. No doubt chapter 1 of this book is open to the same criticism.

5 W. M. Abbott, ed., *Documents of Vatican 2* (Chapman 1966), p. 253.

6 *Humanae Vitae* (Catholic Truth Society 1968), p. 13.

7 *New Catholic Encyclopedia*, vol. 7 (McGraw-Hill 1967), p. 117.

8 K. Rahner, ed., *Sacramentum Mundi*, vol. 6 (Burns and Oates 1970), p. 86.

9 *Declaration on Sexual Ethics*., op. cit., para. 1.

10 *Declaration*, op. cit., para. 8.

11 Published Sands & Co.
12 L. Dewar, *Moral Theology in the Modern World* (Mowbrays 1964), p. 108.
13 H. Waddams, *A New Introduction to Moral Theology* (S.C.M. Press 1964), pp. 143–6.
14 In 1923 Barry wrote *Christianity and Psychology*, published by the S.C.M. Press. His *Christian Ethics and Secular Society* (Hodder & Stoughton 1966) proved to be one of the more durable books of this genre in the sixties.
15 *Christian Ethics and Secular Society*, op. cit., pp. 178–84.
16 Anon., *A Guide for Spiritual Directors* (Mowbrays 1957).
17 Published in 1974 by SPCK.
18 Op. cit., p. 85.
19 Op. cit., p. 86.
20 K. Barth, *Church Dogmatics* (T. & T. Clark, Edinburgh, 1961), vol. 3, part 4, pp. 164–6.
21 K. Barth, *Romans*, tr. E. C. Hoskyns. O.U.P. 1933 and reprints.
22 D. Bonhoeffer, *Ethics*, ed. E. Bethge. S.C.M. Press 1955.
23 J. Clarke, London. This is, in fact, one volume of his *Theological Ethics* but printed in a separate edition.
24 Quotations from Thielicke, *The Ethics of Sex*, op. cit., pp. 269ff.
25 Darton, Longman, and Todd 1964. Tr. J. A. Baker from the 3rd edn, pp. 120–73.
26 Capper & Williams, *Towards Christian Marriage* (I.V.F. Press 1962), originally published as *Heirs Together* in 1948.
27 *The Returns of Love*. Inter-Varsity Press 1970.
28 Paternoster Press.
29 N. Pittenger, author of *Time for Consent* (S.C.M. Press), see Chap. 10, C (h).
30 This issue is still being debated in 1979. It was a main provision of the 1885 Act that the age of consent to heterosexual intercourse was fixed at 16, and the 1967 Act set the age at 21 for homosexual behaviour. It seems unlikely that either will be changed in the near future.
31 The author of this pamphlet may have been O. R. Johnston, the Director of the National Festival of Light.
32 *The Truth in Love*, op. cit., p. 9.
33 Op. cit., p. 14.
34 Published by the Westminster Press in 1971.
35 *Is Gay Good?*, op. cit., p. 109–10.
36 *Sydney Diocese Report*, op. cit., p. 19.
37 Op. cit., pp. 32–3.
38 Op. cit., pp. 22–3.
39 L. Scanzoni and V. Mollencott, *Is the Homosexual my Neighbour?* (S.C.M. Press 1978), p. 121.
40 The Lamp Press 1979.
41 Lovelace, op. cit., p. 137.
42 Inter-Varsity Press 1979, an expanded version of an earlier Grove Booklet.
43 Op. cit., p. 30.
44 Article in *Work*, an Albany Trust publication of Autumn 1976.
45 The Interim Report, *Sexual Offenders and Social Punishment*, and *Homosexuality and the Western Christian Tradition*.

46 For the history of these Societies, see Weeks, op. cit., chaps. 11 and 12.

47 D. J. West's *Homosexuality* had been first published by Pelican in 1955. S. Storr's *Sexual Deviation*, Pelican 1964. A. Comfort's *Sex in Society*, Duckworth 1963. B. Magee's *One in Twenty* 1966, Secker & Warburg. E. Chesser's *Human Aspects of Sexual Deviation*, Arrow Books 1970. These were some of the less expensive books of the period, intended for the general reader. There were many others. More recent and larger works are mentioned in chap. 1.

48 This offence, long moribund in English law, was revived in 1962 to ensure the conviction of a Mr Shaw who had published *The Ladies Directory*, a list of female prostitutes. Advertisements for homosexual prostitutes were held to be equally illegal by the House of Lords Decision in R. *v.* Knuller, but the court suggested such offences might also be contrary to the 1956 Act, procuring gross indecency, or under the Obscene Publications Acts. The Law Commission in 1974 recommended the removal of this common law offence of conspiracy. This is recommended by the 1979 Board of Social Responsibility Report, para. 183.

49 See West, op. cit., p. 291 on Civil Liberties; Weeks, op. cit., Part 5, on the Gay Liberation Movement; and Hyde, *The Other Love*, op. cit., chap. 8.

50 J. Babuscio, *We Speak for Ourselves* (SPCK 1976), p. 5.

51 Babuscio, op. cit., p. 86.

52 Quoted from *Towards a Charter of Homosexual Rights*, op. cit., pp. 5–6.

53 Report, p. 18.

54 Report, p. 32 and p. 35.

55 Preached at Canterbury Cathedral, 16 September 1962. Robinson was to become famous the following month for his book *Honest to God* in which he discussed 'The New Morality', but said nothing about homosexuality. The phrase 'New Morality' was revived by the Vatican Holy Office when forbidding discussion of situation ethics in 1956. Robinson was a member of the Albany Trust.

56 Report, p. 36.

57 Report, p. 39.

58 *Seven Pillars of Wisdom* (Cape 1940), p. 456.

59 Published by Collins in two volumes.

60 Published Weidenfeld and Nicolson and paper back reprints.

61 Hyde, *The Other Love*, op. cit., covers this period on pp. 182–9 and hints at some of the links Nigel Nicolson makes plain.

62 Published Michael Joseph 1957. Corgi Paper Backs from 1963 and reprints.

63 A. E. Dyson, *Freedom in Love* (SPCK 1975), p. 27.

64 K. Plummer, *Sexual Stigma* (Routledge and Kegan Paul 1975), p. 175.

65 Lewis, *Christian Behaviour* (Bles 1943), pp. 26–30, and many reprints. Originally a BBC talk.

66 Op. cit., p. 28.

67 Bles 1960, pp. 138–9.

68 R. L. Green and W. Hooper, *C. S. Lewis: A Biography* (Collins 1974), chap. 11.

69 C. S. Lewis, *The Allegory of Love* (Oxford 1953), chap. 1.

70 Denis de Rougemont, *Passion and Society*, tr. M. Belgion (Faber 1962), pp. 283ff. The contemporary writer, John Le Carré, depicts such a relationship between George and Anne Smiley in his recent novels.

71 H. Kimball-Jones, *Towards a Christian Understanding of the Homosexual.* S.C.M. Press 1967 and American Y.M.C.A. 1966.

72 Op. cit., p. 108.
73 Op. cit., p. 109.
74 *Time for Consent*, S.C.M. Press; the 1976 edition is in fact considerably rewritten, and comparison of its text with the 1970 edition shows how Pittenger senses the lessening of homophobia.
75 Op. cit., p. 53.
76 Whether this should be legally possible in England has been questioned.
77 Op. cit., pp. 97–8.
78 On the meaning of this phrase see *Teaching Christian Ethics* (S.C.M. 1974), pp. 41–5. Other books in which the Situationist debate is considered are P. Ramsey, *Deeds and Rules in Christian Ethics* (Oliver and Boyd 1965), and G. H. Outka and P. Ramsey, *Norm and Context in Christian Ethics* (S.C.M. Press 1969), part 4.
79 S.C.M. Press 1963, chap. 6. The two books were: *Situation Ethics*, S.C.M. Press 1966; and *Moral Responsibility*, S.C.M. Press 1967.
80 W. Frankena, *Ethics* (Prentice Hall, London, 1963), p. 43.
81 *Moral Responsibility*, op. cit., p. 134.
82 Ed. W. D. Oberholtzer.
83 Quoted from *Is Gay Good?*, op. cit., chap. 3.
84 *Is Gay Good?*, op. cit., pp. 120–2.
85 English publication, Darton, Longman, and Todd, 1977.
86 Op. cit.
87 Op. cit., p. 11.
88 K. Thom, *Liberation Through Love*. G.C.M. 1978. A. E. Dyson's *Freedom in Love*, op. cit., is a longer example of a book which finely demonstrates this widening of love's freedom, but without disregarding order, somewhat in the same style as C. S. Lewis. He teaches English at the University of East Anglia. K. Thom is Chaplain at that University.
89 2nd edn published by War on Want 1978.
90 English edn SPCK 1976. Reference to this important book is included here because celibacy is an issue for G.C.M. Obviously Fr Georgan's work is not thereby being identified with other publications reviewed here as emanating from G.C.M. Cf. H. A. Williams, *Poverty Chastity & Obedience* (Beasley 1975), pp. 76ff.
91 Op. cit., p. 109. Georgan is a difficult writer to précis and the tone of this quotation may be misleading unless seen in the context of the whole passage on homosexual friendship, pp. 188–96.
92 This crucial issue is, of course, of great importance, and much space has been devoted to it in Section B of this book.
93 English edn, ed. A. Kosnik. Search Press 1977.
94 Op. cit., p. 211.
95 Op. cit., p. 214–16.
96 Op. cit., pp. 114–28.
97 Op. cit., p. 217. The English Catholic Social Welfare Commission responding to a request from the National Conference of Priests, published an initial response in November 1979 entitled 'An Introduction to the Pastoral Care of Homosexual People'. This brief pamphlet reiterates Section 8 of the 1975 Vatican Declaration that homosexual acts are objectively immoral, and stresses that pastoral guidance must take account of this, and of the special circumstances of homosexual people (p. 8).

98 The Report was published in October 1979 and attracted immediate Press and Media comment. Both the Archbishop of Canterbury and the Bishop of St Albans, his designated successor, were reported to have expressed doubts concerning the Report's suggestions for homosexual clergy. When the General Synod met in November, requests for an immediate debate on the Report were met with the assurance that the subject, rather than this Report as such, would be put on the Synod's agenda in 1980 or 1981.

CHAPTER 11
A Shift in the Limits of Tolerance

1 *The Enforcement of Morals* (O.U.P. 1959), p. 19.

Bibliography

Babuscio, Jack, *We Speak for Ourselves*, SPCK 1976.
Bailey, Derrick Sherwin, *Homosexuality and the Western Christian Tradition*. Longmans 1955.
—— *The Man–Woman Relation in Christian Thought*. Longmans 1959.
Baldwin, James, *Giovanni's Room*. Corgi Books 1963.
Barrett, C. K., *Epistle to the Romans*. A. & C. Black 1962.
—— *First Epistle to the Corinthians*. A. & C. Black 1967.
—— *The Pastoral Epistles*. Oxford 1963.
Barth, Karl, *Church Dogmatics Vol. III, The Doctrine of Creation, Part 4*. T. & T. Clark 1961.
—— *A Shorter Commentary on Romans*. S.C.M. Press 1959.
Bell, A. P., and Weinberg, M., *Homosexualities*. Mitchell Beazley Publishers 1978.
Beyerlin, Walter, ed., *Near Eastern Religious Texts Relating to the Old Testament*. S.C.M. Press 1978.
Blamires, David, *Homosexuality from the Inside*. Social Responsibility Council of the Religious Society of Friends 1973.
Bright, John, *A History of Israel*, rev. edn. S.C.M. Press 1972.
Carter, C. O., *Human Heredity*. 2nd edn Penguin 1977.
Darlington, C. D., *Genetics and Man*. Penguin 1964–66.
Davies, W. D., *Paul and Rabbinic Judaism*. SPCK 1948–55.
Devlin, Patrick, *The Enforcement of Morals*. Oxford University Press 1965.
The Documents of Vatican II, Geoffrey Chapman 1966.
Dodd, C. H., *The Epistle of Paul to the Romans*. Fontana Books 1959.
Dyson, A. E., *Freedom in Love*, SPCK 1975.
The Ethics of Aristotle, Penguin 1955.
Freud, Sigmund, *On Sexuality*, vol. 7. Penguin Books 1977.
Georgan, Donald, *The Sexual Celibate*. The Camelot Press 1974.

Graves, Robert, *The Greek Myths*, vols. 1 and 2. Pelican 1955.

Hall, M. Penelope, and Hawes, Ismene V., *The Church in Social Work*. Routledge and Kegan Paul 1965.

Hayes, John, and Miller, J. Maxwell, ed., *Israelite and Judaean History*. S.C.M. Press 1977.

Homosexual Relationships—a Contribution to Discussion. Church Information Office 1979.

Hyde, H. Montgomery, *The Other Love*. Heinemann 1970.

Kelly, J. N. D., *The Epistles of Peter and of Jude*. A. & C. Black 1969.

Kimball-Jones, H., *Towards a Christian Understanding of the Homosexual*. S.C.M. Press 1967.

Kosnik, A., and others, ed., *Human Sexuality*. Search Press 1977.

Kummel, W. G., *Introduction to the New Testament*. S.C.M. Press 1975.

Lewis, C. S., *The Allegory of Love*. Oxford University Press 1936.

—— *The Four Loves*. Geoffrey Bles 1960.

Lohse, Eduard, *The New Testament Environment*. S.C.M. Press 1974.

Loraine, J. A., ed., *Understanding Homosexuality*. Medical and Technical Publishing Co. 1974.

Lovelace, Richard F., *Homosexuality and the Church*. The Lamp Press 1978.

Macourt, Malcolm, ed., *Towards the Theology of Gay Liberation*. S.C.M. Press 1977.

McNeill, John I., *The Church and the Homosexual*. Darton, Longman, and Todd 1977.

Metzger, Bruce M., *An Introduction to the Apocrypha*. Oxford University Press 1977.

Moule, C. F. D., *The Birth of the New Testament*. A. & C. Black 1962.

Nelson, James B., *Embodiment—an Approach to Sexuality and Christian Theology*. SPCK 1979.

Nineham, D. E., *The Use and Abuse of the Bible*, The Macmillan Press 1976.

—— ed., *The Church's Use of the Bible*. SPCK 1963.

Noth, Martin, *Leviticus*, rev. edn. S.C.M. Press 1977.

Oberholtzer, W. Dwight, *Is Gay Good?* Westminster Press 1971.

Osborn, Eric, *Ethical Patterns in Early Christian Thought*. Cambridge University Press 1976.

Peake's Commentary on the Bible. Thomas Nelson & Sons 1962.

Phillips, Anthony, *Ancient Israel's Criminal Law*. Basil Blackwell 1970.

Pittenger, *Time for Consent—a Christian Approach to Homosexuality*. 3rd edn. S.C.M. Press 1976.

Plato, *The Symposium*. Penguin Classics 1951–78.

—— *The Laws*. Penguin Classics 1970.

Plummer, Kenneth, *Sexual Stigma: an Interactionist Account*. Routledge and Kegan Paul 1975.

von Rad, Gerhard, *Genesis*. Published in England, W. L. Jenkins 1961.

Ramsey, Paul, *Deeds and Rules in Christian Ethics*, Scottish Journal of Theology: Occasional papers No. 11. Oliver and Boyd 1965.

Report of the Committee on Homosexual Offences and Prostitution. H.M. Stationery Office, Cmnd. 247, 1957 (Known as Wolfenden Report).

Robinson, John A. T., *Re-dating the New Testament*. S.C.M. Press 1976.

Russell, D. S., *Between the Testaments*. S.C.M. Press 1960.

Sanders, E. P., *Paul and Palestinian Judaism*. S.C.M. Press 1977.

Sandmel, *A Jewish Understanding of the New Testament*. SPCK 1977.

Scanzoni, Letha, and Mollenkott, Virginia Ramey, *Is the Homosexual My Neighbour?* S.C.M. Press 1978.

Sexual Offenders and Social Punishment, compiled and ed. Derrick Sherwin Bailey. Church Information Board 1956.

Soggin, J. Alberto, *Introduction to the Old Testament*. S.C.M. Press 1976.

Thielicke, Helmut, *The Ethics of Sex*. James Clarke & Co. 1964.

Towards a Quaker View of Sex. Friends Home Service Committee 1963.

de Vaux, Roland, *The Early History of Israel to the Period of the Judges*. Darton, Longman, and Todd 1978.

—— *The Early History of Israel from the Beginnings to the Exodus and Covenant of Sinai*. Darton, Longman, and Todd 1978.

Vermes, Geza, *The Dead Sea Scrolls*. Collins 1977.

Weeks, Jeffrey, *Coming Out*. Quartet Books 1977.

West, D. J., *Homosexuality Re-examined*. Duckworth 1977.

Wolff, Charlotte, *Bisexuality*. Quartet Books 1977.

Index of Names and Subjects

Index of References

OLD TESTAMENT

NEW TESTAMENT

APOCRYPHA AND PSEUDEPIGRAPHA